Tao, Nature and Man

英汉对照

道、自然与人

金岳霖 著

外语教学与研究出版社
FOREIGN LANGUAGE TEACHING AND RESEARCH PRESS
北京 BEIJING

图书在版编目（CIP）数据

道、自然与人 = Tao, Nature and Man ：英汉对照 ／ 金岳霖著. -- 北京 ：
外语教学与研究出版社，2019.9（2022.3重印）
ISBN 978-7-5135-9769-2

Ⅰ．①道… Ⅱ．①金… Ⅲ．①社会科学－文集－英、汉 Ⅳ．①C53

中国版本图书馆 CIP 数据核字 (2019) 第 223529 号

出 版 人　王　芳
系列策划　吴　浩
责任编辑　张路路
责任校对　仲志兰
装帧设计　视觉共振设计工作室
出版发行　外语教学与研究出版社
社　　址　北京市西三环北路 19 号（100089）
网　　址　http://www.fltrp.com
印　　刷　三河市北燕印装有限公司
开　　本　650×980　1/16
印　　张　26
版　　次　2019 年 9 月第 1 版　2022 年 3 月第 2 次印刷
书　　号　ISBN 978-7-5135-9769-2
定　　价　65.00 元

购书咨询：（010）88819926　电子邮箱：club@fltrp.com
外研书店 https://waiyants.tmall.com
凡印刷、装订质量问题，请联系我社印制部
联系电话：（010）61207896　电子邮箱：zhijian@fltrp.com
凡侵权、盗版书籍线索，请联系我社法律事务部
举报电话：（010）88817519　电子邮箱：banquan@fltrp.com
物料号：297690001

记载人类文明
沟通世界文化
www.fltrp.com

"博雅双语名家名作"出版说明

　　1840 年鸦片战争以降，在深重的民族危机面前，中华民族精英"放眼看世界"，向世界寻求古老中国走向现代、走向世界的灵丹妙药，涌现出一大批中国主题的经典著述。我们今天阅读这些中文著述的时候，仍然深为字里行间所蕴藏的缜密的考据、深刻的学理、世界的视野和济世的情怀所感动，但往往会忽略：这些著述最初是用英文写就，我们耳熟能详的中文文本是原初英文文本的译本，这些英文作品在海外学术界和文化界同样享有崇高的声誉。

　　比如，林语堂的 *My Country and My People*（《吾国与吾民》）以幽默风趣的笔调和睿智流畅的语言，将中国人的道德精神、生活情趣和中国社会文化的方方面面娓娓道来，在美国引起巨大反响——林语堂也以其中国主题系列作品赢得世界文坛的尊重，并获得诺贝尔文学奖的提名。再比如，梁思成在抗战的烽火中写就的英文版《图像中国建筑史》文稿（*A Pictorial History of Chinese Architecture*），经其挚友费慰梅女士（Wilma C. Fairbank）等人多年的奔走和努力，于 1984 年由麻省理工学院出版社（MIT Press）出版，并获得美国出版联合会颁发的"专业暨学术书籍金奖"。又比如，1939 年，费孝通在伦敦政治经济学院的博士论文以 *Peasant Life in China—A Field Study of Country Life in the Yangtze Valley* 为名在英国劳特利奇书局（Routledge）出版，后以《江村经济》作为中译本书名——《江村经济》使得靠桑蚕为生的"开弦弓村"获得了世界性的声誉，成为国际社会学界研究中国农村的首选之地。

　　此外，一些中国主题的经典人文社科作品经海外汉学家和中国学者的如椽译笔，在英语世界也深受读者喜爱。比如，艾恺（Guy S. Alitto）将他1980 年用中文访问梁漱溟的《这个世界会好吗——梁漱溟晚年口述》一书译成英文（*Has Man a Future? —Dialogues with the Last Confucian*），备受海内外读者关注；

此类作品还有徐中约英译的梁启超著作《清代学术概论》（*Intellectual Trends in the Ch'ing Period*）、狄百瑞（W. T. de Bary）英译的黄宗羲著作《明夷待访录》（*Waiting for the Dawn: A Plan for the Prince*），等等。

有鉴于此，外语教学与研究出版社推出"博雅双语名家名作"系列。

博雅，乃是该系列的出版立意。博雅教育（Liberal Education）早在古希腊时代就得以提倡，旨在培养具有广博知识和优雅气质的人，提高人文素质，培养健康人格，中国儒家六艺"礼、乐、射、御、书、数"亦有此功用。

双语，乃是该系列的出版形式。英汉双语对照的形式，既同时满足了英语学习者和汉语学习者通过阅读中国主题博雅读物提高英语和汉语能力的需求，又以中英双语思维、构架和写作的形式予后世学人以启迪——维特根斯坦有云："语言的边界，乃是世界的边界"，诚哉斯言。

名家，乃是该系列的作者群体。涵盖文学、史学、哲学、政治学、经济学、考古学、人类学、建筑学等领域，皆海内外名家一时之选。

名作，乃是该系列的入选标准。系列中的各部作品都是经过时间的积淀、市场的检验和读者的鉴别而呈现的经典，正如卡尔维诺对"经典"的定义：经典并非你正在读的书，而是你正在重读的书。

胡适在《新思潮的意义》（1919 年 12 月 1 日，《新青年》第 7 卷第 1 号）一文中提出了"研究问题、输入学理、整理国故、再造文明"的范式。秉着"记载人类文明、沟通世界文化"的出版理念，我们推出"博雅双语名家名作"系列，既希望能够在中国人创作的和以中国为主题的博雅英文文献领域"整理国故"，亦希望在和平发展、改革开放的新时代为"再造文明"、为"向世界说明中国"略尽绵薄之力。

外语教学与研究出版社

人文社科出版分社

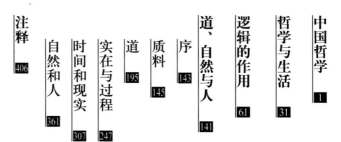

Chinese

中国哲学

Philosophy[1,2]

Of the three main flows of philosophical thought, it has been maintained that the Indian is otherworldly, the Greek unworldly and the Chinese worldly. No philosophy is ever plainly worldly; to say that it is so is merely an attempt to caricature it in order to bring out certain features into striking relief. To those who know something of Chinese philosophy the word "worldly" merely emphasizes certain features in comparison with the Indian and the Greek schools of thought; but to those who do not know anything about it, that word is liable to be quite misleading. What is meant is probably that Chinese philosophy sticks to the kernel of its subject matter; it is never propelled by the instruments of thinking either into the dizzy heights of systematic speculation, or into the depth of a labyrinth of elaborate barrenness. Like machines in an industrial civilization, intellectuality in philosophy drives; and whether it drives us into blind alleys or not, it may lead us far away from the wide boulevards or spacious squares. Intellectually, Chinese philosophy has always been in the open air.

We are accustomed to thinking of Chinese philosophy as consisting of Confucianism, Buddhism and Taoism. It is rather as religions that these are exclusively mentioned. In the early stages both Confucianism and Taoism were only philosophies, and as such they were in the pre-Qin period members of a whole democracy of different schools of thought, the variety of which during that period was unparalleled in Chinese history. Since terms are inadequate, we shall refrain from any attempt at description. It is misleading enough to apply the familiar philosophical terms to Western philosophy, it is much worse to apply them to the Chinese. One might say for instance that there were logicians in the pre-Qin period; but if so, readers might be led to think that there were people who brooded over syllogism, or the laws of thought, or even obversion and conversion. The Yin-Yang-ists have been described in a recent article as the precursors of science, and not without foundation either, but then they were precursors of something which strictly speaking never arrived; and if as a result of this description readers imagine them to be ancient Keplers or Galileos, they entertain a distorted view of a whole brand of thinkers.

Confucianism and Taoism are indigenous to China, they are properly Chinese; Buddhism, however, was introduced from India and it might

一

在三大哲学思想主流中，人们曾经认为印度哲学是"来世"的，希腊哲学是"出世"的，而中国哲学则是"入世"的。哲学从来没有干脆入世的；说它入世，不过是意图以漫画的笔法突出它的某些特点而已。在懂点中国哲学的人看来，"入世"的说法仅仅是强调中国哲学与印度、希腊两派思想相比有某些特点；但是对于那些不懂中国哲学的人，这个词却容易引起很大的误解。它的本意大概是说，中国哲学是紧扣主题的核心的，从来不被一些思维的手段推上系统思辨的眩晕云霄，或者推入复杂枯燥的迷宫深处。正像工业文明以机器为动力一样，哲学是由理智推动的，这理智不管是否把我们赶进死胡同，总可以把我们引得远离阳关大道、一马平川。而在理智方面，中国哲学向来是通达的。

人们习惯于认为中国哲学包括儒、释、道三家。这三家在单提的时候又往往被说成宗教。在早期，儒家和道家本是地道的哲学，即先秦百家争鸣的两家，那个时期的学派纷纭是中国历史上无与伦比的。由于词语未尽恰当，我们不打算对此进行任何描述。把一些熟知的哲学用语加之于西方哲学足以引起误会，用于中国哲学则更加不妙。例如有人可以说先秦有逻辑家，这样说就会引得读者以为那时有一些人在盘算三段论，研究思维律，甚至进行换质换位推理了。最近有一篇文章把阴阳家说成科学的先驱，这也不是全无道理。于是这样一来，阴阳家就成了某种严格说来从未实现的事业的先驱。读者如果根据描述把阴阳家想象成古代的开普勒或伽利略，那是接受了一批思想家的歪曲观点。

儒家和道家是中国固有的，是地道的国货。释家则是从印度

be wondered whether it could be said to be Chinese. The introduction of a foreign philosophy is not quite the same as the importation of foreign goods. In the last century, for instance, the English were alarmed at the invasion of German Idealism. "The Rhine," they declared, "has flowed into the Thames." But however alarmed they might be, their Thames has not since become a mere Rhine; British Hegelianism while acknowledging its origin and impetus from abroad is distinctly English, though it is not so characteristically English as the philosophies of Locke and Hume. Buddhism in China, in the early stages, at any rate, had been modified by Chinese thought: indeed for a time it was robed in Taoistic garbs, and Taoism, it might be said, became its chief agency of distribution. But there was something stubborn in Buddhism which resisted Taoistic manipulations, hence although it became Chinese to some extent, it is not distinguished by the features characteristic of the indigenous Chinese philosophy.

In the following sections we shall single out certain features for discussion. We shall refrain as much as we can from proper names, technicalities or details.

传入的，不知能不能算中国哲学。传入外国哲学
与进口外国商品不完全一样。例如在上个世纪，
英国人曾经惊呼德国唯心论侵入英国，他们说
"莱茵河流进了泰晤士河"。但是英国人尽管惶恐，
他们的泰晤士河并没有就此变成一条纯粹的莱茵
河。英国的黑格尔主义虽然承认来自外国，是外
国引起的，却分明是英国哲学，尽管它的英国色
彩不像洛克哲学和休谟哲学那样鲜明。释家在中
国，无论如何在早期是受到中国思想影响的，实
际上有一段时间披上了道家的法衣，道家可以说
成了传播佛法的主要代理人。但是释家有一种倔
强性格抵制了道家的操纵，因此它虽然在某种程
度上变成了中国哲学，在基本特色方面却与固有
中国哲学不是没有区别的。

　　下面几节要挑出几个特点来讨论。我们尽可
能不用固有名词，不用专门术语，不谈细节。

II

One of the features characteristic of Chinese philosophy is the underdevelopment of what might be called logico-epistemological consciousness. Undoubtedly such a statement has been made frequently, and perhaps too frequently it has been taken to mean either that Chinese philosophy is illogical or that it is not based on knowledge. Obviously this is not what is meant. We needn't be conscious of biology in order to be biological, or of physics in order to be physical. Chinese philosophers could easily manage to be logical without a developed sense of logic; their philosophy could be founded on the knowledge then accepted as such, and yet devoid of a developed sense of epistemology. To be conscious of logic and epistemology is to be conscious of the instruments of thought. Not having a developed consciousness of epistemology and logic, the Chinese philosophers presented their ideas with a barrenness and disconnectedness that might suggest to those who are accustomed to systematic thought a feeling of indeterminateness unexpected of philosophies, and possibly also dampening the enthusiasm of the students of Chinese thought.

Not that there was no such consciousness. Perhaps inevitably from the nature of the impetus concerned, this consciousness started with what impatient thinkers are liable to dismiss as mere sophistries. The underlying reality behind the so-called sophistries, however, was only a switch of the muses from the problem of ultimate realities to those of language, thought and ideas, realizing perhaps that the latter must be tackled before the former could be solved. Such a switch took place in the pre-Qin period when a number of thinkers started to maintain the distinction between the universal and the particular, the relativity of terms, the separation of hardness from whiteness, the doctrine of infinite divisibility of the finite, of the staticity of quickly moving arrows, etc., in the midst of speculations which were obviously more directly concerned with the problems of that turbulent age. Students of philosophy will inevitably think of the parallel in Greek thought. It was from similar doctrines arising out of reason itself that the intellectual finesse in Western philosophy was obtained; and it was by them that philosophy was in some sense converted into mental gymnastics. In China, however, the tendency was short-lived; admirable as it was for a beginning, it yet died a precocious death. The logico-epistemological consciousness remained underdeveloped almost to the present day.

二

中国哲学的特点之一，是那种可以称为逻辑和认识论的意识不发达。这个说法的确很常见，常见到被认为是指中国哲学不合逻辑，或者中国哲学不以认识为基础。显然这个说法并非此意。我们并不需要意识到生物学才具有生物性，意识到物理学才具有物理性。中国哲学家没有发达的逻辑意识，也能轻易自如地安排得合乎逻辑；他们的哲学虽然缺少发达的认识论意识，也能建立在以往取得的认识上。意识到逻辑和认识论，就是意识到思维的手段。中国哲学家没有一种发达的认识论意识和逻辑意识，所以在表达思想时显得空洞不连贯，这种情况会使习惯于系统思维的人得到一种哲学上料想不到的不确定感，也可能给研究中国思想的人泼上一瓢冷水。

这种意识并不是没有。可能受有关刺激的特点影响，这种意识从一开始就不可避免地容易被没有耐性的思想家斥为诡辩。然而，这类所谓诡辩背后的实质，其实不过是一种思想源头的大转变，从最终实在的问题转变到语言、思想、观念的问题，大概是领悟到了不碰后者就无法解决前者。这样一种大转变发生在先秦。那时有一批思想家开始主张分别共相与殊相，认为名言有相对性，把坚与白分离开，提出有限者无限可分和飞矢不动的学说。这些思辨显然与那个动乱时代的种种问题有比较直接的关系。研究哲学的人当然会想到希腊哲学中的类似情况。从这类来自理性本身的类似学说中，可见他们已经获得了西方哲学中那种理智的精细；凭着这些学说，哲学在某种意义上变成了锻炼精神的活动。然而这种趋向在中国是短命的；一开始虽然美妙，毕竟夭折了。逻辑、认识论的意识仍然不发达，几乎一直到现在。

Whatever the causes may be, and a large number may be suggested, the effect on philosophy and science is far-reaching indeed. Science in the West is linked up in an intimate way with Greek thought. While it is untenable to regard the former as a direct offspring of the latter, it is none the less true that the former owed part of its development to certain tendencies in Greek thought. Technique in experimentation was comparatively a late arrival in the history of European culture, and while it is of the utmost importance to science it is not its only necessary condition. Certain tools of thinking are equally required, and what was actually supplied might be most conveniently called mathematical patterns of thinking. The emergence of calculus was a great impetus to science, thus indicating that the instruments for handling data are just as important as their collection through observation and experiment. The patterns of thought to which Europeans had long been accustomed were Hellenistic. Hellenism is thoroughly intellectual; its intellectuality is characterized by developing ideas and carrying them ruthlessly and relentlessly either to their sublimities or to their absurdities. *Reductio ad absurdum* is itself an intellectual instrument. It was this element which was responsible for the early development of logic, which on the one hand supplied the tools of early science, and on the other gave Greek philosophy that admirable articulateness which was the envy of later thinkers. If the development of this logico-epistemological consciousness was partly responsible for the presence of science in the West, the lack of this development must be partly responsible also for the absence of science in China.

The effect on Chinese philosophy is equally far-reaching. While Chinese philosophy is not adorned with intellectual frills and ruffles, it is also not burdened or stifled by them. This is not meant to portray earthiness. There is hardly any philosophy less earthy than that of Chuang Tze. John Middleton Murray has somewhere said that while Plato was a good poet, Hegel was a bad one. On some such basis, Chuang

Tze should be regarded as a great poet perhaps even more than a great philosopher. His philosophy is expressed in exquisite poetic prose in delightful parables, extolling as lofty an ideal of life as any philosophy in the West. There is a certain whimsicality that yet manages to be robust, a kind of finality that is not dogmatism, together with that liveliness and graspability which appeal to the understanding as well as to the emotion

其所以如此，可以举出一大堆原因；但是不管出于什么原因，哲学和科学受到的影响确实是深远的。科学在西方与希腊思想有紧密联系。虽然不能把前者看成后者的直接产物，却可以说前者的发展有一部分要归功于希腊思想中的某些倾向。实验技术是欧洲文化史上比较晚起的，尽管对科学极为重要，却不是产生科学的唯一必要条件。同样需要的是某些思维工具；人们实际提供的这类工具，很可以称为思维的数学模式。微积分的出现是对科学的一大促进，这表明处理数据的手段同通过观察实验收集数据同等重要。欧洲人长期用惯的那些思维模式是希腊人的。希腊文化是十足的理智文化；这种文化的理智特色表现为发展各种观念，把这些观念坚决地、不间断地推到崇高之极致，或者荒诞之极致。归谬法本身就是一种理智手段。这条原理推动了逻辑的早期发展，一方面给早期的科学提供了工具，另一方面使希腊哲学得到了那种使后世思想家羡慕不已的惊人明确。如果说这种逻辑、认识论意识的发达是科学在西方出现的一部分原因，那么这种意识不发达也就该是科学在中国不出现的一部分原因。

中国哲学受到的这种影响同样是深远的。中国哲学没有打扮出理智的款式，也没有受到这种款式的累赘和闷气。这并不是说中国哲学土气。比庄子哲学更不土气的哲学是几乎没有的。约翰·米德尔顿·默里大约曾说过，柏拉图是个高明的诗人，黑格尔则是个拙劣的诗人。根据这个说法，也许应该把庄子看成大诗人甚于大哲学家。他的哲学用诗意盎然的散文写出，充满赏心悦目的寓言，颂扬一种崇高的人生理想，与任何西方哲学不相上下。其异想天开烘托出豪放，一语道破却不是武断，生机勃勃而又顺理成章，使人读起

of the readers. And yet to those who are accustomed to the geometrical pattern of thought in philosophy, there is even in Chuang Tze a sort of intellectual bleakness or disconnectedness as well. Although deduction and inference must have been at the service of the thinker, there was no attempt to weave ideas into a closely knitted pattern. As a result, there isn't that systematic completeness which is so soothing to the trained mind.

But ideas that are worked out to their systematic completeness are liable to be such that we have to take them or leave them. Through them the author is irrevocably committed. They could not be eclectically taken without having their pattern revoked as well. Here as elsewhere the advantage or disadvantage is not entirely on any one side. It may be, as it has often been claimed, that the world will always be divided between Platonists and Aristotelians, and that probably in a number of senses; but other reasons aside, Aristotle, in spite of Aristotelians, may turn out to be much more short-lived than Plato, on account of the former's articulateness; for the more articulate an idea is, the less capable also is it of suggestion. Chinese philosophy is so brief and so inarticulate in terms of the interconnectedness of ideas that its suggestiveness is almost unbounded. The result is that for centuries annotations and interpretations never stopped. Much original thought was disguised in the cloak of ancient philosophies which were never revoked, nor yet, peculiar as it may seem, completely accepted. Whether the numerous Neo-Confucianisms or Neo-Taoisms in the different periods in Chinese history were recrudescence of the original impulses or not, they were not at any rate repetitions of the original thought. In reality there was no lack of originality, but in appearance there was an absence of what might be called free adventures of thought. We are not here speaking of the practical reasons why Chinese philosophy stuck to the beaten path from certain periods onward. Even long before some philosophies acquired the intolerance of religions, the tendency to clothe original thought in terms of existing philosophies was already in evidence. Whatever mundane reasons there may be, Chinese philosophy in the form in which it was presented was particularly suited to being made use of by original thinkers in that it could gather original thought into its mold or structure almost without any effort.

来既诉诸感情，又诉诸理智。可是，在惯用几何模式从事哲学思考的人看来，即便在庄子哲学里，也是既鲜有理智，又缺少连贯。虽然这位思想家必定使用了演绎和推理，却无意于把观念编织成严密的图案。所以，他那里并没有可供训练有素的心灵得以抚慰的那种系统完备性。

然而，安排得系统完备的观念，往往是我们要么加以接受，要么加以抛弃的那一类。作者不免要对此负责。我们不能用折中的态度去看待它们，否则就要破坏它们的图案。这里也和别处一样，利和害都不是集中在哪一边。也许像常说的那样，世人永远会划分成柏拉图派和亚里士多德派，而且分法很多。可是撇开其他理由不说，单就亚里士多德条理分明这一点，尽管亚里士多德派不乐意，亚里士多德［学说］的寿命也要比柏拉图［学说］短得多，因为观念越是分明，就越不能具有暗示性。中国哲学非常简洁，很不分明，观念彼此联结，因此它的暗示性几乎无边无涯。结果是千百年来人们不断地加以注解，加以诠释。很多原初的思想，为了掩饰，披上古代哲学的外衣；这些古代哲学是从来没有被击破，尽管看似奇特，也从来没有得到全盘接受的。中国历史上各个时期数不清的新儒家、新道家，不论是不是独创冲动的复萌，却绝不是那独创思想的再版。实际上并不缺乏独创精神，只是从表面看来，缺少一种可以称为思想自由冒险的活动。我们在这里谈的并不是中国哲学从某个时期开始故步自封的实际原因。早在某些哲学蒙上宗教偏见之前，用现存哲学围裹原初思想的倾向已经很显著了。不管出于什么现实的原因，这样的中国哲学是特别适宜于独创的思想家加以利用的，因为它可以毫不费力地把独创的思想纳入它的框子。

III

Perhaps most people at all acquainted with Chinese philosophy will single out the unity of nature and man as its most distinguishing characteristic. The term "nature" is illusive and the more one grapples with it, the more it slips through one's fingers. In the ordinary sense in which it is most often used in our everyday life, it is not adequate to stand for the Chinese term *"t'ien."* Perhaps if we mean by it "both nature and nature's God," with emphasis sometimes on the one and sometimes on the other, we have something approaching the Chinese term. This doctrine of the unity of nature and man is a comprehensive one indeed; in its highest and broadest realization, it is a state in which the individual is identified with the Universe through the merging of the subject into the object or vice versa, by sticking to the fundamental identity and obliterating all obvious differences. To express this idea adequately requires a special set of terms which it is not the intention of this article to introduce. We may confine ourselves to the mundane consequences. If the ideal is approached to any appreciable extent, there won't be that unhealthy separation of a self or an ego from his fellow beings on the one hand, nor a demarcation of things human from things natural on the other. The resultant attitude both in Chinese philosophy and in popular thought towards nature in the ordinary sense is quite different from that in the West: Nature is hardly ever something to be resisted, to be struggled against, or to be conquered.

In the West, there is quite a pervading desire to conquer nature. Whether human nature is regarded as being "nasty, brutish and short" or human beings as angelically cherubic babes in the woods, they seem to be always battling against nature, claiming a sort of manifest destiny over the whole natural domain. The result of this attitude is a sort of anthropocentricity on the one hand and a certain malleability of nature on the other. The effect on science is tremendous. One of the incentives to the advancement of science is to acquire the power needed for the conquest of nature. Nature cannot be conquered without an adequate knowledge of it. It can only be made malleable for human beings by our making use of it through our knowledge of its laws. All the engineering marvels, all the medical achievements, in fact, the whole modern industrial civilization, including the armaments, for good or for evil, may be regarded in one sense at least as the conquest of nature by natural means towards a state of affairs desired by human beings. From the point

三

多数熟悉中国哲学的人大概会挑出"天人合一"作为中国哲学最突出的特点。"天"这个词是扑朔迷离的，你越是抓紧它，它越会从指缝里滑掉。这个词在日常生活中用得最多的通常意义，并不适于代表中国的"天"字。如果我们把"天"理解为"自然"和"自然神"，有时强调前者，有时强调后者，那就有点抓住这个中国字了。"天人合一"说确是一种无所不包的学说；最高、最广意义的"天人合一"，就是主体融入客体，或者客体融入主体，坚持根本同一，泯除一切显著差别，从而达到个人与宇宙不二的状态。恰当地表达这个观念需要用一整套专门术语，本文不打算一一介绍。我们仅限于谈谈它的现实影响。如果比较满意地达到了这个理想，那就不会把自己和别人强行分开，也不会给人的事情和天的事情划下鸿沟。中国哲学和民间思想对待通常意义的天，基本态度与西方迥然不同：天是不能抵制、不能反抗、不能征服的。

西方有一种征服自然的强烈愿望。人们尽管把人性看成"肮脏的、野蛮的、短暂的"，或者把人看成森林中天使般的赤子，却似乎总在对自然作战，主张人有权支配整个自然界。这种态度的结果，一方面是人类中心论，另一方面是自然顺从论。这对科学的影响是巨大的。促进科学的因素之一，是获得征服自然所需要的力量。没有适当的自然知识，就不能征服自然。只有认识自然规律，从而利用自然，人才能使自然顺从。一切工程奇迹、一切医药成就——实际上——全部现代工业文明，包括功罪参半的军事装备，至少在某种意义上都可以看成用自然手段征服自然以达到人类愿望

of view which regards nature as something quite apart from humans, the issue is clear—victory so far belongs to the human beings; but from the point of view which regards human beings as having a nature of their own and therefore also problems of mutual adjustment arising out of it, the issue is not so clear—it may even turn out that the victor is also the vanquished.

The separation of nature and man results in a sort of anthropocentricity which is clearly exhibited in Western philosophy. To say that man is the measure of things, or that the essence of a thing is the perception of it, or that understanding makes nature, reveals the attitude that nature is somehow not simply given. In the language of philosophy, there is a certain constructability in the concept "nature" in which there is free play of intellect; and in the language of everyday life, there is a certain manoeuvrability over nature which human beings either do enjoy or want to enjoy. We are not speaking here of Idealism or Realism which are after all conscious constructions. We are speaking rather of the difference in attitude between China and the West such that while in the latter the world is almost taken for granted to be dichotomized into nature and man, in China it takes quite an effort to detach man from the nature of things. Of course different schools of thought in China interpret nature in different ways, attach to it different degrees of interest or importance; different thinkers of the same school, and the same thinker at different times may also have different notions of nature. But whatever the notion may be, man is not set apart from nature and in opposition to it.

Thus far we have merely touched on the nature of man. The partial conquest of nature in the West seems to have left human nature more assertive than before, and far more dangerous. The attempt to humanize science and industry is an attempt to temper human nature so that the results of science and industry would not be implements of cruelty, slaughter and general destruction. If civilization is to be preserved some such attempts at individual and social control are necessary and calling attention to them is surely a credit to a number of thinkers. We should however be careful about suggesting a conquest. In a sense and a significant one too, nature whether human or non-human has never been conquered. No natural law has ever been nullified or suspended for human benefit and at human will; what has been done is to bring about a state of affairs such that certain natural laws operate against certain others

的实例。从自然与人类隔离的观点，产生的结果是清楚的——胜利到目前为止属于人类。但是从人类有自己的自然天性，因而也有随之而来的相互适应问题这个观点，产生的结果就不那么清楚——甚至可以变成胜利者也是被征服者。

自然与人分离的看法带来了西方哲学中彰明昭著的人类中心论。说人是万物的尺度，说一物的本质即是其被感知，或者说理解造成自然，说明人们以为自然不知怎么并非一成不变。在哲学语言中，"自然"概念包含一种可以构造的意思，心智是在其中自由驰骋的；在日常生活语言中，人类所享有或者意图享有的自然，是可以操纵的。我们在这里说的并不是唯心论或实在论，那毕竟是意识的构造物。我们是说中国和西方的态度不同：西方认为世界当然一分为二，分成自然和人；中国则力图使人摆脱物性。当然，中国的不同学派以不同的方式解释自然，给予自然不同程度的兴趣或重要性；同一学派的不同思想家，同一思想家在不同时期，也可以对自然有不同的理解。可是尽管理解不同，都不把人与自然分割开来、对立起来。

到此为止，我们仅仅接触到了人性。西方对自然的片面征服似乎让人性比以往更加专断，带来更大的危险。设法使科学和工业人性化，是设法调和人性，使科学和工业的成果不致成为制造残忍、屠杀和毁灭一切的工具。要保存文明，就必须设法控制个人，控制社会，而唤醒人们设法这样做的则是一些思想家。不过，我们应当小心谨慎，不能随便提征服。在一种意义上，而且在一种重要的意义上，人的天性和非人的天性是从来没有被征服过的。自然规律从来没有为了人的利益、顺从人的意志而失效或暂停；我们所做的只是安排一个局面，让某些自然规律对另一些自然规律起抵制作用，

so that the results desired by human beings are sometimes realized. If we try to conquer nature by damming it up, nature will overwhelm us with vengeance; there will soon be leakages here and there and later there will be floods, landslides and explosions. The same is true of human nature. The doctrine of original sin, for instance, results either in psychological subterfuges which make human beings undignified, or else in explosions which make them destructive or anti-social.

While certain internal restraint through philosophy or religion and certain external restraint through law are required in any society and admitted by Chinese philosophy, it does not advocate the frustration of the functioning of the primary instincts. There is as a result something which, for lack of an adequate term, might be described as natural naturalness or contented contentedness. By these terms we do not mean to insinuate that there are fewer instances of cruelty or barbarity in Chinese history than in that of any other nation; evidences of want on destruction, or blood-thirstiness, or of desires running rampant seem to abound in Chinese history as anywhere else. What is meant is rather that there isn't that unnaturalness which Oscar Wilde saw in the naturalness of a Victorian. The Chinese may have something to say against unnaturalness, but they do not make a fuss over being natural on the one hand, and seem to be quite contented with their contentedness on the other. Perhaps in modern times we are accustomed to regarding contentedness as stagnation, as mental laziness, or as spiritual snuggery. The modern point of view is essentially one that encourages revolts against one's self, producing as a byproduct such psychological wear and tear that ease and equanimity in life can no longer be maintained. It is a point of view that is opposed to the one we are trying here to describe. The Chinese are contented with their contentedness, exhibiting ideologically the attitude that each to himself is something that is given, and therefore something to be accepted; to borrow a phrase so admirably employed by F. H. Bradley, each has his "station and life," and in them or it he has his natural dignity. We are not speaking here of the heightened philosophical state attainable only by the few. Although Confucianism allows everybody the possibility to become a saint, failure to do so does not cause any psychological strain. Given this attitude concerning one's station and life, one is not merely at one with nature, but also at one with society.

俾使人的愿望有时得以实现。如果我们想用堵塞的办法来征服自然，自然就会重重地报复我们：不久就会在这里或那里出现裂缝，然后洪水滔天，山崩地裂。人的本性也是一样。例如原罪说就会造成颓废心理，使人们丧失尊严；或者造成愤怒的爆发，使人们成为破坏分子和反社会分子。

哲学或宗教给人一种内在的约束，法律给人一种外在的约束。这类约束是任何社会都需要的，也都为中国哲学所承认，但是这并非鼓吹取消各种原始本能的作用。这样就产生了一种情况，由于缺乏恰当的词语，可以姑且把它描述为自然的合乎自然，或者满意的心满意足。我们的意思并不是用这样的词语暗示说，残酷、野蛮的事例在中国历史上比任何其他民族少；杀人如麻、嗜血成性、为所欲为的事情在中国历史上跟别处一样俯拾皆是。我们的意思是说，奥斯卡·王尔德在维多利亚时代的人身上合乎自然的状态里看到的那种不合自然，在中国人身上是没有的。中国人或许反对不合自然，但是一方面并不吹捧自然的状态，另一方面也似乎非常满意于自己的心满意足。在现代，我们大概惯于认为心满意足就是停滞不前、精神松懈、苟且偷安。这种现代观点本质上是鼓励向自己造反，其副产品是心理受折磨，再也不能保持生活上平安宁静。这个观点是与我们在这里试加描述的观点背道而驰的。中国人满意于自己的心满意足，表现出一种态度，认为对他自己来说，每一件事都是给定的，因而都是要接受的；借用弗朗西斯·赫伯特·布拉德利一句名言来说，就是人人各有其"位分和生活"，其中有他自己的自然尊严。这里我们谈到的并非只有少数人才能达到的至高无上的心理状态。儒家虽然认为人人都可以成为圣贤，但是做不到也并不形成心理负担。既然见到人各有其位分和生活，一个人就不仅与自然融为一体，而且也与社会融为一体了。

IV

It is but a truism that individuals cannot live apart from society. Both Greek and Chinese philosophies embody this point of view. From Socrates to Aristotle there was an extraordinary emphasis on the importance of a good political life, and all of those scholars are political thinkers as well as philosophers. The underlying idea seems to be that the fullest or the most "natural" development of an individual can only be attained through the medium of a just political society. Philosophy touches life just as intimately as literature and perhaps more intimately than a number of other subjects. Those who are born philosophers or those who happen to have philosophy thrust upon them through political or social encroachment upon their liberties are bound to take the above truth as one of the premises or active principles. The attempt to furnish what is now called *Lebensanschauung*, to understand life, to give it its meaning, and to lead a good life was a more primitive incentive to philosophy than what is currently valued as pure understanding. Since a good life was desired, the principle of the interrelatedness of life and politics led philosophy straight to political thought and philosophers became directly or indirectly connected or concerned with politics.

This tradition wasn't entirely carried on in the West, and one of the reasons why it stopped will partly be the subject of discussion in the next section. But in China the tradition persisted almost to the present day. Quite without exception, Chinese philosophy is at the same time political thought. One might say that Taoism isn't, but saying so is like saying that those who advocate economic laissez faire are not advocating an economic policy or not formulating economic thought. Surely anarchism is political thought even if anarchy sometimes means the absence of government. In political thought, Taoism might be said to be negative in what was advocated when compared with Confucianism. It regarded political measures of the kind advocated by the Confucianists as artificialities which created problems rather than solved them.

This negative doctrine was based on something positive. The Taoistic political thought was both equalitarian and libertarian; it might even be said to be both carried to the extreme. With the doctrine of universal relativity carried to the sphere of politics, it was opposed to any kind of imposition of standards and political measures are in one way or another standardization. Standards there may be, and yet standardization need

四

　　个人不能离开社会而生活，这是不言而喻的。希腊哲学和中国哲学都体现了这个观点。从苏格拉底到亚里士多德，无不特别强调良好政治生活的重要性。这些学者既是政治思想家，也是哲学家。他们的基本观念看来是认为个人要得到最充分即最"自然"的发展，只能以公道的政治社会为媒介。哲学涉及生活之紧密有如文学，也许比很多其他学科更为紧密。那些生来就研究哲学的人，以及那些由于自由受到政治侵犯或社会侵犯而投身于哲学的人，都不能不把上述真理当作自己的前提之一，或者积极原则之一。人们企图提供现今所谓的人生观，企图理解人生，给人生以意义，过良好的生活——这是研究哲学的动力，是比大家重视的纯粹理智更原始的动因。由于人们要过良好的生活，所以生活与政治相联结这条原则就把哲学直接引到政治思想上，哲学家就直接或间接地与政治发生联系，关心政治了。

　　这个传统在西方没有完全贯彻，中断的原因之一将是下节讨论的主题的一部分。然而它在中国几乎一直保持到今天。中国哲学毫无例外地同时也就是政治思想。有人会说道家不是这样，可是说这话就像说鼓吹经济放任的人并非鼓吹一种经济政策，并非陈述经济思想一样。尽管无政府有时是指没有政府，但无政府主义毕竟还是政治思想。在政治思想方面，可以说道家所鼓吹的同儒家相比是消极的。它认为儒家鼓吹的那类政治准则是人为的，只会制造问题而不解决问题。这种消极学说自有其积极基础。道家的政治思想是平等和自由，甚至可以说都推到了极端。它把一切皆相对的学说搬到政治领域，根本反对硬扣标准，而政治准则就是以某种方式硬扣标准。标准可以有，却不必硬扣标准。因为事物的本性中本来就有

not take place, for the standards that are inalterably given in the nature of things need not be imposed at all, while those that need be imposed must inevitably be alien to the situation that gives rise to such impositions. Taoistic political thought was a sort of political laissez faire and laissez aller, it was negative only in the sense of condemning super-imposed political efforts, not in the sense of having entertained no political goal whatsoever. Like Confucianism, Taoism has its political ideal. That ideal might be described as a sort of equalitarian and libertarian bliss to be attained in a kind of Rousseauistic state of nature with perhaps certain European strenuosity edited out of its naturalness.

Compared to Taoism, Confucianism was much more positive in political thought. Confucius himself was a statesman as well as a philosopher. He abstained very wisely from the role of an original thinker, declaring that he was a transmitter of doctrines already entertained and a describer of institutions that existed in a bygone and somewhat golden age. Whether consciously or otherwise, he succeeded in endowing his creative thought with the objectivity of historical continuity. He might have described himself as a Neo-Confucianist, for in giving his thought the impersonality already mentioned, he succeeded also in rendering it uniquely Chinese. Even without political backing it probably could induce Chinese thought to follow its trail, and with political backing it easily molded subsequent thought into its own pattern. That pattern is both philosophy and political thought woven into an organic whole in which politics and ethics are inseparable and in terms of which the man and his station and life are also united. The unity of nature and man is also a unity of ethics and politics, of the individual and the society.

Philosophy and political thought may be linked up in many different ways. One may erect a metaphysical system and deduce from it certain principles concerning politics, or one may plunge into politics and indulge in political thought which has no systematic bearing with his philosophy. Political thought may be internal to a philosophical system and external to the philosopher, or internal to the philosopher, but external to his philosophy. In either case, there is a sort of dislocation; either philosophy ceases to be politically potent, or political thought loses its philosophical foundation. British Hegelianism for instance furnished a political thought internal to the philosophical system, but so external to the philosophers, with the exception of T. H. Green, that neither it nor they could be said to have exerted any influence on English politics.

不可改变的标准，根本不必硬扣；需要硬扣的标准必定与引起硬扣的情况格格不入。道家的政治思想是政治上自由放任，它的消极意义仅仅在于谴责政治上过分硬扣的做法，并不在于不采纳任何政治目标。道家和儒家一样有自己的政治理想。我们可以把那种理想描述为可以在卢梭的自然状态中达到的自由平等境界，再加上欧洲人那种自然而然的不屈不挠的精神。

与道家相比，儒家在政治思想方面要积极得多。孔子本人就既是哲学家又是政治家。他十分明智地不当独创的思想家，宣称自己只是宪章文武，祖述先王之道。他在有意无意之间，成功地使自己的创造性思想带上了继承传统的客观意义。他是可以把自己描述成新儒家的，因为他使自己的思想不带个人性质，也就成功地使它成为独一无二的中国思想。即使没有政治后盾，它大概也能够引导中国思想沿着它的轨道前进；既有政治后盾，它就很容易把后来的思想捏进它的模式。那模式就是哲学和政治思想交织成一个有机整体，使哲学和伦理不可分，人与他的位分和生活合而为一。"天人合一"也是伦理与政治合一，个人与社会合一。

哲学和政治思想可以有多种多样的联系。人们可建立一个形而上学体系，再从其中推出若干有关政治的原则；也可以投身政治，沉湎于一种与他的哲学并无系统联系的政治思想。政治思想可以与某种哲学体系有内在联系，与这位哲学家有外在联系；或者与某位哲学家有内在联系，而与他的哲学有外在联系。这两类情况都会颠倒错乱，不是哲学在政治上失势，就是政治思想失去哲学基础。例如英国的黑格尔主义提供了一种政治思想，与这种哲学体系有内在联系，但是与那些哲学家们的联系非常外在，以致这一体系和这些哲学家都不能说对英国政治产生了什么影响，只有托马斯·希尔·格林除外。

Confucianist political thought was internal both to the philosopher and his philosophy. Through the doctrine that internal saintliness or sagacity could be externalized into enlightened statecraft, every philosopher felt himself to be a potential statesman. It was in statecraft that one's philosophical ideals found their broadest realization. Since Confucianism has become a sort of unwritten constitution in China, the country has been governed more by flexible social control than by rigid legal discipline; and in such a body politic, the eminent philosopher and teacher was at least as much as, if not more of, an unofficial statesman, as a prominent lawyer in a country that is predominantly governed by law. A prominent Confucianist philosopher was a sort of uncrowned king or an uncommissioned minister of state, if not during his life, at least posthumously, for it was he who shaped and fashioned the Zeitgeist in terms of which life in any society was more or less sustained. It was thus that Chinese philosophers were sometimes said to have changed the customs and manners of the land, and it was thus that Chinese philosophy and political thought were significantly woven into a single organic pattern.

儒家政治思想与哲学家及其哲学都有内在联系。儒家讲内圣外王，认为内在的圣智可以外在化成为开明的治国安邦之术，所以每一位哲学家都认为自己是潜在的政治家。一个人的哲学理想，是在经国济世中得到充分实现的。由于儒家思想在中国成了不成文的宪法，国家的治理多半用柔和的社会制约，而不大用硬性的法纪；在这样的国家里，杰出的哲学家和大师的地位即便不高于在野的政治家，至少与在野的政治家相等，同法治国家的杰出律师一样。一位杰出的儒家哲人，即便不在生前，至少在他死后，是无冕之王，或者是一位无任所大臣。因为是他陶铸了时代精神，使社会生活在不同程度上得到维系。因此人们有时说中国哲学家改变了一国的风尚，因此中国哲学和政治思想意味深长地结成了一个单一的有机模式。

V

The unity of philosophy and politics lies partly at any rate in the philosopher. Chinese philosophers until very recent times were quite different from Western philosophers of today. They belonged to the class of Socrates and Plato. In his *Soliloquies in England*, George Santayana declared with some vehemence and more than a trace of protestation that he was a modern Socrates. Of all the present-day philosophers, he might indeed be singled out as a cultural influence of more than a technical significance, having gone through and beyond the technicalities of philosophy and stepped into the realm of humane letters. But frankly, there can be no more modern Socrates any more than there can be a modern Aristotle. Ever since Herbert Spencer, we have learned to be wise in checking our ambition to unify the different branches of knowledge through the medium of a single scholar. There is so much technique developed in each branch of knowledge that it is well-nigh impossible for the underlings that we are to be the masters of them all. We regret the passing of Socrateses. A living encyclopedia may bring forth a certain unity to knowledge which may be efficacious towards its further advancement, but since knowledge could be nibbled at piecemeal and improved or advanced through the present method of the division of labor, the loss of such a unity need not be regretted. In some sense, the passing of Socrateses is much more regrettable.

Not only is there a division of labor in the modern pursuit of knowledge, there is also that trained detachment or externalization. One of the fundamental tenets in the modern scientific procedure is to detach the researcher from the object of his research, and this can only be done by cultivating his emotion for objective truth and making it predominate over what other emotions he may happen to have concerning his researches. Obviously one cannot get rid of one's emotions, not even a scientist, but if one is trained to let one's emotion for objective truth dominate over his other emotions in his researches, one has already acquired the detachment needed for scientific research. In accordance with this procedure the modern philosopher becomes more or less detached from his philosophy. He reasons, he argues, but he hardly ever preaches. Together with the division of labor, the tendency towards detachment makes him a detached logician, or a detached epistemologist, or a detached metaphysician. Philosophers in former days were never

五

　　哲学和政治的统一，总是部分地体现在哲学家身上。中国哲学家在近代以前，与当代的西方哲学家大异其趣。他们属于苏格拉底、柏拉图那一类。乔治·桑塔亚纳在他那本《英伦独语》里大声疾呼，而不只是发表一般声明，说他是现代苏格拉底。在当代的哲学家中，确实可以说数他发挥了超过学术意义的文化影响，他钻研了并且越出了学术性的哲学，踏进了人文学的领域。可是老实说，现代苏格拉底是再也不会有的，现代亚里士多德也不会有。从赫伯特·斯宾塞起，我们已经意识到应该明智一点，不必野心勃勃地要求某一位学者独立统一不同的知识领域的分支。每个分支都取得了很多专门成就，要我们这些庸才全部掌握是几乎不可能的。可惜苏格拉底式的人物已经一去不复返。一个活的百科全书可以使知识得到某种统一，对发展知识可能非常有效。可是通过现在的分工办法，可以将知识分块消化，加以改进，加以提高，丧失这样一种统一也不一定是憾事。在某种意义上，苏格拉底式人物的一去不复返才是更加值得惋惜的。

　　现代人的求知不仅有分工，还有一种训练有素的超脱法或外化法。现代研究工作的基本信条之一，就是要研究者超脱他的研究对象。要做到这一点，只有培养他对于客观真理的感情，使这种感情盖过他可能发生的其他有关研究的感情。人显然不能摆脱自己的感情，连科学家也很难办到。但是他如果经过训练，学会让自己对于客观真理的感情盖过研究中的其他感情，那就已经获得科学研究所需要的那种超脱法了。这样做，现代哲学家就或多或少超脱了自己的哲学。他推理、论证，但是并不传道。除了分工以外，这种超脱的倾向使他成为超脱的逻辑家、超脱的认识论者或者超脱的形而上学家。

professional. The emergence of professional philosophers may have done some service to philosophy, but it seems to have also killed something in the philosopher. He knows philosophy, but he does not live it.

That something is gained in philosophy after this method of approach is employed, there is no doubt. We do know more of the problems of each branch of philosophy than we did before. Although the personality of the philosopher cannot as yet be entirely divorced from his philosophy, a basis for objectivity is achieved which makes philosophy much more capable of cumulative effort than it ever was before. The advance in this direction is made possible by the improvements in the tools of expression; a kind of technique of articulation is being developed which cannot be ignored. Anyone may still enjoy the privilege of adopting any philosophy suited to his nature or pre-dispositions, but he can hardly express his ideas in any way he wants. Nor is the gain limited to philosophy; the philosopher has also gained an ideal of detachment. It might be described as a sort of sweet skepticism in which, to use familiar terms, Hebraic sweetness is seasoned with Hellenic light and Hellenic light is tempered with Hebraic sweetness. Anyone who is fortunate enough to approach this ideal will acquire the kind of rare charm in which skepticism doesn't make him cynical, nor does sweetness made him effusively or obtrusively good. He will not be militantly virtuous and may therefore lose that social or sociological efficacy or function expected of him, but considering the evil that militantly good people may do, he is bound to be a negative asset and a positive value. The ideal is difficult of attainment. In being detached and externalized philosophy becomes a rather tortuous and thorny path; it has become so strewn with technicalities that their mastery requires time, training and a certain academic single-mindedness and before these are mastered one might lose one's way or else wither away in the process. Even when he succeeds to any extent, he is hardly a modern Socrates.

Chinese philosophers were all of them different grades of Socrateses. This was so because ethics, politics, reflective thinking and knowledge were unified in the philosopher; in him, knowledge and virtue were one and inseparable. His philosophy required that he lived it, he was himself its vehicle. To live in accordance with his philosophical convictions was part of his philosophy. It was his business to school himself continually and persistently to that pure experience in which selfishness or egocentricity was transcended so that he would be one with the universe.

往日的哲学家从来不是专职的。职业哲学家的出现可以对哲学有些好处，但是对哲学家似乎也有所损伤。他懂哲学，却不用哲学。

采用这种做法之后，哲学当然也有所得。我们对每个哲学分支的问题比以前知道得多了。虽然还不能把哲学家的个性与他的哲学完全拆开，毕竟为客观性打下了一个基础，使哲学比以前更能接受积累。其所以在这一方面有所进步，是由于表达工具有了改进，思路得以分明的技术正在发展，这是不容忽视的。任何一个人，可以仍然有权采取任何适合于他的禀性的哲学，却不能随心所欲地表达他的思想。有所得的还不限于哲学，哲学家也得到了一种超脱的理想。我们可以把这超脱描述为一种美妙的怀疑主义：在这种怀疑主义里，可以说希腊的明朗渗透进了希伯来的美妙，希伯来的美妙软化了希腊的明朗。有幸接近这种理想的人会妙趣横生，怀疑主义并不使他尖酸刻薄，美妙也不使他过于清高。他不会因过于清高而失掉人们瞩望于他的社会作用；他有鉴于过于清高之士可以办坏事，就只好既消极又积极。理想是很难达到的。哲学一超脱，就成了一条迂回曲折的崎岖道路，布满技术性的问题。掌握它需要时间，需要训练，需要学究式的专一。在全部掌握之前往往会迷失方向，或者半途而废。一个人即便取得了某种程度的成就，也不能成为现代苏格拉底。

中国哲学家都是不同程度的苏格拉底式人物。其所以如此，是因为伦理、政治、反思和认识集于哲学家一身，在他那里知识和美德是不可分的一体。他的哲学要求他身体力行，他本人是实行他的哲学的工具。按照自己的哲学信念生活，是他的哲学的一部分。他的事业就是继续不断地把自己修养到进入无我的纯净境界，从而

Obviously this process of schooling could not be stopped, for stopping it would mean the emergence of his ego and the loss of his universe. Hence cognitively he was eternally groping, and conatively, he was eternally behaving or trying to behave. Since these could not be separated, in him you have synthetically the "philosopher" in the original sense. Like Socrates, he did not keep office hours with his philosophy. Neither was he a dusty musty closeted philosopher sitting in a chair on the periphery of life. With him, philosophy was hardly ever merely a pattern of ideas exhibited for human understanding, but also at the same time a system of precepts internal to the conduct of the philosopher and in extreme cases it might even be said to be his biography. We are not speaking of the caliber of the philosopher—he might be second rate; or of the quality of his philosophy—it might not be tenable; we are speaking of the unity of the philosopher with his philosophy. The separation of these has changed the social value of philosophy and deprived the world of one kind of colorfulness.

与宇宙合而为一。这个修养过程显然是不能中断的，因为一中断就意味着自我抬头，失掉宇宙。因此，在认识上，他永远在探索；在意愿上，则永远在行动或者试图行动。这两方面是不能分开的，所以在他身上你可以综合起来看到那本来意义的"哲学家"。他同苏格拉底一样，哲学不局限于办公时间。他也不是一个深居简出、端坐在生活以外的哲学家。在他那里，哲学从来不单是一个提供人们理解的观念模式，它同时是哲学家内心中的一个信条体系；在极端情况下，甚至可以说就是他的传记。我们说的并不是哲学家的才具——他可以是第二流哲学家；也不是哲学家的思想——它可能都站不住脚；我们说的是哲学家与他的哲学合一。哲学家与哲学分离已经改变了哲学的社会价值，使世界失去了一抹绚丽的色彩。

Philosophy

哲学与生活

and Life³

It is not merely in China that philosophers have been put on the defense from the point of view of the ever growing irrelevancy of philosophy to life. The philosophers' conference in the spring of last year indicated that the problem has finally succeeded in attracting general attention in America. It seems however that if there is any solution to the problem, it does not lie merely with the professional philosophers. In the following pages we shall urge that the professional philosophers are not alone to blame, that the organization of and for knowledge is unsuited towards a discriminating life and that it is dangerous to the ideals of democracy.

The reason why philosophy is singled out for attack lies chiefly in the comparison between its present status and its ancient and honorable history. Philosophy used to deal with the fundamental problems of life and philosophers had often been great masters, fountains of not merely knowledge but also of wisdom, to whom the less gifted looked for guidance and light. Socrates, Plato and Aristotle were not merely the walking encyclopedias of their time, they were also its statesmen, its priests, its columnists and its radio commentators combined. In China the discrepancy between the ancient and present-day philosophers is perhaps even more striking. The philosophers used to occupy a position more significant if not more powerful than that of the great lawyers in American history in times of peace, and in times of emergency they had even appeared as Catos in the defense of their dynasty or their fatherland. The question arises naturally as to what the present-day philosophers are doing to meet the needs of an essentially medieval country invaded by a ruthless enemy, impoverished and almost disorganized by seven years of modern warfare. The comparison renders philosophy a natural target for dissatisfaction.

Two points might be briefly considered, one of them concerning the scope of philosophy and the other its nature. The fact that the term "philosophy" has changed its scope is known to everybody and yet the consequences of such a change do not seem to have been equally borne in mind. Philosophy has become a sort of impoverished country family with its estate partitioned into small lots managed by city agents. What is known as philosophy that is taught in the universities is merely the scanty

一

　　并非只是在中国，哲学家才面临着被批评哲学与生活越来越脱节的问题。夫年春季的哲学家大会表明，这个问题终于也在美国引起了普遍的注意。但是，即使有什么解决的办法，也不仅仅是职业化的哲学家的任务。下面我们将说明，为此受谴责的不仅有职业化的哲学家，现行的知识结构和追求知识的方式也不利于形成一种有见识、有辨别力的生活，而这一点对于民主的理想来说也是极其危险的。

　　哲学家之所以被单挑出来承受攻击，原因主要在于，哲学目前的状况与它昔日的荣耀形成了鲜明的对照。过去，哲学处理的是生活中最根本的问题。哲学家通常都是大师，不仅是知识的源泉，也是智慧的源泉；从他们那里，后知后觉者寻到了引导和启示。苏格拉底、柏拉图和亚里士多德不仅是他们时代的活的百科全书，同时也是那一时代的政治家、牧师、专栏作家和电台评论人。在中国，哲学家在古今的差异甚至更大。中国哲学家昔日所占据的位置即使不比美国历史上和平时期的伟大律师们更有权威，也比他们更有影响力；而在紧要关头，他们会挺身而出，如加图一样捍卫他们的王朝或祖国。自然有人会问，哲学家眼下都在做什么，去满足一个与中世纪状态相差无几的国家的需要？这个国家正受着凶残的外敌入侵，经过七年的现代战争，早已凋敝不堪、涣散无序。正是古今的对比使哲学成为人们宣泄不满的对象。

　　主要有两个问题需要考虑，一个是哲学的界域，一个是哲学的性质。"哲学"的界域已经改变了，这一事实世人皆知，然而这种改变的结果却似乎没有在思想上获得承认。哲学好像是一个破落的乡村家庭，它的地产已经被分割得七零八落，分别落入都市代理人之手。现在在大学里仍然被称为哲学而教授的，只不过是残留给

lot left to the county seat. Shorn of its ancient glory and splendor, it is yet on the whole efficiently managed. If one takes philosophy in the sense of the original property including the lots entrusted to city agents, it hasn't lost its relevancy to current problems nor has it failed to meet national emergencies. Washington D.C. represents the greatest concentration of philosophy, if we take it in this wide sense. The great master has indeed disappeared being split into a large number of experts who should nevertheless be known as philosophers. But if we take philosophy in the narrow sense, it is doubtful whether it has ever been potent in shaping the destinies of man.

Perhaps more relevant to our point is that philosophizing has changed its nature. A sort of objective research has taken place rendering the approach to philosophy more closely allied to science than to religion. Skepticism seems to be the key note to the new approach and the most important tenet is to detach the researcher from the object of his research or at any rate to relegate him as much as possible to an irrelevant background. It is easily seen that with this approach there is hardly any principle unconditionally accepted and none unswervingly adhered to by any group of philosophers. Dogma disappears and with its disappearance philosophy ceases to furnish life with any motive force. It does not urge people to do anything, it hardly ever advocates, and if it insists upon the acceptance of certain propositions, it does so with discursive argumentation rather than peremptory indoctrination. If a philosopher advocates any doctrine militantly, it is not philosophy that is motivating him, it is rather the priest or the politician or the social reformer. Academic philosophy has ceased to be a moral force, in the sense, let's say, of Confusianism, and in making whatever training that is required more and more technical, it has also become less and less of an educational discipline.

Whether modern philosophy is useful or not depends upon the view as to what kind of use is to be made out of it. The significant fact is not that epistemology dominates philosophy, it is rather that the whole field of philosophy is organized for understanding or knowledge. Ethics does not teach students to be good, it teaches them to understand goodness; esthetics does not teach students to appreciate the beautiful, it teaches them to understand beauty. Groham Wallas should be sympathized with

这个乡村宅第的微不足道的一小部分而已。被剥夺了昔日辉煌和荣耀的光芒之后，哲学在总体上仍然被安置得很好。如果人们考虑哲学原始的地产中仍然包括已被都市代理人托管的部分，那么哲学就没有丧失对当下问题的关切，也没有放弃对民族危机的回应。如果我们在宽泛的意义上理解哲学，华盛顿特区就是哲学的最大集中地。大师确实消失了，分化成了无数的专家，尽管他们可以被认为是哲学家。但是，如果我们狭义地理解哲学，那么哲学是否有效地影响了人类命运，就是值得怀疑的了。

更加值得注意的是，用哲学家的思维来研究问题的性质也已经改变了。一种客观研究的方法兴起来了，它使哲学研究更倾向于与科学而不是与宗教联盟。这种新的研究方法的核心概念是怀疑论，最重要的原则是使研究者独立于研究对象之外，或者至少把他尽可能降为研究的无关紧要的背景。不难看出，采取这种方法，几乎就没有哲学家可无条件接受或坚定不移支持的原则了。教条消失了，随着教条的消失，哲学也不再为生活提供任何动力。它不再敦促人们做任何事，它甚至不再鼓吹什么。如果它要坚持让你接受某些提议，也只是通过东拉西扯的论证，而不是霸道地灌输。如果一个哲学家咄咄逼人地鼓吹某种学说，推动他的绝不是哲学，而是他身上牧师、政治家或者社会改良者的那一部分。学院派的哲学不再像中国古代的儒家学说那样是一种道德的力量；在它的各种训练中，技巧的要求越来越多，而教育的意味越来越稀薄。

现代哲学是否有用，这一问题有赖于我们如何看待哲学所产生的作用。在这里，值得注意的事实不是认识论主宰了哲学，而是整个哲学领域都是为了理解或者说是为了追求知识而构建起来的。伦理学不再教导学生为善，它教学生理解善为何物；美学不再教学生欣赏美，它教学生理解什么是美。格雷厄姆·沃拉斯关心思想

for his solitude in concerning himself with the art of thinking, for the courses on logic at present supply the students with the knowledge of validity rather than train them for valid thinking or thought. If something is regrettably lost, something is also distinctly gained. The modern approach to philosophy renders it more tangible than before as well as more capable of cumulative effort, and with it knowledge in philosophy is capable of compound interest. Knowledge in philosophy can be willed to posterity whereas philosophical experience or insight cannot. It cannot be denied that in being organized for understanding and knowledge, philosophy has had a steady progress and as knowledge is always useful whether directly or indirectly, philosophy cannot fail to be useful even though its usefulness is transferred to a sphere different from what we expect it to be if we have in mind the example of philosophy in the past.

Nevertheless something is regrettably lost. In being thus organized for knowledge, philosophy has become even for those who philosophize a mere aspect in life, an absorbing profession during office hours perhaps, but nonetheless an aspect detached from life in general. The synthetic unity of the philosopher with the man seems to have disappeared. One gets the impression that among scores of professors of philosophy, there is hardly a single philosopher. In becoming the monopoly of a few experts, philosophy has ceased to be a free commodity either in the rough and tumble of the market or in the politeness and gentility of society tea parties. The old earnestness of purpose in philosophy has been replaced by a kind of skillfulness in the manipulation of ideas and whatever philosophical impulse there is in the layman, it is no longer satisfied by technical philosophy. For him philosophy becomes as shrouded in mystery as science, but unlike science its usefulness is not evident in terms of concrete achievements. Is there any reason why philosophy should take up its present trend? There are a large number of reasons, but we shall take up only one of them.

方法的孤独实在值得同情，是因为近来的逻辑课程为学生提供的是合理性的知识，而不是训练他们如何合理地进行思考。有所失必有所得。哲学的现代研究方法使哲学比过去更加清晰明确，也更有助于知识的积累，使蕴藏在哲学中的知识能够唤起广泛的兴趣。哲学的知识能够遗留给后代而哲学的经验和洞察则不能。无可否认的是，从进行理解和获得知识出发而建构起来的哲学已经取得了稳固的进步。因为知识总是有用的，无论直接还是间接，所以哲学不可能丧失其有用性，尽管它的作用已经转移了领域，这个领域与我们按哲学的昔日风范所指望它发挥作用的领域不甚相同。

然而确实有些东西无可挽回地丧失了。为了知识而建构起来的哲学甚至成为可以在八小时以内从事的职业，那些人仅用哲学家的思维来研究生活的某个方面，但是这个部分一般情况下也是与生活分离着的。哲学家与人的合而为一似乎已经消失了。人们得到这种印象，成堆的哲学教授中，几乎没有一个哲学家。哲学为几个专家所垄断，它不再是嘈杂混乱的市井和优雅的沙龙茶会都能够随意取用的日常用品。哲学昔日对意义的渴望已经被操控观念的技巧所取代，然而这种技术哲学满足不了门外汉内在的哲学冲动。在一般人的眼里，哲学已经变得像科学一样云遮雾绕，无比神奇，可是又不像科学能够以有形的成就明确展示其作用。哲学有什么理由走当前的发展之路？理由很多，但我们只谈其中的一个。

In taking up its present trend, philosophy is simply following the example of almost every branch of study. Almost all studies are at present organized for efficiency and in being so organized they are inevitably accompanied by certain characteristics. In the first place there is on the whole a tendency towards further and further subdivision so that a larger and larger number of scholars become experts in narrower and narrower fields of knowledge. Each tiny subdivision becomes a technical retreat and the expert comfortably settled in it cannot be expected to be the master of a whole branch of study. Great masters have disappeared in natural sciences, they are disappearing in economies and sociology, and in the sphere of philosophy there will soon be the logician, the epistemologist, the esthetician, etc., instead of the philosopher. In the second place, in order to obtain results, scholars have to detach themselves as much as possible from the object of their studies. While the attitude is admirable from the point of view of obtaining reliable knowledge or information, it is liable to render the result of the study external to the student. His study is indeed a vital element in his profession, but whether or not it is equally a vital element in his life depends upon whether or not his profession absorbs his life. If it does, he is a single-tracked man with a large number of other aspects of life submerged or undeveloped or brushed aside; and if it doesn't, his study becomes external to his life. Other characteristics may be mentioned, but these two alone are sufficient to indicate the flavor of our present-day scholarship. What is even more important is that these characteristics act and react upon each other to accelerate the direction in which our knowledge is tending for. The more the studies are subdivided, the more they are externalized, and the more they are externalized, the more minute the subdivisions also become.

These characteristics are the direct results of organizing studies on the basis of efficiency and entirely for the advancement of knowledge. There was a time when studies were not so organized, when the educated were almost always the cultural, some of them even living full lives in which a multiplicity of impulses found their natural play. There used to be scholars in China who didn't care to pass examinations and even during the last century in England there were scholars who didn't bother to

二

哲学开始形成当前的发展趋势，只不过是追随其他各学科的榜样而已。当前，几乎所有学科都是为着效率而组织起来的，在这样的结构形式中，它们不可避免地伴随着某些特征。首先，总的趋势是分工日益细密，越来越多的学者在越来越窄的知识领域里成为专家。每一个细小的知识分支都成为一个技术园地，很难指望安居其中的专家会成为整个学科的大师。在自然科学领域，大师已经消失了，他们也正在经济学和社会学的领域里消失。在哲学的领域，也会很快出现逻辑学家、认识论专家、美学家等等，而不是哲学家了。其次，为了获得成果，学者们不得不尽可能使自己与研究对象分离开来。从获得确实可靠的知识或信息的观点来看，这种态度是值得赞赏的；但与此同时，它又具有使研究成果外在于研究者的倾向。毫无疑问，学者的研究是他职业生涯中的一个重要因素，但是，它是否同样是他生活中的重要因素，却在于他的职业是否融入了他的生活。如果融入了，他就是一个偏狭的人，因为他生活中的其他许多方面都被淹没了，或者是没有得到发展，或者是被弃之不顾。如果他的职业没有融入他的生活，他的研究就变得外在于他的生活了。也许还能提到另外一些特点，但仅此两点就足以显示当代学术的风貌了。更重要的是，这两点一再发挥作用和彼此作用，促使当前的趋势加速发展。我们的知识处于此种趋势之下，研究变得越细碎，它们就越外在化；而它们越外在化，研究又变得越细碎。

在效率的基础上组织研究，完全为推进知识而开展研究，其直接后果便是上述这些特点。曾经有一个时期，学术研究不是这种形态。在那时，受过教育的人几乎总是有文化修养的，其中的一些人甚至完全随兴所至，让各种兴趣自然地得到满足。中国过去也有一些学者根本不在乎功名；就在上一个世纪，英国也有不少学者根本

write books. For them it was quite sufficient merely to have lived a life of discrimination. It is true that under the social and economic conditions then prevailing, few could indulge in any such ideal. But then now that the conditions are improved why not extend the ideal to the masses of people? The reason why such an ideal cannot be seriously entertained lies in the fact that for the individual at present, it has no survival value. In a highly industrialized and economically competitive community, each has a function to perform and efficiency in its performance enables and entitles him to survive. The existence of the idle rich should not blind us to the extent as to minimize the prevalence of this tendency towards greater and greater efficiency. It is this tendency that is ultimately responsible for the remarkable strength of the industrial powers exhibited in the present crisis. If this tendency is so prevalent in other spheres of life, we can hardly expect it to be absent in the realm of scholarship and studies.

There is unfortunately an additional reason. Scholarship used to be in China at least an individual and almost private affair. It did not require much property to indulge in, and while scholars constituted a class or a social and political status, scholarship was not a profession. Poverty of course did diminish the possible number of scholars, but those who were so fortunate as to possess the minimum amount of wealth could become scholars and what is more important they themselves owned the paraphernalia with which they worked. In this respect they were somewhat like the artisans of medieval Europe. They didn't have to justify themselves socially or politically. With industrialization and cooperate organization of institutions for scholarship, the paraphernalia for studies have been taken away from the scholars just as with industrialization the instruments or tools have been taken away from the workers. Scientists depend almost entirely at present upon public institutions and while in Humanities one may still indulge in private research if one happens to be comparatively wealthy, the chance for one's doing so is getting shimmer and shimmer every day. Scholars have become employees and in being paid for their work are constantly put on the defense unless they show reasons continuously why they should be so employed. Scholarship has become professionalized and it is scholars' business to produce knowledge. The emergence of professional tennis players seemed to have aroused both resentment and resistance, but the emergence of

不为撰写著作而费尽心思。对于他们来说,只要过一种有辨别力的生活就足够了。确实,在当时盛行的经济及社会条件下,只有极少数人能够醉心于这样的理想。但是,在目前条件已经改善的情况下,为什么不把这种理想普及到广大民众呢?这种理想之所以不能保持,原因在于,对于现代的个人来说,毫无存活价值可言。在高度工业化和经济竞争的社会里,每一个人都要发挥一种作用,只有有效地发挥其作用,一个人才有可能,同时也才有资格存活下来。悠闲的有钱人确实存在,但是这一点不应当蒙蔽我们,使我们看不到总趋势是追求越来越高的效率。正是这一趋势,应当对当前危机中呈现出的巨大的工业化力量承担责任。如果追求效率的趋势通行于生活的其他领域,我们怎么可能指望它在学术研究的领域里缺席呢?

不幸的是,这里还有一个原因。过去,中国的学术活动是个人的事,甚至是私密的事。醉心学术无需大量的财产来支持,虽然学者构成了一个阶层,成为一种社会的、政治的身份,但学术不是一种职业。贫穷肯定减少了学者的可能数量,但那些有幸拥有些许财产的人都有可能成为学者。更重要的是,他们自己就拥有从事学术活动的种种用具。在这一方面,他们有点像欧洲中世纪的手艺人,他们无须在社会上或者在政治上确认自己的身份。随着工业化的到来和学术在研究所里协作组织,学者从事学术研究的用具被拿走了,就像工业化把生产设备和工具从工人那里拿走一样。现在,科学家已经完全依赖科研机构;在人文研究领域,如果相对有钱,也还可以从事私人研究,但这样做的机会在一天天地减少。学者成为雇员,以研究换取报酬,并不断遭受质询,除非他们不断地出示理由,说明他们应当被如此雇佣。学术职业化了,学者的工作就是生产知识。职业网球运动员的出现似乎引起了抱怨和抵制;但是,

professional scholars has taken place unheralded and unsung on the one hand and unresisted and uncondemned on the other. Even philosophy can hardly escape being professionalized and philosophers are now taken to task as to what kind of product they are issuing to the general public. Philosophers may suffer in comparison with the scholars in the other branches of knowledge, but both suffer from the domination by the same tendency.

Let it be thoroughly understood that we are not here condemning the tendency described above. From the point of view of gaining knowledge it should be highly praised. Knowledge is useful directly or indirectly and what is even more significant, it is power. It is power whether we use it in our struggle against nature or merely against other men. Nor is it irrelevant to life; it is probably the most potent factor in improving the conditions under which we live and to use an old phrase it is probably the most effective instrument in hindering whatever natural hindrances there may be to the maintenance of the conditions of a desirable life. What is maintained is rather that however relevant knowledge may be to the conditions of life, it is not, or at any rate has ceased to be, a vital element in the main spring of our actual living. It is somewhat like money which assumes different roles to different people depending on whether it is in the hands of the abjectly poor or fabulously rich. In the hands of the former it may remove certain undesirable conditions of life, while in the hands of the latter it need not be conducive to a more desirable mood of living. Like money again, knowledge is a sort of currency with which desires and passions are satisfied, and a wealth of knowledge need not raise the quality of living.

Nor are we belittling science. We are not suggesting that those in a limitation to the applicability of scientific method; it may very well be that anything under the sun could be scientifically studied. Nor are we saying that the training involved is useless to the general business of living; it undoubtedly is especially from the point of view that the scientific attitude may be carried over to the other spheres of life. What is maintained is that no matter how much we know of the processes of life in terms of scientific concepts, we still have to live our lives as individual and social experiences with the particular endowment that is given to us. A thorough knowledge of nutrition may enable a person to choose the food that is good for his health, but it does not necessarily enable him to

职业学者的出现既没有人宣告和称颂，也没有人抵制或诅咒。哲学自然也难逃职业化，哲学家现在受到的责难是，他们将为公众生产什么产品。与其他知识领域的学者相比，哲学家可能更痛苦，但所有学者都同样在遭受被当前的趋势所支配而造成的痛苦。

希望诸位充分理解，我们在这里并没有诅咒上面所提到的学术趋势。从获取知识的观点来看，这种趋势应该受到高度赞扬。无论直接还是间接，知识总是有用的；更重要的是，它是一种力量，一种我们可以用来对抗自然或者他人的力量。它也并非与生活无关，而可能是改善我们生活条件的最强有力的因素。用一句老话来说，为了维持理想生活的条件，排除自然设置的种种障碍，最有效者无如知识。然而可以肯定的是，无论知识与生活的条件如何相关，它也不是，或者在某种程度不再是我们实际生活的源头活水。知识有点像金钱，在不同的人那里扮演着不同的角色，这取决于它是在赤贫之人手里还是在巨富之人手里。在穷人手里，它可能改变某些不尽如人意的生活条件；在富人手中，它却不会使生活变得更称心如意。还是像金钱，知识是一种通货，拥有它，意愿能够得到满足；但是拥有太多知识并不一定能够提高生活质量。

我们也绝无小看科学的意思，我们并未将其限定在科学方法的应用性上。可以说，普天之下莫非科学研究之对象。我们也没有说，有关的训练对于生活中的一般事务无所补益。相反，从科学态度应该被推广到生活的其他方面的观点来看，这些训练是特别有用的。问题是，无论我们如何根据科学的观点来理解生活的进程，无论这种理解达到何种程度，我们仍然要以自己独特的天赋，形成个体和社会经验，过自己的日子。对营养学的全面了解可以使人挑选有益于身体健康的食品，但是并不必然使他爱好那些有益健康的

prefer what is wholesome to what is tasty. A thorough knowledge of sex certainly does not substitute for sexual experience, and it is extremely doubtful whether experts on sex are ever expert lovers. A drunkard who doesn't know that alcohol is bad for him is merely miserable when he is dead drunk, and he needn't be unhappy; but if he knows that alcohol is bad for him and yet cannot resist it, it is a tragedy when he succumbs to alcohol. It is doubtful whether knowledge by itself had ever been a directing influence; if ever it was, it is no longer so for most people; for them it is a commodity like tooth brush and like tooth brush it is liable to be hung up whenever it is not in use. Whether knowledge in some other sense is virtue or not and, the Greeks claimed it was, we needn't try to ascertain, knowledge as it has come to be today is not a virtue. It is too neutral to influence our preferences or tastes, too properly non-committal to enable us to pass on issues outside of its proper sphere, too external to enable us to act on our beliefs, and too impotent to furnish us with any, and instead of being the master or co-worker of emotions and passions, it has become their slave.

食品胜过符合他口味的食品。对性科学的全面了解肯定不能代替性经验；一个性学专家能否成为性爱高手，这是大可怀疑的。一个醉鬼不知道酒精对他有害，他只是在他酩酊大醉时比较凄惨，而他本人不一定不幸福；但是，如果他知道酒精对他有害却禁不住诱惑依然贪杯，这就成了一个悲剧。知识本身是否具有指导性的影响，这是值得怀疑的。如果它曾经有过这种影响，那么对于大多数人来说，它现在已经不再有了。在大多数人那里，知识像是牙刷一类的用具，只要不用，就被挂起来了。在其他意义上，知识是否是美德——古希腊人认为是——我们无须求证，知识在今天已经不是了。知识是中性的，影响不了我们的爱好和口味；它的分寸感太强，使我们不能靠它来解决它的恰当范围以外的问题；它太外在，不能支持我们根据信仰来行动；它也太软弱，不能为我们提供任何信仰。它未能成为情感和欲望的主宰或伙伴，相反，它成了它们的奴隶。

III

With the exception of Germany, the highly industrialized countries were also democracies. Democracies have been economically imperialistic, but they have not been in recent years at any rate blatant military aggressors. If the world is to be made safe for democracy, democracy should be safe for the world as well as for its own citizens. Since the citizens constitute the ultimate sovereign of a democracy, it is essential that they themselves should be free, independent and discriminating individuals. In order that they may not be blindly led, they should live discriminating lives rather than exist as mere lubricated parts of well-oiled machines. Since the majority rules, it is essential that majority decision represents discriminating choice rather than blind impulse. If power politics is to be condemned in international relations, it should be equally so within a nation or a state. If power politics in international nations leaves the weak states the helpless spoils of the strong, power politics within a nation or a state leaves the citizens identified with the special interests practically without any voice in their government. Internal politics is indeed more fundamental, for if political action within a state represents the resultant force of the pull and push of special interests, there is no guarantee that they will not pull and push beyond the national boundaries. In order to make democracy safe for the world, it should be made safe for its own citizens. The ideal of democracy can only be achieved by having free independent and discriminating citizens who are eternally vigilant over their public duties. It imposes a most strenuous duty on the common man, but for those who believe in democracy, the responsibility assumed by them is well worth their while for it is the only one compatible with the dignity of being human.

In totalitarian countries some special ideology is imposed on all people as that they are whipped into a single purpose resulting in the kind of uniformity of behavior desired by the accepted leader or oligarchy. A certain amount of uniformity of behavior is necessary for any nation. Most nations depend for it upon a common language, a common cultural pattern or historical heritage, as well as upon blood ties. Modern industry contributes to it so subtly that a certain amount of uniformity of behavior is achieved without being suspected that it is imposed, since it is

三

除了德国，高度工业化的国家都是民主国家。民主国家在经济上是扩张性质的，但是，它们在近年以来尚未公然成为军事侵略者。如果这个世界要保障民主国家的安全，那么，民主国家也应当保障这个世界以及本国国民的安全。因为国民是民主国家的最终主宰者，所以他们本身应当是自由的、独立的和有分辨力的个人，这一点非常重要。为了不被盲目引导，他们不应当仅仅充当机器中被润滑油打磨过的零件，而应当过一种有分辨力的生活。由于是大多数人说了算，大多数人的决定就应当是经过分辨的选择而不是源于盲目的冲动，这一点也是很重要的。如果强权政治在国际关系中要受谴责，那么，它在一个国家内部也应当同样受到谴责。如果强权政治在国际上让弱国无助地遭受强国的欺凌，一个国家内的强权政治也会让它与特殊利益联系到一起的国民几乎不能在他们的政府里传达出自己的声音。国内政治确实更加根本，因为，如果一个国家内的政治举措是特殊利益拉锯的最终结果，谁也不能保证这种拉锯不会越到国界之外。为了让民主国家保障世界的安全，民主国家就应当被造就得能够保障它自己的国民的安全。民主的理想只能由自由的、独立的、有分辨力的国民来实现，这些国民永远不放松自己的公共责任。民主理想要求普通人承担重要的责任，而对于那些信仰民主理想的人来说，应当由他们承担的责任却非常值得花费精力，因为只有这些责任与做人的尊严是一致的。

在极权国家，某些特殊的观念被强加于全体人民，以此把他们驱赶至某个单一的目标之下。这就导致某种统一的行为，而这种行为正是他们的领袖或政治寡头所希望的。任何国家都需要一定程度的统一行为，大多数国家除了依靠血缘纽带来实现这一点，还依靠共同的语言、共同的文化类型或历史遗产。现代工业为此所做的贡献是很微妙的，以至于它达到了某种统一的行为方式却不被认为是

not consciously imposed by a person or a group of persons. In America, for example, industry is probably the greatest unifying force. Industrial efficiency contributes to political efficacy; measures that are difficult to be carried out in China for instance are easily enforced in America. Industrial power is also military power. By itself it is merely military power that is economically imperialistic, but not militarily aggressive, so that it is defensive not offensive military power. It has thus far saved the democracies from being vanquished in war, and although it has enabled them to be economically imperialistic, it has made them safe neighbors compared to the totalitarian powers. Back in the days of 1940 when the Nazis overran Holland, Belgium and France, some people in China felt that democracies were woefully weak and inefficient. They were indeed vulnerable and when quick decisions were to be made, they certainly were inadequate. Not many of us know that the power of democracies is latent and when not put to the test not actual; but once the decision is made, the whole apparatus of military action is set up, power becomes phenomenally evident. But power is always dangerous; it could be used for good and evil alike; and whether it is used one way or another depends upon the person or persons who wield it.

We are accustomed to coupling industry with democracy without suspecting that along certain lines of development, they may turn out to be not compatible with each other. What is needed for the citizens of a democracy is the independent and discriminating individual, and what is needed for the workers of any industry is the efficient and mechanically minded expert. Instead of using the terms "spiritual" and "material," let us employ the terms "human" and "mechanical." Democracy requires the human and industry the mechanical. If everything is industrialized or even carried with the industrial spirit behind it, the result may be the destruction of much if not all that is human. Industrialize religion and we may indeed gain imposing churches and even expert preachers, what may also be lost is the old humble spiritual haven and the intimate kind of moral influence. Industrialize our creative impulses, we may indeed gain expert craftsmanship, but then we may lose the genuine artist. The industrial method could be applied to any sphere and whenever it is applied without any ameliorating influence, some measurable criterion

在强加于人，因为没有人感到有人或有一群人在强迫他们。例如，工业在美国可能是最强大的统一力量。工业的效率有助于政治效能的产生，比如在中国难以推行的措施在美国就可能轻而易举地实行。工业的力量还是军事的力量。就它本身而言，它也仅仅是经济上扩张性质的军事力量而已，并不具备军事侵略性。所以，它是防御的而不是进攻的军事力量。它拯救了民主国家，使它们不至于在战争中被击败。虽然工业力量使民主国家可能在经济上是扩张性质的，但与极权的力量相比，民主国家使它们的邻居感到安全。回想1940年，当纳粹入侵荷兰、比利时和法国时，一些中国人感到，民主国家是极度衰弱、无效的。这些国家确实易受攻击；当需要迅速作出决定，他们也确实力不从心。没有多少人知道民主国家的力量是潜在的，不推上火线不会发挥威力。然而，一旦作出了决定，建立起军事行动的全套设置，它的力量会非常惊人。但是，力量总是危险的，它可以用之于善，也可以用之于恶；它究竟被用于何种用途，就要看操作它的人是谁了。

我们习惯于把工业和民主相提并论，丝毫没有想到，沿着一定的路线发展，它们可能会变得互不相容。民主制度下的国民需要成为独立的、有辨别力的个人，而工业制度下的工人需要成为有效率的、有机械化头脑的专家。让我们使用"人"和"机器"这两个词来取代"灵性"和"物性"这两个术语。民主制要求的是人，而工业化要求的是机器。如果一切都被工业化了，或者一切事物的背后都透着工业的精神，那么，结果很可能是极大地（如果不是全部地的话）破坏属于人的东西。如果把宗教工业化，我们可能得到庄严的教堂，甚至得到训练有素的牧师，但可能失去破旧简陋的灵魂庇护所和亲密的道德感化。把我们的创作冲动工业化，我们可能得到熟练的手艺人，却也许会丧失真正的艺术家。工业化的方式可能被应用到各个方面，无论什么时候，只要它被加以应用而没什么改善

will be adopted and in terms of that criterion efficiency will be increased and men who are active in that field will become more and more expert as well as mechanically minded. Add competitive economy to industry, and we can hardly escape baneful results. If one works efficiently for eight hours every week day, the desire to spend the Sunday efficiently is almost irresistible. A sort of gyroscopic activity results, and the free and easy exchange of ideas and feelings, the desire to be whimsical, or to cope with the imponderables, or merely to be lazy will be easily censored by the desire to fill the hours of leisure with a maximum of activity, and a minimum of adventure in feeling or in thought. The expert in one sphere is liable to be an ignoramus in other spheres and the mechanically minded may be as helpless as a new born babe when confronted with novel human situations. It is difficult to expect people so conditioned to react alertly and discriminatingly to the complicated internal and international politics and when any important decision is to be made, they are liable to make it at the dictates of their profession or their industrial interests. The democratic ideal may be defeated even in a democracy.

These are quite a few astounding assumptions probably unconsciously held by people in the advanced democracies. Probably very few people believe in the existence of the economic man, very few believe without qualification in the doctrine of economic determinism and yet an enormous number of persons somehow believe or at least act as if they do believe that economic emancipation is a panacea for all social and political evils. It would be for the economic man, but for most people of flesh and blood the solution of economic problems leaves a large number of other problems unsolved. Probably very few people regard human beings as thinking or knowing machines, and yet the assumption that if people only know what to do and how to do things, all their problems would also be solved. For the thinking or knowing machines, knowledge of solutions would indeed dissolve problems before hand so that they do not even emerge as problems, but for human beings with their passions and desires, their loves and hatreds, hopes and fears, and probably a large assortment of complexes, the acquisition of knowledge not only need not solve problems, it may even render them worse confounded than before. There is at present current in the West a new notion of democracy, a sort of state socialism without its old name, whereby the government

效果的话，就会采取某种度量标准。根据这种标准，效率会上升，活跃在这一领域里的人将越来越技艺精湛、头脑僵化。工业化再加上经济竞争，我们几乎难逃这种灾难性的后果。如果一个人在一周的每一个工作日都高效率地工作，那么，他就不可避免地也想充分安排周末时间。那就会产生像陀螺一样旋转不停的活动，那么自由交流思想和情感、追求奇思异想、处理难以预料的事件或者干脆就无所事事这样的想法就很容易被下面的想法替代：休闲时光也要尽可能多地填满活动，尽可能少地做一些情感或思想上的冒险。某一领域的专家很可能对其他领域一无所知；在面临新的人类境遇时，具有机械化头脑的人可能会像新生的婴儿一样束手无策。很难指望这样的人能够对复杂的国内和国际政治作出警觉的、有辨别力的反应。需要作重大决定时，这些人往往从自己的职业或工业上的利益出发来考虑问题。民主的理想很可能在民主的制度下被粉碎。

这些令人吃惊的假设可能被先进的民主制度下的人们不自觉地接受了。可能很少有人相信经济人的存在，很少有人无条件地相信经济决定论。但是，许多人都多少有些相信，或者他们的行为表明他们似乎相信，经济的解放是包治一切社会和政治邪恶疾病的灵丹妙药。对于经济人来说是这样，但是对于大多数有血有肉的人来说，经济问题解决之后还有大量其他问题有待解决。可能很少有人会说人类是会思想或能认知的机器；然而有不少人假定，只要人们知道该做什么和怎样去做，一切问题都将迎刃而解。对于会思想或能认知的机器而言，知道了解决方案将预先化解一些问题，甚至使之不再成其为问题。但是，对于有情感有追求、有爱有恨、有希望有畏惧、七情六欲无不具备的人类来说，知识的获得不仅不必解决问题，而且有可能使自己比以前更加困惑。现在，西方流行着一种民主的新观念，这种观念放弃了旧名称，即所谓的国家社会主义。

gathers enormous powers to better the living conditions of the majority of its citizens; it is indeed an admirable notion of a new democracy to be put in practice within the frame of the old; but to urge it upon the rest of mankind who are without democratic institutions is dangerous, for apart from the old political democracy, state socialism would be totalitarianism, and may even turn out to be fascism. There seems to be here a preference for the new democracy even in the absence of the old. The assumption underlying the enthusiasm of the advocates of this new democracy seems to be that human nature is intrinsically good, a proposition which most of the advocates wouldn't accept. Just as a wealthy man may be a corrupt citizen, an intelligent man a depraved animal as Rousseau long ago pointed out, so the leaders of the new democracy may not be public spirited if there are no existing political institutions that condition or compel them to be. More in a democracy than in any other form of government or state, the problem of the human material cannot be bypassed.

它主张政府集中很大的权力，以此改善大多数国民的生活条件。在民主制的旧框架中实施这种观念，它不失为一个美妙的民主新观念；但是，把它强加在民主制度之外的人们身上，那就很危险了。因为缺乏旧有政治民主制框架的国家社会主义会成为极权主义，甚至有可能转变成法西斯主义。连旧式民主都没有，却似乎对新式民主有所偏爱。在新式民主拥护者的热情之下，潜伏着一个假定，即人性天生是善的。然而大多数拥护者却不能接受这个观点。罗素早就说过，一个富有的人完全有可能是一个道德败坏的公民，一个聪明博学的人也有可能是一个腐化堕落的畜生。因此，如果没有现行的政治制度的制约或强制的话，新民主制度的领导者可能不会热心公益。在民主制度下，人的物化问题比在其他任何的政府形式之下更值得重视。

IV

While the advancement and requisition of knowledge may be industrialized with advantage, education shouldn't be. Knowledge has become specific and pragmatical, and so far as its advancement and acquisition are concerned, they may properly be made the output of large scale production. Foundations, research institutes and graduate schools may all be looked upon as knowledge advancing industries. On the whole these have been rather efficient, and so long as the criterion continues to be the search for and the attainment of truth, the quality of the products need not deteriorate. The desire for social or political justification for the existence of their industries may operate to the detriment of the adopted criteria, but this is a contingency which need not be entered into in the present connection. The industrialization of knowledge advancement merely means the professionalization of the employees, not their product; knowledge can still be easily marketed for general public use. The marketing of knowledge is indeed a part of education, but it certainly is not equivalent to it. The present method of lecturing to large classes in colleges and universities, of taking notes, of examinations, of accumulating credits, etc., seems to have confounded education with the marketing of knowledge. Education is not merely the preparation of the young for the various vocations of life, it is rather to prepare them to be independent, discriminating, and human individuals. Again the marketing of knowledge could be industrialized with profit and colleges and universities may be regarded at best partly as such industries. There is no objection to this industrialization provided it is not taken to be the whole of education, since in education more than specialized and pragmatized knowledge is involved. The latter may be instrumental for providing the means of earning one's livelihood, it is not and has not been equally germane to the direction and the colors and flavors of one's life. Education is essentially concerned with the development of the individual; its negative purpose is to prevent the young from being anti-social, and its positive purpose is to bring out to the fullest fruition whatever there is in the individual. It shouldn't be industrialized and strictly speaking it cannot be, since there cannot be mass production of individuals. Knowledge has become instrument or the servant to desires and passions, and the more we identify the dissociation of knowledge with education, the more likely we are also to leave desires and passions primitive and untutored and with knowledge as their instrument for

四

　　在知识的推进和应用能够被有效地工业化的时候，教育却不应当走这样的路。知识已经专门化并且变得实用了，从知识的推进和获取来看，它们可能是大规模生产的产品。基金会、研究所和研究生院都可以被视为推进知识发展的产业团体。总体上看，它们都十分有效率。只要标准仍然是探讨、获得真理，产品的质量就不必下降。希望能给出工业存在的社会或政治上的正当理由，这种愿望可能会对采取的标准有所不利。但这种可能此处无须论及。知识的工业化仅仅意味着雇员的职业化，而不是产品的职业化。知识还是很容易推销，以便被公众使用。知识的营销确实是教育的一个部分，但肯定不等同于教育。目前大学和学院里大班授课、记笔记、考试和修学分等等方式，似乎把教育与知识营销混淆了。教育不仅要为青年人未来谋职做准备，更要培养他们成为独立的、有辨别力的、有人性的个体。知识的营销可被工业化并产生利润，大学和学院则充其量是这类团体的一部分。只要这不是教育的全部，就不反对这种工业化，因为教育所涉及的范围远不只是专门化和实用化了的知识。后者有助于提供谋生手段，却不能帮助人们指引自己的生活方向和丰富他们的生活。教育的本质是个体的发展：它的消极作用是防止青年人反社会，积极作用是使个人的潜能得到充分的发展。教育不应当被工业化，严格地说，它也不可能被工业化，因为独立的个体是不可能批量生产的。知识已经变成了欲望和情感的工具或奴仆，我们越是把知识的区分等同于教育，就越可能使欲望和情感停留在原始的和未受教育的状态，使知识变成满足欲望和情感的工具，

satisfaction, also more rampant than in the days of blessed ignorance. The main purpose of education is to mold character, to refine away crudities so that strength may be retained, to establish equilibrium among conflicting propensities, to cultivate certain proclivities so that others might be held in check, to modify whatever nature there is by nurture so that the modified nature is cultured and civilized. A system of values must be consciously accepted and a set of beliefs must be consciously avowed. It is not here urged that education should impose values or instill beliefs. But it certainly should discriminate them, it should encourage the young to be conscious of their own predilections in order to articulate what their values and beliefs are likely to be and to convince them that these are not things to be ashamed of. When one is ashamed of his values and beliefs, one either returns to primitive animalism or succumbs to psychological complexes. The kind of skepticism necessary and conducive to the research of veridical knowledge should be confined to the realm of thought and ideas concerning knowledge. If it is carried over to the realm of values and beliefs, it merely renders a person either an emotional anarchist or emotionally at war with his own intellect. A large number of the generation growing out of the First World War were emotional anarchists; to them life at best was merely "amusing," and a world dominated by "amusing" people is the kind that makes some people, such as Henry Adams, shudder and look to the unity of the 13th century for comfort. We are not arguing for any specific kind of unity, what we are insisting upon is that people should be educated towards certain serenity and unashamedness in avowing their values and beliefs for these are after all the motivating influence in their lives. Individuals who are emotional anarchists, however efficient they may be in their chosen professions, are more or less liabilities to a democracy or with them as citizens great decisions are either made haphazardly or else not made at all.

A thorough going liberal education is needed. There should be character building accompanied by the discrimination of values and unashamed avowal of beliefs. The discrimination of knowledge remains necessary and for their purposes the prevailing system of lectures should be continued. There should be supplemented by free, informal and yet serious discussion of ideals, beliefs, values, desires, preferences,

同时使我们的欲望和情感变得比蒙昧无知的时代更难于控制。教育的主要目的是培养个性，消除野性，使人变得坚定；是在冲突的习性之间建立平衡，养成某些嗜好以便抑制其他嗜好；是通过教育改进本性使其变得有教养和有文化的内涵。因此，必须有意识地接受一套价值观念，必须有意识地承认一套信仰。这里的意思不是说教育应该灌输价值或信仰，但是，教育肯定应当对价值和信仰加以分辨，应当鼓励青年人清醒地意识到自己的偏好，使他们能够明确地表达自己的价值观念是什么，并使他们相信这没什么难堪的。当一个人为自己的价值观念和信仰感到难堪时，他要么退回到原始的动物主义，要么陷溺于心理情结。必要的、有益于研究真实知识的怀疑主义应当局限在有关知识的思想和观念领域。如果把它推行到价值和信仰的领域，它只会使人放纵情感，或者使他的情感与理智发生冲突。"一战"期间成长起来的一代人中有不少是情感放纵主义者，对于他们而言，生活至多是"有趣的"。一个被"有趣的"人主宰的世界难免令亨利·亚当斯之类的人感到可怕，转而指望从 13 世纪的统一性中获得安慰。我们不是在鼓吹任何具体形式的统一性，我们所坚持的只是，在承认自己的价值观念和信仰时，人们应该被教育得内心平和，不会感觉难堪，因为正是他们的价值观念和信仰在推动着他们的生活。那些放纵情感的人无论在自己选定的职业中多么高效，他们对于民主制度而言都或多或少是不利的因素。他们作为公民的地方，重大决定要么是任意作出来的，要么根本就做不出来。

　　一种全面的通才教育是必要的。这种教育应当包括个性养成、对价值观念的辨别和对信仰落落大方的承认。对知识进行区分仍然是必要的，为了这个目的，现行的授课方式应当继续保留，但应当再进行自由的、随意的却是严肃的讨论，对理想、信念、价值、欲望、

hidden assumptions, loves and hatreds, likes and dislikes; professors who are engaged in education and not exclusively in the dissimilation of knowledge should have constant contact with the students to exemplify in actual living, whether conformably or otherwise, whether successfully or unsuccessfully, what they articulate in terms of their own Lebensanschauung. Universities which have grown big for the purpose of marketing knowledge, efficiently and on a large scale should establish a large number of small colleges with the separate tutors for the purpose of leading the young through the slow process of learning to be human. All the liberal arts should be brought to bear on the formative young characters just as all sorts of veridical knowledge should be brought to bear on the formative young minds. No consideration of expense should be regarded as relevant. It must be insisted upon that no matter what one intends to be, whether an engineer or a doctor, a banker or a longshoreman, a musician or a physicist, the serene dignity, the serious business as well as the spontaneous playfulness of being human and an individual has priority over all the other special interests. There seems to be a widespread impatience with the idea of sweetness and light, perhaps on the score that it is anemic, wayward in regard to practical measures, hadgingly discursive concerning principles and totally unrealistic in a thoroughly realistic world. Whether the above evaluation of the idea is correct or not, we need not attempt to ascertain; for the alleged equalities are only vices to racism, they are virtues to a democracy. It is only through the combination of sweetness with light that we may attain to the full height of being human and become masters of our own passions and desires so that knowledge and power may not be disastrously employed. It is only then that human beings become safe to themselves.

爱好、隐含的假设、爱恨、好恶等等进行讨论。从事教育而非仅仅追求知识异化的教授应当不断地与学生接触，无论轻松与否，无论是否成功，他们都应该在实际生活中为学生做榜样践行自己讲授的人生观。出于知识营销的目的，大学发展壮大了，然而大学应当高效地、大规模地建立众多的小学院，配置各自的导师，引导青年人通过一个缓慢的学习过程成长为一个人。所有人文学科都应当与年轻人的性格养成有关，正如各种真实的知识都应当与他们的心智养成有关一样。经费不是需要考虑的问题。必须强调的是，无论一个人将来想做什么，无论他想当工程师还是医生，想当银行家还是码头装卸工，想当音乐家还是物理学家，他作为人类和个体都应当具有宁静端庄、严肃职责和发自内心的活泼，这些比其他一切都重要。人们普遍对甜蜜和光明的观念感到厌烦，也许是因为以现实的标准来衡量，这种观念太缺乏活力，在实际操作上太混乱，涉及原则时漫无边际，在一个完全务实的世界里显得太不实际。我们以上对甜蜜和光明的观念的评价是否恰当，这里无须断言；所谓的平等对于法西斯才是恶，而对于民主制度则是善。只有把甜蜜和光明结合起来，我们才可能成为真正的人，成为我们自己的情感和欲望的主人。这样，知识和权力才不会被用于破坏。只有到那时，人类才不会自己危害自己。

Prolegomena [4]

逻辑的作用

"Douter de tout ou tout croire," said Henri Poincaré, *"ce sont deux solutions également commodes, qui l'une et l'autre nous dispensent de réfléchir."* Either one of them precludes also the possibility of philosophy. No matter from what point of view, philosophy should include not only a thoroughgoing as well as a trained skepticism, but also some kind of belief as one of its necessary ingredients since it must have a starting point. Universal nihilism is not so easy in philosophy as it seems to have been in political thought because any negation, whatever, if it does not affirm anything, denies itself and consequently negates nothing. On the other hand, affirmation is equally difficult. If one does not intend to philosophize, he is in a privileged position, since he does not need anything positive with which to lubricate his wheels of thought. But if, when, and as long as, one philosophizes—and there is no reason why he should do so—he is confronted with the difficulty of starting somewhere with something, whatever it is, which his skepticism may have accustomed him to denying. And to make his position difficult to maintain, almost from the very start, most of the things with which he is conversant in our daily life are beyond our power to affirm in the face of a denial. Even the existence of our world can be denied without affording us any ground for further argument except the cold comfort that something is affirmed which does not happen to be our world. To such a denial no remedy of logic or fact can be applied. To give an inventory of the world or to cite the evidences of our senses avails us nothing.

And yet, we must start somewhere. The difficulty is with what and where. Ordinarily a choice is made for which no reason can be given except our personal prejudice or the interests of the age in which we live. A predilection for mysticism will perhaps decide one person in favor of impassioned passages on eternal consciousness while a robust sense of reality may lead another to start with an examination of our sense-data. Not only do different people effect different choices, but different times also present different problems. The problem of evil remains as unsolved as it was in the age of Plato, but few of us struggle with it at the present time. No solution had been arrived at in the Middle Ages as to how many angels can possibly stand on a pinhead, and yet no efforts that we know of have been directed in modern times towards arriving at

亨利·庞加莱说:"怀疑一切或相信一切,这是两种同样简单的解决办法,二者都使我们不用思考问题。"这两种办法均排除了哲学的可能性。无论从什么观点出发,哲学都应该不仅包括彻底的和经过训练的怀疑态度,而且包括某种信念作为一种必要的组成部分,因为它必须有一个出发点。在政治思想中似乎一直很容易形成普遍的虚无主义,但在哲学中却不那么容易。因为任何否定,如果它不肯定任何东西,那么它就在否定自身,因此什么也没有否定。另一方面,肯定同样是困难的。如果一个人不打算进行哲学思考,那么他就处于一种特殊地位,因为他不需要任何积极有效的东西用以润滑自己思想的车轮。但是,如果、当而且只要一个人进行哲学思考——并且没有他为什么应该这样做的理由——他就会遇到从何处、从何事情出发的困难。无论这个出发点是什么,他的怀疑态度可能使他习惯于否定它。而且,使他难于维持那个特殊地位的是,几乎从一开始,日常生活中他所熟悉的大多数事情被否定时,我们都无力去肯定它们。甚至我们这个世界的存在都能被否定,而不用提供任何进一步论证的理由。我们能得到的仅仅是无用的安慰:能被肯定的恰巧不是我们这个世界。任何逻辑或事实都不能用来弥补这种否定。无论是穷尽世间万事万物,还是调动我们所有的感官,我们也毫无收获。

然而,我们必须从某处出发。困难在于从什么和从哪里出发。除了我们个人的偏好或我们所处时代的兴趣外,一般无法说明作出选择的原因。对神秘主义的偏爱也许使一个人支持永恒的意识的慷慨陈词,而坚定的现实意识可能会使另一个人从研读感觉资料出发。不仅不同的人作出不同的选择,而且不同的时代提出不同的问题。今天,恶这一问题就像在柏拉图时代一样依然没有解决,但是却没有什么人去努力抗争。中世纪没有解决一个针头上可以站多少个天使的问题,然而在现代,我们所知的努力也没有找到解决办法。

any solution. Philosophical problems are rarely solved; oftentimes they are solved for an age; but oftener still they fade away with the fading interest which prompted their emergence as problems. But if one starts a philosophical essay with a thoroughgoing as well as a trained skepticism, then either personal prejudice or the interest of an age needs some kind of justification, failing which neither can serve as a starting point. But justification must be based upon some kind of criterion which itself needs justification. An endless process is thus initiated in which no starting point can be effected other than arbitrary. In the end it is our prejudice that is the foundation of our philosophic thought, though we should bear in mind that prejudices from the point of view of logic may not be prejudices from the point of view of the accumulated experience of mankind.

In this chapter, we shall deal with the relations of logic to philosophy, to life, and to our knowledge of the world in which we live. We shall try to set forth the role which logic plays in all the spheres mentioned, and to see on what criterion our belief in logic is justified. We shall discuss briefly our notion of convenience, of economy and of logic, and we shall try to ascertain their relation. Our discussion is perhaps less organized than it could be, and may appear at times to be beating at a bush where no bird is suspected to be hiding. But a good deal of the accumulated dust may be swept away, and to that extent at least our discussion may not be an utter waste of effort.

哲学问题难得解决；经常是，它们只是对于某一时代来说是解决了；但更经常的是，时代的兴趣促使它们成为问题，随着这种兴趣的消失，它们也逐渐消失。但是，如果一个人以受过训练的和彻底的怀疑态度来开始写一篇哲学论文，那么个人的偏好或时代的兴趣就需要某种理由。没有这种理由，二者都不能用作出发点。但是，理由必须建立在某个标准上，而为什么选择这个标准也需要理由。这样就产生了一个只能由任意的出发点开始的无穷过程。我们的偏好最终成为我们哲学思想的基础，尽管我们应该记住，从逻辑观点看是偏好，但从人类积累的经验的观点看却可能不是偏好。

本章将探讨逻辑与哲学、生活以及对我们所处世界的认识的关系。我们将试图提出逻辑在所有上述领域中所起的作用，并且看一看根据什么标准证明我们对逻辑的信赖是正确的。我们将扼要讨论我们关于便利、节省和逻辑的看法，我们还将试图确定它们的关系。也许我们的讨论本应组织得更好一些，而实际上它可能有时似乎是无的放矢。但是，我们的讨论可以清扫许多沉积的污垢，或许从这个意义上讲，至少我们的讨论不是徒劳一场。

In philosophy, perhaps more than in anything else except logic and mathematics, we deal with propositions which stand or fall upon certain criteria, some of which have long been exploded. If we can find a criterion upon which some propositions are ascertained to be undeniable, we can probably employ these as our starting point. A proposition was once considered established when its opposite was inconceivable. But inconceivability is too elusive a criterion. What is inconceivable to one is easily conceivable to another, and instances abound in history of propositions inconceivable at one age turning to be thoroughly conceivable at the next, and vice versa. Again, propositions were once accepted when they were considered to be self-evident. But the same objections can be raised against self-evidence as are raised against inconceivability. Neither is reliable, because both are psychological resistance to strange and unfamiliar ideas and as such are misappropriated for the criteria of logical validity. If we search for a starting point from ideas that are self-evident or propositions whose opposites are inconceivable we are bound to fail.

Propositions are said to be valid if they are true and they are said to be true, if they correspond with facts. This correspondence with facts is therefore often taken to be a criterion of the validity of propositions. It is easy to see however that here as elsewhere we can hardly derive any consolation. In the first place we have no way of knowing whether our propositions correspond with facts, if both these terms are taken to embody their common sense significance. On the one hand, they are so distinct from each other, and on the other, we are so identified with one of them that we are not in the position of a third party to judge whether or not there is any correspondence. The assertion of such a correspondence is itself a proposition which can only be true, when there is a further correspondence. Consequently, no matter how persistently we assert the truth of a given proposition, we shall find it yet to be ascertained one step beyond. More of this will come to our notice in the third chapter, but for the present it is sufficient to say that even if the criterion holds, we are not in any sense better off in our search for a starting point. The criterion if acceptable merely helps us to discover truths; it does not enable us to

一

　　除在逻辑和数学中外，我们也许只在哲学中探讨命题，它们成立与否取决于某些标准，而且有些标准长期以来已被驳倒。如果我们能找到一个标准，据此确定一些命题是不可否定的，大概我们就可以用这些命题作为我们的出发点。当一个命题的对立面是不可思议的，就完全可以认为这个命题被确定。但是，不可思议是一条难以捉摸的标准。对一个人来说是不可思议的，很可能对另一个人是可以思议的。历史上不乏这样的命题实例，它们在某一时期是不可思议的，在紧接着的时期则是完全可以思议的，反之亦然。同样，当认为命题是自明的，就完全接受它们。但是怎么样反对不可思议性，就可以怎么样反对自明性，二者均不可靠。因为它们都是对奇怪和陌生的思想的心理抵触，并因此被误用作逻辑有效性的标准。如果我们从自明的观点或其对立面是不可思议的命题这两点上来寻找出发点，则我们必然失败。

　　如果命题是真的，它们就被说成是有效的；如果它们与事实相符，它们就被说成是真的。因此，这种与事实相符常常被当作命题有效性的标准。然而很容易看出，从这里与从其他地方一样，我们几乎不能得到任何安慰。首先，如果认为"命题"和"事实"这两个词体现出其常识意义，我们就无法知道我们的命题与事实是否相符。一方面，它们二者极为不同；另一方面，我们十分认同其中一方，以致我们不能够以第三者的身份来判断是否有任何相符。当有进一步的相符时，这样一种相符的断定本身就是一个只能为真的命题。因此无论我们多么固执地断定一个给定命题是真的，我们都将发现它应得到进一步的断定。第三章我们将更多地讨论这个问题，但是现在只需说明：即使这个标准成立，我们在寻找出发点时的处境也绝好不了。如果这个标准是可接受的，则它仅帮助我们发现真理，它不能够使我们选择其中任何一个真命题作为我们讨论的出发点。

select any one of them to begin our discussion. If truths are created equal like the "Americans" of Abraham Lincoln, we have no reason to select any one truth to start our discussion any more than the Americans had in 1860 to elect Lincoln for their President. If, on the other hand, truths are not created equal, then some particular truth must be selected and a criterion for such a selection is yet to be discovered.

There is one criterion which is generally considered to be irrefutable, namely presupposition by denial. It is at any rate strictly logical and self-sufficient. There are some propositions which belong to this category such as the propositions "there are propositions," "there is truth," that "we argue" etc. It is generally considered that to deny any of these is to affirm them and that consequently each stands on its own self-sufficient ground. But if one studies the problem closely, one is liable to be led into two or three lines of thought. To begin with, some at least of these propositions are not strictly presupposed by their own denial. Take for instance, the proposition "there is truth." On the face of it, the denial, if true, affirms the proposition and if false allows the original proposition to stand. It is therefore obvious that the proposition "there is truth" is presupposed by its denial. But if we reason in this fashion we imply suppositions which are not here indicated; we imply, for instance, that truth however defined is of universal application, irrespective of the differences involved in logically prior and logically subsequent steps. The truth of these propositions and the truth affirmed or denied by them belong to different types of logical procedure; and if Mr. Russell's theory of types, of the technique of which I admit complete ignorance, applies to all propositions alike, then the use of presupposition by denial as a criterion in the sense herein discussed is limited to a considerable extent.

The above reasoning may or may not be sound, but it indicates the possibility that some of the propositions which are presupposed by their denial involve other propositions implied in neither the affirmation nor the denial.

In the second place, there are other propositions which deny themselves on similar grounds but which some of us may find it necessary to maintain as embodying our sincere beliefs. The problem of the "lie" is trivial compared with the problem of those who conscript

如果真理的产生就像亚伯拉罕·林肯口中的"美国人"那样是生而平等的，那么正如美国人在 1860 年不必选林肯作为他们的领袖一样，我们也没有理由选择任何一个真理作为我们讨论的出发点。另一方面，如果真理的产生不是平等的，那么必须选择某个特定的真理，并且还要发现这种选择的标准。

一般认为，有一种标准是个可反驳的，即通过否定的预先假设。无论如何，它是逻辑严格的和自足的。有些命题属于这一类，例如"我们认为有命题""我们认为有真"等等。一般认为，否定任何这样的命题就是肯定它们，因此它们均坚持各自自足的立场。但是如果仔细研究这个问题，很容易导致两三种思维方式。首先，在这些命题中，至少有些命题不是其自身否定所严格预先假设的。以"有真"这一命题为例。表面上看，否定如果是真的，则肯定这个命题；如果是假的，则允许原初的命题成立。因此，显然"有真"这一命题被其否定预先假设。但是如果我们以这种方式推论，则我们暗含着这里没有指明的假设。例如，我们暗含着，若不考虑逻辑上优先和逻辑上在后的步骤所包含的差异，则以任何方式定义的真都可以普遍应用。这些命题的真和由它们肯定的或否定的真属于逻辑过程的不同类型；如果罗素先生的类型论（我承认对它的方法一无所知）适用于所有这样的命题，那么用通过否定的预先假设作为这里讨论的意义上的一条标准，就受到很大程度的限制。

以上推理也许可靠，也许不可靠，但是它表明一种可能性，即在被其否定预先假设的命题中，有些命题包含另一些既不在肯定中也不在否定中蕴涵的命题。

其次，还有其他一些命题，它们根据类似的理由否定自己，而我们有些人可能发现有必要坚持这种命题，因为它们体现了我们真诚的信念。"说谎"这一问题比起那些为了自己的哲学目的而使用

the relativity theory of Einstein for the purpose of their philosophy. It is true that the constant velocity of light and the absoluteness of the "interval" are somewhat ignored by those who assert that everything is relative, but if this proposition embodies the sincere belief of its propounders, it is almost heart-breaking to see it fade away through a self-denial that must seem at times to be purely verbal. The theory of types I am told, is intended to remove the difficulties arising from these propositions, and whether or not it has already attained the technical perfection it seeks, it seems to involve the non-technical problem of its application. Wherever it is applied it is likely to resolve the criterion of presupposition by denial into greater complexities than we can see at a glance, and our attempt to find a starting point has so far produced no definite gain.

In the third place, the criterion of presupposition by denial itself presupposes a belief in logic. If one refuses to believe in logic, propositions can never be established for him merely because they cannot be denied by him according to the rules of logic. While logic is conceivably convincing to most people, it need not be effective with children or lunatics or philosophers. The latter can easily believe that there is truth at the same time that they believe that there is not. If one does not believe in logic, there is no logical reason for him to change his mind, though there may be other reasons why he should do so. That there are other reasons will be the subject of this chapter.

Symbolic logicians can justifiably congratulate themselves for having discovered a few primitive ideas from which most if not all of the logical principles can be deduced. A logical pyramid is thus made possible through the technical skill of the mathematicians. It is questionable, however, whether similar results will be achieved in philosophy by introducing into it the same method elsewhere so profitably employed; for philosophy is less restricted in its sphere than logic, it deals with topics of a more heterogeneous nature and its various problems have not been and are not likely to be linked into a gapless chain. The starting point for any system of logic need not be a starting point for philosophy; consequently the success of symbolic logic has not so far been followed by a corresponding success in philosophical thought.

爱因斯坦相对论的人的问题，是微不足道的。确实，断定每个事物都是相对的那些人，不太知道不变的光速和"间隔"的绝对性。但是，如果这个命题体现了其提出者真诚的信念，那么看到它因为有时似乎仅仅是字面的自我否定而逐渐消失，几乎要痛心疾首。据我所知，类型论旨在消除这些命题中产生的困难。它是否已经达到它所追求的技术完善，这似乎包括它的应用这一非技术问题。无论在哪里应用它，结果很可能是：把通过否定的预先假设这一标准变成比我们一眼可以看出的更复杂的东西。因此我们要发现一个出发点的尝试至此没有得到确切的收获。

第三，通过否定的预先假设这一标准本身预先假设了对逻辑的相信。如果一个人拒绝相信逻辑，那么对他来说，仅仅因为他不能根据逻辑规则而否定命题，因此命题绝不能建立起来。虽然大多数人都可以感到逻辑的说服力，逻辑对小孩、疯子或哲学家却不必是有效的。后者可以很容易相信有真，同时他们又相信没有真。如果一个人不相信逻辑，那么他就没有逻辑的理由改变自己的思想，尽管他可能有其他这样做的理由。这些其他理由将是这一章讨论的主要问题。

符号逻辑学家完全有理由祝贺他们自己发现了一些基本思想，从这些思想即使推不出全部逻辑规则，也可以推出大部分逻辑原则。这样通过数学家的技术可以形成一座逻辑的金字塔。然而，在哲学中引入在其他领域中运用得卓有成效的相同方法，是否也将取得类似的结果，却值得怀疑。因为哲学并不像逻辑一样限定在自身范围内，它探讨具有更为复杂多元性质的论题，它的各种不同的问题一直没有并且也不可能被连成一条无缝隙的链条。任何逻辑系统的出发点不必是哲学的出发点，因此，虽然符号逻辑学已获成功，在哲学思想中却迄今并未出现相应的成功。

The terms "philosophy" and "philosopher" have been used with extraordinary vagueness. Goethe has been claimed by some as a great philosopher and Shakespeare by others. What is meant by either statement is probably that both men had great insight into human nature and life, but whatever the statements may mean, few of us dispute it. Shelley is regarded as a great philosopher, by no less a thinker, I understand, than Mr. Whitehead, but none of us ever dreams of writing controversial poems setting forth ideas to refute that angle, ineffective or otherwise. If silence means consent in philosophy as it does in law, then Shelley's philosophy may claim universal acceptance. At the same time, all philosophers are said by some to be poets; Mr. John Middleton Murry regards Plato as a good poet and Hegel a bad one. Whether or not poets feel insulted by the sentiment herein expressed, philosophers seem to remain quite undisturbed in their philosophical serenity. What seems to account on this state of affairs is that philosophy is not concerned with ideas qua ideas; like science, it is interested in the method from which they are derived and through which they are correlated with each other.

The case of Mr. Bergson is illuminating at this point of our discussion. Here is a man whose poetry is supposed to take the form of philosophy rather than that of the winged words and sonorous phrases of verse, with the result that each suffers from the other. While his Élan Vital has successfully penetrated into the perfumed atmosphere of pink tea parties, his philosophy is regarded by a large section of his own profession as being vitiated through self-destruction. Had he allowed his reader to derive inspiration from him through intuition, his hold on the public might have been stronger; he might even have become a religious leader, but then he would not have been in the modern philosophical world. Having selected to be active in the latter field, he has to convince people through argumentation and the moment he argues, he is bound by logic to emphasize intellect at the expense of intuition, since as far as his reading public is concerned it is through the former that the latter makes itself felt.

One cannot very well argue for the importance of intuition simply because argumentation involves elements with which intuition as differentiated from intellect by definition is incompatible. We hold no brief for intellect, at least not for the moment; for all we know, intellect might very easily be

　　"哲学"和"哲学家"这两个词的使用一直极为含混。有些人称歌德是一位大哲学家，另一些人称莎士比亚是一位大哲学家。这两个陈述的意思大概均是说这两个人深刻洞察人的本性和生活，但是无论这两个陈述可能意味着什么，却没有什么人反驳它。雪莱被怀特海之类的思想家看作是一位大哲学家，但是无论效果如何，从未有人想要撰写富有争议的诗篇罗列观点去反驳这一观点。如果在哲学中同在法律中一样，沉默意味着同意，那么可以说雪莱的哲学得到了普遍的接受。同时，所有哲学家都被某些人说成是诗人；约翰·米德尔顿·默里先生认为柏拉图是一个优秀的诗人，黑格尔是一个低劣的诗人。无论诗人是否觉得此处表达的意思是一种侮辱，哲学家似乎依然安于达观的平静当中不受任何影响。这种情况的原因似乎在于：哲学与作为思想的思想本身无关；与科学一样，哲学关心的是那些获得这些思想和使这些思想相互联系的方法。

　　伯格森先生的情况对我们讨论的这一点很有启发。这个人的诗采用哲学的形式，没有充满诗意的文字和抑扬顿挫的词句，结果哲学性和诗性相互干扰。他的"生命冲动"成功地融入社交界的高雅气氛，而他的哲学却被他的广大同行视为因自我毁灭而效果顿减。如果他允许他的读者通过直觉从他的作品获得灵感，那么他对公众的影响可能更大，他甚至可能成为一个宗教领袖。但是这样，他就不会待在现代哲学界之中。由于他选择要积极从事哲学界的活动，他就必须以论证服人。而当他进行论证的时候，他受到逻辑的约束，必须强调理性而不要直觉。因为就其广大读者而言，正是通过理性，人们才感知到直觉。人们不能充分地论证直觉的重要性，仅仅因为论证包含着这样的因素，这些因素与从定义上不同于理性的直觉是不相容的。我们不是为理性辩护，至少现在不是；因为我们都知道，理性可能很容易附属于直觉，伯格森先生可能强烈地感到

subordinate to intuition; Mr. Bergson probably feels strongly that it is; but if the less endowed portion of mankind cannot share his insight except through arguments, it is naturally to intellect rather than to intuition that they attach the greater importance. Thus only one of two alternatives is open to Mr. Bergson, not both: either he adopts the method of systematic philosophy, in which case he may have to abandon his philosophical position; or he gives up argumentation in which case he may have to propagate his idea in the style of Shelley or Keats.

A criticism of a veteran philosopher cannot be crowded into one short paragraph, and a lengthy exposition is totally out of place here. What is intended is merely to show that philosophy is mainly concerned with arguments not with random ideas gathered from here and there. Those who believe in God are not in a better or worse position in philosophy than those who do not, for philosophy offers no criteria upon which particular emotional attachment can be justified. The moment a belief is supported by arguments, philosophy begins to have something to say. But arguments involve analysis and synthesis in which premises and conclusions play a great part and if arguments are the main concern of philosophy, then logic is its essence. A large amount of insight is desirable, a robust sense of reality is probably more convincing in modern tunes than a rich imagination, but a rigorous reasoning power is in any case indispensable. Philosophers are much less criticized for their ideas than for the way in which they develop them, and many a philosophical system has perished on the one rock of logic.

Special definitions aside, philosophy is for most people a sort of Weltanschauung more or less systematized. While the "world," whatever it is, is generally regarded as common to everybody, our reactions against it and our ideas about it are admittedly different for different individuals. Nature is persistent in her peculiar manifestations, she insists on having her own way; she may not frown at the courtship of the scientists, but she has shown hardly any excitement over philosophical systems. She is indifferent alike to our hopes and fears, our beliefs and doubts, which are after all the articulate or the inarticulate premises of most philosophical systems. Nature reveals no preference for any one set of them over any other, and our preferences are essentially our own prejudices. Our

是这样。但是如果不那么聪明的人只有通过论证才能分享他的高见，那么他们自然会认为理性更重要而不是直觉更重要。这样，伯格森只能在两种情况中选择一种，而不能选择两种：要么他采取系统哲学的方法，在这种情况下，他可能不得不放弃他的哲学立场；要么他放弃论证，在这种情况下，他可能不得不以雪莱或济慈的文体传播他的思想。

评论一位资深的哲学家只用短短的一段话是不够的，并且在这里也不合适去详细地展开论述。我们仅仅是想说明，哲学主要与论证有关，而不是与这里或那里搜集的任意一些思想有关。相信上帝的人在哲学中的地位不会比不相信上帝的人高，也不会比他们低，因为哲学不提供能够判断特定感情依属的标准。一旦你论证支持一种信仰的时候，哲学就有话要说了。但是论证包括分析和综合，其中前提和结论起着重大作用；而且如果哲学主要与论证有关，那么逻辑就是哲学的本质。大量的见识令人神往，对于现实强有力的感知在今天大概比丰富的想象更有说服力。但是无论如何，缜密的推理能力是必不可少的。哲学家受到批评往往不是因为他们的思想，而是因为他们形成这些思想的方式，许多哲学体系都是由于触到逻辑这一块礁石而毁灭的。

除专门定义外，哲学对大多数人来说是一种或多或少系统化的世界观。无论"世界"是什么，一般认为它对每个人是共同的；我们对它的反应、我们关于它的思想，在不同的个体却是不同的。自然界有自己一贯的特有现象，她坚持有自己的方式；她可能不会对科学家的求爱紧皱眉头，但对哲学系统几乎也没表现出过兴奋。她对我们的希望和恐惧、我们的信念和怀疑一样地无动于衷，而这些希望和恐惧、信念和怀疑毕竟是大多数哲学体系的已经表达的或未经表达的前提。自然界不会对哲学体系厚此薄彼，然而我们会因自己的偏见偏爱某些哲学体系。我们对世界的

ultimate beliefs about the world are incapable of justification; they do not need any and are therefore not open to argument. That is why it is just as futile for us to argue with priests as it is for them to try to convince us. Once, however, our beliefs are put on a rational basis, as philosophical ideas are supposed to be, then logical validity becomes a question of supreme moment. Mr. Bradley has every right to believe in his Absolute as Mr. Bergson has in his Élan Vital; without arguments in support of their beliefs, their position is philosophically not worse than that of a Christian with his belief in God, or better than that of a commercial traveler with his belief in the number thirteen; but if both these philosophers regard their beliefs as rationally derived, then their positions must stand or fall upon the soundness of their reasoning, that is to say, upon logic.

But is logic in better luck than our beliefs? Is it any less elusive? Obviously, Mr. Bradley's logic is not the same as Mr. Russell's, the logic of both is different from that of John Stuart Mill; and in the hands of the Germans, with their unrivaled academic apparatus and the rich possibilities of their polysyllabic language, the subject has come to be endowed with a wealth of form, of color, and of light and shade, compared to which even modern painting can hardly boast of richness and variety. Logic not only differs with different logicians, but also varies with different ages. Until very recent times, it did not show any capacity for cumulative effort. It seems to be just as chaotic as philosophy itself and it is difficult to see how it can possibly be made a criterion for philosophical criticism.

Factually there are different logical systems, but theoretically there is only one implied logic. The question is obviously not one of the logician's. He may be personally as different from any other logician as he can possibly be, but within his subject matter, he must come into some kind of agreement with his fellow logicians. Whenever he advocates his logical system, he must justify it, but he can only justify it on logical grounds since other grounds are totally irrelevant. He cannot however justify his own logical system upon the principles of his own logic, since his problem is to justify these as well. He has to justify his logic by some other logic if he cannot claim that his logic justifies itself; but if his logic

终极信念是不能证实的；这些信念不需要任何论证，因而是不可论证的。因此，正像神父试图说服我们是毫无用处的一样，我们与神父进行争论也是毫无用处的。然而，我们的信念一旦建立在理性的基础之上，正像哲学思想应该的那样，那么逻辑的有效性就成为最重要的问题。正像伯格森先生完全有权相信他的生命冲动一样，布拉德利先生也完全有权相信他的绝对。没有论证支持他们的信念，他们的观点在哲学上不比基督徒信仰上帝的观点更糟，也不比一个旅行推销员相信数字13的观点更好。但是如果这两位哲学家都认为他们的信念是由理性得出的，那么他们的观点成败必定由他们推理的可靠性来决定，即由逻辑来决定。

但是，逻辑比我们的信念更幸运吗？它是不太难以理解的吗？显然，布拉德利先生的逻辑与罗素先生的逻辑不同，而二者的逻辑又与约翰·斯图亚特·穆勒的逻辑不同。在德国人手中，由于他们拥有无与伦比的学术工具和多音节语言丰富的可能性，这个课题逐渐被赋予丰富的形式、色彩、光泽和色调；相比之下，甚至现代绘画几乎也不能斗胆言称丰富性和多样性。逻辑不仅在不同的逻辑学家那里是不同的，而且在不同的时期也是不同的。直到最近，它才表现出某种累进成就的能力。它似乎与哲学本身一样混乱，很难看出如何能够使它成为进行哲学批评的一条标准。

实际上有不同的逻辑系统，但是理论上只有一种暗含的逻辑。这个问题显然不是逻辑学家的问题。作为一个人而言，一个逻辑学家可以与仟何其他逻辑学家尽可能地不同，但是对于他研究的课题，他必须与他的逻辑学同仁达到某种一致。只要他提倡他的逻辑系统，他就必须证明它是正确的，但是他只能基于逻辑证明它是正确的，因为其他原因都完全无关。然而，他不能根据他自己的逻辑原则证明他自己的逻辑系统是正确的，因为问题是他也要证明这些逻辑原则是正确的。如果他不能声称他的逻辑自身是正确的，他就必须以其他某种逻辑证明他的逻辑是正确的；但是如果他的逻辑证

justifies itself, he cannot justify his advocacy of it, since logically in that case he has no reason to advocate. If, when, and in so far as, he advocates a system of logic he is bound to suppose that there is some kind of logic which is not entirely his own and which he has reasons for not preferring to his own. Whether factually he has it or not, theoretically he must be credited with the intention either of convincing his opponent or enabling his readers to effect a choice in his favor. If his expectations are to be fulfilled, he must argue with a process of reasoning that is not exclusively his own nor his opponent's logic, for otherwise he cannot be theoretically impartial. Consequently wherever two systems of logic are competing for our preference, one logical system is implied according to which our preference is to be made. Without this implied system, not only can neither side gain ascendency over the other but there will also be no ground for argument. If each argues with a reasoning implied in his own logic, he is not merely doing injustice to his opponent, he is also arguing with something to which his opponent finds himself in opposition from the very beginning. Without an implied system of logic, the argument of the logician is very much the same as that of the English lady who claimed that what the French called "pain," and the Germans "Brot," is really and simply bread.

Logic is in fact never self-explanatory. It is generally explained in terms of something which is not quite itself. A system of logic may be forged into a continuous chain; if so, each link can be explained in terms of the chain, but the whole chain cannot be explained in terms of the links without extraneous elements, for otherwise it has to repeat itself each time it is called upon to explain and consequently can never explain itself. As a matter of fact our logic is much looser than that. It generally includes elements which cannot be explained by its own principles. It must however be logical, but it cannot be logical according to its own logic. The question of its ultimate logicality necessarily resolves any given logic into a portion of a greater logic, whatever that is, which fares no better with the question, if it is again raised. A process of infinite regression is thus initiated which logically allows no end. Thus while an implied system of logic is required when the logicality of a given system is questioned, no such implied system is obtainable. The only alternative

明自身是正确的，那么他就不能证明他提倡它是正确的，因为从逻辑上看，在这种情况下他没有理由提倡它。如果、当并且只要他提倡一个逻辑系统，他就必然假定有某种逻辑，它不完全是他自己的，而且他有理由认为它不如自己的逻辑。无论实际上他有没有这种逻辑，埋论上必须认为他有说服对手或使读者作出有利于他的选择的意图。如果要实现他的愿望，他必须以一个推理过程进行论证，而这个推理过程不专门是他自己的逻辑，也不专门是对手的逻辑，否则理论上他就不公正。因此，只要两个逻辑系统竞争让我们选择，就暗含一个逻辑系统；根据它，我们作出取舍。如果没有这个暗含的系统，不仅双方均不能胜过对方，而且也将没有论证的基础。如果各自以自己的逻辑所暗含的推理进行论证，则不仅对自己的对手是不公正的，而且他所论证的东西其对手从一开始就是反对的。如果没有一种暗含的逻辑系统，逻辑学家的论证与一位英国女士说法国人叫做"pain"而德国人叫做"Brot"的东西实际上就是面包，是完全一样的。

实际上，逻辑从来就不是自我解释的。它一般是由完全不同于逻辑的东西解释的。一个逻辑系统可以构造成一个连续的链条。如果这样，则可以用这个链条解释其每一个链环；但是如果没有外来因素，以这些链环就不能解释这个链条，因为否则每次它需要解释时都必须重复自己，因而绝不能解释自己。事实上，我们的逻辑比这松散得多。它一般包括不能由它自己的原则所解释的因素。然而，它必须是符合逻辑的，但是它不能根据自己的逻辑来符合逻辑。它的终极逻辑性的问题必然将任何给定的逻辑分解为更大的逻辑的一部分，但是无论这种逻辑是什么，如果又提出其终极逻辑性的问题，则它的进展依然好不了。这样就形成了一个逻辑上不允许终止的无穷倒退的过程。因此，如果询问一给定系统的逻辑性，则要求一种暗含的逻辑系统，而这样暗含的系统是无法得到的。唯一

is not to ask the question at all, regarding it either as meaningless or as unanswerable. The latter alternative is merely an admission of our impotence which some of us are not willing to acknowledge, while the former alternative will eventually result in our putting logic on the basis of belief. That amounts to saying that there is no logical reason why there should be logic except that as a matter of fact those who believe in it will find their belief resulting in a chain of reasoning each individual step of which is not itself a matter of belief.

What is meant by the latter part of the preceding paragraph may be stated in another way. For those who do not believe in logic, the rigorous reasoning which is its essence is by no means compelling. Arguments no matter how well founded are notoriously ineffective with religious fanatics and impassioned lovers. It is not always because arguments are illogical that they are ineffective; often they are so because the persons to whom they are applied are at the moment of application disbelievers in any rigorous process of reasoning. Martin Luther is said to have believed that he preached better sermons when he was angry than when he was not. A number of observations may be made in the present connection, but the one that is relevant to our discussion is that moments of anger are the moments during which reasoning power is suspended because a belief in logic is no longer compatible with the impatience with which emotional excitement such as anger is necessarily accompanied. Historically a belief in logic may be the result of an acquaintance with logic, but logically it cannot be so derived, since it is itself a necessary condition for the effectiveness of logical reasoning.

We seem to be now in a dilemma which brings us exactly to the point where we started. On the one hand, in order that logic may be effective there must be a belief in it; on the other hand our belief is irrelevant to its effectiveness, since effectiveness depends upon logical rigor, not upon our belief. But the dilemma is only apparent, and not real. A child must be born of some parents, but once it is born, it can get along without them. The dilemma is thus seen to be no dilemma at all, for the word "effectiveness" is used in two different senses. The effectiveness in logical rigor to a person who believes in logic, is not the same as the effectiveness of the conviction which logic may carry to a person who

的选择是根本不问这个问题，要么把它看作是无意义的，要么认为它是无法回答的。后一种看法不过是承认我们的无能，这是我们有些人不愿承认的；而前一种看法最终使我们将逻辑基于我们的信念。这等于说，除了事实上那些相信逻辑的人将发现他们的信念产生一个推理链条，而这个推理的每一步本身却不是信念的问题外，为什么应该有逻辑，这是没有逻辑理由的。

可以用另一种方式阐述上段后一部分的意思。对于那些不相信逻辑的人来说，作为逻辑本质的严格的推理绝不是必须接受的。众所周知，在宗教狂和激情满怀的恋人那里，无论多么严格地建立起来的论证都是无效的。论证并非总是因为不合逻辑而是无效的，相反，它们无效常常是因为它们所施用的那些人在应用时不相信任何严格的推理过程。据说，马丁·路德相信他生气时比不生气时讲道更好。对目前这一点上可以发表一些看法，但是与我们的讨论相关的一个看法是，生气的时候是丧失推理能力的时候，因为对逻辑的信念与必然同生气相伴的情感激动的急躁是无法相容的。历史上，对逻辑的信念可能是懂逻辑而产生的结果，但是逻辑上却不能这样得出，因为对逻辑的信念本身是逻辑推理的有效性的一个必要条件。

现在我们似乎陷于一种困境，它把我们恰恰带到我们开始的地方。一方面，为了逻辑可以是可行的，必须相信逻辑；另一方面，我们的信念与逻辑的有效性无关，因为有效性依赖于逻辑的严格性，而不依赖于我们的信念。但是这种困境只是表面的，而不是实在的。一个小孩必须是父母所生，但是他一旦出生，就可以没有父母而生活。因而可以看出，这种困境根本不是困境，因为"有效性"一词是在两种不同的意义上使用的。逻辑严格性的有效性对于一个相信逻辑的人来说，与逻辑可能带有的使人确信的有效性对一

does not believe in it. In the one case, it is within the framework of logic, and in the other, it is totally out of it; the system of reference being different in each. But while the dilemma is dissolved the difficulty still remains. Logic is no more and no less convincing to one who does not believe in it than the existence of God is to an agnostic.

个不相信逻辑的人来说是不同的。在一种情况下，有效性是在逻辑的框架之内；而在另一种情况下，有效性完全是在逻辑的框架之外，因为两种情况的参照系统是不同的。但是，尽管困境消除了，困难却依然存在。正像上帝的存在对于一个不可知论者来说并没有更具或更没有说服力一样，逻辑对于不相信逻辑的人也并没有更具或更没有说服力。

II

Our search for a starting point is so far admittedly a failure. Perhaps if we start from a different point of view, we may get further than we have been able to up to the present. Thus far we have tried to justify our position before we know exactly what it is. We have searched for an a priori justification for whatever view we take, and we found that a priori, there cannot be any justification whatsoever. Suppose however we start from the other way around, and assume for the moment that there is a world, that it is possible for us to know more and more of it, and that whether we can justify it or not we are to come into contact as well as to arrive at some kind of working arrangements with it. If we start with such a point of view, the question as to whether the world is chaotic or orderly is meaningless. We may sound the future with Mr. Balfour and learn that "the energies of our system will decay, the glory of the sun will be dimmed, and the earth, tideless and inert, will no longer tolerate the race which has for the moment disturbed its solitude." Or we may prophesy with Mr. Russell and agree "that no fire, no heroism, no intensity of thought and feeling, can preserve an individual life beyond the grave; that all the labors of the ages, all the devotion, all the inspiration, all the noonday brightness of human genius, are destined to extinction in the vast death of the solar system, and that the whole temple of Man's achievement must inevitably be buried beneath the debris of a universe in ruins." We may predict with Henry Adams that the dissipation of solar energy will bring us a sure and steady extinction and yet we do not consciously commit suicide in anticipation. We may be doing so unconsciously, and of course none the less effectively, but on the whole we do not intentionally expedite our journey to our final destination, with the same industry, the same assiduity and the same zeal with which we eat watermelon or play tennis.

As long as we live, we have to come into some kind of working arrangements with the world. If the world is chaotic, we have to create some kind of order by which we may live in harmony. If the world is harmonious, we have to discover what that harmony is. The problem may be different in each case from that of the other, but the practical result is about the same. We are not discussing here either the Practical or

二

应该承认，到目前为止我们寻找出发点没有成功。如果我们从一个不同的观点出发，也许我们可以比我们迄今所能得到的结果更进一步。至此在我们确切知道我们的立场是什么之前，我们却试图证明它是正确的。我们对我们采取的任何一种观点寻找先验的证实，我们找到了那个先验，然而却丝毫不能证实。然而假定我们以另一种方式出发，暂时假设有一个世界，我们可以越来越多地认识它，无论我们能不能证实它，我们都可以接触它并且达成某种可行的安排。如果我们从这样一种观点出发，世界是混乱的还是有秩序的这个问题就毫无意义。我们可以随贝尔福先生探测未来并得知，"我们这个宇宙的能量将衰灭，太阳的光辉将暗淡，没有潮汐、没有生气的地球将不再容忍目前搅扰它清净的种族。"或者我们可以随罗素先生预言并同意，"任何激情、任何英雄行为、任何深刻的思想和感情都不能保持一个个体生命不进坟墓；所有时代的努力、所有奉献、所有灵感、所有如日中天的人类才华，注定要随太阳系的毁灭而消亡，整座人类成就大厦必然埋葬在毁灭的宇宙废墟之下。"我们可以随亨利·亚当斯预言，太阳能的消耗肯定将为我们带来灭亡，然而我们却不预先有意识地自杀。我们可能会毫无意识地这样做，当然仍然产生预期的效果，但是我们大体上不会以吃西瓜或打网球所具有的那种勤奋、刻苦和热情故意加快我们通往最终归宿的旅行。

只要我们活着，我们就必须达成某种与这个世界的可行安排。如果世界是混乱的，我们就必须制造某种秩序，以此我们可以生活得和谐。如果世界是和谐的，我们就必须发现这种和谐是什么。在两种情况下，问题可能相互不同，但是实际结果大致相同。这里我

the Pure reason, we are simply insisting that some kind of arrangement must be made by which we may be enabled to do the best we can with our lives. The question is therefore whether the world helps or hinders our life. We seek facility and avoid hindrance. In other words we follow the line of least resistance, which however is historically ascertained. It is found that with whatever we are concerned in our dealings with the world, our line of least resistance can only be followed by following certain *définie* relations implicit either in nature or in human thought, that is to say, by following logic. We are not here concerned with the question as to whether logic is the law of nature or the law of human thought, it may be neither and it may be both; what we want to point out is that without logic our life is so thoroughly burdensome as to be almost impossible.

But life, as it is generally thought of, has nothing to do with logic. It is said to be illogical. Reason seldom plays any significant part in it. We come without our consent and we go against our will; while we live, we are slaves to our passions, our desires, our hopes and our fears on the one hand, and on the other, we are now and forever after under the power of the blind forces of nature, of what Mr. H. F. Osborn called a tetra-plasmic environment. We sometimes hate because we love, we often smile because we are sad; we weep for joy and we dance to the music of death; pain is to us occasionally pleasurable, and gaiety is sometimes the expression of our spiritual torment; we strive for what we know to be unattainable, we live and let live, and whether the path we take is spacious and easy or narrow and straight, we have no clear view of our destination.

The donkeys of Peking were once noted for their sagacity; they were supposed to have seen the futility of a gallop; neither the threat of whips, nor the commands of their drivers could persuade them to budge an inch from the green grass of the roadside pastures. But they were discovered to be passionately fond of carrots and were sometimes seen galloping after a carrot at the end of a stick held by their riders. The donkeys are perhaps not sagacious enough but then are they less so than we? It is much easier to see the shortcomings of the donkey than our own. A certain American professor once saw a water weasel in a lake and paddled his canoe directly after it. Both were going at a rapid rate, "A weasel is only a weasel," thought the professor, "it does not even know how to escape."

们不是在讨论实践理性或纯粹理性，我们不过是坚持认为必须作出某种安排，以此也许我们能够为我们的生活尽最大努力。因此问题是，世界是帮助了我们的生活还是阻碍了我们的生活。我们追求便利，避免障碍。换言之，我们采用最省事的办法，然而这种办法是历史确定的。人们发现，在我们与世界打交道时，无论我们考虑什么，采用最省事的办法只能是遵循自然界或人类思想中蕴含的某种被定义的关系，就是说，遵循逻辑。我们这里不是考虑逻辑是自然界规律还是人类思维规律的问题，逻辑可以二者都不是，也可以二者都是；我们要指出的是，没有逻辑，我们的生活十分沉重，甚至几乎是不可能的。

但是，正像人们一般认为的那样，生活与逻辑没有丝毫关系。生活据说是没有逻辑的，理性很少在生活中起任何重要作用。我们未经我们的同意而来到世间，我们违反我们的意愿离世而去；我们活着，一方面我们是我们的感情、我们的欲望、我们的希望和我们的恐惧的奴隶；另一方面我们现在并将永远处于自然界（即亨利·费尔菲尔德·奥斯朋先生称之为四重原生质环境）的神秘力量的统治之下。我们有时因爱而恨，我们常常由于难过而笑；我们为高兴而落泪，我们随哀乐而起舞；有时痛苦对我们是欢乐，有时欢乐表达我们的精神痛苦；我们为我们知道不可及的东西而努力，我们自己活也让别人活；无论我们选择的道路是宽广、容易，还是狭窄、平直，我们都看不清我们的目的地。

北京的毛驴过去曾以它们的灵性而闻名。据猜测，它们认识到飞快奔跑是没用的；鞭子的恐吓、驭手的命令都不能使它们从路边的绿草地移动一步。但是后来发现它们非常喜欢吃胡萝卜，有时看见它们为驭手棍棒末端上绑的胡萝卜而飞快地奔跑。也许这些毛驴还不够机灵，但是它们比我们更不机灵吗？看见毛驴的缺点要比看见我们自己的缺点容易得多。有一次某位美国教授在一个湖里看见一只水獭，于是划起自己的独木舟紧追不舍。双方的速度飞快，这位教授想："水獭不过是只水獭，它甚至不知道怎么逃跑。"

The idea of the superiority of man is comforting no less to the plain man than it was to the professor, but before the latter had time to enjoy it, his canoe dashed itself into fragments on a piece of rock and he himself was hurled into the water. Is not our life galloping for a carrot or chasing after a weasel and dashing upon a rock? Is it rational?

But to say that life is either rational or irrational, either logical or illogical is probably the result of a confusion of thought. Life with a capital L is an impossible concept. It is too vague to permit of predication in any way. It may be used to advantage in poetry, but in systematic philosophy it indicates mental poverty rather than mystic insight. It is to some of us frankly meaningless. If it means anything at all, it must mean the lives we live, and the lives we live are so different in quality from each other that hardly any general proposition about them can be philosophically valid. But if some general proposition is actually asserted about life, it must be a vague concept, and as such, we have pointed out, it is incapable of any valid predication.

Suppose, however, we waive the point, and regard Life as a concept capable of predication. The question is whether it is correctly predicted. It is asserted here that life is illogical. Now Logic has hardly anything to do either with things, or concepts or individual propositions. Things and concepts cannot be related to logic in any way, because logic is strictly speaking a special relation between propositions. That is why disconnected ideas or concepts or beliefs, or propositions are neither logical nor illogical. That is why a belief in the devil is on the same level, from the point of view of logic, as a belief in God. That is why philosophy is not concerned with random ideas. Life is not a group of clearly stated propositions between which any relation subsists. It is on our assumption a concept and as such it cannot be predicated in any way by logic. It is neither logical nor illogical.

The statement that life is illogical probably means that there is little logic in life. But in this form, the proposition is extremely vague. It is susceptible of many different interpretations, two of which may be cited for our discussion. It may mean on the one hand, that the people of a community do not generally have one purpose, or having it, they do not take the same steps to satisfy it, or taking the same steps for

对于普通人也好，这位教授也好，人的优越性这种思想令人欣慰。但是，教授还没有来得及高兴，他的独木舟就被礁石撞裂，他被一下子掀入水中。我们的生活不也是为胡萝卜而飞快奔跑，或是追逐一只水獭而撞上礁石吗？这是合乎理性的吗？

但是生活是合乎理性的或不合理性的，是合逻辑的或不合逻辑的，这种说法大概是思想混乱的结果。真正的生活是一个不可能的概念。它十分含混，对它不能作出任何断定。在诗中，用它可能是有利的；但是在系统的哲学中，与其说它表明神秘的洞察力，不如说它表明思想的贫乏。坦白地说，它对我们有些人是无意义的。如果它确实有什么意义，那么它一定意味着我们所过的生活；而我们所过的生活相互性质极为不同，以致几乎任何关于它们的一般陈述都不能是哲学上有效的。如果实际上断定有关生活的某些一般陈述，那么它必定是一个含混的概念，而作为这样的概念，正像我们已经指出的那样，它不能作出任何有效的断定。

然而，假定我们放弃这种观点，并把"生活"看作一个能够断定的概念。问题是它是不是得到正确的预测。这里断定了生活是不合逻辑的。现在，逻辑几乎与事物、概念或个别命题没有任何关系。事物和概念不能以任何方式与逻辑联系起来，因为严格地说，逻辑是命题之间的一种特殊关系。因此，没有联系的思想、概念、信念或命题既不是合逻辑的，也不是不合逻辑的。因此，从逻辑的观点看，信恶和信上帝是同等的。因此，哲学不考虑随意的思想。生活不是一组得到清楚陈述的、其间存在某些关系的命题。根据我们的假设，生活是一个概念。作为这样一个概念，不能用逻辑对它做任何表述。它既不是合逻辑的，也不是不合逻辑的。

生活是不合逻辑的，这个陈述大概意味着生活中没有什么逻辑。以这种表达，这个命题极端含混。这允许有许多不同的解释。这里为我们的讨论可以举出其中两种解释。一方面它可以意味：一个群体的人一般没有一个目的；或者有一个目的，但他们没有采取共同的步骤

satisfaction, they do not arrive at the same conclusion, or arriving at the same conclusion, they do not start from the same purpose. In other words, there is neither common aim, nor common effort. On the other hand, the statement may mean that our individual lives are bundles of contradictions. A mentally comfortable person may feel himself in harmony with nature, but a sensitive and striving soul is likely to be constantly at war with himself. Since it is only the mentally restless who are to any extent reflective, it is probably by them that the contradictions of life are the most keenly felt. But whether they are keenly felt by many or only a few, they seem to be recognized by all.

In order to decide whether the above discussion is to the point or not, we have to clear up one ambiguity contained in the statement referred to in the beginning of the preceding paragraph. We have to point out that whether there is little or much logic in life, we are not justified in saying on that account that life is either illogical or logical. The vagueness of the term "life" and the definiteness of the term "logic" do not permit such an inference. A room may possibly be asserted to be dusty when "it" contains much dust, because that which contained much dust is presumably that which is asserted to be dusty, and the degree of dustiness of a room bears some kind of a relation to the quantity of dust contained in it. But in the case of life and logic, such a presumption is quite impossible. The "life" that contains little logic cannot be the life that is asserted to be illogical; because strictly speaking the term "logic" does not permit of degrees, so that the expression "more or less logical" is meaningless and the predication of logicality of any subject for our consideration bears no relation to the amount of logic contained in that subject. If life contains little logic, it simply means that life has few aspects that are logical, and many that are not. The "life" that is said to contain little logic is a generic term that includes everything that is life and the "life" that is asserted to be illogical is limited to those aspects of life to which logic is denied.

It now remains to consider whether there is little or much logic in life. The question can never be statistically answered. Our answer is necessarily a matter of speculation or belief, and like most beliefs, it is likely colored by our personal temperament. But while a statistical answer can hardly be given, any confusion of thought involved in the

来实现它；或者他们采取共同的步骤来实现它，但没有达到相同的结局；或者他们达到相同的结局，但没有从相同的目的出发。换言之，既没有共同的目标，也没有共同的努力。另一方面，这个陈述可以意味：我们的个体生活充满矛盾。一个思想上轻松自在的人可能感到自己与自然界和谐一致，但是一个敏感而奋发的人很可能不断地与自己做斗争。由于只有思想活跃的人才能在某种程度上进行反思，因此很可能是他们最敏锐地感受到生活的矛盾。但是，无论是许多人还是只有少数几个人敏锐地感受到它们，似乎所有人都承认它们。

为了判定以上讨论是否切题，我们必须消除上一段开始提到的那个陈述所包含的一种歧义。我们必须指出，无论生活中是没有什么逻辑，还是有许多逻辑，我们都没有理由因此说，生活要么是不合逻辑的，要么是合逻辑的。"生活"这个词的含混和"逻辑"这个词的明确不允许这样的推论。如果一间屋子有许多灰尘，可能就可以断定"它"是布满灰尘的，因为有许多灰尘的东西大概就是被断定为布满灰尘的东西，并且一间屋子布满灰尘的程度与它具有的灰尘的量有某种关系。但是在生活和逻辑的情况下，这样的设想是根本不可能的。没有什么逻辑的"生活"不能是被断定为不合逻辑的生活；因为严格地说，"逻辑"这个词不允许有程度，因此"或多或少符合逻辑的"这个表达式是无意义的。我们考虑的任何主体的逻辑性的断定，与这个主体中具有的逻辑的量没有关系。如果生活没有什么逻辑，这不过意味着生活没有什么合逻辑的方面，并有许多不合逻辑的方面。被说成没有什么逻辑的"生活"是一个通称，它包括一切是生活的东西；而被断定为不合逻辑的"生活"则限于没有逻辑的那些生活方面。

现在需要考虑生活中是没有什么逻辑还是有许多逻辑。绝不能以统计学的方式回答这个问题。我们的回答必然是猜测或信念的问题，而且正像大多数信念一样，它很可能带有我们个人气质的色彩。但是尽管几乎不能作出统计学的回答，仍必须清除一般为这两种可能的回答之一列举例子而引起的任何思想混乱。一般认为，生活中

instances generally cited for either of the two alternative answers must be removed. It is ordinarily supposed that conflicting desires in life are logical contradictions. Such however is not necessarily the case. Thus the desire to be in Europe and America at the same time is said to be self-contradictory, because presumably a person cannot be in two places at the same time. Such a desire may be split into two, which may be put in the form of statements such as "I desire to be in A at T" and "I desire to be in B at T" where B and A represent different places and T the same time. These statements are only contradictory by assuming that no one at the same time can possibly desire to be in two different places. But such an assumption is quite different from the more or less recognized fact that one cannot be at two different places at the same time. Factual limitations need not have anything to do with our desires. The fact that we cannot visit the moon is no reason why logically we cannot desire to visit it.

The satisfaction of one desire does sometimes preclude the possibility of the satisfaction of another desire. But the satisfaction of desires is generally believed to be different from entertaining them; it may be obtained in the sphere of feelings or emotions, or it may result in some reaction from the external world. To desire the Venus de Milo is by no means the same as to desire a lady of flesh and blood. In the former case no behavioristic response is expected, while in the latter case such response is actively hoped for. The satisfaction of different desires may therefore be different. If it takes place in the sphere of desires, feelings or emotions, the satisfaction of one desire need not result either in logical contradiction to or logical consistency with the satisfaction of another desire. If it occurs in some kind of response in the external world it does not affirm logical contradiction in the sphere of desires, even where these desires are supposed to conflict; it merely affirms a place for logic in the external world. My desires to be in Europe and America at the same time do not logically contradict each other as desires; their respective satisfactions do contradict each other if we assume that we cannot be in different places at the same time. But a logical contradiction in the external world does not mean a logical contradiction in the world of desires.

有冲突的愿望是逻辑矛盾，然而情况并非必然如此。期望"同时在欧洲和在美洲"被说成是自相矛盾的，因为一个人总不能同时在两个地方。这样一种愿望可以一分为二，例如这可以以陈述的形式表达如下："我期望 T 时在 A 地"，"我期望 T 时在 B 地"，这里 B 和 A 表示不同的地点，T 表示相同的时间。仅仅当假定任何人都不可能期望同时在两个不同的地点，这些陈述才是矛盾的。但是这样一个假定与一个人不能同时在两个不同的地点这一或多或少公认的事实是十分不同的。事实的限制无须与我们的愿望有任何关系。我们不能探月，这一事实不能解释为什么逻辑上我们不能期望探月。

满足一种愿望有时确实排除满足另一种愿望的可能性。但是一般人相信，满足愿望与满怀愿望是不同的；它可以在感情或情绪的范围内实现，或者它可能产生某些来自外界的反应。期望得到米洛的维纳斯雕像与期望得到一位有血有肉的女士截然不同。在前一种情况，不指望得到行为主义的反应；而在后一种情况，则渴望得到这种反应。因此，不同愿望的满足可以是不同的。如果满足一种愿望是在愿望、感情或情绪的范围内发生，那么它不必导致与满足另一种愿望的逻辑矛盾或逻辑一致。如果它在外界引起某种反应，则它不证实愿望范围内的逻辑矛盾，即使假定这些愿望在这里是冲突的；它仅仅证实逻辑在外界的一席位置。"我想同时在欧洲和在美洲"，作为愿望这是相互没有逻辑矛盾的；如果我们假定我们不能同时在不同的地方，那么分别满足这些愿望确实就是相互矛盾的。但是一个外界的逻辑矛盾并不意味着一个愿望范围内的逻辑矛盾。

Our discussion thus far has resulted only in this: that we cannot say that life is either logical or illogical, that whether life contains little or much logic cannot be statistically determined, that our view concerning it is a matter of belief, and that some at least of the so called logical contradictions in life are not so in a strict sense. However, none of the above conclusions has any very direct bearing on the important point at issue. The point is that without logic life would be so burdensome as to be almost impossible. One instance alone of the function of logic in life is sufficient to establish its importance. The relation of "if-then" when reduced to its last analysis is a logical relation; it is also a relation which must be reckoned with if we want to satisfy our desire for self-preservation. If our Lebensanschauung does not happen to be either materialistic or idealistic, we are liable to regard our lives as some kind of adjustment between ourselves on the one hand and nature on the other. We may be a part of nature, or nature may be a part of ourselves, each may be inseparable from the other; but the moment we discuss their relation, we are bound to regard them as two entities, at least during the time of our discussion. Our ideals, our purposes, our wills, and our instincts must be distinguished from their field of satisfaction, a field that must be regarded as beyond what Mark Twain called "the remotest frontiers" of our persons.

We seem to be gyrating towards the cesspool of free will and necessity from which many a philosopher has never emerged. Fortunately for us, a lengthy discussion of the problem is here out of place. It is only necessary to mention that without some kind of comparatively rigid relationship in nature, our will, whether determined or not, will not be freely satisfied. If we will to be warm in our room, during the Arctic winters of Peking, it is quite obvious to the much-maligned plain man that we had better heat our stoves. Only fools and philosophers are puzzled over the relation between our will to be warm on the one hand, and the heating of the stove on the other. Whatever result the philosophers may arrive at in their discussion of this relation, the plain man recognizes that if we want such and such a thing, we must then do such and such other thing. The relation of "if-then" is not less appreciated by the plain man than by the philosopher, only the latter can describe the steps involved in greater detail than the former. At any rate this is the kind of relationship that

因此，我们的讨论至此只得出如下结果：我们不能说生活是合逻辑的或不合逻辑的；不能以统计学的方式确定生活是没有什么逻辑还是有许多逻辑；我们关于生活的看法是信念的问题；至少生活中有些所谓逻辑矛盾不是严格意义上的逻辑矛盾。然而，以上任何结论与争论的重点都没有任何直接的关系。争论的重点是，没有逻辑，生活就会十分沉重，以致几乎是不可能的。逻辑在生活中的职能仅以一例就充分建立起它的重要性。"如果——则"这一关系归根结底乃是一种逻辑关系；如果我们要满足我们自我保护的愿望，就必须认真考虑这种关系。如果我们的生活观恰巧不是唯物主义的或唯心主义的，那么我们很可能把我们的生活看作我们自己和自然界之间的某种适应。我们可以是自然界的一部分，或者自然界可以是我们自己的一部分，二者也许不能相互分离；但是当我们讨论它们的关系时，我们必定把它们看作是两个实体，至少在我们的讨论过程中是两个实体。我们的理想、我们的目的、我们的意志和我们的本能，必须区别于对它们的满足，必须把后者看作是超出马克·吐温称之为我们人的"最边远区域"的范围。

我们似乎又转向那个许多哲学家从未走出来的自由意志和必然的泥潭。幸亏我们在这里不必详细讨论这个问题。只需要提一点：在自然界若没有某种相对严格的关系，就不能自由地满足我们的意志，不论是确定的还是不确定的意志。如果在北京的严冬，我们要在屋里感到暖和，则一个很普通的人显然也知道，我们最好在屋里生炉子。只有傻瓜和哲学家才会对我们要在屋里感到暖和和生炉子之间的关系困惑不解。无论哲学家在对这种关系的讨论中会得到什么结论，普通人都认识到如果我们要某种东西，那么我们必须做另外某某事情。普通人和哲学家同样懂得"如果——则"这个关系，只不过哲学家能够比普通人更详细地描述其中所包含的步骤。无论如何，

facilitates our lives. Most of us can see for ourselves that the discovery of such relationships removes the burden with which we are loaded when we happen to have desires concerning which such relations when discovered indicate the direction of our activity.

But is such a relation a logical one? The logical relation, "if A, then B," whatever A and B may happen to be, does not lead us to the knowledge "if such and such a fact, then such and such other fact or facts." The latter is limited to the sphere of facts or events. It is the relation of cause and effect, and as such it is itself burdened with logical difficulties. Whatever the law of causality may be, however it is stated, it must be rigid in order that it may be effective from the point of view of our everyday life and it cannot be quite rigid from the point of view of logic. It probably was not invented by nature merely for its service to mankind, but if it is to be serviceable to mankind it must be valid not merely for the facts of the past, but also for possible similar occurrences that are yet to come. It must in other words afford us some ground for prevision. But such a rigidity of relationship cannot subsist between facts and occurrence that are not yet facts. Nothing certain can be said about the future, so that if the law of causality is to be applied to the future, it cannot be rigid, and if it is not rigid, its usefulness as an instrument is to that extent, diminished.

Besides, there is a more fundamental difficulty. The abstract relation "if A then B" can never lead us to a knowledge of any particular causal relationship in the world of facts, and the causal relationship discovered to be subsisting between certain facts can never lead us to the abstract generalization of the nature, if A then B. The difficulty is traditional, and whether or not it has been solved by scientists and logicians, it remains unsolved among philosophers. It is a difficulty of the general problem of the relation between a priori and a posteriori reasoning. Inductive generalization always involves something that is not inductive, and a priori ideas, as we have already pointed out, are in the last analysis incapable of a priori justification. Each seems to be dependent in a measure upon the other, and while we are not here concerned with the solution of the general problem of their mutual relationship, we are nonetheless interested in it in so far as it effects the question as to whether or not the relation of "if-then" in the world of facts is such a relation in the world of logic.

这是一种方便我们生活的关系。我们大多数人都能亲身看到：当我们恰巧有了某种愿望，而与这种愿望有关的关系一旦被发现，就会指明我们行为的方向时，发现这样的关系，就解除了我们身上的负担。

但是，这样一种关系是逻辑关系吗？无论 A 和 B 可能恰巧是什么，"如果 A，则 B"这一逻辑关系都不能让我们知道"如果如此如此一个事实，则这般这般另一个事实或另一些事实"。后者限于事实或事件的范围。这是原因和结果的关系。作为这样一种关系，它本身有许多逻辑困难。无论因果律可以是什么，可以如何陈述，它必须是严格的。这样，从我们日常生活的观点看，它才可以是有效的；而从逻辑的观点看，它不能是完全严格的。自然界创造它大概不仅是因为它对人类有用；但是如果它要为人类提供帮助，那么不仅对过去的事实，而且对还将出现的可能类似的情况，它都必须是有效的。换言之，它必须为我们提供某种预见根据。但是，关系的这种严格性不能存在于事实和目前尚不是事实的事件之间。关于未来不能说出任何确定的东西，所以如果把因果律用于未来，它就不能是严格的；如果它不是严格的，那么在这种程度上就削弱了它作为一个工具的有用性。

此外，还有一个更根本的困难。"如果 A，则 B"这种抽象关系绝不能引导我们认识事实范围内的任何特殊因果关系；而且，这种被发现存在于一定事实之间的因果关系绝不能引导我们抽象地概括出"如果 A，则 B"这种性质。这个困难是历史的，无论它在科学家和逻辑学家那里是否得到解决，它在哲学家那里仍然没有被解决。这是关于先验和后验推理之间关系的一般问题的困难。归纳概括总是包含不是归纳的东西，而且先验的思想，正像我们已指出的那样，归根到底不能得到先验的证实。它们似乎有些相互依赖，而且虽然我们这里不考虑解决它们的相互关系的一般问题，但是我们依然对它感兴趣，因为它产生下面的问题：事实范围中的"如果——则"这种关系是不是逻辑领域中的这样一种关系。

The answer to the above question depends to a large extent upon a reconciliation between the looseness of the factual relation of "if-then," and the rigidity of the logical relation. If the two can be reconciled, there is hardly any reason why one of them should not be considered, for our purpose at least, as the other. Such a reconciliation is possible only by making the logical relation logically less rigid. Factual relations may become less and less loose in the advance of knowledge, but they can never attain to logical rigidity in the traditional sense. But the traditional sense of logical rigidity is very much modified by the introduction into logic of the calculus of probabilities. The development of this comparatively new branch of knowledge is itself a recognition of the uncertainties that seem to permeate the world of facts. At the same time, these uncertainties, once recognized, lead us to regard our knowledge of facts or factual relations as statistical rather than absolute. We have therefore on the one hand, a development of the logic of probabilities and on the other a recognition of the statistical nature of our knowledge of facts.

These two tendencies or two aspects of one tendency produce the reconciliation desired between factual and logical relations. On the one hand, the more we improve our statistical method, the more nearly certain factual relations become. (We are here dealing with facts that are known and are assuming that our calculation of the future is based upon our knowledge of the past.) On the other, the logic of probabilities is gaining in rigidity day by day and although it cannot attain to the rigidity of formal logic, the calculation of probabilities has become a logical procedure. We do not of course claim that the general problem of the relationship between inductive and deductive reasoning is solved; it may be, and it probably remains, as thorny as it ever was before. We merely point out that the factual relation of "if-then," including such concomitant variations as cause and effect can become very nearly certain through an improvement in statistical method and that some logical relations of "if-then" are conceded to be not quite certain by the introduction into logic of the calculus of probability. We are therefore in a position to say that the factual relation of "if-then" may be considered for specific purposes a logical relation and that if such relations remove some of the burdens of life, we are ready to apprcciatc what role logic plays in it.

We see then that whether life contains little or much logic, it is logic that enables us to live with the least resistance. We may be able to show

　　回答这个问题在很大程度上取决于"如果——则"的事实关系的松散性和逻辑关系的严格性之间的调解。如果二者可以调解，那么几乎没有任何理由为什么不能把它们一方（至少为了我们的目的）看作另一方。只有使逻辑关系在逻辑上不太严格，这种调解才是可能的。事实关系可以随认识的深入变得越来越不松散，但是它们绝达不到传统意义上的逻辑严格性。但是由于逻辑中引入了概率演算，因而大大修正了逻辑严格性的传统意义。发展这一比较新的认识分支实际上是认识到事实范围中似乎到处可见的不确定性。同时，一旦认识到这些不确定性，就可以使我们对事实或事实关系的认识看作是统计的，而不是绝对的。因此，我们一方面发展了概率逻辑，另一方面认识到我们对事实的认识的统计性质。

　　这两种倾向，或一种倾向的两个方面，造成事实关系和逻辑关系之间理想的调解。一方面，我们越改进我们的统计方法，事实关系就变得越接近确定。（我们这里探讨已知的事实并且假定我们对未来的计算基于我们对过去的认识。）另一方面，概率逻辑正在变得越来越严格，尽管它不能达到形式逻辑的严格性，但是概率演算已成为一个逻辑过程。当然，我们不是说演绎和归纳推理之间关系的一般问题得到解决；它可能并也许依然像以前那样难以解决。我们仅仅指出，通过统计学方法的改进，"如果——则"这种事实关系，包括相应的原因和结果这样的变异，可以变得很接近确定；并且必须承认，在逻辑中引入概率演算，某些"如果——则"这样的逻辑关系却不是非常确定的。因此我们可以说，为了特殊的目的，可以把"如果——则"这种事实关系看作一种逻辑关系。如果这样的关系解除我们的某些生活负担，那么我们很乐意重视其中逻辑所起的作用。

　　于是我们看到，无论生活是没有什么逻辑还是有许多逻辑，正是逻辑能够使我们最容易地生活。后面我们也许能够说明，随着我们

later that logic will play a greater and greater part in life as we travel into the unknown future, but it remains for us to point out in this paragraph that logic facilitates life only in the satisfaction of our desires that are given; it does not have anything to do with the value, or quality or quantity of desires as desires, nor does it have anything to do with the psychology of their mutual relations. Life, whatever it means, may be just as romantic or poetic, or absorbingly interesting, or just as dull, or prosaic or commonplace with a flourishing sense of logic as it would be with no development of logic at all. Spiritual sufferings or strivings, ambitions beyond one's capacity, emotional excitement centering around one's ego, or imaginations that are unconditioned by time and space, or religious feelings or Freudian complexes are, from the point of view of those who are a part of them, those aspects of life with which logic is not concerned.

探讨未知的未来，逻辑将在生活中起越来越大的作用。但是在这一段我们仍需要指出，逻辑为生活提供便利，仅仅在于满足我们既定的愿望；它与作为愿望的愿望的价值、性质和数量没有任何关系，与探讨它们的相互关系的心理学也没有任何关系。生活无论意味着什么，有丰盛的逻辑意义它可能是浪漫的、诗一般的或令人神往的，或者是枯燥的、无聊的或平凡的那样，没有逻辑的发展照样如此。精神上的痛苦或斗争、超出人的能力的雄心、围绕自我的情绪激动，或不受时空限制的想象，或者宗教感情或弗洛伊德学说中的情结，从构成部分的角度来看，都是生活中逻辑所不考虑的那些方面。

While logic has been criticized by most people as irrelevant to life, it has been attacked by philosophers as inadequate for and inapplicable to the problem of knowledge. The attacks come from a number of sources, three of which will be discussed here. In the first place, there is the attack from the point of view of science. The fruitfulness of science is undeniable, and even if philosophers were to ignore it, they can only do so at the expense of their own philosophical ruin. In its history, science was constantly at war with tradition, and in its struggle for existence, it received no aid from syllogistic logic. While it involves principles not empirically derived, its progress was mainly a result of experimentation and empirical observation. Since its accumulated data are too complex to be organized and systematized by syllogistic logic on account of its limited range, it is easily, rather too easily, concluded that logic is of no use to science; and for those positivists who regard science not merely as the royal road, but also as the only road to genuine knowledge, logic, because of its inadequacy for science, is further asserted to be equally inadequate for knowledge.

A second line of criticism comes from skepticism. The arguments of some Greeks against the possibility of knowledge were essentially arguments against logic, since epistemology in those days was more closely interwoven with logic than it probably is today. But historically at any rate the light of the Greek skeptics was a dim one compared to which that of Aristotle and Plato shone with dazzling brilliance. Besides, European philosophy was subsequently captured by Hebraic emotionalism and by the Church, any deviation from which was liable to incur unphilosophical treatment, and skepticism was not such a doctrine as to stir its adherents into willing martyrs. Thus the skepticism of the Greeks affects us only indirectly, if at all. It was rather the skepticism of David Hume that led many to a renewed attack on logic. The philosophy of that great iconoclast implied an extreme incapacity of logic not merely by excluding metaphysics and theology from the sphere of philosophy, but also by making science itself irrational. The subsequent development in philosophy might be regarded as replies to Hume, but while the anti-intellectualism of today may be regarded as a survival of Hume's thought, it has its own distinctive elements derived chiefly from the Darwinian theory of evolution.

三

　　大多数人批评逻辑与生活毫不相干，而哲学家却抨击逻辑不适于并且不能用于认识问题。这些抨击有种种来源，这里将讨论其中三种。首先有来自科学观点的抨击。科学成就辉煌，这是不容否认的；甚至哲学家要无视这一点，其代价只能是毁灭自己的哲学。在科学史上，科学一直与传统发生冲突，在其生存斗争中，它没有得到三段论逻辑的帮助。科学包含不用经验得出的原则，而科学的进步却主要是实验和经验观察的结果。由于科学的累计数据十分复杂，以致应用范围十分有限的三段论逻辑不能组织它们并使它们系统化，因此容易，并且有些过于容易得出逻辑对科学没有用处的结论。对于那些把科学看作不仅是通往真知的康庄大道而且是唯一途径的实证主义者来说，由于逻辑对于科学是不适宜的，因此逻辑被断定对于认识同样是不适宜的。

　　第二种批评来自怀疑论。一些古希腊哲学家反对认识的可能性的论据，实质上是反对逻辑的论据，因为认识论那时比今天大概更紧密地与逻辑交织在一起。但是历史上，与亚里士多德和柏拉图的绚丽多彩相比，古希腊怀疑论者毕竟黯然失色。此外，欧洲哲学后来受到希伯来人的唯情论和教会的统治，只要违背教会，就可能招致不理智的待遇，而怀疑论不是一种鼓动其信徒乐于献身的学说。因此古希腊的怀疑论即使有影响，也只是间接地影响我们。倒是大卫·休谟的怀疑论引导许多人重新攻击逻辑。这位对传统观念进行攻击的伟人的哲学意味着逻辑极为无能，因为它不仅从哲学领域排除形而上学和神学，而且使科学本身成为非理性的。以后哲学的发展可看作是对休谟的回答，但是尽管今天的反唯理智论可看作是休谟思想的残存，但它却有自己不同的、主要得自达尔文进化论的要素。

The third attack on logic comes from the anti-intellectualism of both Pragmatism and Vitalism. Since the world evolves, the Pragmatists are not slow to infer that logic and truths also evolve. Thus at a single stroke, any particular system of logic is deprived of its eternal validity, and any permanent system is a mere contradiction in terms. Like everything else, it rises and passes away; it is an instrument adapted to the purpose of life only for a given time, and presumably also only for a given place. Not only is logic considered to be always evolving, but also its evolution is asserted to be its saving grace, for otherwise it would be powerless to cope with the events of a changing world. This is particularly emphasized by the Intuitionism of Mr. Bergson, who probably feels, as Li Po felt before him, that the world is a hotel, and time, only a passenger. It probably hurts his sensitive soul to see logicians claiming a knowledge of the world by their manipulation of static concepts, terms and relations, when with everything at a flux, and ourselves a part of the stream, the only way to be intimate with our environment and to know its realities is, according to him, to move with its onward march.

These attacks may be met by three lines of argument. In the first place, syllogistic logic should not be confounded with logic; in the second place, logic can account for certain facts or problems hitherto considered unaccountable; and in the third place, the static nature of logic is not an argument against it.

Science is said to have gone far beyond the limits of logic. The statement is hardly objectionable, if the term "logic" means syllogistic logic. But there is no reason why the two should he confounded with each other. It is true that syllogistic logic is too narrow to meet the requirements of science, but it is also true that science is itself logical. Science, it need hardly be affirmed, is not merely a body of knowledge. Nor is it merely, as it is often claimed to be, empirical knowledge. If it is at all different from the practices of the ancient medicine men, or the weather forecasts of uneducated peasants, it must have some quality that is peculiarly its own.

It seems to imply order, organization and systematization. It is not merely what it contains; it includes the method by which its contents are brought into correlation. In fact, it is chiefly its methodology that is entitled to the credit of its success. But scientific method means a very rigid procedure which is none the less logic, even though it is not mere syllogism.

对逻辑的第三种攻击来自实用主义和生机论的反唯理智主义。由于世界是进化的，实用主义者很快推论逻辑和真理也是进化的。这样一举剥夺了任何特定的逻辑系统的永恒的有效性，任何永久的系统不过是一种用词矛盾。它像任何其他事物一样，产生并且消亡；它是仅在某一时间，大概也仅在特定地方适合生活目的的工具。不仅逻辑被看作是永远不断进化的，而且逻辑的进化也被断定是一个可取之处，因为否则它就不会有能力处理变化着的世界中的事件。伯格森先生的直觉主义特别强调这一点，像李白在伯格森之前感受到的那样，大概觉得世界是一个旅馆，时间仅是一位过客。看到逻辑学家通过使用静止的概念、词项和关系而声称认识了世界，大概伤害了伯格森敏感的心灵，因为在他看来，由于一切事物都是流动的，我们自己是这长河中的一部分，因此熟悉我们周围环境和认识其实在性的唯一途径是随其前进而运动。

这些批评可能遇到三种论证。首先，三段论逻辑不应与逻辑混为一谈；第二，逻辑可以说明迄今认为无法说明的某些事实或问题的原因；第三，逻辑的静态性质不能反驳逻辑。

据说，科学大大超出逻辑的限度。如果"逻辑"这个词意味着三段论逻辑，那么这个陈述几乎是令人无法反对的。但逻辑和三段论逻辑却没有理由混为一谈。三段论逻辑过于狭窄，不能满足科学的要求，这是真的。但科学本身是合逻辑的，这也是真的。几乎不需要证实，科学不仅仅是大量的知识。它也不像人们常常声称的那样，仅仅是经验知识。如果科学确实有别于古代巫医的实践或没有文化的农民所做的天气预报，那么它一定有某种专属于自己的性质。它似乎暗含着秩序、组织和系统化。它不仅是它所包含的东西，还包括将其内容相互联系起来的方法。事实上，科学成功的荣誉主要应归于它的方法论。但是科学方法意味着十分严格的程序，而这个程序仍然是逻辑的，尽管它不仅仅是三段论。

Much of the familiar criticism of logic centers around this confusion of terms. Another instance of it is the claim that logic is incapable of dealing with a number of very fundamental concepts. The problems of Zeno, the antimonies of Kant, as well as the notions of infinity and continuity are problems which logic is supposed to be powerless to solve. What is meant by logic here is again syllogistic logic, the limitations of which, true or false, are not properly limitations of logic. Some of the problems that are deemed logically insolvable are at any rate already logically solved. The notions of infinity and continuity are now firmly constructed through logical analysis and are likely to remain with us, unless a revolution such as that of the theory of Relativity in mathematical physics takes place in philosophy, necessitating a general house-cleaning of our fundamental concepts. Our notions of time and space, of change and motion have not yet received any widely accepted formulation, but it is much more probable than ever before that such a formulation will soon be offered for criticism and perhaps acceptance.

What seems to be very generally overlooked by the students of philosophy is that logic has developed far beyond its original confines. It embodies at present a good deal of the methods of pure science. Not only scientific knowledge, but also scientific procedure, is capable of mathematical expression, and through the merging of mathematics with logic, much of what was once exclusively scientific, or exclusively logical is no longer separated by a clear and distinct line of demarcation. A higher synthesis is obtained through the use of symbols so that, as Mr. Russell tells us, it is difficult to say where mathematics begins or where logic ends. Symbolic logic has been criticized by various people on various grounds. But whatever the criticisms may be, it can claim at least one advantage; it is capable of greater expansion than the traditional logic. On the one hand, it is susceptible of greater generalization; on the other, it is reducible to a fewer number of primitive ideas. It is much more of a closed system than ever before; it is perhaps too abstruse and technical to be of general interest, but in ceasing to be a mere plaything for philosophical dilettantes, it has become a more reliable instrument than it ever was for serious philosophical criticism and construction.

The above paragraphs are intended to show that some attacks on logic are based on a confusion of thought, that the logic of today is different from syllogism, and that in its most developed form, it is capable of

　　对逻辑的许多类似批评都是围绕这种用语的混乱而产生的。它的另一例情况是声称逻辑不能处理一些非常基础的概念。芝诺的问题、康德的二律背反，以及无穷和连续的概念被认为是逻辑没有能力解决的问题。然而这里的逻辑指的又是三段论逻辑，它的局限性，无论真假，准确来说，都不是逻辑的局限性。那些所谓在逻辑上不可解决的问题，有些不管怎样在逻辑上已经解决了。现在通过逻辑分析确切地构造了无穷和连续的概念，并且我们很可能依然使用它们，除非在哲学中发生一场像数学物理学中的相对论一样的革命，对我们的基础概念进行大扫除。我们关于时间和空间、变化和运动的概念尚未得到任何广泛接受的表述，但是今天比以往任何时候都更加可能提出这样的批评或接受的表述。

　　似乎哲学研究者总体上忽视了一个问题，即逻辑已发展得远远超出原来的范围。今天逻辑包含了大量的纯科学方法。不仅科学认识，而且科学程序都能够以数学方式表达。由于数学与逻辑的结合，许多过去一度专门是科学的东西或专门是逻辑的东西，今天已无法由一条清晰和鲜明的分界线分开。逻辑和数学通过使用符号达到了更高程度的综合，因此正像罗素先生告诉我们的那样，很难说数学在哪里开始或逻辑在哪里结束。不同的人根据不同理由一直批评符号逻辑，但是无论这些批评可能是什么，至少可以声称符号逻辑有一种优越性：它能够比传统逻辑的范围更大。一方面它允许更笼统的概括，另一方面，它可以化简到很少几个初始思想。它是前所未有的封闭系统，也许它十分深奥、技术性很强，以致问津者极少，但是由于它不再是一些肤浅的哲学家手中简单的玩物，因此它成为严肃的哲学批评和构造的空前可靠的工具。

　　以上几段旨在说明：对逻辑的一些批评根源在于思想混乱；今天的逻辑与三段论不同；逻辑以其最发达的形式能够处理棘手的

dealing with the thorny problems of knowledge. It remains for us to meet the arguments of both Pragmatism and Vitalism. The argument that logic evolves and that therefore there is no one logic is met by what has been said in one of the previous sections. The different systems of logic that exist as a matter of fact imply one system that may or may not exist. The existing systems may perish, but the implied system is logically applicable to all time and all possible worlds. If one argues about logic, one is obliged, I believe, to come to the above conclusion, whether one believes in it or not. The only way to escape it is to refrain from logical arguments altogether.

The argument that logic is static and therefore it is incapable of dealing with the facts of a continuously changing world is worth a few remarks in that it is urged with a good deal of persistence.

Mr. Poincaré has somewhere pointed out that if our idea of evolution evolves with biological evolution, we would not be able to say anything about it. A constancy of concepts, and an inevitability of the sequence of propositions are indispensable to the advance of science. The world may change, but our generalizations about the changing world cannot change with it; for if they change with the changing world, they would not have the validity credited to them for more than a mathematical instant of time. That of course does not mean that our ideas of the changing world do not change; it simply means that they do not change at a one-one ratio with the changing world. For a given period of time, some generalizations must be assumed to be valid at least for that period of time, for otherwise there cannot be any system of reference in terms of which the past can be described and the future appraised in large outlines.

It is not only the past and future that present difficulties of the nature described; the very process of description and appraisal of nature will be quite impossible if the terms or names employed in such description change with the ever-changing world. Science is now regarded as a systematic and minute description of nature, rather than an explanation of it. We who are mere students of philosophy, are not in a position to dispute the validity of such a view of science; we only accept what is offered and if a large number of scientists maintain the position that science is a description of nature, we may be required to justify their position.

认识问题。我们依然要面对实用主义和生机论的论证。前面有一节讨论已遇到这样的论证：逻辑是进化的，因而不存在某种特定的逻辑。存在的不同的逻辑系统实际上暗含着一种可能存在也可能不存在的系统。存在的系统可以消亡，但是暗含的系统在逻辑上却适合于一切时间和一切可能世界。我相信如果一个人论证逻辑，那么他一定会得出上述结论，无论他信不信它。避免这一结论的唯一方式是绝对不要对逻辑展开论证。

逻辑是静止的，因而不能处理不断变化的世界的事实，这一论证值得讨论几句，因为有人极其坚持主张这种论证。

庞加莱先生曾指出，如果我们关于进化的思想随着生物进化而进化，那么我们实际上对它不能发表任何看法。概念的恒定性，命题序列的必然性，是科学的进步必不可少的。世界可以变化，但是我们关于这个变化世界的概括却不能随它而变化；因为如果这些概括随着变化的世界而变化，那么它们哪怕精确的片刻都不会被赋予这样的有效性。当然这并不意味着我们关于变化的世界的思想不变化，这只不过意味着它们的变化与变化的世界没有一一对应的比例。对于某一特定时期，必须假定有些概括至少对这一时期是有效的，因为否则就不能有任何可用以粗略地描述过去和评价未来的参照系统。

不仅过去和未来表现出具有上述性质的困难；而且如果描述中的用语随着不断变化的世界而变化，那么对自然的描述和评价过程本身将是完全不可能的。科学现在被看作是对自然的系统而详细的描述，而不是对自然的解释。我们不过是哲学的研究者，没有能力怀疑这样一种科学观点的有效性，我们仅接受提供给我们的东西；并且如果许多科学家坚持认为科学是对自然的描述，那么就可能要求我们证实他们的观点。

Formulas are according to this view descriptions. As such, the terms used must be either statistical summaries of a general nature or exact equivalents of individual objects in all particulars. The latter is both impossible and useless: its impossibility will be dealt with later, and its uselessness has already been mentioned, viz, it does not enable us to say anything about the world.

The only alternative left is to regard the terms used in formulas as statistical summaries. Regarded as such, the term "human being" includes the notion that man lives to an age anywhere from one minute to one hundred years and that though some men die the moment they are born and others live to 110 years, the notion contained in the term is not thus invalidated. But if we look at the problem in this light, the terms or names or symbols used in descriptions are only less permanent than concepts, they are by no means the equivalent of objects in all particulars. They do not change continuously with the objects they describe, because the statistical average does not change in the same ratio with the variation of particular individuals contained in a class statistically studied. Statistical descriptions cannot therefore change with the objects described; they are relatively permanent. The very notion of a statistical description involves a relative permanence of its terms.

It is probably this tendency of ideas not to change with the changing world that has led some people to emphasize intuition at the expense of intellect. Let us not concern ourselves for the moment with the question of whether or not it is desirable that our ideas should change at the rate of the changing world. Let us merely make one or two brief observations on intuition. Is it dropped out of thin air for us to exercise our religious belief, or is it capable of analysis and consequently of intellectual justification? If the former, we need not say anything about it, since it is no longer a question of argument and conviction. If the latter, it loses its distinctive quality in the sense that it will be discovered to be different from intellect only in degree and not in kind. It is quite possible as some of us maintain that intuition is only a quick process of reasoning where the premises and the sequence of propositions are merged into the conclusions arrived at almost in an instant. Those who know intuitively, if there are such, may not be able to analyze the process by which they obtain their knowledge, but it can be analyzed for them by others who are

根据这种观点，公式就是描述。因此，用词必须是具有一般性的统计概括或在所有细节方面与个体对象的确切对应物。后者既不可能，也无用处。其不可能性以后将讨论，其无用性已经提到，或者说，它个能使我们对世界发表任何看法。

剩下的唯一选择是把公式用词看作统计概括。如果这样看，则"人类"这个词包括这样的概念：人活到从一分钟至一百岁这个区间的任何时候。尽管有些人一生下来就死了，也有些人活到一百一十岁，但是这个词包含的概念并不因而无效。但是如果我们根据这种观点看这个问题，那么描述中使用的词、名字或符号仅仅不如概念持久，但绝不是在所有细节方面与对象的对应物。它们不会随着它们描述的对象而不断变化，因为统计的平均数不会与统计研究的类别中包含的特殊个体的变化以相同的比例而变化。因此，统计描述不能随描述的对象变化，描述是相对持久的。统计描述这个概念包含着用词的相对持久性。

也许正是受到了"不随变化的世界而变化"这种思想倾向的引导，有些人强调直觉而放弃理性。我们现在不考虑是否我们的思想最好应该随变化的世界而变化这个问题，而仅仅对直觉发表一两点意见。对我们来说，直觉是凭空掉下来就可以形成我们的宗教信仰的，还是可以分析，因而可以理性证实？如果是前者，我们对它就不必再说什么，因为这不再是一个论证和可以说服的问题。如果是后者，那么它就失去了其特有的性质，因为显然它与理性仅是程度上不同而不是类的不同。很可能正像我们有些人主张的那样，直觉仅是一个迅速的推理过程。在这个过程中，前提和命题序列几乎一下子并入得到的结论之中。如果有人可以凭直觉认识，那么他们也许不能分析获得认识的过程，但是那些不太喜欢神秘主义的人可

less given to mysticism. The essential difference between intuition and intellect is probably one of speed. If our reasoning is quick, it is liable to involve ambiguous steps which we are far from being sufficiently detached to recognize and analyze when we are identified with our intuition. The steps involved probably do not follow each other with much logical rigor, and some alternatives may very likely have been ignored. That is where intuition is so often unreliable. And that is why the slow and steady process of reasoning is preferred to the dazzling and quick.

Those who believe in intuition are seldom open to argument. By the kind of psychology that attributes evil to the devil and good to God, they attribute success to intuition and failure to mere "feelings." If they feel that it is going to rain in an hour and find that in an hour it does not rain, they merely "felt," but if within an hour it actually rains, they exalt and exuberate and go into ecstasies over the profundity of their intuition. Fortune telling is still extensively practiced in Peking and fortune tellers are still objects of curiosity for tourists. Within the short period of six months, I have personally heard a number of remarkable successes in fortune telling, but to my amusement, none of its failures. Nothing seems to succeed more than success either in business, or in fortune telling or in intuition. It is futile to urge that the results are accidental in the sense that so far as we know no logical or statistical relation subsists between future events and intuition, since it is the successful feelings alone that are entitled to the name of intuitional insight.

But at any rate one of the reasons that have led some people to emphasize intuition is that intellect is unable to keep pace with the changing world and that such inability is regarded by them as a limitation of and therefore a disadvantage to our knowledge of that world. Whether or not this is a limitation of our knowledge need not engage our attention for the present, but whether or not it is therefore a disadvantage is worth a few remarks. Try as I may, I for one do not see the advantage of a knowledge that runs side by side with the changing world. If our knowledge of a tree can and does vary with the variation of that tree in every particular from one mathematical instant of time to another we should be in a nightmare, infinitely more puzzled and involved in our daily life than Tristram Shandy ever was in his "Autobiography." Life, if

以为他们分析这个过程。直觉和理性之间的本质差别大概是速度问题。如果我们的推理迅速，则很可能包含含混的步骤；当我们认同直觉的时候，则我们绝不能十分公正地认出并分析这些步骤。这些步骤可能不是十分严格的逻辑顺序排列，而且一些选择也可能被忽略。这就是直觉常常不可靠的地方。因此推理过程最好是缓慢而稳健，而不要快得令人瞠目。

相信直觉的人很少愿意接受论证。根据把恶归于恶魔、把善归于上帝这样一种心理，他们把成功归于直觉，把失败归于纯粹的"感觉"。如果他们感到一小时后要下雨并发现一小时后没有下雨，则他们仅仅"曾感到"。但是如果实际上一小时内下雨了，则他们欢呼雀跃，对他们的直觉的深奥心醉神迷。算命在北京依然很普遍，算命先生仍然是旅游者好奇的对象。在短短的六个月时间里，我自己就听说好几起算命显著成功的案例，但是使我饶有兴趣的是没听说算命失败的案例。成功似乎莫过于做生意、算命或直觉上的成功。强调结果是偶然的，这是毫无用处的，因为据我们所知，在未来事件和直觉之间没有逻辑或统计关系，因为只有成功的感觉才配直觉的见识这一名称。

但是，之所以一些人强调直觉，原因之一毕竟在于理性不能跟上变化的世界，而且他们把这种无能看作是我们对这个世界的认识的一种局限性，因而是一种缺陷。这是不是我们的认识的一种局限性，现在无须考虑；但是，这是否因而是一种缺陷却值得说几句。无论我怎样努力，我自己也看不出一种与变化的世界并驾齐驱的认识的优点。如果我们对一棵树的认识能够并且确实从某一精确时刻到另一精确时刻随着那棵树的每一细小变化而变化，那么我们就会像做噩梦一样，比《项狄传》中的特里斯舛·项狄更加困惑不解并

it includes such knowledge, would be not only burdensome but even impossible. We cannot live because we cannot even begin to live. We can possibly live if our lives are infinite in duration, but whatever our spirits may do after our bodies are turned to dust, our lives are conceded by everybody to be altogether finite.

In order therefore that our knowledge may be useful to our lives it must be comparatively more static than the world known. Its names, or symbols or terms must be crystallized for a time at least into statistical summaries or rigid concepts and their relations must be generalizations of a comparatively permanent nature so that they may be used as data for further and more elaborate inferences. If our knowledge is absolute and abstract, it involves relations of concepts and sequence of propositions and if it is statistical and descriptive, it involves a calculus of probabilities. It cannot escape logic in either way; it may involve different kinds of different systems of logic, but it cannot get along without some kind or some system of logic.

且更深陷日常生活。如果生活包括这样的认识，那么生活不但十分沉重，甚至是不可能的。我们不能生活，因为我们甚至不能开始生活。如果我们的生命是无限延续的，我们也许可以生活；但是无论我们的精神在我们的肉体化为灰烬后可能做什么，任何人都认为我们的生命总是有限的。

因此，我们的认识若要对我们的生命是有用的，那么与已知的世界相比，它就必须是相对静止的。它的名字、符号或用词必然至少暂时具体地形成统计概括或严格的概念，它们的关系必然是具有相对持久性质的一般概括，因此它们可用作进一步的更复杂的推论的数据。如果我们的认识是绝对的和抽象的，则它包含概念和命题序列的关系；如果它是统计的和描述的，则它包含概率计算。无论哪种方式，认识都不能逃避逻辑；它可能包含不同的逻辑种类或不同的逻辑系统，但是没有某种逻辑或某个逻辑系统，认识就不能发展。

IV

It is thus seen that logic is indispensable to life, knowledge and philosophy, and probably to a number of other things which need not be enumerated. This, however, does not mean that logic is capable of logical justification. In so far as any a priori reason for its being is concerned, we have not advanced a step. And yet as we have already seen, if we want to live with the least resistance, if we want to philosophize, if we want to know the world in which we live, we have to have logic. The position we intend to take is thus, or at least seems thus to be clearly indicated by our discussion. If we cannot justify logic logically, we have to justify it by the results it yields. Metaphysically we have to be pragmatic, for otherwise we cannot start any discussion. There is no reason why we should be logical any more than there is reason why we should know the world, or recognize its existence, or entertain desires and strive for their satisfaction. "I think, therefore I am" may seem to be certain to Descartes, but it is by no means certain to a large number of the rest of mankind.

But what kind of results? Obviously there may be many kinds of results and a choice of any one of them involves again the notion of a criterion with all the difficulties already discussed. We have repeatedly declared quite frankly that any starting point is arbitrary. It is essentially prejudice from the point of view of logic. Some prejudices are more suited than others to the life we live and the world we live in, but they are none the less prejudices. Our particular prejudice is convenience. The fundamental notion with us is that it is convenient to believe in logic, at least more so than not to believe in it. Logic is sometimes said to drive people mad, because it involves complications and ramifications of all kinds which are supposed to be beyond the intellectual naivete of the plain man. It is seldom recognized as affording us greater convenience than probably any other element in our life. It affords us convenience, because it is probably the greatest economizing agent. It is that which economizes our life, our thought, and our knowledge of the world in which we live.

Our notion is beset with difficulties like any other. To begin with, convenience if it is used as a starting point cannot be justified until almost the end of the discussion is reached. An a priori procedure requires the

四

这样就可以看出，逻辑对生活、认识和哲学是必不可少的，大概对其他一些这里无须列举的事物也是必不可少的。然而，这不是说，逻辑能够得到逻辑的证实。就逻辑存在的任何先验原因而言，我们还未前进一步。然而正如我们已看到的那样，如果我们要最容易地生活，如果我们要进行哲学研究，如果我们要认识我们所在的世界，我们就必须有逻辑。这样，我们的讨论清楚地说明或至少似乎清楚地说明我们企图采取的观点。如果我们不能在逻辑上证明逻辑是正确的，我们就必须用它取得的成果证明它是正确的。在形而上学上，我们必须是实用主义的，因为否则我们就不能开始任何讨论。没有理由说明我们为什么应该认识世界，承认世界的存在，或有愿望并努力满足我们的愿望，同样也没有理由说明我们为什么应该合逻辑。也许"我思故我在"似乎对笛卡儿是确定的，但它对其他许多人绝不是确定的。

但是结果怎样？显然可以有许多种结果，而且任何一种结果的选择又包含所有上述讨论过的困难的标准这一概念。我们多次相当直率地宣布，任何出发点都是任意的。从逻辑的观点看，这基本是一种偏好。一些偏好比另一些偏好更适合我们过的生活和我们所在的世界，但是它们仍然是偏好。我们的特殊偏好是便利。我们的基本概念是相信逻辑是很便利的，至少比不相信逻辑更便利。有时人们说逻辑使人发疯，因为它包括各种各样错综复杂的情况，而这些情况被认为是超出常人的天真的理性行为的。很少有人承认，逻辑大概比我们生活中任何其他要素为我们提供了更大的便利。它为我们提供便利，因为它大概是最节省的力量。正是这种力量，节省了我们的生活、我们的思想和我们对我们生活的世界的认识。

我们这种看法与其他看法一样困难重重。首先，如果用便利作为出发点，那么几乎到讨论结束时才能证明它是正确的。一个

conclusion to be dependent in some measure upon the starting point. Convenience as a criterion, however, requires the starting point to be interpreted in terms of the conclusion. Its essential nature seems to be primarily embodied in the effect the choice leads to when once it is made. But here we are confronted with the difficulty of not knowing what the effects will be. We cannot say beforehand which is convenient and which is not. We have to experiment. But experimentation implies that we know what is convenient even if we do not know which is convenient. We are driven to a definition of convenience, which as we shall see later is quite impossible if it is to be ultimately intelligible. And if our definition cannot be thoroughly intelligible, we are driven to admit that although we have selected convenience as a starting point, we do not know exactly what our starting point is.

But speaking roughly, we assume that convenience means something like following the line of least resistance, or the direction of the greatest economy. It remains to say something about either the notion of resistance or the notion of economy. Neither however is easy to grasp. The notion of economy may be worked out mathematically into some kind of formula derived from still more fundamental and primitive ideas, but it is not a notion which can justify itself, for after all there cannot be such a thing as an economy of economy. Economy is generally considered to be relative, that is, there should be something to which economy is related. We may have an economy of thought, or we may have an economy of action, but if we are pushed to the very last limit, we are bound to conclude that the greatest economy is to have no thought in the one case and no action in the other. If so, there is no need for economy at all. Consequently, the very notion of economy involves things for which economy is desired.

Here again we are in difficulty. Those things for which we desire economy cannot be logically derived. They are only assumed in metaphysics for the sake of convenience. We are therefore reasoning in a circle. The difficulty may be real, but it may just as well be said that we have not yet recognized logic and that logical objections, whether or not valid, are as yet inapplicable. And even if they are applicable, they may be removed by regarding the terms to a relation on such a basis that neither is logically prior nor subsequent to the other. It is probably easier

先验的过程要求结论在某种程度上依赖于出发点。然而，便利作为标准，则要求以结论解释出发点。它的本质性质似乎主要体现在作出选择后，选择所导致的结果里。但在这里我们会遇到困难，我们不知道结果将会怎样。我们不能预先说哪个是便利的，哪个不是便利的。我们必须试验。但是试验意味着我们知道什么是便利的，即使我们并不知道哪个是便利的。我们被迫定义便利，正像我们后面将看到的那样，如果要这种定义是根本上可理解的，则是完全不可能的。如果我们的定义不能是完全可理解的，我们就不得不承认，尽管我们选择便利作为出发点，我们仍不确切知道我们的出发点是什么。

但是大体上说，我们假定，便利的意思类似采取阻力最小的方法，或沿着最节省的方向。阻力或节省的概念有待说几句，然而二者均不易把握。可以用数学方法将节省的概念设计成某种从更基础、更初始的思想得出的公式。但它不是一个可以证实自身的概念，因为毕竟不能有节省的节省这样的东西。一般认为，节省是相对的，即应该有节省与之相联系的东西。我们可能有思想的节省，或者我们可能有行为的节省；但是如果穷究底蕴，则我们必须得出这样的结论：最大的节省是一方面没有思想，另一方面没有行为。如果这样，就根本不需要节省。因此，节省这个概念包含需要节省的东西。

这里我们又陷入困境。不能逻辑地得出那些我们需要节省的东西，只是为了便利的缘故而形而上学地假定它们。因此我们在循环推理。这可能真是困难，但是这可能就是说，我们迄今尚未识别逻辑；逻辑的反对无论是否有效，至此都是不适宜的。即使逻辑的反对是适宜的，通过把用词看作二者在逻辑上互不为先后的一种关系，也可以排除它们。一方面节省的概念即使不暗含也包含譬如行

for most of us to see that the notion of economy involves, if it does not imply something, for example action and thought, for which economy is a convenience, than to realize that thought would be impossible without economy and action without economy would be such a waste of energy as to be totally self-destructive.

To such ideas as the above that are by no means clear and distinct, we are tempted to bid a speedy farewell, leaving them to their "lucid vagueness." But we are not yet through with the notion of economy as an instrument. Professor Pearson is probably the most recent propounder of the view that science is but an economy of thought and whether the view is widely accepted or not, it is as plausible as any. In a later chapter we hope to discuss the relation between science and philosophy in which we will set forth, in greater detail, views similar to those of Professor Pearson, but for the moment we only want to point out that not only is science an economy of thought, but also thought an economy of life, and knowledge and facts are but economies of nature.

That thought is an economy of life has been recognized almost from time immemorial. The old proverb, "Reflect two times before you act" was probably meant to avoid mistakes, but mistakes, though complicated by our moral notions, customs and mores, are from the point of view of our action chiefly those results that are miscalculated towards the realization of our aim. That is to say, they are a waste of effort. Reflection has therefore long been recognized as an economy of activity. The difficulty is not with the horse sense of the hunters and nomads, nor with the common sense of the commercial travelers. These have long been acknowledged as having economized our efforts. It is rather with the reasoning of what may be called the higher region of intellectual solitude that the difficulty of seeing its economizing effects in life is so often confronted. Skeptical philosophy seems to be upon its face value much less of an economy than dogmatic belief. Our beliefs are sources of comfort. When they are dogmatic they obviate the necessity of strenuous thought. They may even economize our activities, but unfortunately they do not economize and historically have not economized our efforts towards the realization of our aims for which an advance of knowledge offers a statistically surer guidance. As contrasted with dogmatic belief, skeptical philosophy offers an economy that is more far-reaching and

为和思想这样一些东西，对这样的东西，节省是一种便利。另一方面没有节省，思想将是不可能的；而且没有节省，行为就会是一种能力浪费，以致彻底自我毁灭。对我们大多数人来说，看到前者也许比认识到后者更容易。

我们想与上述绝非清晰明确的思想尽快告别，任其处于"清晰的含混"之中。但是我们尚未放弃作为一个工具的节省的概念。皮尔逊教授大概是"科学不过是思想的节省"这种观点的最新倡议者。无论这种观点是否得到广泛接受，它像任何观点一样有道理。在后面一章我们希望讨论科学和哲学的关系，其中我们将更详细地提出与皮尔逊教授相似的观点。但是现在我们仅想指出，不仅科学是思想的节省，而且思想是生活的节省，认识和事实不过是自然的节省。

几乎从远古以来就认识到思想是生活的节省。"三思而后行"这句老话大概是指避免犯错误；但是尽管我们的道德观念和风俗习惯把错误复杂化了，但是从我们的行为观点出发，错误主要是那些由于失算而未实现目的的结果。这就是说，错误是白费努力。因此长期以来，思考被看作是行动的节省。困难不在于猎人和游牧民的起码常识，也不在于旅行推销员的常识。人们早就承认它们节省了我们的努力。相反，是在那些可以称为理性孤独的更高领域，常常很难看出其在生活中所起的节省作用。就其表面价值而言，持怀疑态度的哲学比教条主义的信念似乎更不节省，我们的信念是安逸的根源。如果它们是教条的，就排除费力思考的必要性。它们甚至可能节省我们的活动，然而不幸的是，它们不节省而且在历史上没有节省我们实现我们的目的的努力，而认识的发展为我们的目的提供了统计上更为可靠的指南。与教条主义的信念相对照，持怀疑态度的哲学提供了一种尽管也许不太明显，然而却更为深远和更为广泛

more comprehensive though perhaps less obvious. We need not concern ourselves for the present with the detailed steps in which philosophy, no matter how abstruse, economizes our activities; we need merely to say that it bears a very close relation to science such that if science economizes thought and thought economizes life, philosophy achieves practically the same results.

That facts are economies of nature will be seen in the next chapter and need not before claim our attention here. Our main concern for the rest of this chapter will be to discuss the role logic plays as an economizing agent and the nature of metaphysical assumptions. We repeat that our business is not to decide as to whether logic is a law of nature or a law of thought. Whether it is nature or thought is a problem in epistemology with which we are not here concerned. The logical way is to start with a definition of logic, but if we resort to such a procedure, we have to admit our ignorance from the very start. Logic has been defined in various ways, and the definitions are generally, perhaps unconsciously influenced by the metaphysical position of the logician concerned. Frankly we do not know exactly what logic is, we cannot define it with any degree of rigidity, quite apart from the difficulties involved in any definition; but we are, and perhaps most people are, impressed with the subject matter of the textbooks on logic. We are struck with the fact that whether we call propositions judgments or vice versa, we do not deal with them as such; we only deal with them to ascertain their relationship, to see whether one follows from the other, and to establish their sequence.

Whether logic is nature or thought does not make much difference to our point of view. Both these terms are extremely vague. A certain professor at Johns Hopkins University has gathered forty-eight or forty-nine different meanings of the word "nature" current in Europe from Aristotle onward. The Chinese term for nature may shed some light for us with reference to the above view of logic. Strictly interpreted, it means "itself-so." Such a term suggests objectivity in the sense that if a thing is itself so, it does not depend upon any external agency either to will it so, or to will it otherwise. It also suggests immutability of relations, and a rigidity of its course, in the sense that any other relation or any other course would be incompatible with its antecedents. In other words, it suggests predetermination. But predetermination is not a natural event; it

的节省。无论哲学怎样深奥，它节省了我们的活动。现在我们不必考虑哲学节省我们活动的详细步骤，我们只需要说，哲学与科学有十分密切的关系，以致如果科学节省了思想，并且思想节省了生活，那么哲学实际上获得相同的成果。

下一章将看到事实是自然的节省，因此这里不必考虑它。这一章的其余部分主要是讨论逻辑作为一种节省因素所起的作用和形而上学假设的实质。我们再次声明，我们的任务不是判定逻辑是自然规律还是思维规律。它是自然还是思维，这是认识论中的问题，我们在这里不予考虑。逻辑的方式是从逻辑的定义出发，但是如果我们诉诸这样一种过程，我们从一开始就必须承认我们的无知。逻辑得到各种方式的定义，定义一般受到、也许无意识地受到有关逻辑学家的形而上学观点的影响。坦白地说，除了任何定义中涉及的困难外，我们并不确切地知道逻辑是什么，我们不能在任何严格程度上定义它。但是我们，也许是大多数人，都对逻辑教科书的主要内容留下深刻的印象。不管我们称命题为判断，还是称判断为命题，我们都不这样探讨它们——这一事实使我们深思。我们探讨它们仅为确定它们的关系，看是不是一个从另一个得出，并且建立起它们的序列。

逻辑是自然还是思想，这对我们的观点没有多大区别。这两个词都是十分含混的。约翰·霍普金斯大学某位教授收集了自亚里士多德以来"自然"一词在欧洲流行的四十八九种不同的意义。汉语中的"自然"一词也许会对我们上述逻辑观点有所启示。严格地解释，它意味"本身——如此"。这样一个词意味着这样一种客观性，如果一事物本身如此，则它都不依赖于任何外在因素让其如此或让其不如此。它还意味着关系的不变性和它的过程的严格性，即，任何其他关系或任何其他过程与其前例是不相容的。换言之，它意味着预先决定。但是预先决定不是一个自然事件，严格地说它是一种

is strictly speaking a logical relation. An event is never predetermined by its antecedent in the rigid sense in which a conclusion is predetermined by its premises. While the term "itself-so" means natural, it suggests that which is logical. It is by no means impossible that nature and logic are one and the same thing with a separation necessitated only by thought.

Whether or not logic is one with nature, it is at any rate that which is itself-so. That which follows is logical, logic is therefore a sequence of propositions or judgments or whatever one may call them which follow one from the other. But it is not any kind of sequence, or one of a large number of alternative sequences. It is one sequence and only that one. It is a necessary sequence. The notion of necessity is notoriously difficult, and we shall not stop even for a rough definition. Some definitions for instance Mr. Russell's involve the meaning of truth and even if it is to be accepted, it has to wait until the notion of truth is made clear. According to our scheme, the notion of necessity is even more primitive than the notion of truth, and cannot therefore be defined in terms of the latter. But an indication of our attitude is desirable, for otherwise we can hardly mean anything when we say that logic is a necessary sequence. A sequence is necessary when in the last refinement of the given premises, one and only one conclusion remains that can follow from these premises.

But what do we mean when we say that the conclusion "follows" from the premises? Evidently, the term "follows" has no signification of either temporal or spatial sequence. Like a river that follows its course, it probably indicates the line of least resistance. But the line of least resistance in thought is the line that meets the least objection. It is the line that continues the meaning of the original thought. This is another way of saying what has often been said before that the conclusion is implied in the premise. Such being the case, no objection can be raised against the conclusion, if none is directed against the premises. The line of the least objection in thought is that line which continues the meaning of the premises. That which continues the meaning of the premises is that which "follows." What is meant by "follow" in thought is the continuity of meaning if once it is given in the form of premises. If the meaning of the premises is concise and precise, only one line of continuity can be traced in which case the notion of necessity is involved.

逻辑关系。一事件从不在结论被其前提预先决定这种严格的意义上被其先例预先决定。由于"本身——如此"这个词意味着自然的，所以它意味着合逻辑的东西。自然和逻辑是仅仅由思想而必然分开的同一种东西，这绝不是不可能的。

无论逻辑与自然是不是一种东西，它毕竟是本身如此这样的东西。得出的东西是合逻辑的，因此，逻辑是一个命题或判断序列，或可任意命名的从一个得出另一个的序列。但是它不是任意一个序列或具有许多可选序列的序列，它是一个序列并且只是这个序列。它是一个必然序列。众所周知，"必然"这一概念很难下定义，但是我们也不会放弃得到一个粗略的定义。有些定义——譬如罗素先生的定义——包含关于真的意义，即使接受这一定义，也要等到说明"真"这一概念之后。根据我们的设想，"必然"这一概念甚至比"真"这一概念更基本，因此不能用"真"定义"必然"。但是最好说明我们的态度，因为否则当我们说逻辑是一个必然序列时，我们几乎不能说明任何意思。如果经过对给定前提的最终完善，一个并且仅有一个能从这些前提得出的结论保留下来，那么这个序列就是必然的。

但是，我们说结论从前提"得出"是什么意思？显然，"得出"一词没有时间或空间序列的意思。就像一条河有自己的流向，它大概说明阻力最小的方向。但是思维中阻力最小的方向是遇到最小反驳的方向，这是使原初思想的意义得以继续的方向。这是前面常说的结论蕴涵在前提之中的另一种说法。如果情况是这样，那么提不出对前提的反驳，就提不出对结论的反驳。思想中遇到最小反驳的方向就是使前提的意义得以继续的方向。使前提的意义得以继续就是"得出"。思想中"得出"的意思是指意义的继续，如果一旦以前提的形式给出意义。如果前提的意义是简明精确的，那么只能找到一个继续的方向。在这种情况下，就包含"必然"这一概念。

The essence of logic is now somewhat clear. It is of course by no means rigid. A rigid formulation of what logic is probably requires mathematical skill which does not happen to be a gift of most people, students of philosophy included. We will have to be content with a rather vague notion and to see how, as it stands, logic serves as an economizing agent. But that has already been shown in this chapter. We have seen that logic is the essence of philosophy, it is the structure of science, it is that through which sense-data are grouped into facts, and it is the practical instrument by which life seeks to satisfy its desires.

There is moreover one economy which has been very summarily mentioned and which, on account of its importance, deserves a little more emphasis. It is the economy of beliefs. A belief in a God does not involve a belief in a Goddess or even a belief in British foreign policy. Each of these requires a separate belief in the sense that a belief in any one does not lead to a belief in any of the others. But a belief in logic involves a belief of the whole logical procedure. If one believes in a group of premises which lead to a conclusion, one believes in the conclusion as a matter of course. Logic economizes belief in the sense that the step involved in any process of reasoning does not require separate beliefs.

That is one of the reasons why science has gained ascendency over religion. Science economizes our beliefs. Once believed in, it accounts for itself; the theories of individual scientists may be open to doubt, but the accepted truths form a whole, self-consistent body which may be believed in once, and as a whole for any particular period of time. Especially is this true of the procedure science adopts. Religion on the contrary involves no immutable relations between its separate special tenets. The belief in Christianity involves a whole set of logically heterogeneous beliefs for instance the belief in creation and the divinity of Christ, neither of which is deducible from the other and logically each requires a separate belief. In other words religious beliefs are based upon emotion whereas a belief in science is supported by intellect. The difference is that with the former separate emotions are required while with the latter, a few fundamental beliefs are sufficient for all. Because a religion involves separate beliefs, it is not a subject for argumentation. As soon as one argues about a religion, he destroys it. When Eduard Zeller went to his classroom to construct the idea of God, he destroyed the Creator more effectively than the swords of the infidel.

　　现在，逻辑的本质有些清楚了。当然这绝不是严格的。逻辑是什么，这一严格表述大概需要数学技术，而大多数人，包括哲学的研究者恰好没有这种能力。我们将不得不满足于一个相当含混的概念，并且看看在目前情况下逻辑实际上是如何用作一种节省的因素。但是这一章已经说明这一点。我们已经看到逻辑是哲学的本质，逻辑是科学的结构，正是通过逻辑将感觉材料组成事实，而且逻辑是生活寻求满足其愿望的实际工具。

　　前面还非常扼要地提到一种节省，由于它十分重要，应该再强调一下。这就是信念的节省，相信一个神并不包括相信一个女神，或甚至相信英国的外交政策。这些东西均要求独立的信念，因为相信某一东西并不导致相信其他任何东西。但是，相信逻辑包含相信整个逻辑过程。如果一个人相信导致一个结论的一组前提，按照常规那么他就相信得出的结论。任何推理过程包含的步骤不要求独立的信念，在这种意义上，逻辑节省了信念。

　　这是科学比宗教优越的原因之一，科学节省我们的信念。一旦相信科学，科学就能解释自己。可以怀疑科学家个人的理论，但是公认的真理形成一个自身一致的整体。这个整体可以相信一次，而且作为一个整体，在任何特定时期都是可以相信的。科学采用的过程尤其是这样。相反，宗教不包含其独特的信条之间永恒不变的关系。信仰基督教包含一整套逻辑不同的信念，例如相信创世和基督的神圣，二者均不能相互推出并且逻辑上均要求独立的信念。换言之，宗教信仰基于情感，而科学的信念是由理性支持的。不同之处就在于前者要求独立的情感，而后者只需要少数几条基本信念。因为一种宗教包含若干独立的信念，它就不是能够进行论证的题目。一个人只要论证一种宗教，他就摧毁了这种宗教。当爱德华·策勒尔到他的教室构造有关上帝的思想时，他比异教徒的宝剑更有效地摧毁了这位造物主。

V

It is now necessary to say a few words about our basic metaphysical assumptions. If we say that we believe in logic for the sake of convenience, we do not mean that logic can be created by will. Frankly we do not know what creation by will means. If it means creating something out of nothing, then it seems to be impossible. If God created the world in the sense that a Swiss creates a watch, then, as Walter Bagehot has long ago pointed out, he created a world out of something which he did not create. If creation means producing something out of some substratum, then the raw stuff must have long been there and is there beyond our creative effort. Creation in this sense is practically the same as discovery. If we believe in logic for the sake of convenience, we believe in something that is already there for us to believe in, and to believe in it is more convenient than otherwise. This means metaphysical pragmatism.

A pragmatist in metaphysics need not be a pragmatist in any other branch of philosophy. He may be in every other sphere a realist except that he sees no reason why he should be so when he is pushed by persistent questioning into regions where ideas are neither provable nor disprovable and where the method of proof or disproof is itself open to doubt. His point of view is frankly unpoetic and to the pedantic academician, even undignified; he is almost like the American Y.M.C.A. Secretary who believes that honesty is the best policy, because it pays to be honest. Metaphysically he sees no reasons why he should be a realist except his belief, itself unprovable, that to be realist would turn out to be of greater convenience than otherwise.

But if one is a realist should he meddle with metaphysics at all? Is not metaphysics open to all sorts of ridicule at the hands of our modern realist thinkers? The word "metaphysics," we must bear in mind, is a perfectly good word meaning above or beyond the physical or the natural. But in recent times it has been identified with the transcendentalism of

Kant and the idealism of Hegel as well as the theories of recent idealists and theologians and as such it seems to be characterized by Mr. Russell and others as more or less of a London fog carried into the academic world where intellectual lights are so much dimmed as to make us

五

现在有必要对我们基本的形而上学假设说几句话。如果我们说，为了便利的缘故，我们相信逻辑，那么我们并不意味着逻辑能够由意志创造。坦白地说，我们不知道由意志创造是什么意思。如果这意味无中生有，那么这似乎是不可能的。如果上帝在一个瑞士人创造一块手表的意义上创造世界，那么正像沃尔特·白哲特早就指出的那样，上帝从他没有创造的某种东西里创造了世界。如果创造意味从某种基质造出某种东西，那么原料一定早就在那里并因而在我们的创造努力之外。在这种意义上，创造与发现实际是一样的。如果我们为了便利的缘故而相信逻辑，那么我们就是相信某种已经在那里让我们相信的东西，而且相信它比不相信它更便利。这意味形而上学的实用主义。

一个形而上学的实用主义者不必是哲学任何其他分支的实用主义者。他可以在任何其他领域都是一个实在论者，除了当不断的询问将他逼入思想既不可证明也不可反驳而且证明或反驳的方法本身也令人怀疑的领域时，他看不出他为什么应该这样。他的观点根本没有诗意，而且在那些迂腐的院士看来，甚至有失大雅。他几乎就像美国基督教青年会的秘书一样相信诚实才是上策，因为诚实不会吃亏。在形而上学上，除了他的本身不可证明的信念，即作为一个实在论者结果会比不是一个实在论者更为便利，他看不出他为什么应该是一个实在论者。

但是，如果一个人是一个实在论者，那么他到底应不应该参与形而上学呢？形而上学在现代实在论思想家那里不是受到各种各样的嘲笑吗？我们必须记住，"形而上学"一词完全是个好词，意味着高于或超出物理事物或自然事物之外。但是在近些年，它被等同于康德的先验论和黑格尔的唯心主义以及近代唯心论者和神学家的理论。作为这样一种理论，它似乎在某种程度上被罗素先生和其他一些人描述成进入学术界的伦敦的大雾，因而理性之光变得十分昏暗，致使

suspect air castles looming at a distance. But such a limitation of the word "metaphysics" is a waste of a good and useful term. It is used here as a branch of philosophy, which deals with those ideas or concepts which are so primitive as to be neither provable nor disprovable. It is the sphere where assumptions or postulates or hypotheses or fundamental premises or whatever we may call them are examined and analyzed so as to effect a choice with which to serve as a starting point for any kind of philosophical discussion.

But a choice involves the idea of a criterion which if a logical justification is required is beset with difficulties. The only resort left is to effect a choice without any kind of justification, in which case one choice is just as valid philosophically as any. That is why our fundamental beliefs, viz., those that are not deduced from other beliefs, are essentially prejudices. Our own choice of convenience as a criterion is itself a prejudice. It may have advantages over other selections as we shall try to show but these advantages are not its a priori justifications. They bear no logical relation to its being our choice. That is to say, its advantages are seen only after it has been made our choice. They may lead us as a matter of fact to adopt our choice, but they do not justify it as a matter of logic. Besides our belief in logic is itself a matter of convenience.

As we have already said our belief in logic does not necessarily create logic. Logic may be somewhere, just as somewhere a state of affairs may exist known either as the world or the universe. Neither of them necessarily depends upon our belief for its own existence. But its existence for any of us depends upon our beliefs and our belief is a matter of choice. If one refuses to believe in logic, no amount of logical arguments will convince him, and if one refuses to believe in the existence of the world, no amount of empirical arguments will ever convert him. For those who do not believe in convenience, there is probably no argument in its favor but for those who believe in it, there are advantages.

There is at least one metaphysical advantage. Our notion of

convenience carries with it the notion of economy. It does not tolerate a multiplicity of assumptions. It need not have anything to do with either the zeitgeist or the world-will, either the life force or the Élan Vital, either Spencer's unknowable or Kant's thing-in-itself, either the immanent or the

我们怀疑远处隐隐出现的空中楼阁。但是对"形而上学"一词的这样一种限制是对一个有用的好词的浪费。这里用这个词表示哲学的一个分支，这个分支探讨那些非常基本以致既不能证明也不能反驳的思想或概念。它是一种领域，在这个领域中，对假设、公设、假说、基础前提，或我们可随意命名的这些东西进行检验和分析，以便作出一种选择，以此作为任何一种哲学讨论的出发点。

但是，选择包括关于标准的看法。如果需要进行逻辑的证实，则这种标准困难重重。剩下的唯一办法是作出一种不要任何证实的选择。在这种情况下，一种选择就像任何选择一样是哲学上有效的。因此，我们的根本信念，或那些不是从其他信念推出的信念，基本是偏好。我们自己选择便利作为标准，这本身就是一种偏好。它可能正像我们将试图说明的那样，有超过其他选择的优点，但是这些优点不是它的先验的证实。它们与我们选择它没有逻辑关系。这就是说，只有当它成为我们的选择之后，我们才看到它的优点。实际上，这些优点可能导致我们采取我们的选择，但是它们并不证明它逻辑上正确。此外，我们相信逻辑，这本身是一个便利的问题。

正像我们已经说过的那样，我们相信逻辑，这并不必然创造逻辑。某处可能有逻辑，就好像某处可能存在着一种事态，我们称之为世界或宇宙。逻辑与世界或宇宙就其自己的存在而言，均不必然依赖于我们的信念。但是对我们任何人来说，其存在却依赖于我们的信念，而我们的信念是个选择的问题。如果一个人拒绝相信逻辑，那么多少逻辑论证也不会说服他；如果一个人拒绝相信世界的存在，那么多少经验论证也绝不会转变他的看法。对于那些不相信便利的人，大概没有有利于便利的论证，但是对于那些相信便利的人，却有优点。

至少有一种形而上学的优点。我们的便利概念带有节省的概念。它不容忍大量的假设。它与时代精神或世界意志、生命力量或生命冲动、斯宾塞的不可知论或康德的"自在之物"、超越者或内在者等等，

transcendent. It makes use of Ockham's razor to cut off all the fundamental ideas that we do not need. It is satisfied with a minimum that is required at any given time; it may add or subtract according to the demands of our positive knowledge at any one time, but it does not multiply concepts to suit religious biases or emotional idiosyncrasies. It aims at philosophical economy though it may and as we shall see, it probably will result in greater complications in the sphere of positive knowledge. And it complicates our knowledge for the convenience of our life.

Another advantage is that our criterion fosters positive knowledge. It recognizes a real world with real problems that demand realistic solutions. In other words it encourages science. Neither materialism nor idealism encourages positive knowledge, because each of them tries to account for the world according to its own bias which does not happen to be a bias that is compatible with our positive knowledge as it is historically developed and as it is developing today. That realism is more in accord with science will be set forth in a later chapter. It is only necessary to mention here that the encouragement our position offers to science, once granted, is an important argument in its favor.

There is still another advantage. Our belief in convenience involves as we have seen our belief in logic, and logic, once believed in, is one of the most powerful instruments in philosophy. It is one that justifies some fundamental propositions which through the adoption of the rules of logic may become unassailable. Such propositions are the ones mentioned at the beginning of this chapter. We have mentioned one or two, and others may yet remain to be discovered. Some technical difficulties may be encountered, but they may also be removed by technical devices. With an improvement in logical technique, more and more irrefutable and self-consistent propositions may be discovered upon which a thoroughgoing, solid firm and withal skeptical philosophy may yet emerge at a not far distant date. It is perhaps just as futile to hope in philosophy as in other spheres of life, but since students of philosophy are none the less human beings, they have about as much need for consolation as the so-called plain man.

Whether the hope is futile or not, the above paragraph is misleading in the sense that an advance in logic is itself taken to be almost an advance in philosophic speculation. Logic is a structure, a sort of link, but

不必有任何关系。它利用奥卡姆剃刀清除所有我们不需要的基本思想。它满足于在任何给定时间所要求的最低限度，它可能根据我们在任何一个时间的实证认识或加或减，但是它不增加概念以适合宗教偏见或情感的怪癖。它旨在哲学的节省，尽管它可能并且大概最终将使实证认识领域变得更为复杂，正像我们将看到的那样。而且，为了我们生活的便利，它使我们的认识变得复杂。

另一个优点是我们的标准促进实证认识。它认识到一个有实在问题的实在的世界，而这些问题需要实在的解决。换言之，它促进科学。唯物论和唯心论都不促进实证认识，因为它们均试图根据自己的偏见对世界作出说明，而这种偏见恰巧与我们在历史上发展的并且今天正在发展的实证认识是不相容的。实在论与科学更一致，这个问题将在以后的章节提出。这里只需要说，我们的观点对科学提供的支持一旦得到承认，就是一个有利于科学的重要论证。

还有另一个优点，正像我们已看到的那样，我们相信便利包含我们相信逻辑。逻辑一旦被相信，就是哲学中最强有力的工具之一。逻辑是证明一些基本命题的工具，通过采用逻辑规则，这些命题可以成为不容置疑的。这样的命题是这一章开始时提到的命题。我们提到一两个，其他的可能有待发现。可能会遇到一些技术困难，但是通过技术手段也可能清除它们。随着逻辑技术的改进，可能会发现越来越多不可反驳的和自身一致的命题。在不远的将来可能会出现一种基于这些命题的彻底的、坚固可靠的而又持怀疑态度的哲学。对哲学寄予希望大概同对其他生活领域寄予希望是同样没有用处的。但是，既然哲学的研究者毕竟是人，因此他们与所谓普通人一样需要得到安慰。

无论这种希望是不是没有用处，在哲学的进步本身几乎被当作哲学思辨的进步这种意义上，上面一段容易使人误解。逻辑是一种

it is not itself a philosophical chain. It may help us to decide as to which ideas are consistent with a given set of ideas, but it does not help us to choose the ideas that are to each of us *personae gratae*. With regard to fundamental ideas, we follow our personal bias, and if they are detached each from the other, there is no question of their logical validity. Logic does not originate ideas, it does not indicate to us what kind of ideas we should form about the world any more than it fishes out the lady whom we should adore. Given a certain reaction against the world in which we live, logic merely indicates the way by which our ideas about it can be linked together into a comprehensive whole. It has hardly anything to do with the direction of our thought. It offers us as yet no criteria for a choice of premises. With the development of logic, different philosophical systems may become somewhat similar to different geometries; the reasoning may be the same, and yet the thought different.

How does logic help philosophy? The perfection of logical technique is an aid to philosophical criticism. Ideas that are vague, or ambiguous or meaningless may be clarified or removed altogether by a strict logical analysis. With an improvement in logic foggy sentiments may not pass as philosophic profundities. A proposition is first split into its terms to see whether they are clear and distinct, that is, to see whether they have any definite meaning. They are then reorganized into the original proposition to see whether it has significance. It may be significant without being true, that is to say, without being consistent with other propositions. The proposition that men walk on their heads seems to be quite significant, but it is not true in the sense that it is not consistent with a number of other propositions in which "men" are predicated. Logic helps positive philosophy almost to the same extent as it helps critical philosophy, because in so far as philosophy is critical, it is also positive.

It is hardly necessary to point out that we are not logicians. The arguments so far advanced reveal only a superficial, or to be more generous to ourselves, only an amateurish acquaintance with the subject which we are laboring at great pains to emphasize. But while we emphasize logic, we are not trying to produce a *Principia Logica*, or even a modest text book setting forth its principles and methods. Our subject matter is primarily a logical analysis of fundamental philosophical ideas;

结构，是一种联系，但它本身不是一个哲学链条。它可能帮助我们判定哪些思想与一组给定的思想是一致的，但它不帮助我们选择我们每个人所欢迎的思想。关于基本思想，我们遵循自己的偏见。如果它们是相互分离的，它们就没有逻辑有效性的问题。逻辑并不发明思想，它不会挑出我们应该心仪的女子，也不会向我们说明我们关于世界应该形成什么样的思想。如果逻辑对我们所在的世界作出某种反应，那么它仅仅表明那种能够使我们关于世界的思想联系起来形成一个综合整体的方式。它与我们的思想方向几乎没有任何联系。迄今它没为我们提供选择前提的标准。随着逻辑的发展，不同的哲学体系可能变得与不同的几何学有些相似了；推理可能是相同的，而思想却可能是不同的。

逻辑怎么帮助哲学呢？逻辑技术的完善是对哲学批评的帮助。严格的逻辑分析可以彻底澄清或清除含混、模糊或无意义的思想。随着逻辑的改进，含糊不清的想法或许不能再冒充为哲学的深奥思想。首先将一个命题分为几个词项，看它们是不是清晰明确，就是说，看它们是否有确切的意义。然后再把它们重新组成原来的命题，看它是否有意义。它可能有意义，却不是真的，这就是说，与其他命题不一致。"人倒立行走"这个命题似乎是完全有意义的，但是它与其他一些表述"人"的命题是不一致的。在这种意义上，它不是真的。逻辑帮助批判的哲学，它几乎在相同的程度上帮助实证哲学，因为只要哲学是批判的，它也就是实证的。

我们不是逻辑学家，这一点几乎是不必指出的。至此提出的论证说明我们对我们苦心费力强调的问题只有肤浅的理解，或更宽容地说，只有不太在行的理解。但是我们强调逻辑，而不是在试图制造逻辑原理，甚至也不是在创作一部提出逻辑原则和方法的适宜的教科书。我们的问题主要是对基本的哲学思想进行逻辑分析，而不

it is not a philosophical treatment of logical concepts. In other words, we are trying to analyze philosophical ideas logically, not logical ideas philosophically.

The following chapters intend to deal with a number of ideas the recognition of which seems to afford us convenience in the fundamental sense we have discussed in the present chapter. We shall first deal with our notion of facts, then with that of truth. We shall assume the world or at least a part of it to be constantly and continuously changing, and we shall analyze our notion of change. Thence we proceed to a discussion of time, space and motion, and will conclude this book by a disquisition on metaphysics and science.

We are bound to say, however, that the attempt will be on the whole a failure. This is not false modesty; it is a mere recognition of the inadequacy of the means towards the end. The critical part of this book, if any, is mainly a question of logical analysis, and the positive part, if any, is chiefly a question of logical construction. The whole attempt depends upon logical rigor for its success. But logical rigor is very likely an unattainable ideal in these pages, since we have from the very beginning neither a distinct notion of what logic is, nor a clearly defined method of logical procedure. If our logic is lacking in rigor and definiteness, our analysis cannot very well be clear and distinct, and the system of ideas herein set forth may prove to be as muddled as those of which it is intended to be a criticism.

But if the attempt is suspected to be a failure from the very beginning, why indulge in it at all? This is a very fundamental question. It cuts to the very root of life. The answer is already implied in these pages. We do not do things capable of any abstract justification. We do not generally live for a purpose, and the purpose for which we are said to live is itself incapable of justification. While I am thinking, I am smoking the third cigarette in succession, not because I am as yet unsatisfied with aromatic stimulation, but because so long as I am not actively pushing my pen, my hands need be occupied with something, and it might just as well be a cigarette. Some of us philosophize, because we are interested in truth; others philosophize, because we want to derive consolation. Many are tumbled into philosophy, because they have nothing else with which to occupy themselves. If we

是对逻辑概念进行哲学探讨。换言之,我们在试图用逻辑方法分析哲学思想,而不是用哲学方法分析逻辑思想。

后面的章节想探讨一些思想,承认这些思想似乎为我们提供我们在这一章所讨论的这种基本意义上的便利。首先我们将探讨我们关于事实的看法,然后探讨关于真的看法。我们将假定世界或至少世界的一部分是不断持续变化的,我们将分析我们关于变化的看法。由此我们进而讨论时间、空间和运动,最后将以对形而上学和科学的研究来总结这本书。

然而,我们必定会说,这种企图总体上要失败。这不是虚伪的谦虚,这不过是承认达到目的的方法很不胜任。这本书如果确有关键性的部分,则主要是逻辑分析的问题;如果确有积极的部分,则主要是逻辑构造的问题。整个企图的成功依赖于逻辑的严格性。但是逻辑的严格性很可能是在这寥寥数页达不到的理想,因为我们从一开始既没有关于逻辑本质的清晰概念,也没有明确定义了的逻辑过程的方法。如果我们的逻辑缺乏严格性和明确性,那么我们的分析就不能非常清晰确切,结果就可能证明这里提出的思想系统与它所要批判的那些思想系统同样混乱不堪。

但是,如果从一开始就怀疑这种企图要失败,那么究竟为什么还要一味地尝试它呢?这是一个非常根本的问题,它深及生活的本质。这几页已经暗含着回答。我们不做能够得到任何抽象证明的事情,我们一般不为一个目的而活着,所谓我们为之而活着的目的本身是不能证明的。当我正在思考的时候,我正在连续抽第三支烟。这不是因为我仍不满意香味的刺激,而是因为只要我没有挥笔疾书,我的手就要拿点东西,这可能正好是支香烟。我们有些人进行哲学研究,是因为对真感兴趣;也有一些人进行哲学研究,是因为想得到安慰。许多人涉足哲学,是因为没有其他事情可干。如果我们不期待各个哲学体系最终得到相同的结论,

do not expect philosophies to end in the same conclusion, we can hardly expect philosophers to start from the same motive.

With us, philosophy is frankly a form of play. We may be playing it with a naivete that is at once amusing and exasperating to the experts, but we are trying as far as possible to play the game according to its rules. With either success or failure we are not concerned, for the result with us does not count half as much as the process. That is where play is one of the most serious activities in life. Other activities have too often some kind of axe to grind. Politics is a sphere where people aim at power. Finance and industry are spheres where people aim at wealth. Patriotism is sometimes a matter of economics, and philanthropy is for some persons the only road to fame. Science and art, literature and philosophy, may have behind them mixed motives, but a game of solitaire in a dingy garret is the pure expression of a soul abandoned to the stream of life.

那么我们就几乎不能期待哲学家从相同的动机出发。

坦白地讲,哲学对我们来说是一种游戏。我们可能天真地做哲学游戏,这使专家感到可笑又可气,但是我们尽可能努力根据哲学规则来做哲学游戏。我们不考虑成功或失败,因为我们并不看重结果而看重过程。正是在这里,游戏是生活中最严肃的活动之一。其他活动常常怀有私心。政治是人们追求权力的领域,财政和工业是人们追求财富的领域。爱国主义有时是经济的问题,慈善事业是某些人成名的唯一途径。科学和艺术、文学和哲学可能有混杂的背后动机。但是在阴暗的小阁楼上的单人游戏,就是一颗被抛入生活之流的心灵的纯粹的表达。

Tao, Nature
道、自然与人
and Man[5]

PREFACE

During the academic year of 1943-1944 I accepted the invitation of the State Department in Washington D.C. to visit America. It was a great pleasure to me to meet many persons whom I would not otherwise have met and to be acquainted however haphazardly with the climate of American opinion. But whenever the idea that something was also expected of me in return managed to emerge above the level of my consciousness, I was preyed by a guilty sense of woeful inadequacy for the job on hand. Although a professor merely professes, and needn't profess more than Protestants nowadays protest, yet there should be a subject which he could offer as a sort of cultural barter. I have taught logic and epistemology in China for a number of years, but to talk about either in America would be merely carrying coals to Newcastle. I am not a sinologist; and to settle problems of Chinese history in terms of the West System would be quite beyond my capacity. I was interested in introducing Chinese ideas to America, but here again I was hardly the person to do it; people much better suited to the work either could be persuaded to do so, or else like Dr. Hu Shih had already been doing so for quite a number of years. I have certain ideas. It is distinctly immodest of me to air them anywhere; fairness however requires me to pass them as my own rather than to attribute them to the thinkers of the past merely to burden them in the end with perhaps untenable thought. In the following pages I am giving in English a much abridged version of a book published some years ago under such conditions in China that not only it is not found in libraries, but also I myself haven't a single copy. The bulk of this following was done in the peace and quiet of Lowell House, Cambridge, and in the Oriental Institute, Chicago. I have added a chapter on Nature and Man which is not in the original book in order to bring ideas somewhat out of the unpopular level.

Whether or not the book is worth writing or publishing, it gives me at any rate an opportunity to express my gratitude to Harvard University, to the University of Chicago, and above all to the U.S. Department of State.

序

在 1943—1944 那一学年，我接受美国国务院的邀请，访问了美国。这对我来说是一件很好的事，它使我认识了许多朋友，否则我是不可能认识他们的；它也使我可以很自由地感受到美国公众舆论的走向。但是，当意识到作为回报我必须要做的事情时，我就有一种内疚感，因为对于要做的工作我没有充分的准备。虽然教授只是做教授，而不必比新教徒的抗议做得更多些，但是他必须提供一个主题作为一种文化交流的内容。我在中国多年以来是教逻辑和认识论的，但是如果在美国来教这样的课程就显得多此一举。我本人不是一位汉学家，因此以西方思想系统的术语来解决中国历史的问题完全是我力所不能及的。我倒有兴趣在美国介绍中国的思想，然而我也不是做这一工作的合适人选。有更合适的人选或可被劝说来做这件事，或同胡适博士一样已多年尽心于此。我对中国思想有某些看法，然而在任何地方来谈论我的看法就太过傲慢了。公平的原则要求我把这样的看法视为我自己的，而不是历史上的思想家们的，以免这些可能是站不住脚的思想被归罪于这些思想家们。在下面的篇幅中，我用英语缩写了几年前出版的一本书 [6] 的部分。在中国目前的条件下，不要说在图书馆里找不到这本书，就是我本人手头上也无此书。下文的主体是我在剑桥洛厄尔大厦和芝加哥东方研究院的和平宁静的环境中完成的。我增加了关于“自然和人”的一章。这一章在原来的书中是没有的，增加它的目的是使本书的思想多少易为人接受。不管这本书是不是值得写或出版，但是它却给了我一个机会向哈佛大学、芝加哥大学，尤其是向美国国务院，表示我由衷的谢意。

STUFF⁷

I

Let us take what we ordinarily call a particular thing or object, for example, the magnolia in the side palace of Lo Shou T'ang [the Hall of Happiness and Longevity], near to the lake, in the Summer Palace in Peking. I have already described and located for you a particular object; it is located in a well-known palace in a well-known city and it is classified under the catalogue of magnolia. Those who had paid special attention to that tree will recall its "shape" and "character" and the place it is located; to them nothing further need be said. They may take an excursion into their past experiences, and if their recollections were vivid, they would see that tree in their mind's eye. But to those who do not remember or never have seen the tree before, nothing avails so far as a substitute for direct experience is concerned.

Suppose that some of them do not know what a magnolia is or how it looks like. We might say a lot of things which are trees of this particular tree since it does belong to the family of magnolias. But while these statements are true of that magnolia, they are not uniquely true of that magnolia. There are ever so many magnolias for which these statements are equally true, for example, the two magnolias in front of the Library of Congress. Thus while these statements tell us what a magnolia is like, they do not indicate the shape of that magnolia, or its age or its size, or how many trunks it has or whether its trunks are straight, etc. To get at that particular magnolia, something else is needed. If we were scientists or literary men we might describe that tree in greater detail, not merely in answer to the questions listed, but also to questions that might be asked along other lines. If words fail, we might be tempted to draw, and if drawings are inadequate, we might resort to photographs. But how are we to be sure that the picture was taken in Peking other than in Hollywood? It seems obvious that no matter what we do, we are doomed to failure so long as revealing the "thatness" of that magnolia is concerned. While we are convinced that as a matter of fact there is no other tree exactly suited to the description or the drawing or the photograph, we are at least equally convinced that the possibility if there being one cannot be

质料

一

我们以通常所谓的特殊事物或客体为例，如北京颐和园乐寿堂偏殿湖边那棵玉兰树。我在此已经向你描述了这一特殊的客体及其位置：它在远近闻名的城市中远近闻名的颐和园之内，而且它被划归为木兰科。曾经注意过这棵树的人当然会回忆起它的"形状"和"特性"及它所在的位置。对于他们没有必要做什么进一步的介绍。他们能够回到过去的经验中；如果他们的记忆是生动的话，他们就会在自己的脑海中看见那棵树。但对那些记性不好或以前从未看见过这棵树的人来说，在他们的直接经验的范围内就没有这样的印象。

假如他们中的某些人不知道什么是玉兰树或不知道它长什么样，那么我们就得说上好多属于木兰科的树的知识。尽管所有这些陈述对于那棵玉兰树而言都是正确的，但它们并不仅仅对于那棵玉兰树才是正确的。这些陈述对于许多木兰科的树同样是正确的，如它们也同样适用于国会图书馆前的那两棵玉兰树。可见，这些陈述虽然告诉了我们玉兰树是什么样的，但它们并未确切地指示那棵特定的玉兰树的形状、树龄或大小，或它有多少树干，或它的树干是否是直的，等等。因此要确切地知道那棵特殊的玉兰树，我们还需知道关于它的其他一些信息。如果说我们是科学家或饱学之士，那么我们就会更加详尽地描绘那棵树，而不仅仅回答那些已经提出的问题，也同样应该回答那些可能提出的其他种种问题。如果拙于言辞，我们可以尝试着去画画。如果画画还是不能达意，我们可以照相。但我们又何以能确信这样的相片是在北京照的，而不是在好莱坞照的？显然，不管我们怎么努力，我们在显示那棵玉兰树的"那个"的特殊性时注定是要失败的。当我们确信，事实上并没有其他的树和这一描述或画或照片完全一样的时候，我们至少同样确信

denied. The question of possibility is not one that is contingent before a conglomeration of related facts; anything that is not contradiction is possible. The minutest description of an x may possibly be equally adequate for y; x is φ, ψ, θ, … and y is φ, ψ, θ, … are not contradictions. Americans who are so accustomed to mass production will grasp the point more easily than the Chinese.

We were speaking of describing that magnolia tree. Description is made of abstract ideas which are instruments for segregating one universal or a set of universals from any universal or any set of universals. To say that a fine apple is red may be perfectly true, and if true, it rules out certain possibilities, for instance that it is green. It keeps you in ignorance about other possibilities, for instance it may be large compared to other apples, or almost perfectly spherical unlike other apples. Neither size nor shape is revealed by the proposition that it is red; its function is to single out one universal, to leave the rest untouched and to rule out certain possibilities. The usefulness of abstract ideas should not be minimized; they are the basis of communicability of experiences. Particular experience cannot be communicated. I cannot ask you to meet at the station a friend of mine whom I have known for years but whom you have never met or seen by just mentioning his name; I have to describe him in abstract terms, to say for instance that he is tall, has a lot of white hair, or that he stoops and is a bit lame, etc. and trust to the probability that there is not another man of the same description at the train. Descriptions are eminently useful, but they do not always prepare you for your experience of the described objects. To say that a certain tree is a tall magnificent magnolia does not prevent you from having surprises when you are confronted with that tree and see it to be "that" tall and "that" magnificent.

A particular thing or object is never merely either one universal or a set of universals. Winston Churchill is one of the most colorful personalities of their age, but describe him as much as you like, and no matter how adequate and full you aim your description to be, you merely arrive at a combination of universal, a sort of Churchillianity which may possibly be shared by another Englishman or American. Neither is Aristotle the sum of the Aristotelianness. The usual reaction to the joke

不可否认有那么一棵其他树的可能性。在一堆相关的事实面前，关于这一可能性的问题不是偶然的。任何不矛盾的事物都有可能。对 x 的最细致的描述对于 y 也可能同样是充分的；"x 是 φ，ψ，θ，……" "y 也是 φ，ψ，θ，……" 并不矛盾。习惯于批量生产的美国人比起中国人会更容易理解这一点。

我们刚才谈到的是关于玉兰树的描述的问题。描述就得运用抽象的意念。抽象意念是一种工具，把一共相或一类共相同其他的共相或其他一类共相区别开来。说一个好苹果是红的可能是完全正确的。如果这是正确的，那么它就排除了如它是绿的这样的可能性。它使你忽略其他的可能性，如这一苹果可能比别的苹果更大一些，或它比别的苹果更圆一些。它是红的这一命题没有揭示出这一苹果的大小或形状，它的功能只是彰显某一共相，而不涉及其他的共相，排除掉其他的可能性。不应看轻抽象意念的作用，它们是经验具有可传播性的基础。特殊的经验就不能传播。比如我不能仅仅告诉你一个朋友的名字，就让你去火车站接我认识了多年而你却不认识的那位朋友。我必须用抽象的词语来描绘他，比如说他个子高、有不少白发，或他有点驼背并有点瘸等等，而且要依赖于这样的可能性即在同一列火车上再没有和这样的描绘相像的其他人。描述是非常有用的，但它们并不总能使你的经验与被描述的客体协调一致。说某一棵树是高大壮观的玉兰树并不能保证当你遇到那棵树，发现它"那样"高、"那样"壮观时，你不会感到意外。

一特殊的事物或客体从来就不仅仅是一共相或一类共相。温斯顿·丘吉尔在他那个时代是最有个性的人物之一。你可以尽可能多地对他进行描述，而且不管你力图对他描述得多么充分和完满，你所能得到的也只不过是一堆共相，一类所谓的丘吉尔性的东西，它们可能为另外一个英国人或美国人所具有。亚里士多德也不是亚里士多德性的东西的总和。有这样一个玩笑，说所有亚里士多德的

that all Aristotle's books were written by another man of the same name is that no difference is made; this is so because we are merely his readers not for instance his wife in a monogamous society; if we were we would pay more attention to one of them than to the other. And though it is hardly imaginable that there could be two Aristotles exactly alike, it is by no means impossible that Aristotleness is shared by many, each one of whom is a particular individual. Since each one of them is a particular object sharing a common set of universals, no particular object in so far as its particularity is concerned is ever merely a set of universals. Hence no description in terms of abstract ideas will ever reveal the particularity of a particular object.

Besides description we employ other means to get at particular objects. The very first sentence with which we started our discussion makes use of proper names in order to get at the particular magnolia we have in mind. Particular objects might be named or pointed to or referred to in terms of ordered frames. To point things out is probably the easiest, the most convenient since with regard to most things we don't bother to give names. But pointing to is an operation that requires co-temporal and co-spatial experience. You cannot point to the past any more than you can point to an unnamed and unreferred tree and ask a friend in a distant city to appreciate its shape and color. Naming has certain advantages; names stick faithfully to the things named. John Doe might have been thin and now he may be fat; but fat or thin, he remains John Doe. When a particular thing cannot be pointed to or is not named, it is often referred to in terms of ordered frames. The most frequently-used ordered frames are that of time and space. A thing at such and such time and place particularizes the thing mentioned. In particularization, sometimes one implement alone is used, but more often a combination of these implements together with descriptions is necessary. This is what we have done with the particular magnolia tree in our very first sentence.

But implements of particularization are only applicable to a particular or a name of particulars and strictly speaking not applicable to particular things or objects. A particular is different from a universal only from the point of view of its particularity, not from the point of view of its being an object. Even a pattern of particulars is only a pattern of aspects. As

著作都是由另外一个同样姓名的人所写的。对这一玩笑的通常的反应是，不管亚里士多德的著作是谁写的都没有什么本质上的区别。这是因为我们都只不过是他的读者，而不是一夫一妻制下他的妻子。如果我们是他的妻子，那么我们当然会比别人更关心其中的一个亚里士多德而不关注同名的另一个。虽然我们不可能想象有两个完全相同的亚里士多德，但并非不可能的是，所谓的亚里士多德的性质可以为许多人所共享，而其中的每一个人都是特殊的个体。由于其中的每一个人都是享有一类共同共相的特殊客体，因此就特殊性这一点而言，没有一个特殊客体就仅仅是一堆共相。可见，以抽象意念来描述不可能揭示一特殊客体的特殊性。

在描述之外，我们还运用其他的方法来理解特殊客体。我们开始讨论的第一句话就利用了专名，以便我们可以想象到这株特殊的玉兰树。我们命名、以手指示或用有序的结构来提及特殊客体。把事物指示出来可能是最简单的、最方便的一件事，因为对于大多数的事物我们不必麻烦给它们起名。但是用手指是一个行动，它需要经历同一时空。正如你不能用手指示一棵未命名、未曾提及的树并且让你异地的朋友来欣赏它的形状和颜色一样，你也同样不可能用手指示出过去。命名有它的长处。名称忠实地依附被命名的事物。张三可能过去很瘦，现在很胖。但不管他是胖还是瘦，张三还是张三。当一个特殊事物不能被用手指出来或不能被命名时，那么经常的做法就是以有序的结构来指示。最常被运用的结构就是时间和空间。在某某时间某某地点的一个事物使已被提及的事物特殊化了。在特殊的环境中，有时只运用一种工具也就够了。但是更多的时候则有必要运用很多的工具来进行描述。这正如第一句话我们在讨论玉兰树时所做的那样。

但特殊化的工具只能运用于殊相或适用于殊相的名称，严格说来，它们并不能运用于特殊事物或客体。一殊相不同于共相仅仅是因为它的特殊性，而不是因为它是一客体。即便是殊相的样型也只

aspects, particulars do not have the substantiality, the actuality and the potentiality of particular things or objects. A set of universals does not constitute an object, neither does a set of particulars, since neither has got what we ordinarily call "body." Perhaps if we invoke the aid of time, we can see more easily that a particular is different from a particular thing or object. Particulars do not repeat, once they are gone, they are gone forever; whereas in particular things or objects there is something that persists endurance. Implements of particularization merely enable us to get at particulars and strictly speaking not particular things or objects. Let us return to that magnolia with which we started. It is forever changing. And yet in so far as its particular shape and character at any particular moment are concerned, they cannot change, since they don't endure. A succession of different sets of particulars has indeed taken place and may even serve as a criterion for our observation of change, but none of the sets has changed into any other. There is something that has changed and so far that thing has been elusive.

When we describe something we are segregating a universal or universals; when we point to or name or refer to something in terms of ordered frames, we indicate a particular or particulars. As we have already said there is in that magnolia something that is neither a universal or a set of universals, nor a particular or a name of particulars. There is a certain "thatness" that eludes both description and indication which for the sake of convenience let us call "expression." There is then something in every particular thing or object, a "thisness" or "thatness" or an x that cannot be expressed. Mt. Qomolangma is comparatively permanent, but ever in this case it is constantly and continually undergoing a series of changes which is simply another way of saying that in or around or about "it" there is a succession of different sets of particulars or of different realizations of sets of universals. I am smoking now, the cigarette in my hand is extremely mysterious; its paper came from a factory out of materials that were plant life receiving nourishment from the sun, the water and the earth, its tobacco could be similarly traced, but surely waterness or sunshineness or earthness have not been transformed into cigaretteness: there is something that went through all these as if a man changes from his uniform into his business suit. As I know, the cigarette

是外在的样型。作为外在来讲，殊相不具有特殊事物或客体的实质性、现实性和可能性。一套共相并不能组成一客体，一套殊相也不能组成一客体，因为这两者都没有我们通常所说的"实体"。可能如果我们借助于时间的话，那么我们就能更容易地看到，一殊相是不同于一特殊的事物或客体的。殊相并不重复出现，一旦消逝，它们也就永远消逝了。然而在特殊的事物或客体中却有着某种具有永久性的东西。可见，特殊化的工具只能使我们理解殊相，严格说来是不能理解特殊事物或客体的。让我们在此还是回到开头谈到的那棵玉兰树。它总处在变化之中。然而考虑到它在特殊的时间所呈现出来的特殊的形状和特性，它们是不能变化的，因为它们并不会持续。不同的殊相已经连续不断地出现，而且这些连续不断出现的殊相可能会成为我们观察变化的标准，但是这些殊相中的任何一套都不可能转换成另一套殊相。当然在这中间确实有某种东西在变化，就目前而言这种东西是难以捉摸的。

当我们描述某事物时，我们把不同的共相区别开来。而当我们用手指、命名或以有序的结构提及时，我们是在指示殊相。正如我们已经指出的那样，在那棵玉兰树中有某种东西，它既不是一共相或一套共相，也不是一殊相或殊相的名称。为方便起见我们把描述或指示叫做"表达"，那么有这样的所谓"那个性"使表达变得迷惑难解。那么在每一个特殊的事物或客体中都有这样一种东西，它就是"这个性"或"那个性"或 x，它是不能被表达的。在某种相对的意义上说，珠穆朗玛峰是一恒常的存在，但在这里的语境中，它也经常不断地经历着一系列的变化。用另一种不同的方式说，在"它"之中或周围或与之相关，总有连续不断的不同的殊相或连续不断的不同的共相的实现。我现在正在抽烟，我手中的这支烟着实使人感到困惑不解。它的纸的部分来自造纸厂，其原料作为植物需要从阳光、水和土壤中吸取营养。它的烟草的部分也可以同样的方式追溯其来源。然而毫无疑问，水、阳光、土壤的特性并没有转化成为香烟的特性，但有某种东西却经历了不同的转化过程，正如同某人把制服换成了商务套装一样。就我所知，香烟逐渐地

gradually disappears: some of it takes the form of smoke and soon merges into the air, some of it has turned to ashes, and the remaining becomes crumbled up in my ash tray. The "identity" of the cigarette seems to have disappeared and yet if the situation were as simple as that we would find it quite meaningless to say that "this" ash was a part of "that" cigarette. There must be something that goes through cigaretteness and ashness almost as if a student changes from a sophomore into a junior.

Some of you may think in terms of modern physics and interpret the inexpressible x as electrons. You may say that what constitutes this or that particular object is a particular bunch of electrons and is therefore expressible. But this evidently is not what is meant. A particular collection of particular electrons is indeed expressible; in so far as it is particular, it can be indicated, and in so far as it realizes a universal, it can be described. But what underlies both the collection and each of the particular electrons is still the inexpressible x. In urging the above argument you have mistaken the analytical procedure from the expressible to the inexpressible for the scientific procedure from the macroscopic to the microscopic. In the physical sciences there is a reduction of the big to the small, or the complex to the simple—it is an attempt to explain or to describe the macroscopic in terms of the microscopic; it is not the concern of the sciences to tackle the problem that no matter how big a star is or how small an electron is, there is in both an x that is inexpressible. An electron is eminently expressible, and if in future it is to be described in terms of entities a million times smaller yet, these entities are equally expressible. But underlying both there is still that inexpressible x.

Some of you may suggest what is here called an inexpressible x may be a sort of gestalt, a pattern, a unique form or a freak configuration of accidental properties. A particular thing or object is indeed that, but if it were merely that, it would have nothing inexpressible. However freakish a configuration is and may be, it is describable in terms of universals and could be named or pointed to or referred to in terms of ordered frames. Practical difficulties there are bound to be: we may not have adequate ideas or terms to describe the configuration, or we do not know enough to say anything definite about it; we are liable to fumble and fail. But

消失了：它的某些部分变成了烟，不久就消失在空气中；某些部分变成了烟灰；而剩余的部分由我把它摁入烟灰缸内弄碎。这支烟的"同一性"似乎消失了。然而如果情况果真像这样简单的话，那么我们便会发现说"这"烟灰是"那"香烟的一部分是毫无意义的一件事。在这中间必定有某种东西经历了香烟性和烟灰性，这正如大学生从二年级升入三年级一样。

你们某些人可能会以现代物理学来考虑这样的问题，把这不可表达的 x 解释为电子。你们可能会说，组成这或那的特殊客体的是特殊的电子束，所以它们是可以表达的。显然，这样的解释是不正确的。特殊电子的特殊组合的确是可以表达的：只要它是殊相，它就能够被指示出来；只要它实现了一共相，它当然也能被描述出来。但在这特殊的电子及其组合背后的支撑物是不可表达的 x。在推进上述讨论的过程中，你们把从可表达到不可表达的可分析过程误解为是从宏观到微观的科学过程。在物理学中，有从大到小的约简过程，或从复杂到简单的约简过程——这是企图以微观来解释或描述宏观。不论一星球是如何地大或一电子是如何地小，在这两者之中都存在着的不可表达的 x 并非科学所要解决的问题。显然，电子是可以表达的。在将来如果它能以它百万分之一的实体来描述，这些实体同样是可以表达的。但是在这二者背后仍有不可表达的 x。

你们中有些人可能会建议，这里所谓不可表达的 x 可能就是一格式塔、一样型、一唯一的形式或偶然性质的一种畸形结构。一特殊的事物或客体就是这样的东西。但如果它仅仅是这样的东西，那么它也就没有什么不可表达的东西了。不管一结构是如何地畸形，或可能是如何地畸形，它总是可以运用共相来描述，而且可以被命名或用手指示或以有序的结构来提及。肯定会有实际的困难：我们可能没有那么多的意念或术语来描述这样的结构，或者我们不知道足够的信息来确切地表达它。我们可能会显得笨拙，以至最终失败。

154

theoretically it is expressible. If it were described, the description would be to it somewhat as what Aristotleness is to Aristotle and if we were to point out the configuration we would be doing hardly anything more than to point out Aristotle in relation to Aristotleness. If we call Aristotleness or Rooseveltness as synthetic possibilities (a synthetic possibility is such that its constituent possibilities are conjoined but not inferable from each other), they are merely classes for which so far as we know each has only one member. But having only one member to such a class is a question of fact, not of theory. The same is true of freak configurations. However freakish or unique a configuration may be, it is not the inexpressible x.

II [8]

The world with which we are familiar in common sense including that of history and science belongs to the realm of expressibles, even though we are often confronted with experiences which we are at a loss to express. The implements for expression from the point of view of language are symbols, words and sentences. I shall ignore whatever difficult problems there are of language and proceed straight to what is expressed by language usually called meanings. It is necessary to distinguish the content from the object of what is meant. The simplest way of making this distinction clear is to take a simple sentence such as "The desk is low." On the one hand you have the intended meaning of the person who uttered the sentence, and on the other you have a state of affairs usually called a fact which the person who uttered the sentence experienced in some context or others. The former is the content and the latter the object. While both are expressed by the sentence, neither is the sentence. We need not concern ourselves with what is expressed by exclamation or questions; for one purpose only what is expressed by declarative sentences need be considered. These sentences are usually made up of nouns or pronouns or proper names, adjectives, demonstratives and verbs, or other qualifiers or quantifiers. From the point of view of content, some of these stand for ideas and some such as pronouns and names designate sense-data or images. The special content of a sentence in which we are interested is what is now often called a proposition. A proposition is distinguished from the sentence that expresses it as well as from the fact or object

但是，从理论上讲，它仍然是可表达的。如果它是可表达的，那么描述之于它，在某种意义上，正如亚里士多德的性质之于亚里士多德。如果我们准备要去指出这一结构，那么我们所做的可能也仅仅是指出亚里士多德与亚里士多德的性质的关系。如果我们把亚里士多德性或罗斯福性称之为综合可能性（所谓的综合可能性是指，这种可能性是组合在一起的，而不是从相互之间的关系推论出来的），那么就我们目前所能知道的情况来看，它们仅仅是一些类别，每个类别只拥有一个成员。但是类别中只有一个成员是一个实际的问题，而不是一个理论的问题。这样的说法也同样适用于所谓的畸形的结构。不管一结构是多么地畸形或唯一，在理论上讲，它都不是那个不可表达的 x。

二

通常来说，我们所熟悉的世界，包括它的历史和科学，都属于可表达的领域，虽然我们经常遭遇到那种无法表达的窘境。从语言的观点看，用来表达的工具是符号、词语和句子。我打算把那些关于语言的困难问题抛开，而直接从用语言来表达的通常被称作意义的东西开始。在此很有必要把意义的内容和被表达的客体这两者区别开来。作出清晰区别的一个最简单的方式就是以简单的句子为例，比如，"这张桌子很矮。"一方面是你能理解到的说出这一句话的人意欲表达的意思，另一方面是说话者在某些或其他语境中所经历的这种事实，你也可以体会到这种事实。前者就是所说的内容，而后者就是客体。两者都借助于句子得到表达，但它们哪一个都不是句子。在这里，我们无须考虑感叹句或疑问句表达什么这样的问题。为了某种目的，我们现在只需考虑陈述句所表达的东西。陈述句通常是由名词或代词或专名、形容词、指示词和动词或其他的修饰词或量词组成的。从表达内容的角度说，这些词中有的是表达意念，有的如代词和名称则指示感觉材料或意象。我们感兴趣的句子的特殊内容，是所谓的命题。命题不同于表达它的句子，

asserted by it. The constituents of a proposition are ideas, images, or sense-data.

Images and sense-data are concrete-like or particular-like entities in the eminently synthetic process of thinking. In the analytical structure of thought, they are absent. Although they are mental or sensual, they are not ideas. They are in some sense private, hence they cannot be communicated except through the instrumentality of ideas. They are the things that afford us the richness and variety of one sensual and mental life. While they are in some sense private, they are not devoid of objectivity, for they are the basis of communicability of experiences even though they are not themselves the instruments of communication. This can be seen from the words that express them. A string of proper names or pronouns or demonstratives without experiential content express nothing unless they are interwoven with nouns, adjectives and verbs. The location of that magnolia tree is done not merely in terms of proper names, but also in terms of descriptions. If without descriptions we cannot communicate, without ideas we cannot either, in spite of the fact that we have images and sense-data.

It is the abstract ideas that are the agencies for communication. Abstract ideas as contents have universals for their objects. Whatever else any given universal may be, it is at any rate something distinguishable and distinct from other universals. Each universal is just itself, and it includes everything that is itself and excludes everything that isn't. This you can easily see cannot be said of any concrete object, for instance, the red pomegranate on the fireplace shelf is neither merely red, nor merely pomegranate, nor merely both. Naive as the idea may be, it is yet not easily expressed. Perhaps it is its naivete that prevents it from being readily intelligible. What is insisted here is that there is separability or discreteness in universals which in terms of ideas is the basis of abstraction of any one of them from synthetic and concrete wholes. To say that this apple is red singles not redness for consideration quite irrespective of its roundness or sweetness or sourness which presented in the concrete is inseparable. An idea merely articulates an aspect, not a whole; an abstract, not a concrete. Whatever differences there may be in grammar between nouns and adjectives, they are the same one

也不同于由命题表达的事实或客体。命题的构成材料是意念、意象或感觉材料。

在思维的完全综合过程中，意象和感觉材料是类似于具体的或类似于特殊的实体。在思想的分析结构中，它们并不存在。它们虽然是精神的或感觉的，但是它们不是意念。在某种意义上，它们是私人的，因此除非借助于意念这种表达的工具，否则它们是不能传达的。它们向我们提供了有关感觉的和精神的丰富性和多样性。在某种意义上，尽管它们是私人的，但是它们却不是没有客观性，因为它们是经验能够传达的基础，虽然它们本身不是传达的工具。我们从表达它们的词语中可以看到这一点。一串专名或代词或没有经验内容的指示词，如果不与名词、形容词和动词结合在一起，就不能表达任何东西。那棵玉兰树的位置不仅仅是以专名的形式表现出来的，而且也是以描述的形式表现出来的。如果没有描述，我们是不能够进行交流的。同样，没有意念，我们也不能交流，尽管我们有意象和感觉材料。

抽象意念是我们进行交流的中介。作为内容的抽象意念是以共相为其客体的。不管被给定的一共相是什么样的，它至少是可辨认的，是可以与其他的共相区别开来的。每一共相就只是其自身，它包括属于自身的一切，而排除了一切不属于自身的其他东西。你很容易明白对于具体的客体就不能这么说了。比如壁炉架上的红色石榴既不仅仅是红色的，也不仅仅是石榴，也不仅仅是这两者。这一意念尽管很简单，然而要表达它却也不是很容易的一件事。可能正是它的简单才使我们不能容易地理解它。我们在这里所强调的是共相的可分离性或离散性。从意念的角度讲，正是这种可分离性才是使每一共相从综合具体的整体中抽象出来的基础。说这一苹果是红的，并不仅仅是说到红色，而不考虑到它的圆或甜或酸等等。在具体的存在中，这些属性是不可分割的。一意念只反映某一方面，而不反映整体；它只是抽象的，而不是具体的。不管名词与形容词之间在语法上有什么样的区别，

respect; the ideas expressed by them only articulates aspects not wholes. Whenever we say this chair or that desk, we are accustomed to regarding expression as pointing to whole concrete objects. It does so indeed in the content of our early day life, but if you analyze it, you will find that it is the particular context that furnishes you with the feeling of wholeness or concreteness, and that apart from the context the "this" and "that" become variables and the only information supplied by them is that whatever they point to are describable in terms of chair or desk quite irrespective of their being red or green or made of steel or wood.

What is true of ideas is also true of propositions. The latter too only articulate certain aspects of our experience. It is only through leaving an enormous lot unsaid that certain other things can be said. We may achieve a certain degree of completeness by saying things in turn (hence also leaving things in turn) and arriving at making the summary almost a complete description of an object. But no proposition by itself can ever achieve wholeness. If we aim at saying everything we succeed in saying nothing. Such a statement as "After all F. D. R. is F. D. R." may aim at comprehensiveness and conclusiveness, but it really says nothing; however conclusive it may be, Roosevelt couldn't be anybody or anything else. The name is a proper name and unless it is legally changed, it sticks to the particular individual named irrespective of changes, and whatever he is, he simply is. If as a result of a quick turn either to the extreme right or to the extreme left, someone says of him that "untrue to himself, he has betrayed his cause," one is not talking of Roosevelt the concrete individual person from birth to death, but of Rooseveltness definable in terms of political ideas and beliefs formerly describable of that person and now no longer describable of that person. If the statement is true, Roosevelt is still Roosevelt though in certain aspects in politics, he is no longer Rooseveltness. The statement does say something because it leaves certain things unsaid.

Propositions have this property of discreteness. This quality of articulating certain aspects which are abstractly distinguishable and separable from other aspects. This is so irrespective of particular or

它们表现的是同一方面的属性。由它们表达的意念仅仅表达的是部分，而不是整体。当我们说这把椅子或那张书桌时，我们习惯于把这样的表述看作是指示完整的具体的客体。在我们早期的生活中，情形确实是这样的。但是如果你对之进行分析，那么你就会发现是特殊的语境向你提供了这样的整体感或具体感。你也会进一步发现，离开了语境，"这"和"那"就变得不确定了，而且由它们提供的信息也仅仅是，无论它们指示什么，都可以运用椅子或桌子来表达，而不考虑它们是红的或绿的或是由铁或木头做的。

我们关于意念所说的一切也同样适用于命题。命题也同样仅仅是表达我们经验的某一方面。只有通过把大多数东西撇在一旁不说的办法，我们才能说到某些其他的东西。我们可能只有通过依次说及事物（当然也是依次撇开事物），并得出关于客体的几乎是完全描述的结论的办法，才有可能达到某种程度的完整性。但没有一命题自身能够达到完整性。如果我们企图说及一切事物，那么就等于我们什么也没有说。如"毕竟富兰克林·D. 罗斯福就是富兰克林·D. 罗斯福"这样的陈述的目标可能是要达到完整性和确定性，但它实际上并没有真正陈述任何东西。不管它有多大的确定性，罗斯福不可能是任何别的人或别的东西。这一姓名是一专名，除非通过法律手段作出改变，不管其他变化，它只适用于某一以这一专名命名的个人。他是什么样的人，他就是。如果他出现了一会儿趋于极右一会儿又趋于极左这样的情形，于是有人会这样说，他"不忠实于自己，他背叛了自己的事业"。这不是在说从出生到死亡这一时期中具体的罗斯福这个人，而是以政治意念和信念来描述的那个人的罗斯福性质，之前可以那么描述，而现在不能再这样来描述了。如果这一陈述是正确的，那么罗斯福仍旧是罗斯福，虽然在政治上，从某种角度讲，他已不再具有罗斯福所具有的性质了。这一陈述确实说了些东西，因为它没有说及某些东西。

命题具有这样的分离性，即仅仅表达某些方面的性质，使被表达的这些方面能够与其他的方面抽象地区别开来、分离开来。这一特性

general or universal propositions or whether they are true or false. The sum total of our knowledge is simply the sum total true propositions which we can assert. If we know a good deal of history we can assert a rather comprehensive set of particular and general propositions. If we know a lot of natural science, we can assert a rather comprehensive set of universal propositions. Having common sense is also having the capacity to assert a body of propositions some of which are true while others are believed by a large number of people to be true. Knowledge is synthetic or unified in the knower, not in any one of the true propositions which in knowing we can assert. But our knowledge is limited; there are any number of true propositions which we have never been conscious of, have never entertained and never asserted. The sum total of true propositions reflects the kind of world as well as the particular world in which we live our sensual and mental lives. Even when we are often at a loss to express our sensual and conceptual experiences, the whole world of those experiences is yet within the realm of expressibles. We live synthetically, but the fact that we can express how we live is due to the fact that our synthetic lives can be taken successively in aspects, the sum total of true propositions assertable of the whole world is a sum total of aspects which are abstractly distinguishable from each other. Through the abstract distinctiveness of aspects the whole sensual and conceptual world belongs to the realm of expressibles.

It is not merely true propositions with which we are here concerned. A false proposition is different from a true one only in that it is false, it does not cease to have that property of discreteness through its falsity. Whether true or false, propositions are either particular or general or universal. A particular proposition is a content of thought supposedly assertable about a particular object or an event expressed by such sentences as "This is a desk" or "Mr. Huang is a hero." The demonstrative and the proper name indicate sets of particulars and the predicates describe universals. A universal proposition is a content of thought

assertable of the relatedness and connectedness of universals such as
what is expressed by the sentence "Whatever x may be, if it is a man, it
is a mortal." In this case it is quite clear that whether true or false the
proposition deals with distinguishable aspects. A general proposition

不考虑特殊的命题或普通的命题或普遍的命题，也不论它们是真的
还是假的。我们所具有的知识的总和就是我们所能够断定的全部真
命题。如果我们知道很多历史事实，那么我们就能够断定相当广泛
的特殊命题和普通命题。如果我们对自然科学知之甚多，那么我们
也同样能够断定相当广泛的普遍命题。具有常识就具有了断定大量
命题的能力，其中一些命题是真的，而另一部分的命题则是许多人
信以为真的命题。知识是综合的或组合的，体现在知者身上，而不
是在任何我们所能断定的真命题中。但是我们所拥有的知识是有限
度的，确实有相当多的真命题我们从未意识到，从未考虑过，从未
断定过。全部的真命题反映世界，也同样反映着我们感性的和精神
的生活所处其中的世界。即便我们经常因为不能够表达我们的感性
的和概念的经验而大惑不解，整个经验世界也仍然是在可表达的王
国之中。我们的生活是综合的，但我们能够表达我们是怎样生活的
这一事实是由于如下的事实，即我们的综合性的生活能够从不同的
方面进行连续不断的理解。可用来断言整个世界的全部真命题就是
不同方面的总和，这些方面相互之间能够抽象地加以区别。正是通
过这些方面的抽象的特点，完整的、感性的和概念的世界才能说是
属于可表达的世界的。

　　我们在此并不是仅仅考虑真命题。一假命题与真命题的区别在
于它是假的，它并不因为自己的虚假性而不具有分离性。不管是真
还是假，命题不是特殊的就是普通的，或者就是普遍的。一特殊命
题表达的是这样的思想内容，即它断定的是一特殊的客体或由"这
是一张桌子"或"黄先生是英雄"这样的句子表述的事件。指示词
和专名表示的是殊相，而谓词描述的则是共相。一普遍命题表达的
是断定共相间相互联系的思想内容，如"不论 x 是什么，如果它是
一个人，他就是要死的"这样的句子表达的就是共相间的关系。在
这一事例中，有一点是很清楚的，这就是不管这一命题是真的还是
假的，它处理的是能够加以区别的方面。一普通命题介于特殊命题

occupies a midway position: it is neither particular nor universal; it summarizes a collection of particular objects in terms of the ordered frames of time and space such as is expressed by "The people in America before 1492 were Native Americans" or "The Chinese under the Qing Dynasty wear queues." One of the difficulties of the social sciences compared to the natural is that up to the present the former has been able only to discover true general propositions while incapable of inferences beyond its limits of time and space. Obviously we can't expect a Chinese to wear a queue now that he is no longer under the rule of the Qing Dynasty. In spite of time and space limitations, a general proposition still deals with distinguishable aspects.

Before a proposition can be true or false, it has to satisfy certain conditions for significance in order that it is capable of having any meaning. I shall not discuss those conditions from the point of view of pure logic. From that point of view we needn't concern ourselves with epistemology and it is in conjunction with epistemology that our attention is centered at present. Take the so-called laws of identity and contradiction. Both are different aspects of the same condition. The law of identity is the positive aspect; that of contradiction is the negative aspect. These aspects together require the identity of every abstract idea with itself and difference of each from every other. These aspects form the very core of analytic abstraction from the synthetic and the concrete, the very basis of separate distinction of the inseparable or unseparated distinguishables. A proposition can have no meaning, that is, it cannot be a proposition at all, if it isn't itself or can be others than itself. Obviously this condition for significance takes precedence over the problems of truth and falsehood. It is not merely the true propositions that are significant, false propositions are equally significant. And yet as will be mentioned in the next section, the condition itself cannot be expressed in its lumpy completeness. The condition for the significance of expressions is itself merely expressed in terms of its aspects.

The realm of expressibles is the realm of that which can be described in terms of universals or described and pointed to or named or referred to in terms of particulars. As we have already seen, an inexpressible x is neither a particular or a set of particulars, nor a universal or a combination of universals. It cannot be the subject or predicate of

和普遍命题之间，它不是特殊的，也不是普遍的。它是根据时间和空间的有序的结构对许多特殊的客体而作出的总结。如"1492 年之前居住在美洲的是土著居民"或"在清朝统治下的中国人留着长辫子"表达的就是这样的命题。社会科学与自然科学相比的一个困难是，直到目前，前者仅能够发现真的普通命题，而不能做超越时间和空间的推论。显然我们不能够期望中国人现在仍然留着长辫子，因为他们现在早已不在清朝的统治之下了。尽管有时间和空间的局限性，一普通命题处理的仍然是可以相互区别的方面。

在一命题成为真的或假的之前，它为了能够具有任何意义，必须要满足某种关于意义的条件。在这里，我不准备从纯粹逻辑的角度讨论这些条件。因为从那样的条件，我们不必考虑认识论，而我们目前关心的重点是与认识论有密切关系的问题。以同一律和矛盾律为例，这两个思维律都是相同条件的不同的方面。同一律是这一条件的积极的方面，而矛盾律则是其消极的方面。这两个方面同时要求每一个抽象意念与自身要有同一性，而与其他的方面要能够区别开来。这些方面形成了不同于综合和具体的分析性抽象的核心。这一核心是对不能分离的或能够分离却未经分离的可区别义项的单独差别的基础。如果一命题不是它自身或者可以是自身之外的其他东西，那么这一命题可以没有意义，这就是说，它根本就不是命题。显然，这一意义的条件较之于真假的问题具有优先性。不仅真命题是有意义的，而假命题同样是有意义的。我们将在下一部分讨论它。这一条件本身不能以它笨重的完整性来表述。表达意义的条件只能在它本身的各方面中得到表达。

可表达的世界是这样的王国，它可以以共相来描述，也可以殊相来描述或用手指或命名或指示。正如我们所已经看到的那样，一不能表达的 x 既不是一殊相或一套殊相，也不是共相或共相的结合。它不可能是通常意义上的真或假的命题（不管是特殊命题或普

ordinarily true or false propositions whether particular or general or universal. In the sense in which we are said to know history and natural phenomena in their various branches, our inexpressible x cannot be known. Although it is intellectually arrived at, that which is arrived at is yet incapable of being the object of conceptual knowledge or sensual experience. What is required in order to grasp it is a sort of intellectual projection, a recognition of intellectual limitations accompanied by a leap out of intellectual processes with a proposition into the great beyond instead of returning to the essence of intellectuality. In this I am maintaining a distinction between intellectual projection and intellectual reflection, for whereas the latter is a return to pure intellectuality such as a study of logic, the former is a dashing at a tangent into the inexpressibles making it negatively intelligible and therefore also non-sensually experiencible.

III

There are inexpressibles which through intellectual ingenuity succeed in getting presented for human contemplation. Incredible as it may seem, logic the object to be studied as distinguished from the content of our studies cannot be expressed either in its entirety or in its essence. The content does not quite correspond to the object in at least two ways. In the first place, you have the logocentric predicament. Any attempt at dealing with logic in any way always assumes it. Try to squeeze logic as much as you can into a system and you discover that some of it remains outside. This is more easily felt when we examine the beginnings of any system of logic. Take the primitive ideas and the propositions of the *Principia Mathematica*. If one recognizes them to be the beginnings of a system of logic, one assumes their related ideas and propositions which as yet are outside the system, and if one does not assume them, one wouldn't recognize them to be the beginnings of the system of logic. I am not talking now of the problem of alternative systems of logic. The admission of alternative systems automatically also admits some logic to be outside any one system. Our point is rather that even admitting one system to be the unique system, one has to assume logic and the logic that is assumed is yet outside the supposedly unique system. To express logic in any way seems to be essentially to leave it unexpressed

通命题或普遍命题）的主语或谓语。在某种意义上，我们可以说知道历史和各个方面的自然现象，但我们却不能说我们同样知道不能被表达的 x。虽然我们在思维上能够理解它，但此种理解到的对象却不是概念知识或感性经验的客体。要把握它，我们所需要的是一种思维的想象，这是对思维的局限性的一种认识，要带着命题裁出思维的过程，不是回到思维的本质，而是要超越思维的范围。这里，我主张在思维的想象和思维的反映之间作出区别，因为后者是对纯粹思维的回归，如研究逻辑；而前者却快速地越过思维而进入不可表达的事物，使它们变得不可理解，因此也使它们具有了非感性的可经验性。

三

　　确实存在着不可表达的东西，但思维的创新却可以使它们成功地呈现出以供人类沉思。尽管这似乎是不可想象的，但逻辑作为研究的客体而非研究的内容，不能在其整体性或本质中表达出来。至少在两个方面，其内容与客体是不相符合的。第一个方面是，你处在以逻辑为中心的困境之中。任何与逻辑打交道的企图在任何方面总是设定了它的存在。你可以尽你所能把逻辑塞进一个系统之中，但最终你却会发现某些属于逻辑的东西留在了该系统之外。当我们考察任一逻辑系统的开头部分的时候，我们就能更容易地看到这一点。我们在此以《数学原理》中初始意念和命题为例。如果你认识到它们是一逻辑系统的开端，那么你就会假定到目前为止都留在该系统之外的与它们相联的意念和命题。如果你不假定它们，那么你也就相应地不能把它们看作是该逻辑系统的开端。我现在讨论的并不是不同的逻辑系统的问题。承认了不同的逻辑系统也就自然而然地承认了有些逻辑留在了任何的系统之外。相反，我们的观点是，即便承认一个系统为唯一的系统，那么我们也就必须要假定逻辑，这一假定的逻辑在这所谓的唯一的系统之外。试图以任何一种方式来表达逻辑，似乎意味着实质上

in other ways and attempts at completeness in this sense have been failures.

We may also examine the sequence of a system of logic. Implication is different from inference, and bearing the distinction in mind, you discover two sequences in *Principia Mathematica*. The horizontal sequence is one of implications, and the vertical one is that of inferences. From the point of view of the organization of the system, inference is more important in the sense that without it the system cannot unfold itself. And yet inference is not formally a part of the system. Although the principle of inference is listed as one of the primitive propositions, it isn't like any of the others, and what is more important, every inference in the system is formally outside the system, for whereas every horizontal sequence is a formal expression of implication (or equivalence etc.), no vertical sequence is a formal expression of inference. In the former, it is not the reader's business to "imply," something implies something, but in the latter, it is eminently his business to infer, for it is he who infers. Every inference in the latter sequence is a datum very much as this patch of color on my desk is a datum to be expressed by me. The bracket reference to the principle merely enables me to recognize the datum to be inference very much as experience teaches me to recognize that patch of color to be brown. There is nothing formal about it. Returning to expressions, we may say that while implicatives are formally expressed, inferences are not, for while the horizontal lines express implications, the vertical line is itself a sequence of events or activities. Thus a very important element in the unfoldment of a system is yet outside of the system.

In the second place, from the point of view of essence, logic can hardly be expressed either. Suppose we take the different systems of logic, ignoring for our purpose the question as to whether there are merely different systems of the same logic or different systems of different logics or even whether they or some of them are systems of logic at all. Take the principle or the law of identity. We have in *P.M.*

p⊃p, in the so-called three valued system p⊆p, in a four valued system
p→p and in the five valued system of Prof. Lewis p→p. They are not the
same, and yet they are all of them claimed to be principles or laws of
identity. Since according to the claim every one of them expresses the

其他方式的不表达。在这种意义上，要达到完整性的企图也就失
败了。

我们也可以审查一下逻辑系统的秩序问题。蕴涵不同于推论。
如果能够记住这一区别，你就会发现在《数学原理》中实质上有两
种秩序。一种是水平的秩序，它是一种蕴涵的方式。另一种是垂直
的秩序，它是一种推论的方式。从组织一个系统的观点来看，在某
种意义上，推论更为重要，因为没有它，这一系统就不能展开。然
而在形式上，推论并非系统中的一个部分。虽然推论的原则被视为
初始命题的原则，但它与其他的部分不同。更为重要的是，系统中
的每一推论形式上是外在于系统的，因为虽然每一个水平的秩序
是蕴涵（或类似的东西，等等）的形式表现，但没有一个垂直的秩
序是推论的形式表现。在前者，读者的职责不是要去作出蕴涵，如
某些东西蕴涵某些东西。但在后者，很明显他的职责就是去作出推
论，因为正是他在作推论。在后一秩序中的每一推论就是材料，这
正如我的书桌上的这块颜色就是我所要表达的材料一样。括号中提
到的原则仅仅引导我认识到这样的材料是推论，如同经验告诉我那
颜色是棕色的一样。关于它没有形式的东西。回到表达式的问题上
来，我们可能会说，蕴涵能在形式上得到表达，而推论却不能够，
因为横线表示蕴涵，竖线本身表示一连串的事件或活动。这样，在
系统的展开过程中的一个很重要的因素就不得不处在这一系统之外。

第二个方面是，从本质的观点着眼，逻辑自身也很难得到表
达。假定我们以不同的逻辑系统为例。为了更好地说明问题，我们
暂且不管以下的问题，即同一逻辑是否有不同的逻辑系统，或不同
的逻辑有不同的逻辑系统，或是否它们或它们中的某些是逻辑系
统。我们以同一律或同一原则来说明问题。在《数学原理》中同
一律表示为p⊃p，在三值系统中表示为p⊆p，在四值系统中表示为
p→p，在刘易斯教授的五值系统中表示为p→p。这些表示都是不一
样的，但它们却都被认为表示的是同一律或同一原则。由于每一个

principle, none expresses it uniquely. No expression has grasped all its essence so that given any expression one feels that although it expresses some aspect of the principle, others are left out. You may say that this is so under the assumption that the different systems enumerated are systems of logic. While the assumption is not discussed, it is yet made, and making it we feel that we succeed only in expressing aspects of the principle of identity. This may very well be, but if we take any one system, we have the same phenomenon. In *Principia Mathematia* for instance, we have p⊃p, p≡p, x=x, A⊂A, R⦁R... What are we to think of these as the expressions of the principle of identity? All of them are in some sense the same, and in other senses different. If we were logicians we could probably resort to an expression variable for which the listed expressions are values and say that the expression variable embodies the essence of the principle of identity without any of its inconsequential aspects. But an expression variable is neither any nor all of its values, and what is more important, being an expression for expressions, it expresses nothing on the same level of any of its values. It does exhibit something, namely the form in which the principle of identity is to be expressed, but it is not itself an expression of the principle of identify. The latter is elusive so far as complete and essential expression is concerned.

The above merely point out the presence of inexpressibles even in the sphere of logic. But if we do not aim at essence or completeness, we have no fault to find with the current expressions of propositions of logic. By granting the essential separateness of expressions and what is expressed and projecting ourselves intellectually beyond them we can transcend them and arrive at what is expressed in its essence and entity. As logicians we must remain at the analytical level and look at p⊃p, p≡p, A⊂A, ... separately so as to be fully conscious of their difference. It is desirable that we should remain at the analytical level and be fully conscious of distinctions and differences. But as philosophers, we should also be able to look at these expressions or any one of them and through them grasp the essence and the entity of what is expressed. The logician helps the philosopher. The advance in logic during the last half century or so has made logical expressions clearer, much less lumpy and much more integrated than they were before, and while it has not enabled us to

都被认为表示的是同一律，所以没有一个表述是唯一的。也可以说，没有一个表述穷尽了它的本质，因此对于任何一个表述，我们会感到它虽然表示了这一原则的某些方面，然而这一原则的其他方面却被遗漏了。你可能会说，之所以如此是因为我们假定了列举的不同系统都是逻辑的系统。虽然这样的假定没有给予讨论，不过我们就这样假定了，我们觉得我们只能成功地表示同一律的某些方面。这一说法应该说有其一定的理由，但是如果我们采取任何一个系统，那么我们得到的是同样的现象。比如在《数学原理》中，我们看到 $p\supset p$、$p\equiv p$、$x=x$、$A\cap A$、$R\supset R$……我们是否把这些都看作是对同一律的表示呢？在某种意义上，它们都是一样的，但在另一种意义上它们却彼此不同。如果我们是逻辑学家，我们可能会求助于一个表达变量，上述的表述都是这个变量的值。我们会说表达变量体现了同一律的本质，而没有任何微不足道的方面。但是，表达变量既不表现它的部分的值，更不表现它的所有的值。更为重要的是，作为同一律表达中的一个表达，在表现其值的同一层面上，它什么也没有表达。然而它也确实展示了某些东西，即表达同一律的形式。但是，它本身却不是同一律的表达。就同一律的完整的和本质的表达来说，后者令人费解。

上面的讨论仅仅是要指出，即便在逻辑的领域内也有着不可表达的东西。但是如果我们的目标不是本质或完整性，那么我们就不会在逻辑命题的这些表达中发现错误。只要承认表达和被表达的东西是相分离的，只要我们在思维上超越了它们，那么我们就能得到所要表达的东西的本质及其实体。我们作为逻辑学家必须坚持分析的立场，必须分别地看待 $p\supset p$，$p\equiv p$，$A\cap A$……以便能够充分地认识到它们之间的差别。能够站在分析的立场上来充分地认识它们的特点及其区别，这是令人向往的。但作为哲学家，我们应该能够审查这些表达或其中的任何一个，并通过它们来掌握被表达的对象的本质和实体。逻辑学家能够帮助哲学家。在过去的半个多世纪中，逻辑学所获得的进步使逻辑的表达更为清晰了。与过去相比，它们显得不那么笨拙了，并且显得更为完全综合。即便进步还不能使我们去表达逻辑中不能被表达

express the inexpressible in logic, it has enabled us to grasp it more firmly than before. So far as the expressible is concerned, the recent advance in logic has made its expression extremely articulate in terms of the interrelatedness of ideas.

It is now a part of the common sense of the philosophical world to regard a tautology as being that truth function of propositions which asserts no fact and entertains every possibility. It cannot be false on the one hand and must be true on the other. That it cannot be false need not be dwelt on at all; exhibitions of this aspect abound in text books on logic. The more important aspect to a philosopher is rather that a tautology must be true. There are even so many things which cannot be false and yet can in no sense be said to be true. But this is not what we have in mind. We are not concerned with how a tautology must be true, since the reasons why it cannot be false also account as to how it must be true. The question uppermost in our minds is rather: what is it that a tautology is true of? It is true of Reality with a capital R, or underlying reality, or to use Prof. Spaulding's intentionally nondescript phrase, a state of affairs? Or is it true of a transcendental mind? Perhaps from the point of view of each tautology being a norm for thought, we are tempted to regard it as being uniquely associated with the mind. But if it were merely true of the mind, we do not see either that it must always be true or that it need ever be true. That which is true of the mind is of course a truth—it may even be a sort of transcendental truth, but in order that it may be a truth in the sense of a tautology, it has to be true of something else as well. I shall not enter into the complexities this line of inquiry inevitably leads to. I shall say bluntly that a tautology is true of Tao or to use a term more familiar to you, logos.

The significant thing about a tautology for us at present is not that it is true of Tao or logos, but that it is so without mentioning Tao or logos either as a subject or as a predicate. From the point of view of unstable objects, fleeting events or contingent facts in terms of science or history, logic is indeed a subject in which we do not know what we are talking about or whether what we say is true. But ontologically we know that we are talking of Tao or logos and what we say is true of it. By asserting nothing to be a fact and entertaining everything as a possibility

的东西，却使我们比以前更牢固地把握住它。就目前我们所讨论的表达问题而言，逻辑学的最近进展使它对意念之间的相互联系性表达显得极为清晰。

哲学世界的一个常识性的看法是认为重言式是命题的真值，它不断定事实，却考虑了一切的可能性。在一个方面它不可能是假的，在另一方面它必须是真的。关于它不可能是假的这一点，我们无须讨论，逻辑教科书对此有较多的论述。对于哲学家来说较为重要的是重言式必须是真的这一点。有很多的事物是不可能假的，但也决不能说是真的。然而我们现在不关心这样的问题。我们现在不讨论重言式为什么必须是真的，因为为什么它不能是假的也就是它为什么必须是真的理由。我们所最关心的主要问题是：重言式对于什么是真的？对于真正的实在是真的？或者说是在实在背后的东西是真的，或者用斯波尔丁教授有意使用的普通词语，情状是真的？或者说是对于先验的心灵是真的？可能，从每一重言式都是思想的规范这样的观点来看，我们倾向于把它看作是与心灵有独特联系的。但如果仅仅对于心灵是真的，那么我们实在是看不出重言式必须总是真的，或者说它需要任何时候都是真的。对于心灵是真的，这当然是真理，而且它可能就是先验真理。但如果它是重言式意义上的真理，那么它对于其他某种东西必须也是真的。讨论这一问题将必然会涉及很复杂的问题，我不打算在此讨论这样的复杂问题。而只是坦率地指出，重言式对于道是真的，或者运用一个更为熟悉的术语说，对于逻各斯是真的。

就目前而言，对我们来说，关于重言式的重要性并不在其对于道的真或者逻各斯的真，而是在没有将道或逻各斯作为主词或谓词的情况下，它对其是真的。就科学和历史而言，从不稳定的客体、稍纵即逝的事件或者视条件而定的事实的观点来看，逻辑确实是这样的主词，我们并不知道我们在谈论的是什么或我们所说的是否是真的。但是从本体论的角度，我们知道我们在谈论道或逻各斯，而且知道我们关于它们所说的一切是真的。由于没有断定任何的事实，更由于考虑到每一事情都

a tautology does manage to be non-committed in relation to history and science; but this does not mean that it is also neutral in relation to ontology. It is through saying nothing about facts that a tautology manages to say something about the ultimate reality. Therein lies the skill of the logician. What is said, however, is the barest minimum of the universe. Is it possible to have another class of statements which assert the fullest maximum? A tautology is sometimes called a pseudo-proposition. Could we have another set of pseudo-propositions which assert everything about neither of fact? We must confess that we are bewildered by the vista. While we see that something extremely important might be done along this line, we are at a loss so far as developing the technique for making such statements is concerned. I myself do not have the ingenuity, and the only thing I can think of is to return to an inexpressible x. Drafting the inexpressible x, however, carries with it difficulties. It cannot be sensed, not pointed to, not referred to in time and space, nor could it be described. We arrive at it through intellectual projection. Either we grasp it or we don't. If we don't, nothing could be done about it.

If we do grasp it, we are also in difficulties. Let us give inexpressible x a proper name. We cannot think of a better name than "Stuff" in spite of the fact that it is liable to leave with us a taste of excessive stuffiness. Proper names are innocuous in the sense that they have no conceptual deducible meanings and yet if we are thoroughly acquainted with the thing named, we do acquire from some names a feeling of adequacy and propriety as compared with other names. Stuff seems to us to be an adequate name for the inexpressible x. It must be admitted that in the structure of ordinary sentences the name Stuff can only enter as a subject, not a predicate. What is even more important is that the statements expressed by these sentences are not propositions in the ordinary sense, nor are the pseudo-propositions in the sense of tautologies. Unfortunately we have to use language, and since according to Whitehead "Philosophy is to express the infinity of the universe in terms of the limitations of language," we might as well recognize these limitations and ineffective thought our attempts are bound to be, try to transcend as much as possible these limitations. In the following sections I shall make use of

是可能的，所以重言式并不企图忠于历史和科学。但这并不意味着，它对于本体论也是中立的。正是通过不断定任何的事实，重言式才有可能谈论终极实在。在此，确实可以看出逻辑学家的技巧。然而所说的是关于宇宙的最基本的东西。是否可能拥有另一套陈述，给出最充分、最完备的描述？重言式有时被称之为伪命题。我们是否可能有另一套伪命题也不断定每一件事实？在这一方面，我们确实一筹莫展。当我们看到某些十分重要的事情必须要据此而做的时候，就发展出构造这样的陈述能力而言，我们也实在是不知所措。我自己本人没有这一方面的创造力，我所能想到的就是回到不可表达的 x。然而要征用这不可表达的 x 却也有着很多的困难。我们不能感觉到它，也不能指出它来，也不能在时间和空间下提及它，更不可能描述它。我们只能依靠思维的想象。或者我们理解了它，或者我们不能。如果我们不能理解它，那么对于它我们就无能为力。

如果我们能够理解它，我们也同样是处在困难之中。让我们现在给这不能表达的 x 一个专名。尽管"质料"一词可能会使我们感到一种沉闷、乏味的感觉，但我们不能够想出一个比"质料"更好的名字了[9]。专名并不具有概念所具有的可推断的意义，因此它就无害。但是如果我们完全了解被命名的事物，那么我们借助于名字而获得一种从其他名字不可能获得的恰当的感觉。我们认为，"质料"对于不可表达的 x 来说是一适当的名字。必须承认，在日常的语句结构中，质料这一名字只能是主词，而不能是谓词。更为重要的是，由这样的语句表达的陈述不是普通意义上的命题，也不是在重言式意义上的伪命题。遗憾的是，我们必须使用语言，而且根据怀特海的"哲学是运用语言的有限性来表达宇宙的无限性"的思想，我们同样可以认识到这样的有限性。我们的努力不可避免地成为无效的思想，但我们应该尽可能地努力去超越这些局限性。在下面的章节中，我将利用消极的陈述和

both negative and positive statements in order to enable those who have already grasped Stuff to grasp it more firmly.

IV

The expressions that are used in this section with the name Stuff as the subject are not definitions, though they resemble definitions. Definitions are of terms which stand for concepts and concepts are idea versions of universals. Stuff is not a universal. Hence the sentences in which Stuff appears as the subject are not definitions. In the sphere of expressibles we have another class of statements to introduce individuals such as in speeches and addresses. The resemblance of some sentences in this section to introductions is obvious, for the function is similar; only in the case of Stuff one cannot be introduced to it as one could to a Tom or Dick or Harry. Stuff is not an individual. Though these statements are not definitions or introductions, they are yet made to enable us to grasp Stuff more firmly than we did before.

The justification for the positive statements lies in the negative ones. One previous analysis reveals that concerning any particular concrete individual thing the sum total of universal and particular propositions that can be truly asserted of "it" from the point of view of what "it" stands for leads us to an x that is inexpressible. The very way in which x is arrived at justifies a number of negative statements provided of course that the discussion in the first section is agreed to and the inexpressible x is grasped. Certain negative statements concerning Stuff are obvious. Stuff is not a universal, for if it were, it would be describable in terms of universals. Stuff is also not a particular, for if it were, it could be named by ordinary names, or pointed to, or referred to in the ordered frame of time and space. It is not an individual, for if it were, it would have characteristics that would make it different and distinct from other individuals. Although each individual thing has its Stuff, Stuff that is common to all individual things is obviously not any of them. It is neither concrete nor abstract, for if it were concrete, it could be sensually experienced, and if it were abstract, it could be conceptually received. It cannot be said to be either existent or nonexistent, for the former is an affirmation of a certain characteristic and the latter a denial of the same, and in either case, Stuff would have to be describable. It neither begins

积极的陈述来使那些已经理解了质料的人更确切地理解它。

四

在这一部分中所有以质料这一名字为主语的表述都不是定义，虽然它们类似于定义。定义是关于术语的，术语代表着概念，而概念则是共相的意念形式。质料不是共相。因此，以质料为主语的句子也就当然不是定义。在可表达的领域内，我们有另一类陈述以在讲话和演说时介绍自己。这一部分的一些句子跟自我介绍的句子的相似之处是很明显的，因为其功能是相同的。只是你可以把自己介绍给张三李四，但却不能介绍给质料。质料不是个体。虽然这些陈述并不是定义或介绍，但是它们却使我们能比以前更确切地理解质料。

对积极陈述的辩护存在于消极陈述之中。在此之前的一个分析已经揭示出这样一点，即对任何一个特殊具体的个体事物而言，从"它"所代表的观点看，所有关于它的普遍和特殊命题的总和引出了不可表达的 x。达到 x 的方式证明了一些消极陈述，当然前提是第一部分中的讨论已经达成以及已经理解了不可表达的 x。有关质料的某些消极陈述是显而易见的。质料不是共相。如果它是共相，它就能以共相来描述了。质料也同样不是殊相。因为如果它是殊相，那么它也就相应地可以以日常的名词来命名了，或用手指出来，或借助于有序的时间和空间而提及。它也不是个体。因为如果它是个体，那么它就具有自己的特点，并借此使自己与别的个体区别开来。尽管每一个体事物都有自己的质料，通用于所有个体事物的质料却显然不是其中的任何一个。它既不是具体的，也不是抽象的。因为如果它是具体的，那么它就能在感觉经验中被经验到；如果它是抽象的，那么它就能借助于概念的思维而得到。它也同样不能说是存在或非存在。因为如果说它存在，那么它就肯定具有某种特征；如果说它非存在，那么就是对这种特征的否定——在任一情况下，质料

nor ends for if it does, it could be referred to in terms of time. I shall point out later that it is the very condition for time, but for the present we needn't dwell on the point. An enormous number of such negative statements could be made. We may summarize by saying that Stuff does not belong to any universe of discourse and that is simply another way of saying that it is inexpressible. On the level of the expressibles, we are of course contradicting ourselves, but having projected ourselves beyond the realm of the expressibles, we are merely using instruments in the form of ordinary statements to enable us to grasp Stuff more firmly than before.

These negative statements enable us to pronounce some positive ones. As will be seen from the above Stuff is pure potentiality. In the sphere of expressibles, potentiality means the capacity of a thing to be something which isn't at any given moment. A has a potentiality to be B, if it can become B at t_2 although it isn't at t_1, however short or long the interval between t_1 and t_2 may be. The term does not exclude nor is it limited to values. Thus Mr. A may have the potentiality for a great actor, while Mr. B may merely have the potentiality of a mathematician whether good or bad or indifferent. In the realm of expressibles we are inclined to say that a given A (an individual thing, let us say) has the potentiality for being B, when none of its universal or its particular has any potentiality for any other universal or any other particular. Obviously a particular cannot change for that particular which a thing changes out of merely dies, and that particular which a thing changes into is merely born. If a third particular is interfered as a medium, we merely have an infinite regress with a set of particulars for which there is a series of birth and death in which none of the particulars has changed. This series of birth and death of particulars may indeed characterize the change of something that does change, but a particular by itself does not change. Neither can a universal. If in the autumn we find that some leaves have changed from being green to being red, it is obvious that the universal greenness has not changed into the universal redness. There may be what we shall later call a succession of realizations of possibilities and this succession may characterize the change of something that does change, but none of the universals in the succession has changed. Since a universal is something

一定会被描述。它既不是开端，也不是终点。因为如果它是，那么它就以时间来提及。我将在后面指出，它是时间的非常重要的条件，但是在目前我们无须考虑这一点。像这样的消极陈述，真是可以说举不胜举。我们可以这样总结，质料不属于任何的论域，这就是以另一种方式说它是不可表达的。在可表达的层次上，我们当然会使自己自相矛盾，但是既然我们已经超越了可表达的王国，那么我们只不过以日常陈述的形式运用工具来使我们比以前更确切地理解质料而已。

这些消极陈述使我们能够发表一些积极陈述。通过上面的叙述，我们将会看到，质料是纯粹的潜在的可能性。在可表达的领域中，潜在的可能性是指使某一东西不在特定时间内成为某种事物的可能。如果 A 在 t_2 能够变成 B，尽管在 t_1 它还不是，那么 A 具有成为 B 的性能，不管 t_1 和 t_2 之间的间隔是长还是短。这一术语并不排除也不限制于真值。这样，A 先生或许有成为一个大演员的可能，而 B 先生则只有成为一个数学家的可能，而不管是优秀的或拙劣的或一般的数学家。在可表达的领域内，我们倾向于这样说，当一个给定的 A（比如一个个体事物）的哪一个共相或殊相都没有变成其他共相或其他殊相的可能时，这个 A 就有着成为 B 的可能。显然，一殊相不能变化，因为自其变化而出的殊相方死，变化所成的殊相方生。如果第三个殊相作为中介出现，那么我们也只不过有着一个殊相的无穷回溯的系列，在其中不断地有殊相死亡，也有殊相不断地诞生，然而没有殊相发生变化。这一殊相生灭的过程可能确实描述了某些事物的变化，但是殊相本身是不会发生变化的。共相也不会发生任何的变化。在秋天，如果我们发现某些树叶由绿色变成了红色，很显然作为共相的绿色并没有变成作为共相的红色。这里存在着我们将在后面称之为可能性实现的连续序列。这一连续序列可以描述某些事物的变化，但是共相本身在这样的序列中是没有发生变化的。由于共相是这样的一种东西，它不依赖于时间和空间，

that is independent of time and space, it would be a contradiction to say that it changes at all.

However, changes can be observed anywhere. In the world of common sense, we are justified in attributing change to the supposedly expressible things or events, states and processes. But if we proceed in the way we have been so far proceeding, we find that the expressibles cannot change and that we only succeed in expressing changes by a very lumpy use of pronouns, demonstratives and proper names. Stuff cannot change either. But it is responsible for all the changes. If we borrow the term "potentiality" from the realm of expressibles, we may say that Stuff is pure potentiality. It is Stuff underlying this table that makes it an object and not merely a collection of a universal or particulars, that together with the universal and particulars makes it capable of being lumpily designated by pronouns, proper names and demonstratives, and renders it capable of change in spite of the unchanging universal and particulars. Expressibility, however, is based on separability and discreteness. Hence all that which are expressed are limited items in our total experience; they are aspects that have their own respective limitations. This wooden desk, so long as Stuff designated as the "this" is cramped in "this wooden desk," has potentiality during a certain period for certain things for example, "kindling wood," but it has no potentiality for other things, for example, a "cow." Ordinarily we say that this wooden desk cannot become a cow though it may become kindling wood. What it does become is, however, not only limited, but also subject to contingencies over which, in being merely this wooden desk, it has no control. But if we talk of Stuff that is not confused to this wooden desk or that red apple, we can easily see that its potentiality is all pervasive and pure. Through wearing and discarding universals and particulars, Stuff can become anything. The richness in the multiplicity of this ever changing world reflects only to a very small degree the all-pervading potentiality of Stuff, for although the latter can be easily seen to be responsible for the present kind of world, it is yet not limited to any kind.

Stuff is also pure activity. In the sphere of the expressible, activity means such behavior on the part of the agent that influence is felt over the patient. Active, action, and actual are all related to activity. Perhaps

因此说共相发生变化就是自相矛盾。

然而，变化终究是随处可见的事情。在常识世界中，我们有正当的理由把变化归之于被假定是可表达的事物或事件、状态和过程。但是如果我们按照我们目前讨论的方式继续进行下去的话，那么我们就会发现可表达的东西是不能变化的，而且我们也只能做到笨拙地运用代词、指示词和专名来表达变化。质料也同样不能变化，但是它却导致了所有的变化。如果我们从可表达的世界中借用"潜在的可能性"一词，那么我们可以说，质料是纯粹的潜在的可能性。正因为有质料潜伏在桌子中才使桌子成为一个客体，而不仅仅是一大堆的共相或殊相。也正因为质料与共相和殊相在一起才使其本身有可能通过代词、专名和指示词被笨拙地指示出来，使它有变化的能力，尽管共相和殊相是不变化的。然而，可表达性是以可分离性和离散性为基础的。因此，所有可表达的东西都是我们全部经验中有限的各项事物，它们都是具有各自的限制的方面。只要被命名为"这"的质料在"这张木头桌子"里，这张木头桌子在一定的时间内就有变成某种东西的潜在可能性，比如"引火柴"，但是它却绝对没有变成比如"奶牛"等其他东西的潜在可能性。通常，我们会说这张木头桌子虽然可能变成引火柴，但却不可能变成奶牛。不过，它变成什么东西非但是有所限制的，而且也要受制于像这张木头桌子不能控制的偶然事件。但是如果我们谈论不与这张木头桌子或那个红苹果混淆的质料，我们就能够很容易地看出，它的这种潜在的可能性是无所不在的，是纯粹的。不管是否拥有共相和殊相，质料都可以变成任何东西。不断变化的世界的这种丰富多样性仅仅在一种很小的程度上反映了质料的无所不在的潜在性，因为虽然我们可以很容易地看出其潜在性导致了目前这一形态的世界，但是它却不会局限于任何一种形态。

质料也是纯粹的能动性。在可表达的领域内，能动性是指对对象施加影响的一种行为。能动的、活动、现实的都与能动性有关。

the English term "actual" has been so much mixed with the term "real" that we lose the connection between it and action or activity. Anyhow I am using the word "actual" to mean that which is acting at present. The actual is of course indulging in activities: it is not merely active; it is also being acted upon. This brings us to the old problem of causal relations. Perhaps some readers of the preceding paragraph have felt the emergency of epistemological considerations when the idea of contingence is introduced. Epistemological considerations are unavoidable and are not limited to this preceding paragraph, but for us contingency is not merely epistemological. I hold a view which I do not propose here to elucidate or to depend on. For the present I merely say that I believe in the contingency of the birth and death of particulars and in terms of activities this contingency may be expressed by saying that while universal causal relations always hold, they interfere with each other so that it is nowhere determinate as to which of them is actualized at any particular place or time. That is to say, although the universal relation A—B always holds under equal conditions, it is by no means determinate that in the sphere of particulars when "a" occurs "b" also happens or whether b happens or not depends upon conditions which are never actually equal. Evolution in the broadest sense possibly never repeats itself. If it does, time has stopped during the repetition. Anyhow I assume the above views and assuming it I have to hold also that in the sphere of expressible particular things or events, states or processes, the activities are limited and contingent. The activities of a, b, c, d... are not pure, but the activity of Stuff underlying a, b, c, d... is pure and unconditioned.

Since we have already spoken of causal relations, we might as well make use of them further by saying that if we were speaking of universal causal relations, we cannot entertain the notion of a first cause in time since universals are independent of time. Neither can we speak of a first cause in time in the sphere of particulars, for unless we give up the doctrine of universal causation, this would involve a beginning of the universe which is its all-comprehensiveness, and it cannot have a beginning. In the language of cause and effect we cannot speak of an uncaused cause. If now we switch to Stuff, we can

可能在英语中,"现实的"一词与"真实的"一词经常混为一谈,所以我们也就不容易发现它与行动或者能动性之间的联系。不管怎么样,我用"现实的"一词来指现在正在行动的。当然,"现实的"沉浸在能动性之内,它不仅仅意味着主动,而且也意味着受动。这就使我们想起了因果关系的老问题。可能某些阅读到先前段落的读者,当提及偶然性的时候,他们已经感觉到了考虑认识论的紧迫性。认识论的考虑当然是不可避免的,而且也并不局限于先前那一段落。但是对我们而言,偶然性并不仅仅是指认识论方面的。我不拟在此阐述我的某些看法。在这里,我只是说,我相信殊相生灭的偶然性。就能动性而言,这里的偶然性可以用这样的说法来表达,即作为共相的因果关系始终是有效的,它们之间相互影响,以致不能确定其中的哪一个在特定的地点或时间能够实现。这就是说,虽然作为共相关系的A—B在相同的条件下总是有效的,但在殊相的领域内,当"a"发生时"b"是否发生是不确定的,或者b是否发生所依赖的条件在现实中从来就不是相同的。在最广泛意义上的进化论可能从未重复自身。如果它重复了自身,那么在所谓重复过程中时间一定是停顿的。无论如何,我采取上面的观点。既然如此,我必须同样指出,在可表达的特殊事物或事件、状态或过程的领域内,能动性是有限制的,是偶然的。a、b、c、d……的能动性不是纯粹的,但潜伏在a、b、c、d……之中的质料的能动性却是纯粹的和无条件的。

由于我们已经涉及因果关系问题,我们可以接着这一话题继续进行讨论。如果我们谈论到共相的因果关系问题,那么我们就不能有时间中第一原因的观念,因为共相是脱离时间的。同样我们也不能在殊相领域内说什么时间中的第一原因,其理由是除非我们放弃共相的因果观念,否则我们就会涉及宇宙的开端问题,而宇宙本身是无所不包的,所以它不能有开端。以原因和结果的语言来谈论,我们就不能说什么没有原因的原因。如果我们把话题转到质料上去,

easily see that there is uncompelled and unceasing activity. While we cannot speak of Stuff in terms of uncaused cause we may indicate what it is like in terms of free will. The notion of free will may or may not be tenable as a philosophical doctrine to be applied to the realm of expressibles; the term "free will" is not quite so open to objection as the phrase "uncaused cause" unless we define the former in terms of the latter. If we borrow the term "free will" and strip it from its ordinary content, we may make use of it and say that in its activity Stuff is self-willed and therefore free. The impression that is meant to be conveyed is that the activity of Stuff is absolutely unhampered and purest of the pure; it is entirely for its own sake that Stuff is active and actual.

Stuff is also pure substantiality. We are accustomed to the term "substance." We often say this or that substance. What is characteristic of a substance is a certain amount of stuffiness, certain rigidity, certain resistance to manipulations independent of the essence of whatever a given substance is endowed. In the sense in which we often use the term, substance is eminently describable and can also be classified into different categories. Stuff is not any of the substances, just as it is not any of expressible potentiality or activity of things or events, or states and processes. Since Stuff is pure potentiality, it cannot be limited to any specific category; since it is pure activity, it is not itself in the chain of the changes of fleeting events, unstable objects and contingent facts. But while Stuff is not itself a substance, it is that which underlies all substances, and it is pure substantiality. Without it, universals would be empty possibilities and particulars would cease to be since there wouldn't be things or events. It is that which give substantiality to substances, for without it, even substance itself would be an empty possibility, definable in terms of rigidity without anything that is rigid, or in terms of resistance with nothing that resists. Perhaps the old notion of substratum as that which qualities and properties adhere may give us an idea of pure substantiality, but in so far as the notion is definable, it does not stand for a Stuff. Nor is our Stuff the lowest common denominator of all substances; we cannot build a tree or pyramid in which Stuff bears the burden of anything and everything.

那么我们就能很容易地看到，存在着无须推动、不会停顿的能动性。我们虽然不能以没有原因的原因来谈论质料，但我们却可以指出，就自由意志而言它是怎样的。自由意志的观念作为哲学思想运用于可表达的领域内，或许能站住脚或许站不住脚。"自由意志"这一术语还不像"没有原因的原因"那样容易遭到反对，除非我们以后者来定义前者。如果我们借用"自由意志"这一术语并进一步剔除它的通常内容，那么我们就可以运用它来这样说，质料的能动性具有自我意志的属性，因此它是自由的。这一说法所要传达的意念是，质料的能动性是没有阻碍的，是纯粹中最纯粹的。质料是能动的，是现实的，这完全是因其自身。

质料也是纯粹的实质性。我们已习惯于"实体"这样的说法。我们经常说这一或那一实体。所谓的实体的特征所指的就是一定的质料性、一定的刚性，以及对影响的抗性，这种抗性独立于给定实体所具有的本质。在这一术语的常用意义方面，实体明显具有可描述性，而且也可以划分为不同的范畴。质料不是任何这样的实体，正如它不是任何可表达的事物或事件或状态或过程的潜在性或能动性一样。由于质料是纯粹的潜在的可能性，所以它不能局限于任何特殊的范畴；由于它是纯粹的能动性，所以它本身不在转瞬即逝的事件、不稳定的客体和偶然的事实的变化的链条之中。但是既然质料自身不是实体，而是潜在于所有的实体之中的，所以它就是实质性。没有它，共相只不过是空洞的可能性；由于不存在事物或事件，殊相也将停止存在。正是质料将实质性给了实体，因为没有它，即便是实体自身也只不过是空的可能性；可以用刚性来描述，却没有任何刚性的东西；可以用抗性来描述，却没有用以抵抗的东西。可能，以前提到的特性、特征等基本特征的概念会带给我们实质性的观念。但是就这一概念能够定义来说，它并不代表质料。我们所谓的质料也不是一切实体所具有的共同的最小公分母；我们不可能构建一棵树或一座金字塔，使质料在其中承担起任何或所有的事物。

V

A number of other statements could be added to the above, and while some will come later on, one will be singled out for special consideration here. In doing so, we shall expose ourselves to a barrage of arguments against our procedure, for unlike the above statements, the one we intend to single out has as its constituents terms which are ordinarily employed in an operational context. We shall say that Stuff is totally devoid of quality and absolutely constant in quantity. We shall readily agree with the view that looked upon as an ordinary proposition, the statement is meaningless, since the term "quality" involves an experiential context that is here lacking, and the terms "constancy" and "quantity" call for operations which cannot here be applied. It is however not the ordinary meanings that I aim at through ordinary propositions; it is rather the flavor I intend to convey through a set of extraordinary statements.

The first part of the statement really prevents us from describing Stuff in any way whatever. To describe it in any way in the ordinary sense is to attribute certain qualities, and to attribute certain qualities to Stuff is to deny its certain other qualities. To describe it in any way is to hamper it, to infringe upon its pure potentiality and activity. It is not merely that such adjectives as "red" or "green," or "square" or "circular," cannot be applied, for obviously Stuff cannot be described by any of them; but also such adjectives as "real" or "existent" cannot be applied either. The term "real" can be defined, even though we may have failed in doing so, which means that the concept "reality" can be related to other concepts, and the universal corresponding to it is understandable through a combination of other universals. If Stuff were real, it would be expressible. We know that like the word "natural" the term "real" is capable of a multiplicity of meanings. I have once gathered more than twenty, and I cannot claim that I have exhausted the whole list of different meanings. But each meaning is different from any other; hence each is definable, that is to say each is a concept, and therefore also an idea version of a universal or what I shall later call a possibility. Anyone who has grasped Stuff at all must be committed that it cannot be said to be either a universal or a possibility. The same is true of existence, and perhaps here the point is even more

<h1 style="text-align:center">五</h1>

对于上面的讨论，我们还可以补充一些东西。其中有些东西我们将在后面涉及，在此我们将要讨论的是一个比较特殊的问题。这么做我们将面临一系列对我们程序的论据轰炸，因为与上述陈述不同，我们将要挑选出的这一问题包含着一些在可操作环境下的常用术语。我们可以说，质料是完全没有特性和数量上绝对恒久不变的。我们很容易同意这样的看法，即把这一陈述看作普通命题的话，它是没有意义的。因为"特性"这一术语包含着经验性的语境，而在这里却没有这样的语境。像"恒久性"和"数量"这样的术语需要运用，而在这里却不能有这样的运用。不管怎么样，我在这里并不以通过常见命题获得普通含义为目标，而是想要通过一套非常的陈述来表达想法。

这一陈述的前半部分确实使我们不能以任何的方式来描述质料。在通常的意义上以任何方式去描述它，就是把某种特性赋予了它。而把某种特性赋予质料就是否认它具有其他的某些特性。以任何方式去描述它就是去限制它，也就是侵犯了它的纯粹的潜在的可能性和能动性。这不只是因为"红的""绿的""方的""圆的"之类的形容词不能适用于质料，因为很显然质料不能以这些形容词中的任何一个来描述；而且"实在的""存在的"之类的形容词也不适合用来描述质料。"实在的"这一术语能够被定义，尽管我们在这样做的时候可能会失败。这就说明概念"实在"是与其他的概念相联的，与之相关的共相能够通过与其他共相的联合而得到理解。如果质料是实在的，那么它就是可以表达的。我们知道，像"自然的"一词一样，"实在的"这一术语可能具有极其丰富的含义。我曾经搜集过二十多个，而且我相信这些含义也并没有穷尽它所有的不同的含义。但是其中每一个含义都是相互不同的，因此每一个含义都是可以定义的。这就是说，每一个都是一个概念。因此我们也可以说，它是共相或我将在后面所说的可能性的意念形式。任何一个人只要他理解了质料，那么他就必须承认，质料既不是共相，也不是可能性。对于存在也同样如此，这一点

easily driven home. To say that Stuff exists is to limit it in other ways just as to say that it is real is to prevent it from being unreal and to say that it is green denies it to be red. The word "exist" as it is ordinarily used or at any rate as it is customarily used by me is narrower than the term "real." The past, the present and the future are involved in the idea "existent." Confucius may be said to be real in some sense though he no longer exists, and the ideal of a future world state may be quite real, though it is non-existent at present. To say that Stuff exists is therefore to limit it in a large number of ways. And if you mean by existence the actual occupation of space at the present time, then to say that Stuff exists is to say that it is limited to certain space and time. Stuff cannot be so limited.

Without going on further with any more specific argument, we may say again generally that no adjective can be used to describe Stuff if by doing so one means to attribute any quality to it. But you may say that Stuff must be homogeneous, because if anyone grasps it at all, one is bound to admit that the Stuff in this chair and that apple is absolutely the same in spite of the differences of these two objects. Quite so! Provided that homogeneousness is not meant to have qualitatively predicated of Stuff. For negatively if Stuff is qualitatively homogeneous, it cannot enter into the core of such diverse things as this chair or that apple, and positively since it does enter into the core of such diverse things, it is not qualitatively homogeneous. It is only homogeneous in the sense of an absence of qualities, not in the sense of having the same qualities throughout. Obviously if it has any quality at all, it would be expressible in terms of that quality, and to borrow a word so often used in the present war, it would be "frozen" in that universal. And being "frozen" in one universal it couldn't enter into any other possibility and its potentiality and activity and substantiality wouldn't be pure. The very core of the matter is that Stuff must be absolutely free in its potentiality, activity and substantiality in order that it may be the underlying reality of such a multiplicity of things in the actual world and of the infinite richness of things in an infinity of possible worlds.

The second part of the statement is in some ways more important. Not only is Stuff devoid of quality, but it is also constant in quantity. I am aware that both these terms could have a certain rigidity of meaning

可能更好理解。说质料是存在就是在另一方面限制了它，正如说它是实在的就不能说它是不实在的，说它是绿的就否认了它是红的一样。"存在"一词在日常用法或者至少我本人的习惯用法上较之于"实在的"这一术语含义要狭窄些。"存在的"的意念包含着过去、现在和未来。孔子虽然现在已经不存在了，但是却可以说他是实在的。未来的世界状态现在虽然还不存在，但是它却也可以是相当实在的。因此，说质料是存在的，就是在很多方面限制了它。而且如果你所谓的存在是指在目前占有头在的空间的话，那么说质料存在就是说质料局限于一定的空间和一定的时间。质料是不能有这样的限制的。

在没有进一步运用更为具体的论证来说明之前，我们可以再一次笼统地说，没有什么形容词可以用来描述质料，如果这样来描述是要将某种性质加给质料的话。但是你可能会说，质料一定是同质的，因为如果任何一个人理解了质料，那么他必定会承认这张椅子和那个苹果的质料是绝对相同的，尽管这两个客体是不一样的。这样说并没有错！假如所谓同质不是指质料的性质上的属性。因为从消极方面说，如果质料在性质上是同质的，那么它就不能够进入像这张椅子或那个苹果这样不同的事物中去。从积极方面说，由于它确实进入了这样不同的事物之中，那么它在性质上肯定不是同质的。它只有在没有任何特性这样的意义上，而不是在全部具有相同特性的意义上，才可能是同质的。显然，如果它有任何特性，那么它就能够用那样的特性来表达。借用目前战争中经常运用的一个词"冻结"，那么我们就可以说它被"冻结"在那一共相之中。在一个共相中"冻结"，它就不能成为其他任何别的可能的一部分，它的潜在性、能动性和实质性就不是纯粹的。核心是，质料必须是在其潜在性、能动性和实质性方面绝对自由的，这样它才能成为这个现实世界多种多样事物的真正的实在性和无限可能世界的事物无限丰富性的真正的实在性。

这一陈述的第二个部分在某些方面更为重要。质料不仅不具有任何特性，它在数量方面也是恒常的。我意识到，这两个术语只有

only if certain operations were exhibited, and where Stuff is concerned, no such operations can apply. However, we have to borrow such terms to convey what is in our minds and what is intended to convey is that "the total amount" (if we could use the term at all) of Stuff is neither ever increased nor ever decreased. There is no old or new Stuff, no old Stuff dying or dead, nor new Stuff being born or struggling to be born. The idea or something similar to it is a very old one; we have the ancient intuition and perhaps more or less lumpy idea that nothing cannot become something nor can anything become nothing. From a certain point of view, this is a very important insight, but from the point of view of certain articulateness required of ideas, it is somewhat lumpy, though immensely rich. It is not easy to ascertain the sphere where it is supposed to hold. Subsequent developments of the idea made it more articulate in certain spheres, for instance, the indestructibility of matter-energy in physics. What I am concerned with here now is rather that the insight applies to Stuff. Stuff cannot increase for any increment must be new and dated and then all the subsequent implications cannot be denied of Stuff, and Stuff would then become expressible. The same argument applies to any decrease. If Stuff could be increased but not decreased, then there may be a time when there wasn't any Stuff, and if it could be decreased but not increased, then there may be a time when there shall not be any Stuff. If increase and decrease maintain an equivalent ratio, there must be portions that are new and portions that are old, and although the quantity is constant, where does the new come from and what has become of the old are unanswerable questions. Obviously old Stuff cannot become new Stuff, for in the absence of any quality, it cannot be said to change and neither new nor old can be applied to it. If the new Stuff comes from anything that isn't Stuff, then new Stuff is created out of nothing, and if old Stuff disappears into something that isn't Stuff, then it is destroyed into nothing. In a word, if we speak of any increase or decrease of Stuff, we are confronted with the problem that nothing can become something and something can become nothing. It is an insight to the contrary that leads us to see the eternity of Stuff.

While we must not confuse either the phenomenal world of our common sense, or the objective world of the sciences with the ever

在某种具体的运用中才具有清楚的意义。当涉及质料时，这样具体的运用是不可能的。然而，我们必须借用这样的术语来传达我们的想法，这一想法就是"全部的"（如果我们可以运用这一术语的话）质料既不曾增加，也不会减少。质料既没有旧的也没有新的；没有旧的质料正在消失或死去，也没有新的质料产生或挣扎着形成。这个想法或类似想法是非常古老的：我们自古直觉认为（或许多少有些笨拙）无不能生成有；同样，有也不会变成无。从某些角度来看，这是一种非常重要的思想。但是，从意念所需的清晰角度来看，这样的看法虽然含义丰富，然而却显得有些笨拙。很难确定这种看法的适用范围。这一看法后来的发展使它在某些方面表达得更清晰，例如物理学中的物质能量不可灭性。在这里我现在所关心的问题是，这样的思想适用于质料。质料不能够增长，因为任何增长必有新旧，那么后续的结果也必会有质料，质料那时就是可表达的了。这样的论证也同样适用于质料减少的说法。如果质料可以增长而不能减少，那么就会有这样一个时间，那时候不曾有任何质料。如果质料可以减少而不能增长，那么就会有这样一个时间，那时候不会有任何质料。如果质料的增长和减少保持同样的比例，那么有的部分就是新的，有的部分就是旧的。虽然质料的数量是一个常数，但新的质料从何而来、旧的质料又去向何处都是不可回答的问题。显然，旧的质料是不可能变成新的质料的，因为既然没有任何的特性，就不能说质料是变化的，也不能说新的或旧的。如果新的质料来自不是质料的其他任何事物，那么新质料就是无中生有。如果旧质料消失进入任何不是质料的其他事物，那么它也就是从有变成了无。总而言之，如果我们说质料可增长或可减少，我们就会遭遇到这样的难题，即无可变成有，有也同样可变成无。这是和质料恒常不变截然相反的一个看法。

在我们注意不把我们常识的现象世界或科学的客观世界与真正的、

pervading and ever underlying Stuff, we may gain an insight into the
latter from our ideas concerning the former. Take the principle of the
indestructibility of matter-energy. This is essentially a development from
the old idea that nothing cannot become something and something
cannot become nothing. In the world of common sense, this is probably
more easily intelligible. Nothing can be created or destroyed, if we think
in terms of "material" or "substance" or "matter." The watchmaker may
be said to have created a watch, the hen may be said to have created
an egg or a chick, but in both cases out of material they do not create.
We do have the emergence of patterns some of which we know to be
obeying laws while others either do not obey laws or we do not know
them to be doing so; but in either case the basic material neither emerges
nor ceases to be. Whether the principle could be proved or verified or
met need not concern us here, it certainly succeeds in describing the
natural phenomena or our experience of them. The addition of energy
to matter in the more recent version of this principle in the sphere of
natural sciences merely carries the analysis one step further by making
matter and energy mutually transformable, the uncreatability and
indestructibility of matter-energy is maintained. It is perfectly possible to
discover in future something else the constancy of which may be used as
the criterion for the transformations of matter into energy or vice versa. If
so, the indestructibility of that thing will still be maintained, for otherwise
equations of transformations would be ultimately meaningless.

When we talk of matter-energy or a third or a fourth entity in future,
we are not talking of Stuff, though that which permeates and underlies
it remains Stuff. In the objective world of the physical sciences, matter-
energy is probably taken to be the lowest common denominator of all
existents and its constancy might be utilized as the unmentioned but
none the less assumed middle term in the symmetrical and transitive
equations of transformations of any forms of existence. The principle
of indestructibility may have this function and in the sphere of science

it may be taken to be merely a methodologized principle, that is to say, that it may be justified by this function alone and not necessarily by any correspondence with reality. I do not know whether this is the case, but even if it were, it does not prevent us from seeing that this

无所不在的质料混同起来的时候，我们就有可能从我们关于前者的思想中得到关于后者的一些看法。我们可以物质能量不灭定律为例。这一定律本质上就是从传统的无不能变有、有也不能变无的看法发展而来的。从常识的世界着眼，这一看法可能是很容易明白的。我们一想到"材料"或"实体"或"物质"，我们就知道任何事物都既不能被创造也不能被毁灭。我们可能会说手表匠创造了手表，母鸡创造了鸡蛋或小鸡。但这两个事例都是从某种材料而来，并不是凭空创造。我们确实知道，某些创生模式是遵循一定的规律的，而另一些并不遵循规律或至少是我们不知道它们遵循一定的规律。但是，不管遵循还是不遵循规律，作为基本的材料既无所谓创生也没有什么停止存在。虽然这一原则是否能得到证明或证实或符合不是我们在这里所关心的问题，但是它却成功地描述了自然现象或我们关于它们的经验。在自然科学领域内，这一原则的最新版本是在原有物质的基础上把能量加了进去，这就使分析更进一步，物质与能量可以相互转化了，并确定了物质能量既具有非创造性也具有不可毁灭性。非常有可能，在将来我们可能发现其他事物的恒久不变性可能被利用来作为物质变成能量或能量变成物质的标准。如果是这样的话，那么那个事物的不可毁灭性仍然是确定的，因为如果不是这样的话，转化的方程式最终将没有任何意义。

当我们谈论物质能量或将来所谓的第三或第四实体时，我们谈的不是质料，虽然渗透其中并真正在它们后面的仍然是质料。在物理科学的客观世界中，物质能量可能被认为是所有存在着的事物的最小公分母，它的恒久不变性可以被用作为任何一种存在形式的对称或传递的转化方程式的中项，这种中项我们没有提及但可以假定存在。不可毁灭性的原则可能有这样的功能，在科学领域内它可以被看作是一种方法论的原则。这就是说，它可以仅仅由这一功能得到证实，而没有必要由它和外在实在的符合而得到证实。我本人并不知道事实是否就是如此的。但假如是这样的话，它也不妨碍我们

principle is more than a mere methodologized principle, that it is based on the insight that nothing cannot become something and something cannot become nothing. We are bound to have this insight if we were intellectually projected into the realm of Stuff. I am convinced that there is Stuff, and I claim that the conviction is based on experience and arrived at through intellectual projection. There can be no question of verification or proof, for the former is confined to particulars while the latter is limited to universals, and Stuff is neither a particular nor a universal. If one grasps it, the above statements exhibit its flavor and enable him to grasp it more firmly than before; but if one doesn't grasp it, these statements do not help him in the least. They are neither propositions in the sense of tautologies. They are metaphysical statements neither proved nor disproved by history and science, nor deducible from logic and mathematics; they are negatively justified by the conviction that without them there is a desideratum in experience for which we are sensually and intellectually incapable of accounting. I am aware that this doctrine of Stuff is an old one and therefore no excitement could be attached to it, but I for one do not think that it has ever been discredited since arguments against it are in my mind irrelevant.

看到，这一原则不仅仅只是方法论的原则，它是以无不能变成有、有不能变成无的思想为其基础的。如果我们理性地推测质料的王国的话，我们会毫无疑问地怀有这样的思想。我确信有质料，并且断言，这样的信念是建立在经验基础之上的，且通过理性推测的途径而得到的。在此无须证实或证明，因为证实局限于殊相的领域之中，而证明则被限制在共相领域之中。质料则既不是殊相，也不是共相。如果某人理解了它，那么上述的陈述将显示它的特点并将引导他比以前更为牢靠地理解它；但是，如果一个人没有理解它，那么这些陈述就丝毫也帮不了他。它们在重言式的意义上不是命题。它们是形而上学的命题，既不能由历史和科学来证实或证伪，也不能从逻辑和数学演绎出来；它们只能由下面这样的思想得到证否，这一思想认为如果没有这些陈述，那么我们急需感常和理性方面不可描述的经验。我意识到关于质料的这些说教并不是新的，因此我们当然对此不必大惊小怪。但是就我而言，我也并不因此认为它被怀疑过，因为所有否认它的论据在我看来都是不相关的。

TAO²

I

Let us start with abstraction. Abstraction is the segregation in thought of aspects from synthetic and concrete wholes, it is the separate distinction of inseparable or unseparated distinguishables. In 1943 you cannot separate the President of the United States from the husband of Ms. Roosevelt, that is to say, you cannot deposit one of them in Hyde Park and leave the other in Washington. The gentleman mentioned has both these aspects, and while they are not separate and for the time being inseparable, they are yet distinguishables which could be separately distinguished. Abstraction from the concrete never cuts the concrete individual up into numerous concrete individuals—it cannot, and is never intended to; its whole purpose is to enable us to think and speak of the concrete. There is no other way of dealing with concrete individual things. If you shake Mr. Roosevelt's hand it is his hand that your hand is shaking, and if you embrace him, it is his body that your arms embrace. You cannot come into contact with him in any concrete synthetic and all-comprehensive sort of way. It is through abstraction that we are able to catch him at all in thought. The importance of abstraction is easily overlooked simply because it is done almost every minute in our lives. The moment we speak or think we are abstracting. The importance of synthesis is also easily overlooked because we are also doing it every day, but the argument in favor of it must be done without crying against abstraction, since synthesis is obviously a synthesis of the abstract.

Abstraction is done in thinking and that which is abstracted is in ideas or concepts. I am using the term "idea" exclusively in the sense of abstract ideas. For convenience I shall confine myself to veridical ideas or concepts, excluding impossible or contradictory ideas. I shall also take concepts to be entities or items which occur in thought as units or simples rather than complexes. This does not mean that such an entity or item is itself simple apart from its occurrence. "Squareness" may enter into our thought as a unit in one moment or context and disintegrates in the next moment or in a different context into propositions or associated concepts such as parallelograms, right angles, each side being equal to

道

一

让我们从抽象开始我们的讨论。抽象是在思想中把某些方面从其综合的和具体的整体分离出来。它是把不可分离的东西或可分离而未曾分离的东西区别开来。在 1943 年，你不可能把美国总统和罗斯福夫人的丈夫这两者区别开来。这就是说，你不可能把其中的一个放置在海德公园，而把另一个放在华盛顿。我们现在所提到的这位绅士同时具有这两个方面。这两方面虽没有分开且暂时不可分离，它们却是可分离的东西。这就是说，它们可以分别地加以辨认。由具体而来的抽象从未把具体的个体分割成无数具体的个体。它不能这样做，人们也从未打算这样做。它的全部目的只在于引导我们去思考和去说出具体的东西。除抽象之外，并没有另外的方式去处理具体的个体事物。如果你与罗斯福先生握手，你所握的是他的手；如果你和他拥抱，你所拥抱的是他的身体。你不可能通过具体的合成和所有的综合等方式接触到他。只有通过抽象的方式，我们才有可能在思想上把握住他。抽象的重要性很容易为人们所忽视，这只是因为在我们的日常生活中抽象几乎是在每一分钟中都发生的事。我们说话或我们思想的时候，我们就是在进行着抽象的工作。由于在我们的日常生活中综合也是经常发生的，其重要性也容易为人们所忽视。但是支持这个论点就不能反对抽象的作用，因为综合显然就是对抽象的综合。

抽象是在思想中进行的，被抽象的事物存在于意念或概念之中。我在此所运用的"意念"是严格的抽象意义上的意念。而且为了方便，我也只限于那些真实的意念或概念，排除那些不可能的或矛盾的意念。我也将把概念看作是实体或条目，它们在思想中是基本的单位或单一的成分而不是复合体。这并不是说，这样的实体或条目本身是可以脱离它的发生环境而成为单一的成分的。"方正度"在某一时刻或语境进入我们思想的时候是一单位，而在下一个时刻或不同的语境中却分解成了命题或相互联系的概念，如平行四边形、直角、每一条边都等同于另一条边等。

every other, etc. There is no ultimate simple or ultimate complex in our items of thought. But items do occur in thought as simples or units and those we call concepts provided they are not contradictory. Bearing the distinction between content and object in mind, we see that concepts are the contents in thought, not its objects. When one thinks about a square, one does have the concept square in thought, but one is not thinking of the concept "square," but of squareness, that is to say, of the object. Concepts are idea versions of what we have hitherto called universals and what we shall later introduce as possibilities.

While based on experience, concepts need not be directly based. We can abstract from the concrete and then proceed to abstract from the abstract; hence we not only have structures of concepts but also hierarchies of concepts. There is no limitation to conception except logic, that is to say that concepts cannot be contradictory. A contradictory idea that occurs as a simple item in thought is no concept at all. Experience and fact only limit the use of concepts, not their being. Concepts unsubstantiated by experience or facts can occur in thought; ordinarily they don't. We can think of a "fire-eating dragon" or "unicorn," but unless for the purpose of examples in philosophy, we generally do not think of them, that is, they do not generally occur in thought. Concepts are then neither contradictory nor true or false. If an idea is contradictory it isn't veridical, and though it may enter into our thought as a simple item or unit, it is not a concept. A concept cannot be said to be true, because since it occurs as a simple, we do not assert anything by it, and the lack of an object to the content or of a universal corresponding to the concept merely renders it definitive of a null class—it doesn't make the concept false. With regard to concepts, there is only our adoption or our disuse and in this we are influenced by experience and facts. Thus the idea "square circle" is no concept, while the concept "witch" though neither false nor true is hardly ever used in the present day.

Concepts are the idea versions (versions in terms of ideas) of universals as well as possibilities. Each universal is an aspect shared by a class of objects, for example humanity which is shared by a class of bipeds, or horseness which is shared by a class of quadpeds. I am using the term "universal" in the positive sense, thus while existence is a universal, non-existence

在我们的思想的条目中，不存在着终极性的单一成分或终极性的复合体。但是在思想中出现的条目确实是以单一成分或单位的形式出现的；只要它们不矛盾，我们就将它们称为概念。如果记住了内容和客体之间的区别，那么我们就明白了概念就是存在于思想中的内容，而不是客体。当一个人思考正方形的时候，他就在思想中有着正方形这一概念，但是他不是思考"正方形"这一概念，而是"方正度"的概念。这就是说，他所想到的是客体的概念。概念是我们迄今称为共相而在后面将称为可能的观念形式。

概念是以经验为基础的，但是概念不必直接有其根基。我们能够从具体中抽象地得到概念，进而从抽象到抽象的方式得到概念。因此我们不仅仅有概念的结构，而且也有概念的等级。除了逻辑之外，概念没有限制。这就是说，概念是不能自相矛盾的。在思想中作为单一成分所出现的矛盾的意念根本就不是概念。经验和事实仅仅限制了概念的运用，而不是它们的存在。没有经验或事实内容的概念可以在思想中出现，但在实际上并不如此。我们能够想到"食火龙"或"独角兽"，但是除非为了哲学上举例的目的，我们一般不会想到它们，就是说它们一般不会出现在思想中。因此概念既不是矛盾的，也不是真的，也不是假的。如果一个意念是矛盾的，那么它就不是真实的。虽然这样的意念可能会进入我们的思想成为一个单一条目或单位，但它不是概念。我们不能说一概念是真的，因为它是单一的成分，我们并没有通过它断言任何事情。由于没有与内容相对的客体或与概念相符合的共相，所以它只是限定了一个空类——像这样的概念也不能说它是假的。谈到概念，只能说我们采用或弃用，在这一点上，我们受了经验和事实的影响。因此，"方的圆"这一意念根本不是概念；"女巫"这一概念既不是假的也不是真的，如今我们几乎不怎么使用。

概念是共相和可能的观念形式（形式是观念意义上的）。每一共相都是一类客体所共享的一个方面。比如，人性是两足动物中的一类所共享的，马性是四足动物中的一类所共享的。说"共相"这一术语时我采用的是肯定形式，因而可以说存在是一共相，而非存在则

is not one but an infinity of universals or possibilities. This means that a universal always indicates a class of objects, and a null class is not covered by any one universal or that the very notion of any one universal involves a logical conjure of it with the universal "real." Thus if the world has never had a dragon, "dragonness" is not a universal. Our concepts are neither limited to universals nor do they exhaust all the universals. Some of our concepts are definitive of certain null classes; they are the concepts, for which there are no corresponding universals. There are also universals which we have never conceived, idealistic arguments to the contrary notwithstanding. Thus the realm of concepts reflects the past of the realm of universals. These realms merely overlap—they do not coincide and where concepts reflect universals, they are the idea versions of universals.

A concept that isn't a version of a universal expresses a possibility. The term "possibility" excludes anything contradictory; everything else is possibility. That which is unimaginable, a fantastic to the extremes in so far as it is not contradictory is a possibility. A possibility if thought of as an object of thought, not a content, hence although it may be expressed by a concept which is a content of thought, it is not a concept, since it is an object of thought. Just as there are universals which are not concerned, there are also possibilities for which there are no concepts. Although possibilities may not be conceived they are conceivable, the realm of conceivability and the realm of possibilities are coextensive for the limit to both is contradictoriness. By introducing the term "possibility" we are able to define a universal as a realized possibility. We shall for the moment ignore the term "realization" which will be defined later on. A universal is real whereas a possibility qua possibility isn't. The statements in the previous paragraphs to the effect that a universal is an aspect shared by a class of objects (or events) or that the very notion of our one universal involves always a logical conjunction of it with the universal "real" are meant to show the reality of universals. The universal "squareness" is real, because there are actually existing squares or in other words, there are square objects. Most of us in the level of the world of common sense would admit the reality of certain objects or events; it is they that give us the unquestioned sense of reality. That sense of reality should also be accorded to the possibilities realized through those objects and events.

不是一共相，而是共相或者可能的无穷。这就是说，一共相总是显示一类客体，而空类并不包含于任何的共相之中，或任何一共相的观念都包含着共相"真实"的逻辑构造。因此，如果这个世界从未有过一条龙，那么"龙性"就不是共相。我们的概念并不受到共相的限制，它们也没有穷尽所有的共相。我们的有些概念限定了某些空类：它们是概念，但没有与之相符合的共相。还有那些我们没有想到过的共相，尽管这反过来成了唯心主义的论据。因此概念的世界反映着共相世界的过去。这两个世界是交叉的，并不是完全一致的。当概念反映着共相，它们就是共相的观念形式。

不是共相的概念表达的是一种可能。"可能"这一术语排除了一切矛盾的东西；其他的一切都是可能。那些不可想象的东西，即使是极端荒谬的，但只要它不是矛盾的，就是一种可能。一种可能如果被认为是思想的对象，而不是内容，那么虽然它可以由作为思想内容的概念来表达，但它不是概念，因为它是思想的对象。正如有未被认识到的共相，也有并无对应概念的可能。虽然可能也许没有被想象到，但它们是可以想象的。可想象的世界和可能世界是两个同延的世界，因为这两个世界的界限都是矛盾性。通过引进"可能"这一术语，我们就可以把共相定义为现实了的可能。我们现在暂且不考虑术语"现实"，而在后面给出它的定义。共相是实在的，而作为可能的可能却不是。前面几段陈述的大意是说，共相是一类客体（事件）所共享的一个方面或我们的共相的观念总是包含着其与"实在"的共相的逻辑结合。这些陈述的目的是要表明共相的现实。"方正度"的共相是实在的，因为实际上存在着方形，或换句话说，存在着方形的客体。我们中的绝大部分人是停留在常识的层次上的，所以我们会承认某些客体或事件的实在性，正是这些客体或事件给了我们这一毫无疑问的实在感。那种实在感也应该给予通过那些客体和事件而现实的可能。

But as we have pointed out in our first chapter, particular things or objects present difficulties upon analysis. There is something that changes and yet endures, something that somehow persists by piercing through combinations of universals and sets of particulars. Since universals cannot change and particulars cannot endure, that which changes and endures is neither universals or particulars alone nor both together. Both are aspects; it is Stuff that gives them unity and individuality. A possibility qua possibility is not real, but unless it is contradictory (in which case it is not a possibility at all) it may be real, that is to say it may be realized. What is known as the realization of possibility is merely the entrance of Stuff into that possibility. A universal is merely a Stuffed possibility. We shall not introduce here the principle of concretion and individuation. We shall assume that realization always involves concretion and individuation. Reality that is concretized and individualized is housed in sets of particulars exampling combinations of universals. What is taken to be real in common sense is on our basis simply Stuffed possibilities or universals covering concrete individuals through concretion and individuation. The difference between a universal and possibility is that the former is realized while the latter needn't be. A universal is of course also a possibility since it is a realized possibility.

We started with abstraction and concepts. Concepts are the contents of our thought which however is not limited to its contents. When we think of squareness we are not thinking of the concept "square," not of "squareness" which is shared by all the squares. The objects of our thought corresponding to our concepts are possibilities either realized or unrealized. Obviously our thoughts are not limited to realized possibilities or universals. We sometimes think positively of nothing or of zero or of infinity, if we know that these are mere possibilities. The fact it is through thinking of bare possibilities that we can think of all, and the neglect over zero in the traditional logic has rendered it inadequate as a thinking apparatus. On the other hand, not all the universals have been conceived, unless we hold the idealistic argument to the contrary. We have to grant that at least there are phenomena in the microscopic world that one has yet unheard of. The same applies to possibilities. Thus while the realm of concepts is not a part of the realm of universals or realized

　　但正如我们在第一章中已经指出的那样，特殊事物或特殊客体给分析带来了不少困难。有些事物是变化的，却也有持续性；有些事物透过共相及殊相的结合而持续存在。由于共相不能发生变化，而殊相不能持续，那些发生变化并且持续存在的东西既不是单独的共相或单独的殊相，也不是共相和殊相的结合。共相和殊相是这样的东西的某些方面，是质料给了它们统一性和个体性。作为可能的可能是缺乏实在性的，但是除非它是矛盾的（那样的话它根本就不是一个可能）它才可能是实在的，也就是说它才可以现实。此处所理解的可能的现实仅仅是指质料进入可能之中。一共相也只不过是有质料在其中的可能。我们不打算在此介绍具体化原则和个体化原则，我们只是假定现实总是包含着具体化和个体化的。具体化和个体化的现实寓存于很多殊相的集合，这些殊相可作为共相组合的范例。常识所认为的实在于我们而言仅仅是质料在其中的可能或通过具体化和个体化涵盖具体的个体的共相。共相和可能之间的区别在于，共相是现实了的，而可能却不必。共相当然也是可能，因为它是现实了的可能。

　　我们是从抽象和概念开始讨论的。概念是我们思想的内容，当然并不仅仅局限于它的内容。当我们思考方正度的时候，我们并不是在思考"方形"这一概念，也不是在思考由所有的方形东西共有的"方正度"这一概念。与我们的概念相对应的我们的思想对象或者是已经现实的可能，或者是还未现实的可能。显然，我们的思想并不局限于已经现实的可能或共相。我们有时会积极地想到空无或零或无限，如果我们知道它们仅仅是可能。我们能够思考只是通过思考极小可能这一事实，以及传统逻辑对零的忽略，使它变成一个很不充分的思想工具。在另一方面，并不是所有的共相都在我们的思想范围之内，除非我们抱着相反的唯心主义的观点。我们必须承认至少在微观世界里存在着至今还未曾听过的现象。这也同样适用于可能。因此，虽然概念世界不是共相世界的一部分或现实了的可能，但是任何被想象到的

possibilities, anything that is conceived and conceivable is a possibility. The number of possibilities is bound to be infinite, since all numbers are themselves possibilities. Compared to the number of possibilities, the number of universals is very small indeed. This means that in terms of the number of possibilities, the actual is but a small fraction of the possible, or in terms of the possible worlds in the unfoldment of the universe, our present world is but a small item in the reality and a short stage in the process.

It is perhaps easier for us to be intimate with our concepts since they are the contents of our thought. If we examine our concepts we find a certain interrelatedness that spreads into structures and ascends into hierarchies. Logic alone enables us to see that some concepts imply or are equivalent to others, while experience and science supply us with other relations. Concepts can be woven into patterns. While we do not have a huge single pattern of all our concepts, we do have little patterns along various lines of inquiry in which we happen to have interests. These patterns are partly deductive and partly inductive, and since in them the connecting links are partly true propositions, they indicate a corresponding pattern of the universals and bare possibilities. A branch of knowledge is a pattern of concepts and since it is a branch of knowledge it is also indicative of a pattern of universals and bare possibilities. At the moment we merely assert that they are patterns of universals and bare possibilities; we do not care to discuss as to what they are. In epistemology we are interested in patterns of concepts imposed by and obtained from our experience of the pattern of universals and bare possibilities, but in logic and mathematics we are only interested in that minimum of pattern that is inescapable either from the point of view of concepts or from the point of view of universals or bare possibilities. One of these minimum patterns is what we call Form.

II

Form is a possibility formed by the exhaustive disjunction of all

possibilities. The term or phrase "all possibilities" is probably open to
the kind of objections for which the theory of types is devised. Whether
the thing is adequate or not we need not concern ourselves with in
the present connection, but in view of the difficulties we intend to use

或者可以想象的都是可能。由于所有的数量本身就是可能，因此可能的数量必然是无限的。与可能的数量相比，共相的数量确实非常小。这就是说，从可能的数量角度来看问题，现实的东西只不过是可能的东西的一小部分。或者就宇宙的展现可能的世界来说，我们当前的世界只不过是实在的微不足道的一部分，是这个无限过程中的一个不长的阶段。

由于概念是我们思想的内容，所以我们可能很容易就与我们的概念处在一种非常密切的关系之中。如果审查我们的概念，那么我们就会发现某种内在的关系蔓延至不同结构、上升至不同层次之间。逻辑本身就能引导我们看到，某些概念蕴涵着其他的概念或与其他概念是等同的，而经验和科学却向我们提供了另一些关系。概念能够被编织成图案。虽然我们可能没有包含所有概念的巨大单一的图案，但是我们却确实具有小的概念图案，这些图案与我们碰巧感兴趣的许多探寻方式相似。这些图案部分是演绎的，部分是归纳的。由于在图案中相联系的环节部分是真命题，它们也就显示出共相和极小可能的相应图案。知识的一个分支就是一个概念图案。由于它是知识分支，所以它也表示共相和极小的可能的一个图案。在此我们仅仅是说它们是共相和极小可能的图案，我们并不在意去讨论它们是什么。在认识论中，我们的兴趣是在概念的图案，这样的概念图案是我们关于共相和极小可能的图案的经验加诸并获得的。但是在逻辑和数学中，我们的兴趣只在于最基本的图案。无论是从概念的角度来看，还是从共相或极小可能的角度来看，这样基本的图案都是不可逃避的。式就是这样最基本的图案中的一个。

二

式就是这样的可能，即把所有的可能按照析取的方式排列起来。"所有的可能"这一术语可能会招致这样的反对意见，类型论就是为了应付这一反对意见而产生的。在目前这一部分，我们没有必要考虑事物是充分的还是不充分的。从困难的角度看，我们打算

the term "all possibilities" to cover not merely the totality, but also the different hierarchies, orders or types of possibilities. The disjunction being the familiar logical disjunction renders our Form thus defined to be absolutely fluid, that is to say, Form is absolutely formless. None of the constituent possibilities is fluid no matter how broad or easy of realization it may be. Perhaps we may make use of the terms "connotation" and "denotation" and say that no matter how wide the denotation or how small the connotation of a concept may be, other than the concept Form, the possibility corresponding to the concept is never quite fluid or formless. Any constituent possibility, that is, any possibility other than Form must have at least a modicum of form, hence also a modicum of rigidity. This is equivalent to saying that it has a boundary line dividing what belongs to it from what doesn't, or in terms of analogy with space, what is inside from what is outside; and anything that does not satisfy the definition of the concept is ipso facto also outside the corresponding possibility. Any constituent possibility may admit or else reject. Even such a wide possibility as existence both admits and rejects: it admits the existents and rejects the non-existents. Every constituent possibility can be dichotomized into the positive and negative, but not Form. There is no boundary line to Form that divides an inside from an outside for the simple reason that there isn't any outside. Everything must be inside, and to say that anything is inside is in the context of our everyday life quite meaningless. It is however not meaningless in terms of ontology and metaphysics.

It is the absolute fluidity of Form that makes it inescapable. In one of the Chinese novels we have a mythical monkey who can cover thousands of miles at a single somersault. He could easily jump out of the country, but he couldn't jump out of the Buddha's palm. The inescapability of the palm is like that of Form. It simply is, and is so absolutely fluid that it is also inescapable. We have already spoken of the entrance of Stuff into possibilities, we have defined the realization of a possibility as the entrance of Stuff into that possibility, and we have defined a universal as a realized possibility. Form is inescapable so far as Stuff is concerned. Some of you may see at a glance the return of an ancient doctrine. The Greeks and the Europeans have been talking about form and matter and the Chinese have been talking about *Li* and *Chi*, and here we are again

运用"所有的可能"这一术语不仅仅是指完全性，而且也是指可能的不同的层次、秩序或类型。所谓的析取就是熟悉的逻辑上的析取，这就使我们把式规定为绝对流动的。这就是说，式是绝对的无形式的。式中的任何一个可能不能是流动的，不管它的现实是多么地宽广或容易。或许我们可以运用像"内涵"和"外延"这样的术语来讨论问题。不管一概念的外延有多广，内涵有多小，除去式这一概念，与概念相应的可能从来不是流动的或无形式的。除式之外的任何可能必须至少有一点形式，因此也必须有一点刚性。这等于说，它有一定的界限，清楚地划定什么是属于它的，什么是不属于它的。或者运用与空间类比的语言说，什么在它的范围之内，什么在它的范围之外。任何东西只要不符合这一概念的定义，就事实而言，它也就在这相应的可能之外。式中的任何可能可以接受或拒斥。即便是像存在这样广泛的可能也是既接受又拒斥的。它接受存在，而拒斥非存在。式中的任何一可能都可以分成肯定的和否定的，但是式却不能这样划分。对于式而言，没有这样的界限来确定什么在它的范围之内，什么在它的范围之外。原因很简单，式是无外的。每一事物必须在式之内。说任何事物都是在内的在我们日常生活的语境中是毫无意义的。但是从本体论和形而上学的立场而言，我们就不能说它是没有意义的了。

式的绝对的可流动性使得它是不可逃避的。在中国的一部小说中，我们虚构的一只猴子一个筋斗可以翻十万八千里。他可以很容易地翻出一个国家去，但是他怎么样也翻不出如来佛的手掌。如来佛手掌的不可逃避性正如同式的不可逃避性。式就是这样，是绝对流动的，所以它才可能是不可逃避的。我们已经谈到质料进入可能的话题，我们把可能的现实定义为质料进入可能，而且我们还把共相定义为现实了的可能。就质料而言，式是不可逃避的。某些人可能会一眼看出这是旧说新传，并没有新意。因为古希腊人和欧洲人一直在谈论形和质，中国人也一直在谈论"理"和"气"，现在

with Form and Stuff. It is perfectly true that we are talking essentially of the same thing, but for better or worse we are talking about it differently and it is partly at any rate the modern apparatus for thinking that is responsible for the difference. We do not think that the ancient doctrine has been disproved or useless, neither of which could be attributed to a doctrine merely on the ground that it is ancient. As far as we can see, it is the simplest doctrine that links logic with ontology and metaphysics. Logic is essentially the exhibition of Form, metaphysics the contemplation of Stuff and ontology the Study of Tao. This however is a digression which we must not pursue in these paragraphs. Suffice it to say that Form is inescapable from the point of view of Stuff and what is probably more important the inescapability of Form imposes no limitations whatsoever on the potentiality and activity of Stuff.

We have one metaphysical principle and two metalogical principles or two versions of one ontological principle. The one metaphysical principle says that Stuff enters into and leaves off from possibilities. This principle is metaphysical because it says directly about Stuff through our contemplation of it, and it is important, because it is not only the principle of the whole process and reality, but also that of any finite passage of time or any change that is experienced or unexperienced. In the preceding chapter we have said that any statement concerning Stuff is neither a proposition in the usual sense, nor a pseudo-proposition in the sense of tautologies. It is incapable of formal proof or experiential verification. The former belongs to the realm of the structural content of thought and in the last analysis assumes Form, while the latter belongs to the realm of objects and events in the unfoldment of process and reality which in turn assumes the very principle in question. But while it cannot be proved or verified and therefore cannot be said to be true in the ordinary sense, it yet holds metaphysically and ontologically. It holds metaphysically because if one grasps Stuff at all, one can easily see that its pure potentiality, activity, substantiality, and its total negation of qualities must have its medium of function in terms of its entrance into and departure from possibilities. It holds ontologically, because once Stuff is grasped, the principle mentioned describes any form of reality or process from the microscopic to macroscopic world. If we do not grasp

我们又在谈论式和质料。一点不错，我们讨论的基本是同样的东西，但是不管是好是坏，我们毕竟是从不同角度来讨论式和质料的。无论如何，一定程度上，是现代性的思考工具导致了这种不同。我们并不认为古代的思想已经被证伪是无用的，我们不能仅仅因为某种想法是古代的，就说它不正确或无用。就我们所能看到的而言，是最简单的思想将逻辑与本体论和形而上学联系起来。逻辑本质上是式的表现，形而上学本质上是对质料的沉思，本体论本质上是对道的研究。然而，在此谈论这样的话题有点离题。从质料的观点，只要说式是不可逃避的这样一点就足够了。而更为重要的一点可能是，式的不可避免性并没有给质料的潜在性和能动性带来任何的限制。

我们有一个形而上学的原则、两个元逻辑学的原则或一个本体论原则的两种形式。一个形而上学的原则是说，质料进出于可能。这一原则所以是形而上学的原则是因为它是通过我们对质料的沉思而直接谈到它的。这一原则是重要的，因为它不仅是整个过程和实在的原则，而且也是有限的时间阶段或曾经经验或未曾经验的变化的原则。在前面一章中，我们已经谈到，关于质料的任何陈述既不是通常意义上的命题，也不是重言式意义上的伪命题。它不可能得到形式的证明或经验的证实。形式证明是属于思想的结构内容的世界，归根结底，它假定了式。而经验证实是属于过程和实在的展开过程中的客体和事件的世界，反过来它也假定了我们正在谈论的原则。虽然它不能得到证明或证实，因此从常识的方面我们不能说它是真的，但是从形而上学和本体论的角度它却是站得住脚的。形而上学上它能站得住脚，因为如果我们理解了质料，那么我们就能够很容易地看到，就其进出于可能而言，它的纯粹的潜在性、能动性、实在性和它对特性的完全否定必须有起作用的中介。本体论上它能站得住脚，因为一旦质料被理解了，上述的原则描述了任何实在的形式以及从微观到宏观的任何过程。如果我们不能以任何方式

Stuff in any way, the principle is indeed unintelligible, but if we succeed in grasping it, we will find it exemplified in our smoking a cigarette as well as in events of astronomical propositions. Even a slight twist of one's hand is a case of Stuff entering into and leaving off from possibilities. As one smokes Stuff is leaving the possibility "cigaretteness" and entering into the possibility "smokeness" and "ashness," etc.

The principle not merely holds, but is also of the uttermost importance. It is more important than any of the previous statements concerning Stuff, only it wasn't the time to speak of it in the last chapter. It is in fact the key principle to all assertions concerning reality. It is the basis of the principle of concretion and individuation, of time, of change, of reality and existence. It is the ultimate basis of the core of factuality. The idea is not easily conveyed, but we have to attempt to do so. Suppose you are a logician or a mathematician accustomed to structures or patterns or orders of forms, and you are convinced of their cogency or validity or truth. You may be elated over the results of your labors just as the fishnet-maker may gloat over the perfection of his fishnet which cannot fail to catch the fish, but just as the fishnet-maker does not supply the fish and the net itself contains no fish, you may realize that no matter how facts obey your structures or patterns or orders of forms, neither they nor you supply that basis for reality, that givenness or stubbornness which is the very core of all the facts that you experience. By stubbornness or givenness I do not mean unchanging stability; if ever we were face to face with the unchanging in the concrete, as sometimes we do with the comparatively unchanging in our experience, such as being comported with the same things upon returning after a long absence, we are liable to be preyed by a sense of the unreal. Reality is shot through and through with process, and actuality or existence is but an expression of changes and activities. What is meant is rather that there is something in facts or existents or realities that resists manipulations, that simply is, and that no matter how much we want to account for it through reasoning, we have to take it for granted. This basic stubbornness or givenness is what our metaphysical principle supplies. We may not be able to do justice to the importance of this principle in a few short paragraphs, but as we proceed, its importance and significance will be more keenly felt.

理解质料，那么这一原则就确实是难以理解的了。但是如果我们能够成功地理解质料，那么我们就能发现抽烟和天文学的命题都是它的实例。即便是我们的手略微动一下也是质料进入和走出可能的例子。一个人抽烟的时候，质料就离开"香烟性"这一可能，而进入了"烟性"和"灰性"的可能之中，如此等等。

这一原则不仅能够站得住脚，也非常重要。它要比先前有关质料的任何陈述都重要，只不过上一章不是谈它的时候而已。事实上，它是所有关于实在陈述的基本原则。它是具体性和个体性原则的基础，是时间原则的基础，是变化原则的基础，是实在和存在原则的基础。它是事实性的核心的根本基础。有关这一方面的思想是很不容易表述的，但是我们还是要努力这样去做。假如你是一位已经习惯于形式的结构或图案或秩序的逻辑学家或数学家，你对这一结构或图案或秩序的一致性或合法性或真理性深信不疑。你可能会对自己的工作感觉到很满意，一如渔网的织补者欣赏自己织出的完美的渔网不会漏掉任何鱼。但是正如渔网织补者自己并不供给鱼、渔网里本身并没有鱼一样，你会认识到，不管事实是怎样遵照你的形式的结构或图案或秩序，它们或你本人都没有向实在性提供基础，提供所与性或硬性。而所与性或硬性是你所经验到的所有事实的核心。所谓的所与性或硬性，我不是说它们是静止不变的。如果我们能面对具体不变的东西，如我们有时在经验中所碰到的那些相对不变的东西，像同一个东西在消失了一段时间之后又出现，我们就会很容易感觉到不真实。实在性充满了过程，现实性或存在只是变化和能动性的表现。这里的意思是说，在事实或存在或实在中的某些东西在抵制操纵，它就是这样；不管我们多么想运用我们的理性来作出说明，我们必须把它看作是当然的东西。这一基本的硬性或所与性是我们的形而上学原则所提供的。在这样简短的段落中我们不可能充分展示这一原则的重要性，但是随着讨论的进展，它的重要性及其意义就会为我们更强烈地感受到。

One of the two versions of the ontological principle is that there cannot be un-Stuffed Form. We have already exhibited the inescapability of Form and pointed out that this inescapability is in relation to Stuff. Stuff may enter into and depart from possibilities. With regard to Form Stuff doesn't enter and leave—it is always there. A constituent possibility of Form with a few exceptions may be empty in the sense of having no Stuff in it; if so it is not a realized possibility, that is, it is not a universal. This is so because any such possibility has a certain amount of rigidity, certain rules for admittance; hence if these rules are not satisfied, no admittance is allowed. Thus the possibility "squareness" requires quadrangularity, the equivalence of its four sides and four angles, etc. These rules make a partition so as to result in an inside and an outside. So long as there is an inside and an outside to a possibility, Stuff may be inside or outside of that possibility. Form is not any of its constituent possibilities. Although the concept Form is definite in meaning, the meaning is yet such that the possibility corresponding to it is absolutely devoid of rigidity, and totally leading to any rules of admittance. Compare Stuff to the mythical monkey and Form to Buddha's palm, you can see that Stuff can never get out of Form, because there is no boundary line and no outside. Form cannot but be realized, that is, it cannot but be Stuffed.

The second version is but a converse way of expressing the first: there cannot be un-Formed Stuff. These two versions express one ontological principle. The same reasoning is applicable to the second version; hence it needn't be repeated. Notice however that in regard to both these versions we say there cannot be instead of merely "there isn't." This brings in an element of far-reaching consequence which we have not dealt with before. Although Stuff is inexpressible and the statements concerning it are not ordinary propositions, Form is eminently expressible. We can exhibit its absolute lack of rigidity intellectually, and if one grasps Stuff, we can see quite easily that un-Stuffed Form or un-Formed Stuff are contradictories. They are nothing in the most comprehensive and deepest sense. It is here that logic, metaphysics and ontology are unified. The principles under discussion combine the results of the metaphysical contemplation of Stuff with the intellectual formulation of Form and guarantee the ultimate basis of reality so that what is logically contradictory is also ontological nothingness. These principles do not of course furnish us with one

　　本体论原则有两种形式，其中一个是说，无无质料的式。我们已经表明了式的不可逃避性，而且也指出这样的不可逃避性是与质料相关的。质料出入于可能。从式来看，质料并没有出入，它永远在那里。式中的某一可能，除个别情况外，可能是空的，即没有质料在其中。如果是这样的话，那么它就不是现实了的可能，这就是说，它不是一共相。之所以如此，是因为任何这样的可能都有一定程度的刚性，质料的进入有一定的规则。因此，如果这些规则得不到满足，质料就不能进入。所以，"方正度"这一可能要求四边形、四边相等和四个角相等等等。这些规则使内在的和外在的区分开来。只要对于一可能而言存在着内在的和外在的这样的情形，那么质料可以在可能之内，也可以在可能之外。式不是任何一个可能。虽然式这一概念在意义上是明确的，这意义就是与它相应的可能绝对是没有任何刚性的，完全导致了质料进入的各种规则。把质料比作孙猴子、式比作如来佛的手掌，你就能看到，质料是永远不可能在式之外的，因为式是没有边界的，是无外的。因此，式是不得不现实的，这就是说，式不可能无质料。

　　另一个则与第一个的形式表述相反：无无式的质料。这两个形式表达的是同一个本体论原则。所以，同样的理由也可以适用于第二个形式，所以我们也就无须在此重复了。然而，我们必须注意的是，对于这两者，我们说的是不可能，而不仅仅是"不存在"。这就带进了一个我们至今还未讨论到的很重要的因素。虽然质料是不可表达的，关于它的陈述也并不是通常意义上的命题，但式显然是可以表达的。从理性上，我们尽可以说，式是绝对没有刚性的。而且如果一个人理解了质料，我们就可以非常清楚地看到，无质料的式和无式的质料是相互矛盾的。在最全面和最深刻的意义上，它们是没有任何意义的。正是在这里，逻辑、形而上学和本体论是一致的。我们在此讨论的这些原则将对质料所作的形而上学沉思的结果与对式的理性的表达方式结合起来，确立了实在的终极性的基础，因此逻辑上矛盾的也就是本体论上无意义的。当然，从我们至此一直在

kind of world which from the point of view of what we have been discussing may be a mere contingency, a phenomenon, and at one stage of discussion, even an accident. But they do guarantee a world or a state of affairs, or a form of reality for which tautologies not merely cannot be false, but also must necessarily be true.

These principles differ in that the ontological principle asserts the minimum of reality, while the metaphysical principle asserts the maximum of reality. They also differ in the way in which they are urged upon us. The discussion in the preceding paragraph exhibits the way in which we are urged to accept the ontological principle. An analysis of Form renders it absolutely fluid and the statement that anything can escape it is easily seen to be contradictory. We may say that logically we are forced to accept the principle. Accepting it however does not enable us to say anything about the kind of world in which we happen to live; it merely enables us to accept the universe. The metaphysical principle is urged upon us through a contemplation of Stuff. The denial of this principle is clearly not a contradiction, that is to say, the principle is not logically forced upon us. And yet if one grasps Stuff at all, there is an inevitability about the principle that one can hardly fail to grasp. There is a sort of "mustness" in the inevitability which is different from necessity in logic. Voltaire was supposed to have once met a beggar who upon being asked why he begged replied "Sir, I must live," whereupon Voltaire was supposed to have said that he didn't see the necessity. There was no logical necessity for the beggar to live, but none the less in his circumstance he must. Confronted with that givenness, that stubbornness, we must accept the metaphysical principle.

III

The absolute fluidity of Form, the inevitability of the metaphysical and its necessity of the ontological principle lead us to a discussion of the a priori. Let us take first the problem from the point of view of Form and Stuff. Suppose we regard Stuff as a sort of raw material and Form as a kind of mould. There is always a question as to whether the mould fits in with the raw material. The absolute fluidity of Form makes it a remarkable mould indeed, a mould that has every shape and form in one way and no shape and form in the other way. There is no possibility that

讨论的角度来看，这些原则也并没有给我们提供一个仅仅是偶然的世界，一个现象的世界，甚至在讨论的某一阶段可能是一个意外的世界。但是，它们确实提供了一个世界或一种事物的状态，或一种实在的形式。对此，重言式不仅仅不可能是假的，而且必须是必然的真的。

　　这些原则是有区别的，因为本体论原则断言的是关于实在的最小值，而形而上学原则断言的则是关于实在的最大值。它们也在我们接受的方式上有区别。前一段的讨论显示了我们接受本体论原则的方式。对式的分析使它成为绝对流动的，很容易看出任何东西可以逃离式的陈述是矛盾的。我们可以说，在逻辑上，我们是被迫去接受这一原则的。然而，接受它并不会使我们谈论任何关于我们恰巧生活于其中的世界情形，它只是使我们接受这个宇宙。形而上学原则却是通过对质料的沉思为我们所接受的。否认这一形而上学原则很明显并不是个矛盾。这就是说，这一原则并不是逻辑地迫使我们去接受它。然而如果一个人理解了质料，那么这一原则有这样的一种不可避免性使我们能够成功地理解它。在这不可避免性中有一种"必须性"，它不同于逻辑上的必然性。假设伏尔泰遇到过一个乞丐并问他行乞的理由，乞丐回答："先生，我必须生存。"于是伏尔泰就说他没有看到这种必要性。乞丐并没有逻辑上的生存的必要性，然而他的情形是他必须生存。在所与性和硬性面前，我们不得不接受形而上学的原则。

三

　　式的绝对流动性、形而上学原则的不可避免性和本体论原则的必然性，所有这些使我们不得不讨论先验的问题。让我们首先从式和质料的角度来讨论问题。假如我们把质料看作是原材料，把式看作是一种模型，那就永远有一个模型是否总能和原材料相适应的问题。式的绝对流动性使它成为一个极妙的模型，它在一种方式上是有所有形状和形式的，而在另一种方式上又是没有形状和形式的。

the raw material will not fit the mould. If we start from Stuff we have the same result, Stuff being totally devoid of qualities. Let us look at any constituent possibility with a few exceptions which we needn't consider at the present. Let us take up temporalness and spatiality. We take these up because they have been regarded as a priori forms of intuition through which noumena are moulded into temporal and spacial phenomena. With Stuff as the raw material and temporalness and spatiality as the mould the story is a different one. We have no logical reason whatever to guarantee that Stuff will not refuse to be moulded by temporalness and spatiality. If Stuff refuses to be so moulded, just as at present it refuses to enter into the possibility "dragonness," we simply have neither space nor time somewhat as at present we have no dragons. Having no time or space is not contradictory, though of course it is never true. Hence it is not like saying that there are no horses either, for the latter if false merely is false, and if false it cannot be said to be never true. There are therefore two kinds of a priori forms, one of which is the form that can be escaped, the whole apparatus of logic forbids its escapability and that is what Form is. The other is the form that never was or is or shall be escaped, the givenness or stubbornness of reality makes it inescapable and that is what temporalness or spatiality or some other of the constituent possibilities of Form are. Let us call the first the rational a priori form, and the second the arational a priori form. Having the second implies having the first, but not vice versa. From the point of view of reasoning the former is more important, but from the point of view of experience the latter is more so.

We have already said that having un-Stuffed Form or un-Formed Stuff is a contradiction. But have we obtained anything as a result of granting that Form is always Stuffed? Yes, a form of reality or a state of affairs. Beyond that nothing is said. In this case the denial seems to mean so much and the affirmation so little. Here again we have to call our attention to the fact that fluidity and fruitfulness cannot be combined.

Form is inescapable because it is absolutely fluid, but the inescapability of Form or the necessary realization of it does not result in anything that is at all fruitful. If we want to know what kind of world we in fact live in even in the vaguest sense, we get no consolation whatever out

原材料不适应于模型是不可能的。如果我们从质料开始，我们也会得到相同的结果，因为质料是完全没有特质的。我们来看一下可能，尽管有些例外，但目前无须考虑。让我们从时间和空间开始。我们之所以要以时间和空间开始，是因为它们一直被认为是直觉的先验形式，通过这种形式本体被纳入时间和空间的现象之中。由于质料是原材料，时间和空间是模型，事情就完全不一样了。我们没有什么逻辑上的理由来保证，质料不会拒绝进入时间和空间的模型。如果质料拒绝进入这样的模型，正如在目前它拒绝进入"龙性"这一可能之中一样，我们确实没有时间和空间，有点好比目前我们没有龙。没有时间和空间并不矛盾，但是从来不是真的。然而，这与说这儿没有马是不一样的。因为后者如果是假的就是假的。如果它是假的，那么就不能说它从来不是真的。因此，我们可以看到有两种先验的形式。一种是可逃避的形式，整个的逻辑系统都禁止它的可逃避性。这样的形式就是式。另一种是这样的形式，它以前、现在和将来都是不可逃避的，实在的所与性或硬性使它成为不可逃避的。这样的形式就是时间和空间以及式中的其他可能。让我们把第一种叫做理性的先验形式，第二种叫做非理性的先验形式。第二种先验形式蕴涵第一种先验形式，而第一种却不蕴涵第二种。从推论的观点看，前者显得更为重要些。但是从经验的观点来看，后者显得更为重要些。

我们已经说到，无质料的式和无式的质料是矛盾的。但承认了式永远是有质料在其中的，我们因此得到什么了吗？是的，实在的形式或状态就是。除此之外，我们没有谈及任何东西。在这里，否定似乎意味着更多的东西，而肯定则没有断定什么东西。在这里，我们再一次必须注意这样的一个事实，即流动性与富有成果性是不能共存的。式是不可逃避的，因为它是绝对流动的。但是它的不可逃避性或它的必然的现实并不导致任何富有成果的东西的形成。如果我们想知道即便在最模糊的含义上我们究竟事实上生活在一个什么样的世界之中，那么我们

of our knowledge that Form cannot but be Stuffed. On the other hand the realization of spatialness and temporalness is significant, we do not know as a result that there is Grand Canyon or Niagara Falls, or the sun and the moon, but we do know that there is time and space together with all sorts of facts which are the results of having time and space. This is fruitful, but then we cannot be logically assumed that the situation could not be otherwise. The dilemma seems to be unavoidable. If a form is unquestionably inescapable, its realization is totally devoid of fruitfulness, if the realization of a form is at all fruitful, that form cannot be guaranteed to be inescapable. The rational a priori form is logically inescapable but absolutely fruitless, whereas the arational a priori form is fruitful upon realization, but is by no means inescapable. The former gives us logical assurance for a form of reality, the latter furnishes us with the factual basis for a certain kind of world. It is the acceptance of both that we are able to account ultimately for the universe in which our kind of world must be realized in its process and reality.

Thus far we have said nothing about a priori-ness. Our discussion so far assumes that an a priori form is a form that either cannot but be realized or simply is always realized. We have not said anything about how epistemologically the form is arrived at. Some of you may suspect and suspect rightly that while we do believe in there being a priori forms we do not believe in there being a priori ways in deriving or arriving at those forms; that while we do believe in having a priori knowledge, we do not believe in having a priori ways of knowing or acquiring knowledge. We shall not digress into a discussion of epistemology, we shall merely point out that there are a priori propositions or statements though the methods or processes through which we arrive at or entertain or assert them cannot be said to be a priori. Concerning propositions or statements therefore the problem of the a priori with us is one of validity or truth or workability and not the ways by which they are arrived at or derived. A proposition or a statement is a priori if it is necessarily true or else must be true. There are also two kinds of a priori propositions or statements, one kind cannot but be true, the other must be true. All tautologies are of the first kind, the principle of induction for instance is of the second kind. Concerning tautologies nothing need be said, the principle of induction

从式是必然会有质料在其中的这一点上得不到丝毫安慰。在另一方面，时间和空间的现实是非常重要的。我们并不知道作为一种结果，是否存在着大峡谷或尼亚加拉瀑布、或太阳和月亮，但是我们确实知道有时间和空间及因有了时间和空间而产生的一切事实。这是富有成果的，但是我们却不能逻辑地假定情况不能是另一种样子。看来，这样的困境是不可避免的。如果式毫无疑问是不可逃避的，那么它的现实就是完全没有任何结果的。如果式的现实根本上就是有成果的，那么式就不能保证是不可逃避的了。理性的先验形式在逻辑上是不可逃避的，但绝对是没有成果的。然而非理性的先验形式，它一经现实便是富有成果的，但是绝不是不可逃避的。前者使我们对实在的形式具有逻辑的确信，而后者使我们具有了某种世界的事实性的基础。正是由于同时接受了这两者，我们才能最终解释宇宙。我们的世界就是在这个宇宙的过程及其实在中现实的。

至此，我们还是没有对先验性作出任何解释。到现在为止，我们的讨论假定了先验形式是这样的形式，它或者是不得不现实的，或者是永远现实的。我们没有说到，从认识论的角度讲，我们究竟是如何才能达到形式的。你们中的某些人可能会怀疑，虽然我们相信存在着先验的形式，但我们却不相信有先验的方式取得或达到那些形式。虽然我们相信我们具有先验的知识，但是却不相信我们有先验的方式知道或获取知识。这样的怀疑是有道理的。我们不会在此离题讨论认识论的问题，我们只是要指出，存在着先验的命题或陈述，虽然我们得到或考虑或断定这些命题或陈述的方法或过程不能说是先验的。因此考虑到命题或陈述，对我们而言，关于先验的问题是合理性或真理性或可操作性的问题，而不是达到或取得它们的方式的问题。如果一命题或陈述必然是真的或必须是真的，那么它就是先验的。有两类先验的命题或陈述，一类是不得不真的，另一类是必然是真的。所有的重言式都是属于第一类。而比如说归纳，就属于第二类。关于重言式我们无须在此再说些什么。归纳原则

has been dealt with elsewhere though unsatisfactorily, but the attempt is none the less an exhibition of its a priori character in the sense that it must be true under any circumstance whatsoever.

The ontological principle is the first kind of a priori statement. It cannot be false in the sense that its denial is a contradiction. Our previous discussion dealt with the inescapability of Form from the point of view of its realization and we have said that this absolute inescapability of Form renders its realization totally insignificant or fruitless. The same is true of the ontological principle. That it cannot be false need not be discussed again, but its unquestionable validity gets us nowhere. We merely know as a result that there is eternally a form of reality which needn't be of any specific form, a state of affairs which needn't be of any specific state. A universe is indeed assured to us, but whether in it there was or is or will be one kind of world at all, we have no way of assuring us at all. The validity of the principle merely provides us with the barest minimum. It is this minimum that tautologies also assert, the minimum for which they are valid or true. Otherwise the impossibility of a tautology to be false cannot philosophically be equated to its necessity for being true. Regarded in this light, the ontological principle is also significant; it does say something, though what it says does not describe our experience in this or any specific world. It asserts the barest minimum of reality, although it says nothing about what we usually call facts.

The metaphysical principle is an a priori statement of the second kind. In being arationally a priori, it is much more difficult to deal with. The rationally a priori statements succeed in being a priori by being absolutely negative about our experience or whatever contingencies there may be in our experience. It is this negativity that renders a rationally a priori statement perfectly intelligible. The metaphysical principle is not negative, its denial is not contradictory and its affirmation says everything about all possible worlds, this present one included. To deny that Stuff enters into and leaves off from possibilities may be unacceptable, or contrary to our insight, but it is not contradictory so that the principle is not forced upon us by logic. If we take Stuff to be a thing or an object in the ordinary sense, we may indeed heap all sorts of contradictions upon Stuff, but we have no right so to regard it at all. If we grasp Stuff rightly,

已在别处讨论过了，虽然还不能使人感到满意，但不管怎么样这一讨论是要表明它的先验性，即在任何情况下它都必须是真的。

本体论的原则是上述的第一种先验陈述。它不可能是假的，因为如果否认它就是矛盾。我们先前关于式的不可逃避性的讨论是从它的现实的观点着眼的。我们曾经说过，式的绝对的不可逃避性使它的现实完全没有什么意义或是没有成果。对于本体论原则我们也可以这样说。这一原则是不能假的这一点没有必要在此再作讨论。但是它的无可非议的合理性却不能使我们有什么收获。作为结果，我们仅仅知道有这样永恒的实在的式，它无须是任何特殊的形式；有这样的状态，它无须是任何特殊的状态。确实，我们相信有宇宙存在，但是在这宇宙中过去或现在或将来是否有某种世界，我们却没有办法使我们自己确信这一点。这一原则的合理性仅仅向我们提供了最基本的东西。重言式也断定了这一最基本的东西，对于这最基本的东西而言，它们是合理的，是真的。否则的话，重言式不可能是假的这一点在哲学上就不能等同于它必然是真的这一点。从这一方面考虑，本体论原则也同样是重要的，它确实说了某些东西，虽然它所说的东西并没有描述我们在这一个或某个特殊世界中的经验。它虽然没有说任何我们通常叫做事实的东西，但是它却断定了关于实在的最基本的东西。

形而上学原则是第二种先验陈述。由于形而上学原则是一种非理性的先验原则，所以要讨论这样的原则就显得更为困难。理性的先验陈述之所以是先验的，是因为它对于我们的经验或我们经验中的那些可能是偶然性的东西持一种绝对否定的态度。正是这种否定的态度使理性的先验陈述完全是可以理解的。形而上学原则不是否定的，对它的否定不是矛盾的，肯定它则论说了所有可能的世界，我们当前这一世界当然是包括在其中的。否认质料进出可能也许是很难令人接受的，或者与我们通常的看法是相反的。但是这一点却并不是矛盾的，因此逻辑并没有强迫我们接受这一原则。如果我们把质料看作是通常的意义上的一件事物或一个客体，我们可能会把所有的矛盾堆积在质料之上，但是我们却根本没有权利来这样看待质料。如果我们正确地

we have to grant that the metaphysical principle holds. We cannot help seeing that it is pure potentiality and activity in terms of possibilities that Stuff enters or leaves, since it is at the same time constant in quantity and totally devoid of qualities. We have to say that the principle holds, although we have no way of attributing contradictoriness to its denial. It is through metaphysical contemplation, not through logical analysis, that the principle is urged upon us.

It is one thing to say that the denial of the metaphysical principle is not contradictory and quite another thing to say that the principle says everything about the world. The former merely implies that the principle says something, that it is not absolutely negative, but it needn't say anything about facts or experience, much less implies that it says everything about the world. Further discussion is required to elucidate the sense in which it is said that the principle says everything about the world. We are sufficiently familiar with logic to know that tautology says nothing. This does not merely mean that it does not predict what will happen in future, or unearth what has happened in the past, this means that it asserts no fact whatever. It really says nothing either about its laws which a given fact obeys, or about the underlying activities of which any given fact is the phenomenal or the experiential expression. Our metaphysical principle also says nothing in the sense that with it we gain no knowledge of history or science. And yet it also says everything, not indeed about facts, but ultimately of the very core of factuality. It does so in the sense that given any fact or any item of experience or any change or any passage of nature or time, we find it to be the expression of the activity of Stuff in its entrance into and departure from possibilities. The principle is the most comprehensive way of exhibiting the essence of anything whatever. The ontological principle says nothing about facts and the absolute minimum about reality, the metaphysical principle says nothing about facts and the essential maximum of factuality. An ordinary tautology is necessarily true because it asserts nothing as a fact and entertains every possibility as a possibility. Our metaphysical principle must be true because it also asserts nothing as a fact but exhibits the underlying essence of any and every fact so that whatever possibility turns out to be a fact it also has that essence. If the principle asserts something to be a fact it might be false for contingencies may

理解了质料，那么我们就必须承认这一形而上学原则。我们会不由自主地看到，质料出入的正是可能的纯粹的潜在性和能动性，因为它在同一时间内在数量上是不变的，是完全没有任何特质的。我们不得不说这一原则是有效的，虽然我们没有方法将矛盾归之对它的否认。正是通过形而上学的沉思，而不是通过逻辑分析，这一原则才为我们所接受。

说否认形而上学原则并不矛盾是一件事，说这一原则说了这个世界的所有事情则是另一件事。前者仅仅意味着这一原则说了些什么，意味着它不是绝对的否定的，它无须说关于事实或经验的任何事情，更不意味着它说了这个世界的所有事情。进一步的讨论必须阐述清楚在什么意义上说这一原则说了关于这一世界的所有事情。我们非常熟悉逻辑，知道重言式并没有说什么东西。这不仅仅是说它没有预言在未来会发生什么，或没有揭露过去发生了些什么，这只是意味着它没有断定任何事实。它既没有说任何既定事实遵循的规律，也没有说既定事实作为现象或经验表达的背后的活动。我们没有因形而上学而得到关于历史或科学的知识，在此意义上，我们的形而上学原则也没有说过任何东西。然而，它却说了一切，当然不是关于事实的，而是本质上的事实性的核心东西。我们是在下述的意义上这样说的，即给定一事实或经验中的任何一项或任何变化或自然或时间中的任一阶段，我们发现它是质料进出可能的能动性的表达。这一原则是展示任何事物的本质的最全面的方式。本体论原则没有说及任何事实以及实在的绝对最低值。形而上学原则没有说及事实以及事实性的本质最大值。通常说来，重言式必然是真的，因为它也没有断定任何事实，只是将每一个可能作为可能来考虑。我们的形而上学原则必须是真的，因为它没有断定任何事实，然而却展示了一切事实背后的本质。因此不管可能会成为什么样的事实，它总是具有这个本质的。如果这一原则断定了某一东西是事实，那么它就有可能是假的，因为偶然性有可能发生，

take place under which that something isn't a fact at all; if the principle exhibits the essence of some but not all the facts, it might be false also, contingencies may also rise under which some even most of the facts have no such essence. The combination of these two elements, namely asserting nothing as a fact and exhibiting the essence of any and every fact, is such that the metaphysical principle holds no matter what possibility turns out to be a fact. It is also a priori, though its denial is not a contradiction.

While we discuss a priori forms first, it is after all the a priori principles that are of much greater importance. In the case of Form and the ontological principle we can hardly say which is more important or which is more fundamental, since each is directly involved with the other, the inevitability of Form is the same as the necessity of the principle. But in the case of the metaphysical principle and certain forms or possibilities such as for example spatiality or temporalness, the question of relative importance is quite different. We may feel that temporalness and spatiality must be realized and yet we may not be able to give any ground for our feeling. But if we admit the metaphysical principle, time and space can be seen to be a matter of course. We shall see this much more clearly in subsequent chapters.

IV

It is now time to introduce Tao. Tao is simply Stuffed Form or Formed Stuff. It is therefore neither pure Form nor pure Stuff. To borrow Kantian expressions which are not strictly applicable, we may say that Tao would be empty if it were pure Form and it would be fluid if it were pure Stuff. It simply is and is so in its own right. As we shall see later on, it is the universe, but unlike the latter, it need not be spoken in terms of that totality or wholeness which is an inseparable part of our notion of the universe. The term "logos" might have been used originally to mean both the expression and the content of certain lines of thought, but if it were broadened to mean also the object of thought, it would be what we call Tao here. There is a passage in the Bible in which the English word "word" is used as a translation of the term "logos," in the Chinese version the term Tao is used and no better term could be found. Tao as it is used here however is not confined to the expression and content of thought, it applies also to its

使得某一东西不成为一事实。如果这一原则展示了某些而不是所有事实的本质，那么它也可能是假的，偶然性也可能发生，其中某些甚至大部分的事实都没有这样的本质。这两个因素的结合，即不断定任何事实又展示所有事实的本质，就会是这样的，即无论什么样的可能会成为事实，形而上学原则总是站得住脚的。它也同样是先验的，尽管否认它并不是矛盾。

虽然我们首先讨论的是先验的形式，但是先验的原则却是更重要的。关于式和本体论原则，我们简直不能说哪一个更重要或哪一个更根本。因为每一个都与另一个直接相关，式的不可避免性也就是原则的必然性。但是对于形而上学原则和某些形式或可能如时间或空间来讲，相对而言的重要性的问题就不一样了。我们可能感觉到，时间和空间必须是现实的，然而我们却很难给我们的这种感觉给出像样的理由。然而，如果我们承认形而上学原则，时间和空间就是理所当然的事儿了。在下面的章节中，我们将会更清楚地看到这一点。

四

现在是引进"道"这一概念的时候了。道就是有质料在其中的式或有式的质料。因此，它不是纯式或纯质料。借用康德的表述，当然从严格意义上而言并不合适，我们可以这样说，道如果是纯式，那么它就是空的；如果道是纯粹的质料，那么它就是流动的。它就是那样，本身如此。后面我们会看到，道是宇宙；但是它又不像后者，因为它不必以总体和全体来表述，而总体和全体是我们对于宇宙的概念中不可分割的部分。"逻各斯"这一术语原本可以在其原来的意义上被运用来既指某些思想的表述也指它们的内容。但是如果它的内涵被扩大至也同时指涉思想的客体的话，那么它将变成我们在此所说的道。在《圣经》中有这样的一段，在其中运用了英语的"word"一词来翻译"logos"一词。《圣经》的汉语译本是用"道"一词来翻译的，找不到更好的词来代替道了。不管怎么样，这里所使用的"道"这一词并不局限于思想的表现和内容，也同样指涉

object. In saying that there is Tao, we are not merely talking about there being thought or thinking, but also about there being the universe.

Tao can be spoken of in at least two different ways, namely, Tao-one and Tao-infinite. The former is the Tao of the barest minimum in connotation and the latter is the Tao with a connotation in essence of that minimum. The point might be more easily grasped if we speak of logos and let us say also of physiology. Denotatively physiology might be said to be a part of logos, while connotatively it has something in essence of bare logos. In saying something about physiology we are also saying through implication about logos, but in saying anything about logos we are not saying anything about physiology. The relation of Tao-one to Tao-infinite is similar to the relation of logos to any of the "...logies," only in the case of Tao-infinite we are not specifying which of the "...logies." The comparison may lead us to an idea of the all-pervasiveness of Tao: anything that is at all expressible is a part of Tao, even the expression itself since expressions belong to a sphere covered by a set of "...logies." Nothing escapes Tao. The whole universe is intelligible in terms of Tao-one and any part of it in terms of Tao-infinite.

For the moment however we shall be confined to Tao-one. Tao-one cannot be denied. The ontological principle guarantees Tao-one. To deny Tao-one is itself contradictory. Anything that is generally contradictory is the purest nothing. It is absolutely nothing. There are a number of nothings which have no purity, no absoluteness. To say that there is nothing in this room for instance does not mean that there is in it purely or absolutely nothing; it merely means either that the usual things are absent at a particular time or else that the proposition anything is there is false. Concerning this kind of nothing, there is no problem, at least not in the present connection. The problem of contradiction however may be brought up. You may say that of course there are contradictories; our history of thought is full of them. There are of course contradictory ideas in the history of human thought in the sense that they were entertained and therefore actually occurred in their process of thinking. This however means the occurrence of contradictory ideas as contents of thought, not the emergence of things or objects corresponding to these ideas. Besides, contradictory ideas merely occur in thought processes; they do

思想的对象。当我们说有道存在时，我们并不仅仅是在谈论说有思想或思维，而且也同样是说宇宙的存在。

我们可以在两种不同的方式上谈论道，那就是道一和道无限。前者是指道在内涵上的最小值，后者是指道具有最小值的内涵本质。如果我们说到逻各斯，我们也同样谈到生理学的话，那么这一点可能更容易理解。从外延上说，生理学可以说是逻各斯的一部分；但从内涵上说，它具有逻各斯的本质的最低值。说到关于生理学的某些东西的时候，我们也就同时通过暗示在谈论着逻各斯。但是当说到逻各斯的时候，我们并没有谈论到生理学。道一和道无限之间的关系类似于逻各斯和"XX 学"之间的关系。只是关于道无限，我们没有指明"XX 学"中的哪一种。这样的比较可能把我们引向道无所不在的观念：任何东西只要是可表达的就是道的一部分，即便是表达本身也是道的一部分，因为表达属于由种种"XX 学"所涵盖的领域。没有任何东西可以逃避道。由道一看，整个宇宙都是可以理解的；由道无限看，宇宙中的任何一部分也是可以理解的。

然而我们暂时只讨论道一。道一是不可否认的，本体论原则担保了道一，否认道一本身就是矛盾的。任何一般说来矛盾的东西就是纯粹的无，这是绝对的无。存在着这样一些无，它们没有纯粹性，没有绝对性。比如说在这间房子里没有任何东西并不意味着在那里是纯粹地或绝对地没有任何东西。它只不过是说在特定的时间没有通常的东西，或者说断定有东西在那里的命题是假的。关于这样所谓的无，应该是没有问题的，至少在目前是这样。但是，却可以提出矛盾的问题。你可能说，当然有矛盾存在，我们的思想史就充满着矛盾。在人类思想史上当然是充满着矛盾的，因为人们会考虑矛盾的情况，所以在思维的过程之中也就现实地产生着矛盾。不过，这就意味着矛盾的意念是作为思想的内容而产生的，而不是作为与这些意念相应的事情或客体而产生的。另外，矛盾的意念只是产生在思想的过程之中，它们并不在思想的

not function in thought structures. They may occur in your preparation of an essay, but if you are aware of them, they do not appear in the finished product. We must remember that having a contradictory idea is an event, a happening, it is not itself contradictory, and to follow the method of approach adopted here, it merely means the realization of the possibility "contradiction," it does not mean the realization of any possibility that is itself contradictory. Contradiction as an event happens every day and the occurrence of a contradictory idea is merely a case in which a thinker contradicts himself. Perhaps we are beating about the bush without any clear ideas ensuing. Perhaps we better say that so far as the occurrence of a contradictory idea is concerned, it is not the occurrence that is contradictory, it is the idea that is so, and it is not the idea as an occurrence that is contradictory, it is the idea as a part of a structure that is ruled out as invalid in content because the realization of the corresponding possibility is impossible in the unfoldment of Tao.

The procedure adopted in these pages is meant to facilitate understanding; it is not a formal procedure. Formally we should say that it is Tao-one that condemns contradictories. To say that the denial of Tao-one is contradictory means more than any ordinary statement of this kind, because the very essence of contradictoriness when pushed to the last analysis beyond logic proper is according to our way of thinking simply an affirmation of Stuff without Form or Form without Stuff. To affirm Tao-one is equivalent to ruling out contradictories. Hence in affirming Tao-one, we affirm nothing else either. The ontological principle merely affirms the barest minimum of reality, which is what we have been describing as Tao-one. As we have already pointed out, Tao-one does not imply Tao-infinite. By Tao-infinite we mean the infinite possibility of specific kinds of world. Since we speak generally, we are not concerned with any determinate kind. Thus by affirming Tao-one, we are affirming incidentally the reality of our present kind of world just as by affirming logos, we are not affirming a state of affairs in which physics or chemistry or history describes or explains natural phenomena. We may have Tao-one and yet our specific kind of world needn't exist.

Suppose we describe our present kind of world in the following manner. Suppose we have the kind of world for which the following

结构之中发生任何作用。它们可能在你准备论文的时候产生，但是一旦你认识到存在着这样的矛盾，那么在你定稿的时候这样的矛盾也就不再出现了。我们必须记住，有一个矛盾的意念是一事件，是一种现象的发生，它本身并不是矛盾的。沿用我们在此所采纳的方法，它个过意味着"矛盾"可能的现实，它并个意味着任何本身矛盾的可能的现实。矛盾作为一种现象是每人都会发生的，矛盾意念的产生仅仅是一个例子，表明思想者的自相矛盾。或许，我们是在绕圈子，没有任何清晰的思想产生。或许，我们更应该说，当谈到矛盾意念产生的时候，并不是说矛盾的产生是矛盾的，而是说这一意念是矛盾的；并不是意念的产生是矛盾的，而是作为结构的一部分的意念由于内容的不合理而被排除，因为在道的展开过程之中，相应的可能的现实是不可能的。

在这里所采取的讨论步骤是为了易于理解，它并不是一个正式的步骤。正式来讲，我们应该说，是道一宣告矛盾不适用。说对道一的否定是矛盾的，并不是仅仅指通常意义上的这种陈述，因为归根结底于逻辑之外适当分析，据我们的思维方式而言，矛盾的本质就是一个没有式的质料或没有质料的式的断言。断言道一就等同于排除了矛盾。因此断言道一，我们也没有断言任何别的东西。本体论原则仅仅是断言了实在的最低值，我们把这样的最低值一直描述为道一。正如我们早已指出的那样，道一并不蕴涵道无限。我们把道无限看作是特殊种类的世界的无限可能。由于我们只是在一般的意义上讨论，所以我们没有考虑任何特定种类的世界。因此，通过断言一，我们也就顺便断言了我们当前世界的实在性。正如断言了逻各斯，我们并不就断言了一种状态，在其中物理学或化学或历史描述或解释自然现象。我们可能有道一，然而我们这样特定的世界并不必存在。

假设我们以下面的方式来描述我们目前的世界。假如我们有这

three exhaustive sets of propositions are true, that is to say, all the true propositions are included in the following three sets:

1. A set of universal propositions P, Q, R, ...
2. A set of general propositions p, q, r, ...
3. A set of particular propositions φ, ψ, θ, ...

The sum total of these propositions jointly describes our present kind of world as well as asserts the existence of this particular world in which we happen to live. Some of the universal propositions are scientific principles or natural laws grouped under the different categories of a whole set of "...logies." Some of the general propositions are discovered in history and the social sciences and some of the particular propositions are found in histories and newspaper reports. A really worthwhile encyclopedia should cover a significant part of these propositions most of which however are not as yet discovered by us at the present. What is meant by saying that in affirming Tao-one, we are not asserting the existence of our present kind of world is that while the statement "Tao-one is" or the ontological principle is true, all these three exhaustive sets of propositions may each and every one of them be false. This laborious process is adopted because the state of affairs herein described is more easily conceived than imagined. It is for instance different to imagine a state of affairs in which there is no space, since imagination involves images or pictures which are concrete-like and therefore spacial. But it might be conceived. The state of affairs conceived here might very well be true and yet Tao-one is or the ontological principle holds.

We may extend the above conception. We can easily conceive the possibility that the set of universal propositions is true and yet the remaining sets are false. If so, we have one kind of world, but not this particular one; in which case, nature is as it was in terms of natural laws, but everything else is different from what it is today. It is also possible that the second and the third sets of propositions are partly true and partly false, while the first set entirely false, in which case we have this particular world in some ways but not in others and it does not belong to the kind described by the first set of propositions. We may have three sets of entirely different but true propositions in which case we

样的世界，对于这一世界下面三类包罗无遗的命题都是真的。这就是说，所有真命题都包括在下面的三类之中：

1. 一类普遍命题 P，Q，R，……
2. 一类普通命题 p，q，r，……
3. 一类特殊命题 φ，ψ，θ，……

所有这些命题的总和描述了我们这个当前的世界，也同样断言了我们恰巧生活于其中的这一特殊世界。普遍命题中的某些命题是科学原则或自然律，它们归属在整个"XX 学"的不同范畴之下。普通命题中的某些命题可以在历史学和社会科学中找到。特殊命题中的某些命题可以在历史和新闻报道中找到。一部真正有价值的百科全书应该涵盖这些命题中的相当大的部分。然而这些命题中的大部分，至少在目前，我们还未发现。我们说当断言道一的时候我们并未断定我们目前这一世界的存在，其真正的意思是说，虽然陈述"道一是"或本体论原则是正确的，但是所有这些包罗无遗的命题中的每一个却可能是假的。采取这样颇费心思的过程是因为，在此思议这一被描述的状态其实要比想象这一状态来得更容易些。例如想象一个其中没有空间的状态是不同的，因为想象包含着类似于具体的意象或图像，所以是空间上的。但它却可以是思议的。在此被思议的这一状态很可能是真的，而道一或本体论原则是有效的。

我们可以进一步拓展上述的构想。我们能够很容易地思议这样的可能，即普遍命题是真的，而其他的命题则是假的。如果是这样的话，那么我们就具有一种类型的世界，但不是这一特殊的世界。这样的话，从自然律的角度看，自然还是和以前一样，但其他所有东西却和现在的大大不同了。也有这样的可能，即第二类和第三类的命题部分是真的，部分是假的，而第一类的命题却完全是假的。如果是这样的话，那么在某种方式上我们可以有现在这样特殊的世界，在其他方式上却不是这样，而且这样的特殊世界并不属于以第一类命题描述的类型。同样，我们也可能有三类完全不同但却真的命题，如果是这样，

have an altogether different kind of world and also a particular one different from the one we happen to have. However we may conceive, the important point remains, namely the ontological principle holds and there is Tao-one; whatever can be conceived is possible, because it is not contradictory. Only the contradictory cannot be conceived hence Tao-one cannot but be affirmed. Later on we shall attempt to show that all sorts of possible worlds will be realized, but then that is the result of the metaphysical principle, not the ontological principle.

If we start the other way around we see possibly even more clearly the all-pervasiveness of Tao-one, provided we do not forget certain implications. We are liable to forget because certain implications are tainted with false values which we don't care to keep above our level of consciousness. Thus being human and with false values attached to humanity tends to make a person forget that he is an animal, a living being, a thing, and basically a part of Stuffed Form. Most people would be angry if they were told that they are animals, and to be told that they are things as well probably leaves them flabbergast and fills them with pity for the conspicuous lack of sanity in the one who speaks in such a fashion. And yet while a thing needn't be a person, a person is quite definitely a thing at the same time. To say that one is a psychologist teaching at such and such a university or writing or having written such and such a book gives us much more information than to say that he is a person, or an animal or a living being, and to say that he is a thing gives us very little information indeed while saying that he is a part of Formed Stuff says nothing at all. But this does not mean that the statement is false; in fact the first implies the last. The egocentric predicament often blinds the individual to his basic identity with other individuals and the anthropocentric predicament often blinds humanity to its identity with other animals, other living beings and other things. It may be advisable to speak of universal sympathy here, but we won't do it; we are for the moment rather concerned with the all-pervasiveness of Tao-one. Start from anything whatever, and no matter how high the connotational content of the corresponding concept may be, you merely start from a part of Tao-infinite, and all the time you are within the realm of Tao-one. This applies to existent things, but also to anything imaginable or

那么我们就会具有完全不同的世界，而且这个特殊的世界也与我们恰巧生活在其中的世界是不同的。但是不管我们怎么样思议，重要的一点，即本体论原则是有效的，存在着道一。任何可以思议的东西都是可能的，因为它们并不是矛盾的。只有矛盾的东西才是不可思议的，因此道一也就必然会得到断言。在后面我们将试图指出，所有的可能世界都是能够现实的，但是那是形而上学原则的结果，而个是本体论原则的结果。

如果我们从另一不同的角度来讨论，那么我们将更容易清楚地看到道一的无所不在的性质，只要我们不要忘记某些后果。我们容易忘记，因为这些后果沾染了假的特质，我们只是在意识里知道这个。因此作为一个人，人性附带着假的特质，所有这些都使得人总容易忘记他是一个动物、一个活的存在、一件东西，更基本的是他是有质料在其中的式的一个部分。被告知是动物的时候，绝大部分的人会感到极大的愤怒。被告知是东西可能会让他们大吃一惊，他们会认为说这话的人显然缺乏健全的理智而对他们感到怜惜。然而，一个东西不必是一个人，但一个人却肯定同时是一个东西。说一个人是一位心理学家在某某大学教书或正在写或已经写完了某某书，显然要比说他是一个人或一个动物或一件东西提供了更多的信息。说他是一个东西几乎没给我们提供多少信息，而说是他有式的质料的一部分则什么也没有说。但是这并不意味着这一陈述是假的。事实上，第一个蕴涵着最后一个。自我中心的思想经常使个人看不到他与其他个人基本的同一性。而人类中心的思想则使人们看不到人类与其他的动物、其他有生命的存在和其他的东西的同一性。明智的态度是要说起普遍同情，但是我们不打算这样做，因为我们目前较为关注的是道一的无所不在的性质。从任何一个东西开始，不管相关概念的内涵有多么丰富，你也只是从道无限的一部分开始的，你始终都是在道一的王国之内。这一点适用于存在的事物，但也同样适用于任何可以想象或可以思议的事物。因此，想象

conceivable. Thus imagine or conceive yourself to be anything whatever. You cannot escape your basic identity with anything else. The merest accident, the most frivolous occurrence that can be conceived are but the stages in the process and items in the reality where Tao-one unfolds itself.

Thus far we have been saying that Tao cannot be denied, that in affirming Tao we affirm nothing, and in affirming anything whatever, we are also affirming Tao-one. We are more concerned here with the all-pervasiveness of Tao-one than with the multiplicity of Tao-infinite. We shall soon speak of the relation between these two, but before doing so, we still have to clarify certain points concerning Tao-one. While something can be formally said of Form, and hardly anything can be formally said of Stuff, there is a sense in which nothing can be said of Tao-one and another sense in which a good deal can be said about it. In its entirety and unity nothing can be said about Tao-one since it is simply the universe. It cannot be said to begin or to end, to increase or decrease, to exist or not to exist, to be real or not to be real.... In the form in which there is a subsumption of subject classes into predicate classes, no statement can be made in which Tao-one appears as a subject, and all statements are valid in which Tao-one appears as a predicate. There are of course certain difficulties in such a statement, but in these pages we overlook them. The point is of course that Tao-one cannot be subsumed under anything other than itself. But while in its entirety, Tao-one is simply the eternal all pervasive unity which is but another way of saying that it is the universe, it need not be taken in its entirety. While any part of the universe is not a universe (hence the thing described by physicists and astronomers as a sphere with a radius or a diameter of so many light years is not our universe) any part of Tao-one is none the less Tao-one. It is this separate applicability that enables us to think of and say things about Tao-one which in its entirety and unity we can say nothing about.

V

The ontological principle is responsible for Tao-one and the metaphysical principle for Tao-infinite. The relation between these two can be analyzed into two different aspects both of which are important to our understanding of Tao. One of these is the relation of organic parts to organic wholes and the other is the relation of the inclusion of

或思议你自己就是任何一件东西。你不能够逃避你自己与其他事物共享的那些特性。能够思议的纯粹意外事件、最无谓的东西都不过是道一展开过程中的一个阶段和实在中的一个条目。

至此我们一直在说道是不能否认的，我们断言道等于什么也没有断言，断言任何东西我们也就断言了道一。我们在此更为关注的是道一的无所不在性，而非道无限的多样性，我们不久将谈到这两者之间的关系，但是在这样做之前，我们还需对有关道一的某些问题做进一步的澄清。虽然我们可以在形式上就式谈论一些什么，且几乎不可以在形式上就质料谈论些什么，但是关于道一我们在一种意义上没有什么可以说的，而在另一种意义上却可以说很多。由于道一就是宇宙，因此在整体上和统一性方面关于它是没有什么可以说的。不能说它开始或终结、增长或减少、存在或不存在、真实或不真实……。在形式上，可以把主词归属于谓词，但道一作为主词出现的陈述是不可能作出的，而道一作为谓词出现的所有陈述都是合理的。当然在这样的陈述中是存在着一定困难的，然而在这里我们可以对此略而不计。这里的关键是，道一是不能归属于除它本身之外的任何东西的。但是，在它的整体性上道一就是永恒的无所不在的统一性，这就是在用另一种方式说道一是宇宙，因此不必以整体性来考虑。虽然宇宙的任何部分并不是宇宙（因此物理学家和天文学家描述的以多少光年为半径或直径的球体并不是我们这里所谓的宇宙），但是道一的任何部分却仍然是道一。正是这种独立的适用性使我们可以思想或谈论关于道一的情形，而关于道一的整体性和统一性我们却是无话可说的。

五

本体论原则是针对道一的，而形而上学原则则是道无限的原则。这两者之间的关系可以分析成两个不同的方面。对于我们理解道来说，这两个方面是同样重要的。其中的一个方面是有机的部分对有机的整体之间的关系，另一个方面则是一类包含于另一类的关系。

one class to another class. The class inclusion relation enables us to say that what is true of the including class is true also of the included class. A basic homogeneity is given to both the including and the included classes which may be lacking to the relation of organic parts to organic wholes. Obviously while on the one hand a brave man is a man, on the other although blood circulation is organic to human body, it is not itself a human body. Organicity involves a system of external and internal relations such that while parts may be dependent or interdependent upon and independent of each other, the whole is always dependent upon its parts. Given therefore the nature of parts, something is also revealed of the whole. It is thus out of the bones of the extinct animals that their bodies can be constructed. Either of these relations has its advantages and disadvantages, while a combination of both enables us to talk of Tao-one in terms of Tao-infinite, for Tao-infinite is not only included in Tao-one, but also organic to Tao-one. Perhaps a bit of imagery will help us. Tao might be likened to a piece of silk with a pattern of different but connected designs together with the warp and weft. Any part of it not only exhibits warp and weft but also a part of the pattern and design. The whole thing is so connected that if one lifts a part of it, some other parts are automatically lifted also. The piece of silk here imagined is static while Tao can be taken both in its static and dynamic aspects. Perhaps we might see in our mind's eye a picture of a running brook skimming along a slightly inclined piece of rock that isn't all smooth on the face so that a certain lacy effect is produced by the water. Every drop there is a drop of water and yet every drop also contributes to the general pattern of its face, so that if the flow is disturbed, a different pattern is produced. While a picture clarifies, it also distorts, but if we ignore the distortion, we may gain through analogy a glimpse of Tao. Tao is both a flow and a pattern, and it is neither its flow nor its pattern; it is a class of entities and events in organic unity—it could be talked about separately hence indirectly it could be talked about also jointly. From the point of view of the articulation of ideas, it is the separate applicability that renders Tao the same as and yet different from the universe.

We have already mentioned the possible equivalence of Tao to logos if by the latter we mean not only the expression and content of thought

类的包含关系使我们能够说包含类是真的话，那么被包含的类也是真的。包含类和被包含类具有一种基本的相同性，但是有机部分对有机整体的关系却没有这样的共同特性。显然，虽然在一方面一个勇敢的男人是男人，但在另一方面虽然血液循环是人体的有机组成部分，然而它却不是人体。有机性是 包含有内在和外在关系的系统。它们的关系是这样的，部分可能是相互联系的或相互依存的，部分和部分之间可能是独立的，但是整体总是要依赖于它的部分的。因此给定部分的性质，那么有关整体性质的某些方面也就同时被揭示出来了。正因为如此，我们可以从已绝种的动物的骸骨来恢复它们身体的结构。这两种关系各有其长处，也各有其短处。它们的结合可以使我们用道无限来谈论道一，因为道无限不仅仅被包括在道一之中，同时它也是道一的一个有机组成部分。在此可能意象会给我们很大的帮助。可以把道比作一段丝绸，它有不同的连贯的图案，由经纬编织而成。这一丝绸的任何一部分并不仅仅是经线和纬线，而且也显示出了图案和花样的一部分。这整块的丝绸是紧紧地联系在一起的，如果拎起其中一部分，那么其他的部分也就自动被拎起来了。在此我们想象的丝绸是静态的，而道既可从静态观察，也可从动态观察。或许我们可以想象这样一幅画面，一条流动的小溪跳跃着流过一块表面并不光滑的倾斜的岩石而激起阵阵浪花。每一滴都是一滴水，然而每一滴也同样都属于整个图案。因此当水流受到影响，就会形成不同的图案。画面既可以澄清，也可以歪曲。但是，如果我们不去考虑歪曲的方面，那么我们就可能通过类比而得到关于道的看法。道既是水流，也是图案。它既不是它的水流，也不是它的图案；它是一类有机的整体的实体和事件。我们可以分别谈论它，也从而间接地可以整体地谈论它。从表达意念的角度来看，正是独立的适用性使道与宇宙同一却又有所不同。

我们已经提到，道可能类似于逻各斯，如果后者不仅仅是思想

but also its object as well. The problem of non-veridical thought might be different in details, but we can easily see that even non-veridical thought with its lack of the usual object is also a part of Tao. There is certainly logos to non-veridicality. Suppose we imagine our knowledge to be almost complete in the sense that we know adequately and comprehensively almost everything there is to know. Our encyclopedia can be roughly divided into at least two main spheres: history and science, the part that deals with particular occurrences and the part that deals with the universal pattern. Our knowledge not only reflects Tao, but is also itself an item in the reality and a stage in the process of Tao. What is revealed through this reflection? The history part reveals process and actuality, and the science part reveals the pattern. We shall leave the former for future discussion, and concentrate on the latter. Our view is that the pattern is one of multifarious designs in the form of various "...logies" grouping different sets of natural laws interconnected with each other by natural laws, assumptions and principles of methodology. These different "...logies" as parts or designs are woven into an organic whole which is the pattern itself. A good deal might be said of the interrelations of the different "...logies." Some are more closely related than others from the point of view of intervening distance, some are on a higher plane than others from the point of view of deducibility, some are more closely knit than others from the point of view of internal organization, and some are perhaps richer than others from the point of view of content, etc. But they are connected like the cities of a country. No city is inaccessible though certain roads do not lead to certain cities. Physiology may be far distant from geology, but they are not disconnected; they may not have a direct road of communication, but by the tortuous way of biology, zoology, botany, geography, paleontology one could travel from physiology to geology and vice versa.

This pattern wouldn't be what we call logos or Tao, for taken by itself, it is empty, static and devoid of actuality; it is like a sift with nothing sifted, or window curtain that is rendered colorless by having no light going through it. We are not talking here of contrast between Stuff and Form, but of that between the actual and the hypothetical.

的表现和内容，而且也是思想的对象的话。不真实的思想的问题在细节上可能是不同的，但是我们仍然可以很容易地看出，即便是没有平常客体的不真实思想依旧是道的一部分。在不真实性中也一定有它的逻各斯。假定想象我们的知识几乎是完全的，即我们完全充分知道几乎每一件应该知道的事情。我们的百科全书至少可以大体上分成两个部分，即历史和科学这样两个领域。一部分处理的是特殊的事件，另一部分处理的是普遍的图案。我们的知识不仅仅反映道，而且它本身也同样是实在中的一个条目和道的展开过程中的一个阶段。这样的反映揭示的是什么呢？历史部分揭示的是过程和现实性，而科学揭示的是普遍的图案。我们将在后面谈论前一个问题，而现在集中谈论后一个问题。我们的看法是，这一图案只不过是各种“XX学”之中多种多样花样中的一种，而所谓的“XX学”通过自然律、设定和方法论原则将各种不同的自然律相互之间紧密地联系起来。这些作为部分或花样的不同的“XX学”被编织成一有机的整体，这就是图案自身。关于不同的“XX学”之间的相互联系我们有很多可以说的。从相互间的距离来说，有些要比其他的似乎联系得更紧密；从可推断性方面来说，有的层次要比其他的更高；从内在的联系讲，有的要比其他的组织更紧凑；从内容来看，有的要比其他的来得更丰富些；等等。但是它们之间的联系类似于一个国家内的城市之间的联系。没有一个城市是不可以到达的，虽然某些道路可能并不直接通向某一城市。生理学可能与地质学相去甚远，但这两者之间绝不是毫无关系的。它们之间可能没有直接的联系，但是通过间接的方式，如通过生物学、动物学、植物学、地理学、古生物学等学科，我们就能从生理学走向地质学，或者从地质学走向生理学。

这样的图案不是我们所谓的逻各斯或道，因为就其本身而言，它是空的、静止的、没有现实性的。它就像没有任何东西可筛的筛子，或者就像没有光线照射的窗帘显得毫无颜色一样。我们在此并没有谈论质料和式之间的对比关系，而只限于谈论现实的和假定的之间的关系。

We are speaking analytically of the universal pattern without the flow of passage of particular events and objects. Actually each is dependent upon the other. The case of the moving picture may be drafted again for illustration. All the cross-sectional pictures do not make the moving picture, for they must come in a certain pattern as well, nor is the picture confined to the pattern for if the cross-sections were different, the whole picture would have been different. Just as it takes both pattern and cross-sections to make a moving picture, so it takes both process and pattern to constitute Tao or logos. In the last paragraph we emphasized the pattern; in the present we have to say a few words about the flow or passage of events and objects. Particular objects in so far as their particularities are concerned are the portables, referrables or otherwise expressibles. While their particularities cannot be described, they themselves can be described through the universals they exemplify or the possibilities they realize. That is to say, the particular events or objects sift through and permeate the pattern like light rays that shot through the window curtains. The pattern is after all the interconnectedness of universals with the different "...logies" as the interconnected designs. It is this flow and passage of particular events and objects that gives life and actuality to the pattern and it is the pattern that gives the flow of passage its intelligibility. Tao cannot be said to be rational if by it we mean something associated with conscious decisions, but it is thoroughly intelligible, because it is thoroughly according to pattern.

Given the relation of Tao-infinite to Tao-one, one can see that not only is the sum total of Tao-infinite the entirety of Tao-one, but the organicity of Tao-infinite is also the unity of Tao-one. There is an infinity to the one as well as a one to the infinity. The organicity of Tao-infinite may be discussed in terms of particular events and objects. From one way of looking at things, a particular object or event reflects the whole universe. From the point of view of epistemology I hold that particular objects and events are both internally and externally related to each other. If not, knowledge would be quite impossible. But this view is not incompatible with the doctrine of organicity of particular objects and events. In the first place, internal and external relations are not always or generally symmetrical. That is to say, if x is externally related to y, y needn't be externally related to x. In the second place, there are varieties

我们分析地谈论普遍的图案，而没有涉及特殊事件和客体的流动过程。实际上，任何事件和客体都是相互依赖的。电影在此可以被用来做一个例子。所有截面图并不能组成电影，因为它们必须以某种图案放映才能成就电影。电影也不限于图案，因为如果这些截面是不同的，那么整个电影就将完全不同。正如必须将图案和截面结合起来才能成就一电影一样，只有将过程和图案综合起来才能形成道或逻各斯。在上一个段落中，我们曾经强调了图案，在此我们必须谈谈事件和客体的阶段或流动。特殊的客体就其特殊性而言是可以随带、可以指称或是可以表达的。虽然它们的特殊性不可以描述，但它们本身却可以通过它们所展示的共相或它们现实的可能得到描述。这就是说，特殊事件或客体在图案中筛滤并弥漫于图案之中，就像穿透窗帘的光线。图案就是共相的内在联系，而不同的"XX学"是内在相联的花样。是特殊的事件和客体的过程和流动赋予图案以生命和现实性，是图案使过程的流动具有可理解性。如果我们所谓理性是指与自觉的决定相联系，那么道就不能说是理性的。但是，它是完全可以理解的，因为它是完全与图案相符合的。

如果给定了道无限和道一的关系，那么你就能看出不仅仅完整的道一是道无限的总和，而且道无限的有机性也是道一的统一性。这就是无限和一、一和无限的关系。道无限的有机性可以从特殊事件和客体的角度来讨论。从某一角度来看事物，一特殊事件或客体反映的是整个宇宙。从认识论的角度来看问题，我认为，特殊的客体和事件在内在和外在两个方面都是紧密联系在一起的。若非如此，知识将是不可能的。但是，这一看法并不与特殊客体和事件是有机整体的思想相冲突。首先，内在关系和外在关系并不总是或一般说来是对称的。这就是说，如果 x 在外在关系上是与 y 联系着的，y 未必就与 x 有外在关系。其次，存在

of organicity; while some demand the exercise of mutual influence of the part upon each other in terms of qualities alone, others merely demand a similar influence in terms not of qualities alone but also of relations as well. Relationally no particular object or event is independent from any other particular event or object; each is so and so because the others are or were or will be such and such. Particularity is never merely local or merely the property or the attribute of particular objects or events. If it were, it might be repeated, since it might be detached from its environment, and once capable of detachment, there is no reason whatever why it shouldn't be capable of repetition. But as we have already pointed out before a particular cannot be repeated. That is to say, it cannot be detached from its immediate environment, nor can its immediate environment be detached from its mediate environment. Suppose we refrain from talking about the universe, and confine ourselves to any cross-section of it which we sometimes call the world at t_1. The repetition of a particular in the world at t_1 means also the repetition of the world at t_1. One can easily see that the world at t_1 cannot be repeated, either continuously or discretely. A continuous repetition of the world at t_1 would be a stoppage of time at t_1, and a discrete repetition of the world at t_1 would be detachment of it from its predecessors as well as its successors. This would eventually result in a repetition of the universe, and a repetition of the universe is also its denial, for a universe that can be repeated isn't the universe at all; it cannot be Tao in its entirety and unity. Since a particular cannot be repeated, it must reflect the whole universe; each must be because the others are or were or will be.

With the above in mind we may say something about universal sympathy. It is in terms of this doctrine of reflection that the universe is said to be in us, not merely that we are in the universe. "Heaven and earth and I myself are contemporaneous and I am at one with a myriad of other things" is a doctrine that might be interpreted along other lives, but it certainly is an offshoot of the ideas herein expounded.

Mr. Bertrand Russell has somewhere remarked that people hanker after eternity without desiring to be infinitely fat, that is, they want to function throughout all time without desiring to occupy all space. Esthetics undoubtedly forbids infinite fatness while economics and psychology propel people into a desire for eternity. The latter desire

着各种各样的有机性；有的单从特质方面要求部分之间的相互影响，而有的不仅仅从特质方面而且也从关系方面要求同样的相互影响。就关系讲，没有一个特殊客体或事件可以独立于其他的特殊客体或事件；每一客体或事件都是如此，因为其他客体或事件也是或过去是或将来会是如此。特殊性从来就不仅仅是局部的或仅仅是特殊客体或事件的性质或属性。如果它是这样的话，它就可能被重复，因为它可能脱离它的环境，一旦可以脱离，就没有什么理由说它不能被重复。但是正如我们已经指出过的那样，一殊相是不能被重复的。这就是说，它不能脱离它当下的环境，它的当下的环境同样也不能脱离间接的环境。假定我们不再讨论宇宙，而是局限于讨论宇宙的任何一个截面，我们称之为"在 t_1 的世界"。在 t_1 的世界中殊相的重复也意味着在 t_1 的世界的重复。我们可以很容易地看到，在 t_1 的世界是不能重复的，不管是在连续性的意义上，还是在孤立的意义上。连续性意义上的在 t_1 的世界的重复就是 t_1 时间的停止；而孤立意义上的在 t_1 的世界的重复就是使它从它前后的环境中脱离开来。这最终将导致宇宙的重复，宇宙的重复就是对宇宙自身的否定，因为能够重复的宇宙从根本上说就不是宇宙，它也不是整体性和统一性意义上的道。由于一殊相是不能重复的，所以它必须反映整个宇宙。每一殊相必须如此，因为其他的殊相也是或过去是或将来会是如此的。

将上面所讨论的要点牢记在心，我们就能够进一步说说普遍同情。从反映这一思想的角度来看问题，我们可以说宇宙就在我们之中，而不仅仅是我们在宇宙之中。"天地与我并生，万物与我为一"这一思想完全可以用其他的生命现象来解释，但这样做可能会偏离我们此处所讨论的问题。伯特兰·罗素先生曾经在什么地方这样说过，人们追求永恒，而从不想使自己无限制地胖起来。这就是说，他们想存在于所有的时间之中，而不想占据所有的空间。美学当然不允许无限制的肥胖，而经济学和心理学却驱使人们去追求永恒。

is less pronounced in the East: it is more or less confined to its rulers. Prosperity probably makes it more prevalent in the West. It is essentially a vulgar desire. On our basis here, if we are conscious of the fundamental oneness at which we are with the universe and everything there is in it, there is a sense in which we might be truly said to be all pervasive in space and time; only it is not a sense that gives the vulgar any satisfaction. To the philosophically minded, it is the sense that consoles, for it is the sense that gives him his universal sympathy with everything that surrounds him. To have a body that is ageless is to deprive one of the joys of change, of growth and decay. To have a spirit that is eternal is to punish him with the loneliness and solitude of the Gods. To want either or both of them is simply a hankering after privileges which are denied to some of the rest of the existential beings; it is an attempt to preserve the egoistical status quo by exaggerating the differences and ignoring the identity. It is thus that the Greek and Hebraic tradition in the West has made human beings anthropocentric in relation to the rest of nature and egocentric in relation to the rest of mankind. Universal sympathy is extremely unlikely if at all possible under such conditions. It is only by realizing that one is floating in one ocean of bits of Stuffed Form or Formed Stuff that universal sympathy is gained and with it also one's own all-pervasiveness and one's own eternity.

Are we not going to the extreme in one direction just as the others are doing so in the other? And what are we going to do practically when for instance a mosquito bites? Kill it, if you can, but don't condemn or hate it for biting. It is the mosquito's job to bite. Don't confound the realm of qualities with the realm of values. In the democracy of existents, each has a function pertaining to the different roles that is assigned. Being a man is a job, a station if you like, but not a status; it is a charge for one to keep, not an inheritance for one to gloat over. In the unfoldment of Tao men and mosquitoes have functions assigned to their roles. The human function is the one which those objects which are human at the same time cannot shirk just as the mosquito function is the one which these

objects which are mosquitoish at the same time cannot but perform.
Once a man turns to dust, his function as man ceases and his function as
dust begins. In the roles of a mosquito and a man, one bites and the other
kills; in the role of physical objects, they have a physical contact in which

这后一方面的愿望在东方表现得不这么强烈，它多少只局限于统治者。生活的富裕可能使追求永恒的想法在西方尤其强烈。然而，这样的想法在实质上是很平民化的。以我们在这里讨论的思想为基础，如果我们意识到我们与宇宙及与宇宙中的每一事物所共享的基本的统一性，那么我们就能从这种意义上说，我们是充溢着整个的空间和时间的，不过这样的意义是不能给我们平民以满足感的。对于一个富有哲学智慧的心灵来说，这样的意义是能够慰藉人心的，因为这种意义使他对自己周围的每一事物给以普遍同情。希望有一个不老的躯体的想法会剥夺变化、成长和衰老给人带来的种种乐趣。希望有一个永恒的心灵的想法实际上是以诸神的孤独和寂寞来惩罚一个人。想要上面任一个或想两个都要都不过是在追求别人所不能具有的一种特权。这样的企图是想要借助于扩大差异、忽视同一性来保持自我中心的地位。正因如此，西方的古希腊和希伯来的传统就把人类看作是整个宇宙的中心，把自我看作是整个人类的中心。普遍同情在这样的条件之下一点也不可能。只有认识到人是处在有质料的式或有式的质料的海洋之中，我们才能获得自己的普遍同情，才会有自己的无所不在和自己的永恒。

正如其他的人在另一个方向上走向了另一极端一样，我们不也在这一方向上走向了极端吗？在实际生活中，比如一只蚊子咬了我一口，我们准备作出什么样的反应呢？如果可能的话，就打死它，但是我们不能因为蚊子咬了我们一口而谴责或讨厌它，因为蚊子的工作就是咬人。请不要把特质的世界和价值的世界混为一谈。在存在的民主中，每一事物都有与其相适应的不同作用。成为一个人就是一份工作，你喜欢也可以叫做停泊地，但不是地位；它是人应该持有的职责，而不是沾沾自喜的遗产。在道的展开过程中，人与蚊子都有相应于他们不同角色的作用。人的作用是那些在同样时间内的有人性的客体所不能逃避的，正如蚊子的作用是在同样时间内有蚊子性的客体所不得不完成的一样。一旦人成了尘土，那么作为人的作用也就停止，但作为尘土的作用就相应地开始了。在蚊子和人的角色中，一个咬，一个打。在物理客体的角色中，

there is transference of matter-energy with certain chemical effects. The language of biting and killing is appropriate to two objects of which one is in the role of a mosquito and the other in that of a man; it is not appropriate to either or both in their role of physical objects. We are not asking the mosquito or the man to forget respectively its mosquitoishness or his humanity; we are simply asking them to remember that they are objects at the same time, and this is not much different from asking the President of the United States or the Senator from Nevada to remember that they are also citizens of the United States.

May it not be said that our view here would impede progress? The generally accepted view in the West seems to be that progress is partly due at any rate to the conquest of nature by man and this implies the latter's assertiveness. Greek light, Hebraic sweetness, Roman law, European science and American industry would have been quite impossible if men merely tried to harmonize themselves with nature or nature's God and did nothing themselves. It is difficult to speak of progress, especially in relation to the unfoldment of Tao. Being human ourselves we naturally heap our affections on humanity, but when we come to think of it detachedly, our affection may very well be blind; there may not be any reason whatever why evolution should stop with the emergence of man. If we could be detached, we might be at a loss in trying to find any striking virtue in humanity. But even limiting ourselves to human history, what is known as progress is certainly not entirely on the credit side. And what is ever more to the point is that even taking progress to be what it is generally taken to be, our view does not impede it either. What we urge, you must remember, is not a principle guiding human conduct, it issues no injunctions against killing mosquitoes or building gigantic bridges, or investigating natural phenomena laboratories, it is a view of contemplation, of detached understanding aiming at broadening our outlook without hampering our activities. If we take it to be a sort of cosmic laissez faire imposed by man, progress in the usual sense is indeed impeded, but if we take it to be a recognition of reality and process in which whatever we do, we are functioning in the unfoldment of Tao, we needn't accomplish less as human beings, though we are bound to feel more as elements in the democracy of existents.

他们有物理上的接触，在其中有物质能量的转换及其所产生的化学后果。咬和打的语言在此是与这两个客体相适应的，蚊子的作用是咬，人的作用则是打。而这样的语言对于它们作为物理客体的角色中的一个或两个来说都是不相适应的。我们并不是要求蚊子或人忘记各自的蚊子性或人性，我们只是要求它们记住在同样的时间内它们都是客体，这与要求美国总统或来自内华达州的参议员不要忘记他们也同样是美国的公民一样。

希望不会有人说我们的这些看法会阻碍进步吧。在西方一个被普遍认同的看法似乎是，无论如何进步是由于人在某种程度上对自然的征服。这就意味着人的武断态度。如果人只是一味地努力使自己与自然或自然的上帝和谐相处而无所事事，那么希腊的明朗、希伯来的美妙、罗马的法律、欧洲的科学和美国的工业都将是绝对不可能的。谈论进步是一个很困难的话题，尤其是在与道的展开相联系的这一方面。作为人，我们当然会将自己的感情放在人性方面；但是当我们以超然的态度来看这样的问题时，我们的这种感情可能就是盲目的。没有任何理由使进化的链条在人类出现之后打住。如果我们能够有超然的态度，那么我们会在努力发现人性中使我们赞叹不已的优良品行方面不知所措。但是即便把我们自己限制在人类历史方面，我们所知道的关于进步的一切也显然并不完全是积极方面的。更为重要的是，即便在一般的意义上来谈论进步，我们的看法也不会阻碍进步。你必须记住，我们在此所提倡的不是指导人类行动的原则，它没有发布禁令反对打死蚊子或建筑庞大的桥梁或调查自然现象的实验室，而是提倡一种沉思的看法，一种旨在拓展我们的视野而绝不阻碍我们行动的超然的理解。如果我们把它看作是由人强加的宇宙放任主义的话，那么通常意义上所谓的进步确实受到了阻碍。但是如果把它看作是对现实和过程的认识，在其中不管我们做什么，都是在道的展开过程之中起作用，那么我们作为人没有必要成就更少，虽然我们作为存在的民主中的因素必然会感受到更多。

REALITY AND PROCESS[2]

I

There are four kinds of possibilities from the point of view of their realization. We shall discuss them in turn.

A possibility is necessary if it cannot but be realized. It is a possibility of which the failure of realization is contradictory. Hence it is a possibility that cannot but be a universal. With the previous discussion in mind we can easily show Form to be such a possibility. Although the number of such possibilities is not large, it is not confined to the single possibility Form either. Consequent upon the necessary realization of Form, the possibility realization is realized and with it also the possibility realness. Since a necessary possibility cannot but be a universal, universality is also necessary. From the point of view of logic such possibilities are important in view of what has been said about tautologies. From the point of view of epistemology these possibilities are unimportant, their realization does not result in our present kind of world.

A possibility is eternally realized if it must be realized in the senses discussed in the last chapters. The failure of the realization of such a possibility is not contradictory, but simply never contingent. The term "eternal" suggests time. We should not speak of such a possibility in terms of time, because temporalness is itself such a possibility. But if we do speak in terms of time we can easily see that there is one time in which these possibilities are not realized. These possibilities owe their realization to the metaphysical principle. Their realization is not a matter for pure reason of logic, but belongs to that givenness or stubbornness, that core of factuality with which we are confronted in our experience and from which we are never free no matter how badly we might want to free ourselves from it. The number of such possibilities is not large, perhaps larger than that of the first kind. Change, temporalness and spatialness are such possibilities. We can see here the importance of the metaphysical principle to some extent. The necessary possibilities when realized merely give a minimum of reality which needn't be of any specific shape or character familiar to us. It is the metaphysical principle that says that the reality thus logically forced upon us is also bound to be changing, to be temporal and spatial, etc. As a result we

实在与过程

一

从可能现实的角度看有四种类型的可能。在下面我们将依次讨论这四种可能。

不得不现实的可能就是必然的，这样的可能如果没有现实就是矛盾的。因此这样的可能必然是共相。如果我们记住了前面的讨论，那么我们就会很容易地看到，式就是这样的一种可能。虽然这样的可能的数量不大，但是这样的可能不仅仅局限于式。作为式的必然现实的结果，可能的现实是现实的，与之一起的还有真实这一可能。由于不得不现实的可能必然是共相，共相性也同样是必然的。从逻辑的观点看，从我们在上面已经提到的重言式来看，这样的可能是重要的。但是从认识论的角度来看，这些可能并不是重要的，它们的现实并不导致我们目前这样的世界。

如果一种可能是我们在上面的章节已经讨论过的意义上现实的，那么这样的可能就总是现实的。这样的可能没有现实并不就是矛盾的，只不过并不是偶然的。"总是"这一术语意味着时间。我们不应该在时间的意义上来谈论这种可能，因为时间性本身就是这样的可能。但是如果我们从时间方面说，我们就能很容易地看到有那么一个时间内这些可能是没有现实。这些可能的现实是由于形而上学原则。它们的现实并不是由于纯粹的逻辑方面的原因，而是由于所与性或刚性和现实的核心，这是我们在经验中经常碰到的，不管我们怎么努力都不可能摆脱它们的。这一类可能的数目也并不是很大，然而可能要比第一类可能的数目要来得大些。变化、空间和时间就是这样的可能。在此我们可以看到形而上学原则在某种程度上的重要性。必然现实的可能当它们现实时只不过给出了实在的最基本的东西，不必是我们所熟悉的形状或特性。是形而上学原则指出，逻辑地为我们所接受的实在是必然要变化的，是有时间和空间的，等等。

have already a kind of world which in some broad outline resembles very much the world we live in, for not only have we change and time, motion and space, but also a frame of reference such that reality is disintegrated into multiplicity without chaos. The block universe, not perhaps in the sense in which James meant it, was never an actual state of affairs.

A possibility is contingent, if it may be realized or unrealized or once realized ceases to be realized. The realization of such a possibility is neither necessary nor obligatory and the number of such possibilities is bound to be infinite; the main bulk of constituent possibilities of Form belong to this class. Perhaps instead of contingent possibilities we might speak of contingent realities. Most of the things with which we are faced are contingent realities. We are liable to dismiss "mere facts" with a sneer. If we are interested in universals or their interrelatedness, the sneer may have its cause or even justification, but one is never sure that he is the one who sneers last. "Mere facts" have a givenness that is stubborn; they cannot be dismissed, except by postulating a criterion of relevancy upon which they are declared to be irrelevant somewhat as the fox dismissed the grapes as being sour. In either case, there is a givenness which cannot be tempered with, a givenness which accrues more to the contingent realities than to the necessary realities. Since reason enables us to accept the latter, it is thus made reasonable, and since reason alone does not enable us to accept the former, all that we can do about it is to say "there it is."

Natural history informs us that a large number of plants and animals have come and gone and during their tenure of occupation or realization, if they were given the facility for imagination, they might have imagined themselves to be destined to permanence. There was a time when there were no human beings and there may be a time when there shall not be human beings. Years ago a newspaper man upon being disturbed by Balfour's cold aloofness said that the latter seemed to be always conscious of the interglacial ages and was probably emotionally prepared to face another glacial age. It is difficult to say whether such consciousness is likely to be disturbing to human life, whether it decreases the sound and fury of the stage, but if it is also modifying our view of human significance, important undoubtedly to human beings, but not applicable to the long views of evolution, it is on our basis a very

其结果就是，我们已经拥有一种世界，它大概与我们生活于其中的世界是极其类似的，因为不仅我们有变化、时间、运动和空间，而且也有参照系使实在很有秩序地分解成多样性。这样的宇宙可能并不是詹姆士所说的块状宇宙，它从来就不是现实的状态。

如果一可能已经现实或未曾现实或曾经现实而现在成虚，这样的可能叫做不老是现实的可能。这类可能的现实既不是必然的，也不是强制性的。这一类可能的数目必然是无限的，式中的绝大多数的可能就属于这一类。或许我们可以把偶然的可能称为偶然的实在。我们所碰到的绝大多数的事物就是偶然的实在。我们常常对所谓"纯粹的事实"不屑一顾。如果我们对共相或共相间的关联感兴趣，我们的这种蔑视是有其原因的或者是正当理由的。但是我们却从不能确定我们能一直蔑视到最后。"纯粹的事实"有一种所与性，是非常顽固的。它们是不能被忽视的，除非假定一参照标准，依据这样的标准宣布它们是不相干的，正如狐狸嫌弃葡萄太酸一样。在这两种事例中，都存在着不能被缓和的所与性，所与性逐渐形成偶然的实在，而非必然的实在。因为理性使我们接受了后者，因此它们是有道理的。由于仅凭理性我们还不能接受前者，所以我们所能做的只不过是说"它就在那儿"。

自然史告诉我们，无数动植物生生灭灭。在它们（对时空的）占有或现实阶段，如果它们具有想象的能力，它们可能会想象到它们本身是会永久存在的。曾经有一段时间是不存在人类的，将来也可能人类不再存在。几年前有一个新闻记者为巴尔福冷淡的态度所激怒，他说道，巴尔福似乎总是能注意到间冰期而且也似乎在感情上做好了准备去迎接另一个冰河期。很难说这样的意识是否能使人类的生命深感不安，是否能降低这一时期的喧嚣和躁动，但是如果这样的意识也能够使人类的重要性的观念有所改变的话——这一观念对于人类来说无疑非常重要，但不适用于长期进化——从我们的

249

healthy consciousness indeed. Nor do we have to disturb our emotional equanimity unduly. Whether or not there will be supermen to succeed us doesn't really make much difference. We have already accepted individual death, yearning towards eternity to the contrary notwithstanding. We have also learned to accept with equanimity the passing of great ages in human history. There is no reason to suppose that we need be especially disturbed by the termination of a tenure of existence at a future date. Though evolution does not repeat itself, possibilities are capable of repetitions of realizations. It is by no means impossible to have another period of human beings after we have died a few millions or a few billions of years.

What we are concerned here is however not the fate of humanity, but the restatement of natural history in our own terms. When we say that saber-toothed tigers and dinosaurs have come and gone, we mean here merely that in the unfoldment of Tao, there was a time when the possibilities saber-toothed-tigerness and dinosaurness were realized and subsequently disrealized. In other words Stuff has entered into these possibilities and subsequently has left them. When we say that there are no dragons we mean that the possibility dragonness is not realized at the present. There is no reason to suppose that in the unfoldment of Tao there never was or never will be any dragon, for dragonness is a contingent possibility. It certainly is neither necessary nor impossible, neither eternally realized nor eternally unrealized. It is a possibility the realization of which is contingent. The same is true of humanity. Our existence is merely contingent. It is of course of the greatest importance or significance to us. But then to any class of existents whatever, the realization of the possibility corresponding to its defining concept is always important and significant. We may like to see the extermination of the ants from our point of view, but from the point of view of the ants, if they were given the faculty to reply, they would disagree with us with some degree of violence. The failure of Voltaire to appreciate the beggar's point of view is due to the former's concentration on being Voltaire; if he were more sympathetic towards the beggar's plight, he would see that even a beggar has to live. It may be that on the basis of a certain prescribed criterion of valuation, humanity is more valuable than ants, or Voltaire more valuable than the beggar, but valuation is prescription

观念看来，这样的意识确实是非常健康的。我们也没有必要过分地为此深感不安。在人类之后是否有可能出现超人实际上也不会有太大的影响。我们已经接受了人的个体是要死亡的，尽管会追求永恒不灭。我们也同样着心平气和地接受了人类历史伟人时期的逝去。那么就没有理由假定我们应该为人类将来的终结而苦恼不已、痛苦万状。虽然进化是不会重复的，但是可能却可以是重复现实的。在人类灭绝后的几百万年或几十亿年之后，人类发展的另一个阶段的出现并不是不可能的。

　　我们在此感兴趣的并不是人类的命运，而是以我们的角度来复述自然的历史。当我们说剑齿虎和恐龙出现之后又灭绝，我们在此只是说在道的展开过程中有这样一段时间，那时剑齿虎性和恐龙性现实了而后来却成虚了。换句话说，质料进入并最终离开了这些可能性。当我们说不存在龙的时候，我们是说在目前龙性这一可能并没有现实。我们没有理由假定在道的展开的过程之中从来没有或将来也不会有龙，因为龙性不是老是现实的可能。它当然既不是必然的，也不是不可能的，既不是永远现实的，也不是永远不现实的。它是这样的可能，即它的现实并不是必然的。这样的话也同样适用于人类。我们的存在也只是偶然的。虽然对于我们而言，我们的存在是非常重要的。然而对于任何一类存在来说，与其定义性概念相应的可能的现实总是很重要的，是很有意义的。从我们的观点来看，我们可能想要看到蚂蚁的灭绝。但是从蚂蚁的观点来看，如果它们有能力回应，它们就有可能比较激烈地表示反对。伏尔泰不能理解乞丐的观点是因为伏尔泰只专注于做伏尔泰。如果他对乞丐的窘境有更多的同情的话，那么他就会看到即便是乞丐也必须要生存下去。按照某种既定的价值标准，人类可能要比蚂蚁更有价值，或者说伏尔泰可能要比乞丐更有价值，但是价值是一种规定，而不是

not description. What is prescribed as values does not always coincide with what is described as qualities and relations. Distinguish the realms and one can see clearly that the valuable needn't be the noncontingent in the unfoldment of Tao. On some criterion of values, it is the contingent that is valuable. Consider our own experiences. It is not the span of life that gives most of us satisfaction, but the significant experiences that can be crowded into it. Most people would value an hour of love or of intellectual excitement or the moment of triumphant discovery than a whole year of monotony and colorlessness. Even in more ordinary circumstances it is the anticipation of the emergent, the abandonment to the occasion, the regret over the passing and the recollection of the past that make life and living different from mere existence.

We are not here interested in the special criterion suggested above; we are concerned rather with the role played by the contingent possibilities. It is the realization of these that supplies the universe with its richness, its variety, and its colorfulness. Obviously if the necessary and the eternally realized possibilities were the only realized possibilities, the universe would have been dreary, barren and bleak and it could not have been the universe since so many possible worlds would have been excluded from it. We shall point out later that if the universe were really the all-embracing entity we take it to be, then all the contingent possibilities must be realized in process. The richness, the variety and colorfulness are assured us by the metaphysical principle. While the realization of any contingent possibility is contingent, the realization of the whole class of contingent possibilities is not contingent. If the realization of the contingent possibilities was itself contingent, Stuff might stay in the necessary and eternally realized possibilities and the metaphysical principle would then be multifid.

A possibility is eternally unrealized if it can be realized only when the sum total of contingent possibilities have been or are realized. Since there never was or is or will be a time when all the contingent possibilities are all realized, such a possibility is eternally unrealized. The realization of such possibilities is not impossible, for if it were, the possibility wouldn't be a possibility, it would be an impossibility. Though eternally unrealized, it is yet a possibility, that is to say, the corresponding idea to

一种描述。被指定为是价值的东西并不总是与被描述为特质和关系的东西相一致。辨别不同的领域，我们就能清楚地看到，有价值的东西在道的展开过程中并不总是必然的。从某种价值观来看，正是具有偶然性的东西才是有价值的。想想我们自身的经历：对于我们中的大多数人而言能给我们带来满足感的不是生命的长度，而是生命中充满着的重要的经历。大多数人可能会珍惜瞬间的爱情或短暂的精神上的享受或成功的发现的时刻，而不是整年的机械的、毫无色彩的生活。即使是在日常生活环境中，正是对新情况的期待、对盛大时刻的沉迷、对逝去的懊悔、对过去的回忆，才使得人的生命和生活不同于简单的存在。

在此我们不是对上述的特殊标准感兴趣，我们关心的仅仅是不老是现实的可能的作用问题。正是这种可能的现实才向宇宙提供了丰富性、多样性和色彩。显然，如果仅仅必然的和老是现实的可能是唯一现实的可能，那么宇宙将是沉寂的、荒芜的和惨淡的。由于许多可能的世界被排除在宇宙之外，那么宇宙就不可能存在。我们将在后面指出，如果宇宙的确是我们认为的包罗万象的实体，那么所有不老是现实的可能必须在过程中现实。形而上学原则使我们确信这个宇宙是丰富的、多样的和有色彩的。虽然任何不老是现实的可能的现实是偶然的，但是整类不老是现实的可能的现实并不就是偶然的。如果不老是现实的可能的现实本身是偶然的，那么质料可能会停留在必然的和老是现实的可能之中，而形而上学原则也将不是统一的原则。

如果仅在所有的偶然可能已经现实的情况下，一个可能才能现实的话，那么这一可能永远不能现实。由于在过去或现在或将来不可能有这样的时间，即在其中所有的不老是现实的可能都现实了，所以这样的可能就是老不现实的可能。这样的可能的现实不是不可能的，因为如果不可能，那么这样的可能也就不是可能了，而是不可能。虽然它们是老不现实的，但它们依然是可能。这就是说，与

such a possibility is not a contradiction, but a genuine concept. Perhaps we have better ways of defining such possibilities, but proceeding from a discussion of contingent possibilities we find it most convenient to define such a possibility in terms of contingent possibilities. Take such a possibility as infinity. It can be easily shown to be eternally unrealized. Perhaps we better start with concept corresponding to the possibility. The idea certainly is not impossible, so far as we know it has never been proved to be contradictory. It certainly is not unreal as an idea or a concept for even those who declare it to be unreal are battling against it and do not regard themselves as battling against nothing. Some may have confused imagination with conception and regard infinity which is genuinely unimaginable to be thereby also inconceivable, but if it were really inconceivable, it should have been proved to be contradictory. But it isn't. The problem is therefore not with the concept but with the possibility. As a possibility, infinity must be admitted and yet as a possibility, it is never realized. It is this lack of realization of the possibility that makes the corresponding concept seemingly unreal.

Perhaps a reference to the doctrines of infinite divisibility will bring out the points which we are laboring under some pains to exhibit. To say that a foot of bar is infinitely divisible is really to say that it is never infinitely divided or infinitesimally is to deny that infinite dividedness is ever a fact in or an item of reality. It is because infinite dividedness is never realized that infinite divisibility is a sound doctrine, and vice versa, it is because infinite divisibility is a sound doctrine that infinite dividedness is never realized. Granting the validity of the doctrine of infinite divisibility in a world in which realization takes the form of the concrete and finite, one realizes that infinite dividedness is not an item of reality, but a limit to a process, a limit which the process may approach but never reaches. If we regard the limit as being reachable, the doctrine of infinite divisibility crumbles. The very notion of infinite divisibility requires the possibility of infinite dividedness to be eternally unrealized.

It can be realized only in the sense that its realization is not a priori contradictory; it isn't realized because the process of realization which is essentially a process of the realization of contingent possibilities must be complete before it is ever realized. And its process is never complete.

这样的可能相应的意念并不是矛盾的意念，而是真正的概念。可能我们有更好的方式来定义这样的可能。但是从讨论不老是现实的可能出发，我们发现最方便的方式就是以不老是现实的可能来定义这样的可能。比如说"无穷"这个可能。显然"无穷"是一老不现实的可能。或许我们最好从与这一可能相应的概念开始讨论。这样的意念当然不是不可能的，就我们现在所能知道的而言，它并没有被证明为是矛盾的。作为一意念或概念当然它不是不真实的，因为即便那些宣称它不真实的人也在反对它，而不认为他们自己反对的是无。有些人可能把想象与概念混淆起来了，因此把真正是不可想象的无穷也看作是不可思议的。但是如果它是真正不可思议的，那么它就应该被证明是矛盾的。然而它不是矛盾的。因此问题不在概念方面，而在可能方面。作为一可能，无穷必须得到承认，而它作为一可能是老不现实的。正是由于缺乏可能的现实，所以相应的概念看上去是不真实的。

可能提起无穷可分性会使我们一直在努力展示的东西明确起来。说一英尺长的木棒可以无限地分割下去，实实在在地是在说它从未被无限地分割过；或从无限小的观点看是否认无限分割是实在的一个事实或一种实在。正是因为无限分割是老不现实的，所以以无限可分性是一个合理的理论。反过来说也是一样，正因为无限可分性是一个合理的理论，所以无限分割从未得到现实。在现实采取具体和有限的形式的世界中承认无限可分性理论的合理性，我们就会认识到无限分割不是一种实在，而是过程的一个极限。这一过程会无限地接近于这样的极限，但是永远不可能达到。如果我们认为这样的极限是可以达到的，那么无限可分的理论也就不攻自破了。无限可分的想法要求无限可分的可能是老不现实的可能。它只有在这样的情况下才能现实，即它的现实并不是先验的矛盾。它不能现实，因为现实的过程本质上是不老是现实的可能的现实过程，在它现实之前这一过程必须完成。但是，这样的过程不可能是完成的。

The first two kinds of possibilities are important because one of them guarantees us with the absolute minimum of reality while the other furnishes us with the ultimate basis of factual givenness. The second two kinds of possibilities are also important for different reasons. The realization of contingent possibilities gives us the richness, the variety and the completeness of Tao, whereas the eternally unrealized possibilities are useful in supplying us with the implements in the realm of thinking and thought. These possibilities are not so important as possibilities as they are from the point of view of their corresponding concepts. "Infinity," "nothing," "not," ... are of the greatest importance not from the point of view of their being possibilities since as possibilities they are eternally unrealized but from the point of view of their corresponding concepts since these are the most important lubricant in thought processes and the most significant links in thought structures. In fact, without them we cannot think. Even in ordinary life we make good use of eternally unrealized possibilities such as "the future" or "tomorrow." Tomorrow as a variable never comes, but its value for Jan. 15th 1944, namely Jan. 16th, will be experienced by us in less than twenty-four hours, and when we do experience it, it is of course no longer tomorrow.

II

Reality is concrete if a plurality of possibilities are realized by one and identical Stuff. Take anything that is concrete, you will find that concreteness lies in the plurality of possibilities having one and identical Stuff. Thus, Tao is necessarily concrete because on the one hand with the realization of Form, realization and reality are realized resulting in the realization of a plurality of possibilities, and on the other the Stuff that is in Form must be one and identical. Although we do not say directly that the universe is concrete, we are saying indirectly that Tao is necessarily so. We have three principles which it is our business to formulate and discuss in this section. The first one to be discussed is the principle of congruence: reality unfolds itself with congruence.

The idea of congruence is borrowed from the ordinary idea of starting from different roads and reaching without conflict the same or different destinations. Regard the different possibilities realized as the different roads and the same or different realities arrived at as the destinations our principle furnishes us with a minimal character, namely concreteness. It

前两类可能是重要的，因为其中的一类向我们提供了关于实在的绝对的最低值，而另一类则向我们提供了事实性的所与的终极基础。后两类可能由于不同的理由也是相当重要的。不老是现实的可能给我们以道的丰富性、多样性和完全性。而老不现实的可能是有用的，因为它向我们提供了思想和思考的工具。这些可能作为可能不如从与它们相应的概念来看那么重要。我们说"无穷""空""无"……是极其重要的，这不是从它们是可能的观点来看的，因为作为可能它们是老不现实的可能；而是从与它们相应的概念的观点来看的，因为它们是思想过程中最重要的润滑剂，是思想结构中最重要的联系项。事实上，没有它们，我们根本不可能进行思考。即便是在日常生活中，我们也经常有效地运用像"未来"或"明天"这样的老不现实的可能。明天作为一个变项从未来来到，但是它对 1944 年 1 月 15 日的值即 1 月 16 日却可以被我们在不到24 小时内经验到。一旦我们经验到了它，它当然也就不是明天了。

二

如果各种各样的可能由于同一的质料而现实，那么实在就是具体的。比如任何一个具体的事物，我们都能发现具体性存在于各种可能具有同一的质料之中。因此，道必然是具体的，因为一方面由于式的现实，现实和实在被现实了，结果就是各种可能的现实。另一方面在式中的质料必须是同一的。虽然我们并没有直接说宇宙是具体的，而我们却间接说了道必然是具体的。我们在此的任务就是要确立和讨论三个原则。需要讨论的第一个原则是和谐的原则。实在在展开的过程中是要遵循和谐的原则的。和谐这一意念是从日常生活中借用来的，即从不同的道路出发最终却达到同一的或不同的目标。把不同的现实了的可能看作是不同的道路，把所达到的同样的或不同的实在看作是目标，那么我们的原则就提供给我们最基本

is the principle of concretization only in the sense of the minimal content of the principle. The congruence with which possibilities are realized result in concreteness if we remember that so far as the Stuffed Form is concerned, the Stuff that is there is bound to be one and identical.

The notion of concreteness in connection with this concrete table or that concrete apple is borrowed from our notion applied to Tao. The concreteness of Tao is not open to doubt, because we have on the one hand a plurality of possibilities realized and on the other one and identical Stuff. The entirety or the sum total of anything whatever must be identical with itself, and since the Stuff in Form is all the Stuff there is, it must be identical with itself. But concerning this concrete desk or that concrete apple, the case is different. We have to be sure a plurality of possibilities realized in each case but in either of them the Stuff that realized it can only be roughly and indeterminately spoken of as one and identical. The inexpressible x in this concrete apple, the "bit" of Stuff that realizes the possibilities redness, roundness and sweetness is not the inexpressible x in that desk, the bit of Stuff that realizes the possibilities rectangularity, brownness, etc.; but beyond that our identification fails, since we cannot point to the inexpressible x, we cannot assert the identity of the inexpressible x with itself either in this concrete apple or in that concrete desk. The concreteness of any ordinary concrete object cannot be demonstrated. It is only with rough probability of applicability that the concreteness of ordinary objects can be said to have been experienced.

Concreteness is the minimal content of the principle of congruence. As a maximum the principle is also the basis of the principle of consistency. We are familiar with the rather prosaic dictum that ideas must be consistent. Whatever consistency may mean, the dictum does not prevent the occurrence of inconsistent ideas in thought processes. What it does is to invalidate the presence of inconsistent ideas in thought structures, and this presence must be invalidated because if it weren't, the structure wouldn't reflect the pattern of possible reality. The ultimate basis is that concrete reality is congruent. In the broadest sense consistency merely means the absence of contradictions, that is to say, if two or more propositions or sets of propositions are both or all false they can be also consistent——one certainly can lie consistently. Ordinarily

的特性，即具体性。它是具体的原则仅仅是因为它是具有最少内容的原则。如果我们记得谈到有质料的式，其中的质料必然是同一的，那么可能现实所遵循的和谐就会导致具体性。

与这张具体的桌子或那个具体的苹果相联系着的具体性的思想是从我们运用于道的思想借用来的。道的具体性是不可怀疑的，因为一方面我们有各种现实了的可能，另一方面我们有同一的质料。任何事物的全部都必须与自身同一，而且由于式中的质料就是所有的质料，所以质料也必须与自身同一。但是考虑到这张具体的桌子或那个具体的苹果，情形却有所不同。我们必须得确定在每一情形中有现实了的各种可能，然而在它们中的任何一个之中，使其现实的质料只能够大体上、不明确地说成是同一的。在这个具体的苹果中有不可表达的 x，但使红色性、圆性、甜度这些可能现实的"这一点"质料并不等同于那张桌子中不可表达的 x，即使长方形性、棕色性等可能实现的"那一点"质料。除此之外，我们不可能再辨别什么东西，由于我们不能够指出不可表达的 x，所以我们不能够断言在这个具体的苹果中或在那张具体的桌子中不可表达的 x 是否与自身同一。在日常生活中的任何具体的客体的具体性都不能够展示出来。只有通过粗略的适用性的统计才能说日常的客体的具体性被经验到了。

具体性是和谐原则的最少的内容，但这一原则最高层面也是一致原则的基础。我们非常熟悉这样的一个平凡道理，即意念之间必须是一致的。不管一致有什么样的含义，这一道理并不能阻止前后不一致的意念在思想过程中出现。它所能做的只是宣判思想结构中不一致的意念的出现是无效的。不一致意念的出现必须被看作是无效的，因为如果不是这样的话，那么思想结构将不能反映可能的实在的图案。终极的基础是具体的实在是和谐的。在最广泛的意义上说，一致性只不过意味着排除矛盾。这就是说，如果两个或更多的命题或两类及以上命题都是假的，它们仍然可能是一致的。一个人

we are liable to confine ourselves to the narrower meaning in the sense that given the truth of certain propositions the body of propositions that may be true with it are consistent with the given propositions. Here one is guided by extra logical considerations and the criterion of consistency is often very fruitful. But the fruitfulness of the criterion is obtained only on the condition that a certain givenness is given or that we do have certain non-necessary and yet true propositions. At the level of the necessary and eternal realities, the principle of congruence merely results in the concretization of reality. But given the realization of certain contingent possibilities, the principle also provides us with trends or tendencies. This merely says that if no contingent possibilities were realized, the principle of congruence is merely a principle of concretion or concretization.

Are we sure that there is to be the realization of contingent possibilities? We have already said somewhere that although the realization of this or that contingent possibility is contingent, the realization of contingent possibilities as a class is not contingent. If the ontological principle alone holds we need not have contingency, but since the metaphysical principle holds also, and we have eternally realized possibilities, contingency cannot be excluded. Since time and change must be realized as a result of the metaphysical principle, contingent possibilities as a class must be realized for otherwise there wouldn't be change or time. The metaphysical principle says that Stuff enters into and leaves off from possibilities. The necessary possibilities are those in which Stuff necessarily stays, and the eternally realized possibilities are such that there is no time when they are unrealized. If those alone were the realized possibilities, Stuff cannot be said to enter into or leave off from possibilities. Under such a hypothesis Stuff merely stays and the kind of world we should have would be entirely static. It is on account of the metaphysical principle that temporalness and changeability must be realized and since there is time and change, there is bound to be the realization of contingent possibilities. To say that there is bound to be the realization of contingent possibilities is to say that reality unfolds itself with contingency.

If reality merely unfolds itself with congruence we have a static though a concrete world, but since reality also unfolds itself with

当然可以使他所说的谎话完全一致。一般来讲，我们倾向于将一致的含义局限在这样的范围内，即假定一命题是真的，而包含这一命题的命题总体又是真的，那么这一命题总体就可以说是与这一给定的命题一致。在此我们为逻辑上的考虑所引导，而一致的标准经常是富有成效的。但是这一标准只有在这样的条件之下才有效果，这一条件就是给定了某所与性或我们确实具有某些不是必然的但却真的命题。在必然的和永远的实在的层面上，和谐的原则仅仅导致实在的具体化。但是假定某些不老是现实的可能的现实，这一原则也会向我们提供倾向性。这只不过是说，如果不老是现实的可能没有现实，那么和谐原则也只不过是具体或具体化的原则。

我们确信不老是现实的可能会现实吗？我们已经在某处说过，虽然这一或那一不老是现实的可能的现实是偶然的，但不老是现实的可能作为一个类，它们的现实就不是偶然的了。如果仅仅是本体论原则成立，我们不必具有偶然性，但是由于形而上学原则也同样成立，而且我们也有老是现实的可能，因此偶然性是不能被排除的。由于从形而上学原则的角度看，时间和变化必须是现实的，因此不老是现实的可能作为一个类也必须是现实的，否则就不可能有时间和变化。形而上学原则主张质料进出于可能之间。必然的可能是质料必然在其中的可能，而老是现实的可能是当其不能现实之时就没有时间了。如果仅仅是上述的这些可能为现实的可能，那么就不能说质料进出于可能之间。在这样的假设之下，质料仅停留在可能之中，那么我们所拥有的世界将完全是静止的。正是根据形而上学原则，时间性和变化性必须是现实的；由于有时间和变化，那么必然会有不老是现实的可能的现实。说必然会有不老是现实的可能现实，就是说实在是偶然地展开自身。

如果实在仅仅是和谐地展开自身，那么我们的世界虽然是具体的然而却是静止的。但是由于实在也同样偶然地展开自身，这样我

contingency, we have not only a concrete but also a dynamic world. Both principles together assure us of a world that is both static and dynamic, static in some respects and dynamic in others. The inevitable relativity in human experience in general and the individual or subjective preferences in particular often result in some people attaching greater reality to the dynamic while others more reality to the static. The distinction between conservatives and radicals in so far as one sees the danger of change and the other doesn't does not seem to be confined to politics; some people are perhaps more Parmenides minded while others Heraclitus minded. A different emphasis by different people is perhaps desirable and salutary, but a sense of reality should include both the static and the dynamic. The basic core of factuality or givenness or stubborness as we have pointed out before is not attached to anything that is unchanging, nor is it uniquely associated with the ephemeral or kaleidoscopic. What is known as the nature of things gathered in our experience, no matter how prejudiced our experience may be, furnishes us with a sense of reality that appropriates a more or less adequate amount of staticity or dynamicness to various things; hence in ordinary life we have very little danger of merging the static into the dynamic or vice versa. It is only in metaphysics or in ontology that one of them is declared to be unreal because the other is somewhat the criterion of reality.

While an emphasis on either staticity or dynamicness may be salutary at different times, a divergence of what we conceive to be ultimately real from what is sometimes known as the apparently real is liable to be vicious. There may be causes leading up to such a divergence. It may be that ultimate reality must be eternal and the eternal is easily taken to be the unchanging; it may be that this notion of change is itself full of difficulties with which reality cannot in theory be burdened; and it may also be that it is easier to turn around and regard change as the ultimate reality. But the intellectual processes leading up to the divergence is one thing and its effect is quite another. In epistemology naive realism must be criticized, but it cannot be abandoned without also crumbling the very foundation of epistemology. The theory of private sense-data seems to have accumulated a wealth of detail that does credit to human ingenuity, but no matter how much theorizing we are willing to accord to this

们就不只拥有具体的而且也是能动的世界。这两个原则向我们保证这世界既是静止的，也是能动的，在某些方面是静止的，在另一些方面则是能动的。人类经验总体上必不可免的相对性及个体上的个人或主观偏好经常导致某些人赋予能动更多实在性，而另一些人则赋予静止更多的实在性。就一方看到变化的危险、另一方没看到而言，保守者和激进者之间的区别并不仅仅局限于政治领域。有些人的思想倾向于巴门尼德，而另一些人的思想却倾向于赫拉克利特。不同的人有不同的思想倾向，这可能是件好事，是有益的，但是实在感却应该同时包含静止和能动这两者。正如我们在前面已经指出过的那样，真实性或所与行或刚性的本质并不是始终不变的事物所具有的，也并不仅仅与短暂的或变化万千的事物联系在一起。不管我们的经验多么具有偏见，在我们经验中所具有的关于事物性质的看法，将会向我们提供实在感，从而把或多或少适度的静止性和能动性归之于各种不同的事物。因此在日常生活中，我们并没有将静止性并入能动性的危险，或能动性并入静止性的危险。只有在形而上学或本体论中，它们中的一个才被认为是不真实的，因为另一个有几分是实在的标准。

在不同的时间强调静止或者强调能动都可能是有益的，然而把我们认为终极真实的事物与间或被看作显而易见真实的事物二者偏离开来却容易造成伤害。我们作出这样的偏离是有一定原因的。可能是我们认为，终极的实在必须是永恒的，而永恒的东西容易被看作是没有变化的；也可能是这样的，变化的观念本身充满着种种的困难，从理论上讲实在不能承载这样的困难；也可能是，转而把变化看作是终极的实在更容易一些。但是引导出这样偏离的思维过程是一件事，由此而产生的结果则是另一件事。在认识论中，素朴实在论必须受到批评，但是我们却不可能完全抛弃素朴实在论而不摧毁认识论的基础。私人感觉材料的理论看上去积累了丰富的细节，为人类的机智增光添彩，但是不管我们想给这种方法授予多少理论

approach, we cannot evolve out of these theories the common objective world so conveniently provided for us by naive realism. Once the bottom is left out, no amount of stuffing at the top will give us any solidity or security. The same may be said about theories of reality. One could be easily sympathized with for being dissatisfied with the ephemeral realities in our experience, but if we dash off at a tangent and erect a theory of reality so divergent from our experience we are bound to have the vicious result that either we feel no sense of reality in accordance with the theory propounded or by sticking to it we make ourselves unreal to our fellow men. Our notion of reality is such that on the one hand reality is static in some respects and dynamic in others, and on the other it is in essence not much different from the items presented to us in our experience. The principle of congruence supplies us with a concrete and static world, and the principle of contingency supplies us with a contingent and dynamic one. While the principles are separately stated, they do not operate separately and it is quite senseless to ask which one operated first.

The principle of contingency merely enables us to have variety. But it does not afford us economy. It is quite possible to have a series of realizations that is single file; if so, we have temporal variation or variety in succession, but no spatial richness or richness that is con-temporaneous. We may have a lumpy block of a world that changes, and yet devoid of any richness in shape or color. In order to supply us with the latter, we have to have the third principle, namely, reality unfolds itself with multiple individuality. This is a principle of economy; it assures us that the series of realizations is not in single file, but in multiple file, so that the block world is integrated into individuals capable of realizing almost all the possibilities that can be consistently realized at the same place and at the same time. If the world were one individual, only a few possibilities could be realized at any time, but since the world is integrated into a multiplicity of individuals, an enormous number of possibilities are realized. Lump six blocks together, and you have only six sides, but break the block into six and you have thirty-six sides. The number of possibilities that could be realized is enormously increased with the admission of this principle.

推定，我们也绝对不可能从这些理论中演化出共同的客观世界，而素朴实在论却能够极其容易地向我们呈现出这样的世界。一旦基础被忽视了，那么上层的材料不管多少都不可能给我们提供可靠性或安全性。这样的话也同样适用于实在的理论。经验中转瞬即逝的实在不能带来满足，我们在这点上能轻易得到赞同，但是如果我们突然离开原有的思路，并建立严重偏离我们经验的实在理论，那么就必然会产生这样的不良后果，即或者是我们感觉不到与上面所提倡的理论相一致的实在感，或者是如果坚持这样的理论，那么对我们的伙伴来说，我们自己就是不真实的了。我们所具有的实在的观念是这样的：一方面实在在某些方面是静止的，在其他方面是能动的；另一方面在本质上它与呈现在我们经验中的个体事物并没有很大的区别。和谐原则向我们提供的是具体的和静止的世界，而偶然性原则向我们提供的是偶然的和能动的世界。虽然这两个原则是分别被阐述的，但它们并不是分别起作用的。如果要问哪一原则首先起作用，那么显然这样的问题是毫无意义的。

偶然性原则仅仅使我们具有多样化，但是它并不向我们提供经济原则。很有可能我们具有单一系列的现实。如果是这样的话，我们有连续的时间方面的多样性，但是却没有空间方面的多样性或同时发生的多样性。我们可能有一个大而笨重的块状世界，虽然有变化，然而却没有形色状态方面的多样性。为了向我们提供这后一方面的多样性，我们必须有第三个原则，即实在以丰富的个性展示其自身。这一原则就是经济原则，它向我们保证连续发生的实现不是单列的，而是多列的。因此块状世界与众多的个体融合在一起，这些个体能够实现几乎所有的可能，这些可能在同样的地点在同样的时间可以一致地现实。如果这个世界是一个个体，那么在任何时间内只能有一些可能能够现实。然而由于世界与众多的个体融合在了一起，所以就实现了巨大数量的可能。把六个方块堆在一起只能得到六个面，而把一个方块切割成六个方块则能够得到三十六个面。因此如果我们承认了经济原则，那么可以现实的可能的数量就大为增加。

It is on account of this principle that the realization of the contingent possibilities can come in a rush, and supplies us with a fullness that grows with the passage of time.

Although this third principle is the last mentioned, it is by no means the least important. From certain points of view it is the most fruitful. It is more than a principle of individuation or a principle of negative economy. It is also a principle of the character of series of realizations. We do not intend to make use of the terms of "homogeneous heterogeneity" or "heterogeneous homogeneity," nor do we follow the example of the Bible by starting with one Adam involved with one Eve and proceeding to millions of Adams and Eves. For us the universe has neither a beginning nor an end; it didn't start with utter simplicity nor will it end in ultimate complexity. Since there is no beginning or end, our principles are not these which began to operate in a distant past or cease to operate in distant future. But if we take any time as the "present" or as the point of reference, the principle operates and as time passes from the point onward our principle of individuation enables the world to accumulate multiplicity. Perhaps the point might be gained more easily by bearing in mind the cooperation of the principle of contingency. The more contingent possibilities are realized, the greater is also the contingency in the realization of contingent possibilities once the principle of individuation is granted. Without assuming initial poverty, richness in descriptive qualities and relations if not in prescriptive values increases in the unfoldment of Tao.

III

With the principle of contingency, we have change. The world is an eternally changing one in some respects, that is to say, the possibility "change" is eternally realized. This is not merely implied by the principle of contingency but also by the metaphysical principle. If Stuff enters into and leaves off from possibilities there is obviously change of realizations. When it is said that "change" is eternally realized, it must be understood that change must be realized that in terms of time there was no time in which it was not realized and no time in which it will cease to be realized. The world did not start with being static and proceed to becoming dynamic. In the aspects in which the world is said to be static, it has

因为这一原则，不老是现实的可能的现实就会蜂拥而至。随着时间的推移，这一原则就会给我们提供不断增长的完整性。

虽然这第三个原则是在最后才提出的，但这绝不是说它是最不重要的。从某些观点来说，这一原则是最有成效的。它不仅仅是个体化的原则或负面的经济原则，而且它也是连续发生的现实的特性的原则。我们不打算运用诸如"同质异类"或"异类同质"这样的术语；也不打算追随《圣经》的做法，从一个亚当和一个夏娃开始，然后产生成千上万个亚当和夏娃。对我们而言，宇宙既没有开端，也没有终结。它并不开始于完全的简单性，也并不终结于最后的复杂性。由于没有开端或终结，我们的原则不是那些在遥远的过去开始起作用或在遥远的未来停止发挥作用的原则。但是如果我们以任何一段时间为"现在"或为参照系，那么这个原则就会发挥作用，而且随着时间从现在开始流逝，我们的个体化原则使得这一世界积累多样化。或许我们同时配合偶然性原则，那么我们将会更容易地得到上述看法。一旦个体化原则得到认可，不老是现实的可能现实得越多，在不老是现实的可能的现实过程中偶然性的成分也就越大。用不着假定最初的贫乏，在描述性的而不是规定性的特质和关系中的丰富性在道的展开过程中就会不断地增长。

三

由于有了偶然性原则，我们也就有了变化。在某些方面世界就是一个永远变化的世界。这就是说，"变化"这一可能是老是现实的可能。并不仅仅是偶然性原则蕴涵了这样的思想，而且形而上学原则也蕴涵着这同样的思想。如果质料进出于可能之间，显然就有现实方面的变化。当我们说"变化"是老是现实的可能时，我们必须知道变化必须是现实的。从时间方面来看，没有原来的一段时间变化是没有现实的，也没有未来的时间变化在其中停止了现实。世界并不是开始于静止的状态，继而才开始能动的。在世界是静止

always been and always will be, and in the aspects in which the world is said to be dynamic, it has always been and always will be so. We have no difficulties in our everyday experience. We need not for the present be concerned with abstract ideas or universals which are out of time and space. Even when we confine ourselves to the concrete items of our experience we find some of them to be comparatively permanent and others comparatively ephemeral, thus indicating relative staticity and dynamicness in the objective world. We do not think that philosophers have been so unobserving as to deny change as a fact since as sentients they experience it in their everyday lives.

What seems to be the trouble lies either in the notion of change or in the reasoning associated with it. There we do have difficulties. The notion of change involves identity and difference in which there must be identity in something and difference in others. Either one of them is essential for obviously neither alone constitutes change without the other. If A is said to have changed into B, there must be something identical as well as something different. If there isn't something different, there isn't any change; A and B were simply different names for the same thing. If on the other hand A and B are different without any link that is identical, they are simply two entities between which there may be lapse of time but of which one cannot be said to have changed into the other. The notion is obviously an abstraction from experience in which most if not all changes are partial and with partial changes the problem of identity and difference is not different in practice. Where there is a partial change, experience reveals to us certain identical aspects in the concrete together with certain different aspects. But experience is often rough and ready; it contains inferential elements which are not often well founded. Experienced differences may often be final, but experienced identity isn't. The latter as experienced is one of aspects and identity in aspects is merely an indication, not a conclusion of something else that is identical. The inference of the latter from the experienced identity in aspects may not often lead us to practical difficulties, but theoretical difficulties remain. It is of course unlikely but by no means impossible to have two different objects with identical aspects. Hence experienced identity in aspects is not a

的那些方面，它总是静止的，而且将来也是这样。而在世界是能动的那些方面，它总是能动的，而且将来也是能动的。在我们日常经验中关于这一点是没有任何困难的。目前我们没有必要关注那些尚不在时间和空间之中的抽象意念或共相。即便当我们局限于我们经验中的具体事物时，我们发现它们中的某些是相对长久的，其他的则是转瞬即逝的，这就表明了客观世界中的相对静止性和相对能动性。由于哲学家作为有知觉的人在日常生活中也经验到变化，所以我们并不认为他们始终是不留心观察以至于否认变化这样的事实的。

这里的麻烦恐怕在于变化的观念或在于与之有关的推理之中。在这里我们确实有困难。变化这一观念包含有同一性和差异性，在某些事物中必须有同一性，而在另一些事物中必须有差异性。这两者中的每一方面都是相当重要的，因为很明显如果没有其中的一方那么另一方也就必然不能形成变化。如果说 A 变成了 B，那么必然有某些东西是同一的，当然也有某些东西是有差异的。如果没有这些有差异的东西，那么就没有变化，A 和 B 也只不过是同一个东西的不同的名字罢了。如果在另一方面 A 和 B 是不同的，而且它们之间也没有具有同一性的联系，那么它们也只不过是两个实体。它们之间可能有时间上的间隔，我们不能说一个变成了另一个。这样的观念显然是从经验中抽象出来的。在经验中如果不是所有也是绝大多数的变化是部分的。部分发生了变化，同一和差异的问题在实践中却没有什么不同。哪里发生了部分的变化，经验便会向我们揭示具体事物中某些同一的方面和其他不同的方面。但是经验往往是粗糙的却尚能用的，它包含了某些基础并不牢靠的推论的因素。经验到的差异可能经常是决定性的，而经验到的同一性并不如此。被经验到的后者是某一方面的东西，方面中的同一性也只不过是一种指示，而并不是同一的其他东西的一个结论。从这些方面的被经验到的同一中得到后者的推论可能并不会经常把我们引向实际的困难，但是理论上的困难依然存在。两个不同的客体有同一的方面当然未必是可能的，但是绝不是不可能的。因此被经验到的方面中的同一

conclusive indication of basic or radical identity. If it isn't, no change need have taken place even in cases where there is partial identity and partial difference. That is to say, even when A is experientially said to have changed into B, on account of the fact that there is between them partial identity and partial difference, one is theoretically never quite sure that a change has taken place since A and B might possibly be two different entities to start with.

The criterion therefore is not identity in aspects though it involves in difference in aspects. Identity and difference are not on the same level or applied to the same kind of entities. When we say that it is possible to have two things with identical aspects we cannot possibly mean by "things" identical combinations of identical aspects, for if so, no two things could have identical aspects, since there is no sense of saying that they are "two." What then do we mean by different things or the same identical thing? Aspects can be divided into the universal and the particular. A thing cannot be equivalent to a set of universals, because at any time the thing may change and a set of universals cannot, though in changing something emerges from one set of universals into another set. Neither is a thing a nexus of particulars because a thing can endure while a nexus of particulars cannot, though in changing something emerges from one nexus of particulars into another nexus. There must be something over and above the nexus of particulars which distinguishes it from other kinds of things. That something we have already found to be the inexpressible x or Stuff. An identical thing is not an identical set of particulars or universals, but an identical bit of Stuff. This identical bit of Stuff is what gives a thing "thisness" or "thatness," a "thisness" or "thatness" which might be pointed to through its nexus of particulars, though in being able to endure in not merely a nexus of particulars. What constitutes change in a thing is the wearing of different aspects by the identical Stuff. Any change is like the change of a man discarding his business suit and putting on his evening dress or in his forsaking his brown shoes and taking up his black ones. Nothing has been changed not even the wearer except that he has changed his clothing and his shoes. In the final analysis, it is the Stuff that is the wearer.

In experience we can never be sure of any bit of Stuff being identical.

并不决定性地表明基本的或本质上的同一性。如果它不是，那么即便在有部分的同一和部分的差异的情形中也不必发生任何变化。这就是说，即便在经验上当我们说 A 变成了 B，因为在这两者之间有部分的同一方面和部分的差异方面，那么我们在理论上也从不可能确信变化在实际上发生了，因为 A 和 B 很有可能从一开始就是两个不同的实体。

因此这标准并不是在很多方面的同一，尽管它包含着方面的差异。同一和差异并不在相同的层次上或能够适用于同样的实体。当我们说有两个事物可能具有同一的方面，我们不可能把"事物"当作同一方面的同一的结合。因为如果是这样的话，就没有两件事物可以有同一的方面，因为说它们是"两个"就是没有意义的。那么我们所说不同的事物或同样的同一的事物是什么意思呢？方面中既有共相也有殊相。一件事物不能等同于一套共相，因为在任何时间，这一事物可能发生变化，而共相却不能发生变化，虽然在变化过程中某些事物从一套共相走进另一套共相之中。一件事物也不是一组殊相，因为一件事物能持续一段时间，而一组殊相却不能，虽然在变化过程中某些事物从某一组殊相进入另一组殊相。在一组殊相之外或之上肯定有某些东西使这一事物与其他事物区别开来。我们早已指出这些东西就是不可表达的 x 或质料。同一的事物不是一套同一的殊相或共相，而是一些同一的质料。正是这些同一的质料使一事物具有"这"或"那"的特性。借助于殊相，"这"或"那"是可以被指示出来的，虽然由于它可以持续而不仅仅有在于一组殊相中。在一件事物中形成变化的是同一的质料不同的方面的"改装"。任何变化都类似于一个人脱下西服而穿上晚礼服那样的变化，或类似于这个人脱下棕色的鞋而穿上黑色的鞋的变化一样。没有什么发生变化，即便是那个穿戴者也没有发生变化，除了他变换了他的衣服和鞋。归根到底，质料才是穿戴者。

在经验中，我们从来不能确信任何质料是同一的。不管什么事

The inexpressible in anything whatever, being inexpressible, is not open to empirical distinctions or operational manipulations; strictly speaking, it is meaningless to speak of bit of Stuff, much more so to speak of them as being identical. Stuff is not divided into compartments with various lines of partitions. Whatever partitions there are, they are the boundaries of events and things and are essentially aspects whether universal or particular. The only way in which we can speak of Stuff being identical is to speak of it in its entirety. Since Stuff does not increase or decrease and is totally devoid of quality, it cannot but be identical. The whole world at t_m and the whole world at t_n must be identical and yet since t_m and t_n are different in content, they must have different aspects. The notion of change is therefore eminently applicable to the whole world in its passage of time. The whole world is forever changing and contingent possibilities are eternally realized and disrealized in the scaffolding of space-time. It is only when we are speaking of the whole world that we have any theoretical assurance of Stuff being identical and hence it is also the whole world that we have any assurance of its having changed, or changing or going to change. It is this change which is also basically time. With regard to any other thing the notion of change is somewhat vicariously applied. The vicarious application does not land us in practical difficulties for identity in some aspects is a sort of rough and ready indication of identity of Stuff and difference in other aspects can always be empirically ascertained or inferred from an eternally changing world. When an object is said to have changed from t_1 to t_2, no matter how short the interval may be, no matter how identical all the aspects may be empirically, it is said to have done so only as an inference from the eternally changing world. When an object is said to have remained without changing, it merely means that no difference in aspects has been observed.

The theoretical difficulty in any empirical assertion of A being changed into B lies in the lack of empirical criterion of ascertaining the identity of Stuff. There is no practical difficulty if the data presented are such that there is identity in some aspects and difference in others for although the former is not a conclusive indication of identity of bit of Stuff wearing these identical aspects, yet it is almost overwhelmingly indicative of such basic identity that an assertion of change is not open to empirical

物中的不可表达的东西，由于它们是不可表达的，所以是不能进行经验的区分的或进行实际的操作的。严格说来，说质料就是毫无意义的一件事，更不用说质料是同一的了。质料没有区分成不同的用隔板隔开的空间。不管用什么样的隔板，它们都是事件和事物的界线，而且它们本质上是共相的方面或殊相的方面。我们能够说质料是同一的唯一的方式就是从整体上说质料。由于质料本身是既不增加也不减少，是完全没有特质的，所以它不可能不是同一的。在 t_m 的整个世界和在 t_n 的整个世界肯定是同一的，然而由于 t_m 和 t_n 在内容上是不同的，它们也肯定是有不同的方面。因此变化这一观念显然是能够适用于在时间流逝中的整个世界的。这整个的世界是不断地发生变化的，而不老是现实的可能在时空框架中永远是被现实的和不现实的。只有当我们说整个世界的时候，我们才能有理论上的把握说质料是同一的，而且也只有在整个世界的层面上我们才能有把握说它曾经变化过、正在变化或将要发生变化。而这个变化根本上说就是时间。考虑到其他的事情，变化的观念多少有点间接的运用。这种间接的运用并不会置我们于实际的困难之中，因为在某些方面的同一性粗略但尚能显示质料的同一性，而在另一些方面的差异也总是能够从永远变化的世界中得到确认或推论出来。当我们说一个事物从 t_1 变到 t_2 时，不管它们之间的间隔有多短，也不管在经验中所有方面具有多高的同一性，我们说它变了是从永远变化的世界中推论出来的。当一个客体被说成是毫无变化的，只不过是说它的具有差异的方面没有被观察到。

　　说 A 变成了 B 这样经验性断言的理论上的困难在于它缺乏一种经验的标准来断定质料的同一性。如果所呈现的材料在某些方面是同一的，而在另一些方面是有差异的，那么就没有什么实际上的困难，因为虽然前者并不决定性地表明质料的同一性存在于这些具有同一性的方面之中，但是它却在很大的程度上显示了这样基本的同一性以至对于所断言的变化不可能发生任何经验上的怀疑。当同一的方

doubt. This is particularly so when identical aspects far outnumber different aspects. Since theoretically anything has changed through the passage of time, any assertion of empirical change has an element of directness especially germane to an empirical context, that is to say, either a thing has been observed to be changing or evidences indicate its having changed. In the former case the change is given in the datum; in the latter case the evidences being empirical satisfy empirical requirements even though they may not satisfy theoretical criteria. All this is meant to say that in practice there isn't much difficulty. It is not meant to minimize the fact that the notion of change is borrowed from where it validly applies to where its application is often open to theoretical doubts. If we stick to the empirical world of individual objects and events, and expect the notion of change to be theoretically satisfactory when applied to each individual separately, we are confronted with the kind of difficulties, with which we started this discussion. The solution or the removal of those difficulties lies with us in assigning change property to that of the whole world and applying it derivatively to individual objects and events in experience.

When we say that the whole world is eternally changing, we mean of course the whole concrete world in the universe, not the universe itself; the unfoldment of Tao-infinite, not the being of Tao-one. There are entities in the universe that cannot be said to be changing or not changing, such as for instance possibilities, universal and concepts, etc. The universe being all-comprehensive and all-embracing is not limited to the concrete and the concrete world in succession does not constitute the universe. We may leave out possibilities for as possibilities they are not real, although they are elements in the universe. Universals are real since they are realized possibilities, and yet they cannot be said to be changing or not changing; their reality lies in the particulars subsumed under them and they are both immanent in and transcendental to particulars. The realization of a possibility is an event, so also is its disrealization, but the possibility realized is not an event. It is possible to have a period of time in which a possibility becomes and remains a universal, if so, while the becoming and the remaining are events in history, the universal isn't. If the period of realization is ever repeated, the repetition is a different event in history from the original realization, and yet the

面在数量上远远超过了差异的方面的时候，情形更是如此。由于在理论上，任何事物时间流逝都发生了变化，所以对于经验变化的断言都有几分直接，尤其当它与经验环境有关时。这就是说，或者一个事物被观察到正在变化，或者有证据表明它发生了变化。在前一种情形中，变化是显示在材料中的。而在后一种情形中，经验的证据满足了经验的要求，尽管它们可能没有满足理论上的标准。所有这些都表明了在实际上并不存在多少困难。当然这样说我们并不是要忽视这样的事实，即变化这一观念是从它合理运用之处借用到其用法常引起理论上怀疑的地方。如果我们忠于单独的客体、事件的经验世界，并期待变化观念分别运用于每一个体的时候在理论上是令人满意的，我们就会碰到某些困难，我们正是从困难开始讨论的。这些困难的解决或去除在于我们能否对整个世界赋予变化的特性，而且把它派生地运用于经验中的单独的客体和事件。

当我们说这一整个世界是永远在变化的时候，我们当然是在说宇宙中的整个具体世界，而不是说宇宙自身；说的是道无限的展开，而不是道一自身。在宇宙中的某些实体不能说是变化或没有变化，比如可能、共性和概念等等。宇宙是无外的，是无所不包的，它并不局限于某个具体的世界，而接连不断的具体的世界并不能构成宇宙。我们在此不谈可能，因为可能本身不是实在的，虽然它们是宇宙中的因素。由于共相是现实的可能，所以它们是实在的，然而不能说它们是变化的或不是变化的。它们的实在存于归属于它们之下的殊相之中，它们两者都寓存于殊相又超越殊相。一可能的现实是一事件，它的成虚也是一事件。但现实了的可能本身不是一事件。可能有这样的一段时间，在其中一可能变成并持续地成为一共相。如果是这样的话，变成和持续地成为就是历史中的事件，但共相却不是。如果现实的时段被重复，这重复也是历史上的一事件，

universal is the same. A class of existents to which a universal applies are individually in history, but the universal corresponding to the concept which is the defining concept of the class in question is not in history. The rise and fall of dinosaurs is an event in history but dinosaurness isn't. While dinosaurness is a universal, the proposition that the possibility dinosaurness is realized is only a particular proposition; its truth merely indicates an event having taken place or a fact having been ascertained, not a universal law. Even when we speak of individuals we have the same state of affairs. While there were only one individual Plato and only one individual Aristotle, Platonicity and Aristotelianness are universals. As universals, they are not confined to any particular place or time; they are capable of repeated realizations though it is perhaps difficult to imagine the emergence of people so exactly alike. While the individual Plato must have changed and changed continuously, Platonicity cannot be said to have changed. What we have been driving at is that while the concrete world is forever changing, there are entities that cannot be said to have changed or not changed.

IV

Change brings us directly to time. In this section we shall confine ourselves to time alone, we shall discuss it in relation to space. There are a number of senses in which the terms "time" and "space" may be used and we are not here concerned with most of them. We shall use the term "time" to mean the flow of objects and events and space their containers. There are two aspects of the content and scaffolding. In this section we shall pay attention chiefly to the scaffolding. Temporalness and spatiality are eternally realized possibilities. This is simply another way of saying that there is always time and space. The metaphysical principle assures us of time and with reality integrated into individuals, we are assured of space. Time cannot be said to begin or to end nor can space be said to have boundaries, whether from the point of view of the scaffolding or from that of the content. Since temporalness is an eternally realized possibility, since the world does not begin to change nor does it stop changing, one could see that time neither begins nor ends. The problem of space in connection with its boundaries is somewhat different. One can perhaps easily see that as scaffolding space has no boundaries; given any starting

与原来的现实是不一样的，然而共相却仍然是同样的共相。与一共相相应的一类存在是历史中的个体，但是与讨论中的此类概念相应的共相却不在历史中。恐龙的出现和消失是一历史事件，但是恐龙性本身不是一历史事件。虽然恐龙性是一共相，而命题"恐龙这一可能的现实"仅仅是一特殊的命题。它的真仅仅表明了一事件的发生或一事件被确定了，而不是一普遍的规律。即便当我们说到个体的时候，我们也处在同样情形之中。虽然只有一个柏拉图，只有一个亚里士多德，而柏拉图式思想和亚里士多德性则是共相。作为共相，它们并不局限于某一特殊的地方或时间，它们可以不断地现实，虽然可能难以去想象完全相同人物会再次出现。虽然个体的柏拉图会一再地发生变化，而柏拉图式思想却不能说是有变化的。我们想要传达的是，虽然具体的世界是不断地处在变化之中，然而却有些实体不能说是已经发生了变化或是没有发生变化。

四

变化直接把我们带到了时间之中。在这一部分中我们将只讨论时间，当然我们是把时间与空间联系在一起来进行讨论的。"时间"和"空间"这两个概念可以在很多的意义上来使用，我们在此将不考虑它们所具有的很多其他的意义，我们将用时间来表示客体和事件的流，用空间来表示它们的容器。有两个方面，即内容和框架。在这一部分我们主要是考察框架。时间和空间是永远现实的可能。这不过是永远有时间和空间的另一种说法。形而上学原则向我们担保有时间；实在是融入个体中的，因此我们确信有空间。无论是从框架的观点还是从内容的观点来看，时间不能说是有开端和终点的，同样空间也不能说是有边界的。由于时间是永远现实的可能，由于这世界没有开始变化，也不会停止变化，所以你就可以看到时间是既没有开端，也是没有终点的。空间及其边界的问题却有所不同。你可能很容易地看到，作为框架的空间是没有边界的；在空间中给定一起点，我们就可以从这一

point in space three lines in three different directions can be prolonged ad infinitum in time. If we say that any of these lines if sufficiently prolonged would return to the original point, we are not speaking of the scaffolding, but of the content and what is even more significant, we are probably speaking operationally. The operational way of speaking is inapplicable to our present sphere of discourse. Our problems are anterior to the assumptions and presuppositions of the operational view of concepts, however helpful or fruitful the latter may be as a principle of scientific methodology. The world at t_1-t_2 indeed has boundaries both in time and in space for by setting limits to time one is also setting limits to space. However, we are not speaking of any world at t_m-t_n, but of space and time and with regard to the latter, not only has time no limits, but space also has no boundaries.

If we are to supply significance to a class of statements in which the notion of simultaneity is involved and the operational way of ascertaining simultaneity is not involved we have to have absolute space and time. When we say that an event happened two years ago on a star that is two light years distant from the earth, we have to grant that the time at which that event happened on that star and sometime in the year before last on the earth are one and identical slices of time. Unless we have identical slices of time throughout the world, we cannot speak of a world at t_m-t_n, for the latter is the identification of the content of the flow with its scaffolding, the world being a convenient summary of the content and t_m-t_n being the scaffolding. In fact the world at t_m-t_n is simply t_m-t_n. If there are no identical slice of time common to all parts of the world (not the earth) the latter cannot be identified with any slice. No matter how different it is to ascertain simultaneity, simultaneity has to be granted, since otherwise there would be a multiplicity of durations corresponding to the multiplicity of objects and events. In the latter case the practical difficulty of ascertaining simultaneity has become the theoretical difficulty of having no time whatever. We have to distinguish the practical difficulty of ascertaining simultaneity from the denial of simultaneity. Simultaneity must be held in spite of the fact that ascertaining it is different. If simultaneity were ruled out, not only a whole class of statements is operationally meaningless, but also theoretically incapable

点向三个不同的方向引出三条在时间上无限延长的线。如果我们说这三条线中的任何一条如果充分地延长的话就能回到起点，那么我们在此所说的就不是框架，而是内容。更为重要的是，我们可能是从手术论的角度来谈论的。从这样的角度来谈论问题的方式不适用于我们目前讨论的领域。我们的问题是先于概念的实操观点的假设和先在假设的，而不管后者作为科学的方法论是多么地有用或多么地富有成效。从 t_1 到 t_2 的世界确实既有时间上的界线也有空间上的界线，因为确定了时间上的界线也就同时确定了空间上的界线。然而我们正在谈论的并不是 t_m 至 t_n 之间的世界，而是在谈论空间和时间。由于所谈论的是空间和时间，所以不但时间没有界线，就是空间也同样没有界线。

如果我们看重的是那些包含着同时性的陈述而不是手术论层面上的所谓同时性，那么我们必须有绝对的空间和时间。当我们说一事件在两年以前发生在离地球有两光年距离的某一星球上时，我们不得不承认，该事件在该星球上发生的时间和地球上前年的某个时间是有同一性的时间片段。除非我们在整个世界上具有同一性的时间片段，否则我们就不能说从 t_m 到 t_n 的世界，因为后者识别了流的内容和框架。世界就是内容的方便的总结，而 t_m 到 t_n 就是框架。事实上，从 t_m 到 t_n 之间的世界只不过是从 t_m 到 t_{no}。如果没有对于这一世界（不是地球）的所有部分都适用的具有同一性的时间片段，那么这些部分就不可能与时间片段有同一的关系。不管确定同时性是多么地不同，同时性是必须要得到承认的，否则就有与客体和事件的多样性相应的连续的多重多样性出现。在后面的情形里，确定同时性的实际困难就变成了没有什么时间这样的理论困难。我们必须把确定同时性的实际困难和根本否认同时性这两者区别开来。我们必须要将确定同时性的世界困难与否定同时性区分开来。同时性是一定要坚守的，尽管确定它是不同的。如果同时性被排除了，不仅有整类陈述在实操上是毫无意义的，

of having any significance. These statements are clearly significant even though it is difficult to supply them with any operational meaning.

From now on we shall take up space-time separately and each from the point of view of the scaffolding. A slice of time is a world of objects and events from the point of view of the content of time; it is also a period that can be marked off in the scaffolding. In order to have a purely theoretical and absolute scaffolding of time and space we shall introduce a few terms which stand for limits of abstraction in order to give a more precise theoretical meaning to the structure of the scaffolding. A slice of time is indeterminate from the point of view of duration; it may mean seconds or ages. We need something that is determinate and invariant. What we need is something like the familiar instant, only it is somewhat different from the usual instant. We shall use the term "instant" here to mean the whole of space without any temporal dimension whatever. An instant is three dimensional spatially but it does not endure. It is a temporal surface without temporal thickness. Any finite slice of time has two instants as its boundaries and an infinity of instants in between. No slice of time is the totality of time. Of the two boundary instants to a slice of time, one is in the beginning of the slice and the other the end. Time neither begins nor ends; only slices of time begin or end. We can supply finite units to any slice of time and measure its length. The world at t_1-t_2 is a slice of time with the operationally unascertainable t_1-t_2 as the beginning and end. Hence the worlds that can be said to begin or end are such worlds—they are not the universe or the totality of Tao or reality. All the separate durations are in one slice of time or another and if their beginning or end is in one individual instant, they begin or end simultaneously. Thus the period between 11 and 12 o'clock in Boston on Jan. 20th, 1994 is at least two things combined: one is a duration relative to a number of things among which the position of the sun in Boston and the other is a slice of time that cuts across the whole universe with 11 and 12 o'clock sharp (operationally non-reachable instants) as the boundaries.

The latter is not relative to Boston; it is one of the values for the variable "world at t_m-t_n." Time is not merely a flow of objects and events, but also a flow scaffolded by an infinity of instants and serially ordered by them. It is in terms of this scaffolding of instants that a theoretical if not an

而且在理论上也是没有任何意义的。显然这些陈述是很重要的，尽管很难给它们以任何实操方面的意义。

从现在起我们将分别地讨论时—空，而且讨论两者都是从框架的观点着眼的。从时间的内容来看，一时间片段是一客体和事件的世界，它也是可以用框架标志出来的一段时期。为了得到纯粹埋论上的和绝对的时间和空间的框架，我们将引进一些代表抽象的界线的术语以便给框架的结构更准确的理论意义。从时间持续的角度看，一时间的片段是不确定的，它可能是指几秒或很长一段时间。我们需要某些确定的和不变的东西。我们所需要的是熟悉的"时点"，只不过它多少与通常所谓的时点有所区别。我们将在此把"时点"这一术语看作是指整个空间，而没有任何时间的维度。一时点是三维空间，没有任何时间的延续。它只是时面，没有时间的厚度。任何有限的时间片段都有两个时点作为它的界线，其间有无限的时点。没有一时间片段是整个的时间。在时间片段中作为界线的两个时点中，一个是开端，另一个则是终点。时间是既没有开端，也没有终点的。只有时间片段才有开端和终点。我们可以把有限的单位运用于时间片段，测定它的长度。从 t_1 到 t_2 之间的世界是一时间片段，同时还有未确定的 t_1 和 t_2 作为它的开端和终点。因此，能够说有开端和终点的就是这样的世界，它们不是宇宙或整体的道或实在。所有不同的时间延续都在这一或那一时间片段内，如果它们的开端或终点是在一个单独的时点中，它们就同时开始或终结。因此，1994 年 1 月 20 日波士顿 11 点和 12 点之间的这一时期至少有两件东西是结合在一起的：一个是相对于一定数量的事物如太阳在波士顿的位置等的时间延续，另一个则是以 11 点和 12 点整点（实操上是不可到达的时刻）作为界线横越整个宇宙的一个时间片段。这后者不是与波士顿相对应的，它是可变的"从 t_m 到 t_n 的世界"的一个值。时间不仅仅是客体和事件的流，而且也是由无限的时点框定、由它们顺序排列的流。正是由于时点的框架，理论上的而不

operational meaning is given to statements which say that such and such events take place at such and such a time. It is through this scaffolding that objects and events are referred to their contemporaneous contents in the flow of time.

An instant is an eternally unrealized possibility. It is a possibility, but it is also eternally unrealized. While we can't say that it is impossible, we are convinced that it is unreal. Nor is it unreal in the sense that at present it isn't actual or existing as for instance the possibility dragonness is. It is unreal because it is eternally unrealized. Its realization depends upon the infinite dividedness of any slice of time which no matter how short it may be is infinitely divisible, so that there is no stage reached in which it is infinitely divided. While the possibility is eternally unrealized, the concept corresponding to it is not thereby useless. Thus 12 o'clock as an instant is never realized, but the concept is eminently useful since operations can be performed to approach it and so long as a rough meaning can be given to the concept, it can be made use of for the practical purposes of life. Neither does the unreality of the instants render the scaffolding organized or ordered by them unreal. The scaffolding is real for the slices of time bordered by these instants as well as the order in which they succeed each other are real. I do not know how the scientists will take to the doctrine herein proposed, for it might very well be their exploded doctrine of absolute time. Our scaffolding here is indeed absolute, but it is also non-operational and so far as we can see all the operational objections are inapplicable. The truth of the proposition that operationally there is no absolute time does not include or imply that non-operationally there isn't such absolute time.

Just as an instant in the whole space without temporal dimension, so a space-time-line is the whole length of time without any spatial dimension. Just as an instant or time surface is not the usual instant, so also a space-time-line is not a Euclidean point. Euclidean space is an abstraction of space without time and consequently without events and objects. Its space is the space of a time surface or what we usually call space at a single instant. Like time surface, space-time-line is also unreal. On our basis, Euclidean space is unreal since time surface is unreal. Although it is unreal, the concept corresponding to it is yet

是实操上的意义才被给予了那些断定某某事件发生在某某时间的陈述。也正是通过这一框架，客体和事件才与它们在时间流中的同时性的内容对应起来。

一时点是一老不现实的可能。它是一可能，但是它也是老不现实的。虽然我们不能说它是不可能的，但是我们却确信它是不实在的。它不是实在的不是因为在现在它不是实际的或存在的，正如"龙性"这一可能那样。它不是实在的是因为它老不被现实。它的现实依赖于任何时间片段的无限可分性，这个时间片段不管多短都是无限可分的，因此就不会到达被无限分割的那个阶段。虽然这一可能永远不被现实，但是与它相应的概念并不是没有用处的。因此作为时点的 12 点虽然从未现实，但是这一概念显然是有用的，因为在实操上我们可以接近它；而且只要它具有了粗浅的意义，那么它还是可以在实际的生活目标中加以运用的。时点的老不现实也不会使由它们组织或排列的框架变得不实在。框架是实在的，因为由这些时点为界线的时间片段与它们先后相联于其中的秩序都是实在的。我不知道科学家将会怎么来看这里所提倡的理论，因为这一理论可能就是他们关于绝对时间的分解理论。我们此处所说的框架确实是绝对的，但它也不具有实操性。据我们所知，所有手术论意义上的反对意见是不适用的。在手术论意义上确实没有什么绝对的时间，这样的命题的真并不包括或意味着在非手术论意义上就没有绝对的时间。

正如在整个空间中一时点是没有时间维度的，同样空—时—线也是没有空间维度的整个时间长度。正如时点或时—面并不是通常意义上的时点，同样空—时—线也不是欧几里得意义上的点。欧几里得意义上的空间是没有时间的抽象的空间，结果是其中没有事件和客体。它的空间是一时面的空间或者我们通常称之为在一时点上的空间。像时面一样，空—时—线也不是实在的。在我们思想的基础上，欧几里得意义上的空间是不实在的，因为时面是不实在的。虽然它是不实在的，但与它相对应的概念却是有用的。把时间和欧

useful. Taking together time and Euclidean space form a scaffolding in which time surfaces and space-time-lines intersect. The intersection is a point-instant. A point-instant is the Euclidean point, while a space-time-line isn't. Just as time can be ordered by time surface, so space can be ordered by space-time-lines. We have to introduce spatial lines which are space-time surfaces, spatial surfaces which are space-time volumes, spatial volumes which are hunks of space time. Space-time can be ordered by these entities into a space-time scaffolding in which reality unfolds itself. The concrete content of this unfoldment makes the scaffolding real.

The scaffolding is not something apart from the process and reality; it is so inextricably conjoined with particulars that they are identified by it. Every particular is definitely and uniquely fixed in the scaffolding, in fact, it is its position in time and location in space-time. No particular can change its position in time or its location in space-time. It cannot move. Motion is only possible when we separate absolutely the temporal from the spatial aspects of things. We as enduring individuals can indeed move from A to B at t_n when t_n is taken as a unit of time in which our movement characterizes us, but when t_n is taken to be t_1-t_2 with ourselves identified with the set of particulars uniquely associated with t_1-t_2, we cannot move from A to B, since that set of particulars stays at A^{t_1}-B^{t_2}. This is the old problem of the moving arrow and the insight involved in it was grasped in China as fully as it was in the West. We are not going to digress into a discussion of the problems of motion, what we are laboring under some pains to point out is that a particular not only cannot change, it also cannot move and while it is born and dies in the flow of reality, it stays forever in the position and location in the scaffolding. This is at least one reason why the truth of a particular proposition is not particular in the same sense as the event asserted by the proposition. "John Lackland passed by this morning" is a fleeting event the thorough appreciation of which is attributed to Carlyle, but the historian in Carlyle is probably more interested in the truth of the proposition rather than the particular event asserted by it, for if the truth of the proposition disappears with that particular morning or with John Lackland in his particular passing by, it is doubtful whether Carlyle is

几里得意义上的空间结合在一起就形成了框架，在其中时面和空—时—线相互交叉。这样的交叉就是点—时。虽然空—时—线不是欧几里得意义上的点，而点—时却是这样的点。正如时间能够由时面排列而成，同样空间也能够由空—时—线排列而成。我们在此必须引进空线即空—时面，必须引进空面即空—时量，也必须引进空量即空时的枓量。空—时可以由这些实体排列成空—时框架，实在就是在此框架内展开自身。这一展开的具体内容使框架变得实在。

　　框架并不是脱离过程和实在的某种东西，它与殊相是如此紧密地结合在一起以至于殊相由它来辨认。每一殊相在框架中都有其确定的和唯一的位置，事实上，这就是殊相在时间中的位置或它在空—时中的定位。任何殊相在时间中的位置或空—时中的定位都不能发生变化。它是不能移动的。只有当我们绝对地将时间与空间方面区别开来，运动才是可能的。当 t_n 被认为是时间单位，作为持续存在的个体，我们是能够在时间 t_n 从 A 移动到 B 的，在其中我们的移动表明了我们的特点。但是当 t_n 被看作是从 t_1 到 t_2，并且我们自身就是那些和 t_1 到 t_2 紧密联系在一起的殊相的时候，我们是不能够从 A 移动到 B 的，因为那些殊相是停留在 A^{t_1} 到 B^{t_2} 之间的。这就是飞矢不动的古老问题。在这一中国传统思想命题中所包含的慧见在西方也同样被领悟到了。我们不打算离开正题而来讨论运动的问题，我们现在努力所做的就是要指出一殊相不仅不能够变化，而且它也不能移动。在实在之流中它在那里生灭，它就永远地在框架中的那一位置上。这至少可以算是一个理由来说明为什么特殊命题的真不是命题所断言的事件意义上的特殊。"无地王约翰今天早晨走过"是卡莱尔所作出的评介中的一个转瞬即逝的事件。但是卡莱尔作为一个历史学家可能更感兴趣的是这一命题的真实性，而不是这一命题所断言的特殊事件。因为如果这一命题的真值与那一个特殊的早晨或与那位无地王约翰走过的特殊事件一样消失的话，那么值得怀疑的就是卡莱尔是否有这种艺术家的

sufficiently of the kind artistic temperament as to abandon himself to the enjoyment of the particular occasion. The scaffolding of time and space is a catalogue. It has of course its shortcomings, but compared to most catalogues, it does not seem to suffer more than they from excessive one-sidedness. To the secret service an agent is, let's say, B29 and to the librarian a book is B75M34, although as a man the former eats and drinks, loves and plays, while as a book the latter may be red or blue in its cover and in content full of significant or futile ideas. The scaffolding of space-time is also one sided, but it is not more pronouncedly so than other catalogues. It is probably more indicative of the characteristics of the catalogued than more catalogues.

V

In the previous chapter we have already spoken of the mutual interdependence of the pattern and the flow or passage of objects and events. By pattern we meant there the interrelatedness of universals. Corresponding to it is the more familiar interrelatedness of concepts. Although concepts are all related, they are yet capable of being arranged into groups. A science in the broadest sense—that is to say, not confined to the physical sciences though the meaning of the term "science" is borrowed from them—is a body of knowledge having for its object the interrelatedness of possibilities and universals and for its content the interrelatedness of concepts. We shall not digress into a discussion of epistemology here, what we want is to talk about interrelatedness of possibilities and universals through the interrelatedness of concepts. Euclidean geometry is from the point of view of its contents a pattern of interrelated concepts; so is physics. Since the content is one of the interrelatedness of concepts, scientific knowledge is a knowledge of universals and possibilities. Since concepts are idea versions of possibilities and universals the interrelatedness of the former is also an interrelatedness of the latter. All the "...logies" have for its content an interrelatedness of concepts corresponding to the interrelatedness of universals and possibilities. Hence the sum total of "...logies" reflect the pattern in which reality unfolds itself. At any particular time the pattern is never complete since the process of realization will never end. This means also that there is no day in which scientific knowledge is complete or scientific research will come to an end.

性情而使自己沉湎于欣赏特殊的事件。时间和空间的框架类似于分类目录。当然它有它的缺点，但是与大多数其他的目录相比，它看上去似乎并不甚于它们的过分片面性。对于一个秘密机关来说，一个特工比如说是 B29，对于一个图书馆馆员来说一本书是 B75M34——虽然作为前者的那个人既吃饭又喝水，会爱会玩；而作为后者的书，它的封面可能是红色的或蓝色的，它的内容充满着重要的或很无聊的思想。空—时框架也有它的片面性，但是与其他的目录比较起来它并不显得更是如此。可能它比其他的目录更能表明其中列举事物的特点。

五

在前一章中，我们已经谈到了图案与客体和事件的流或过程是相互依赖的。所谓图案我们是指共相之间的关联。与之相应的是我们更为熟悉的概念之间的关联。虽然所有的概念都是相互联系着的，但是它们也能够被分成不同的类。在最广泛意义上的科学——这就是说，不局限于自然科学，虽然"科学"这一概念的意义是从自然科学借用来的——是一知识系统，它以可能和共相的相互关联为其对象，以概念的相互关联为其内容。我们不打算在此离题去讨论认识论的问题，我们在这里关心的主要问题是通过概念间的关联来谈论可能和共相之间的关联。从欧几里得几何学的内容来看，它是关于相互关联的概念的图案。物理学也是这样。由于内容是概念相互关联的一个方面，科学知识就是关于共相和可能的知识。由于概念是可能和共相的观念形式，所以前者的相互关系也就是后者的相互关系。所有的"XX学"都是以与共相和可能的相互关系相对应的概念的相互关系为其内容的。因此，"XX学"的总和就反映了实在展开自身的图案。在任何特殊的时间点，由于现实的过程永远不会终结，所以图案也是永远不会完满的。这也就意味着，不会有科学知识完整呈现或科学研究走到尽头的一天。

The term "natural law" is sometimes used to mean the object, sometimes to mean the content and in extreme cases even the expression of the content of scientific knowledge. We shall ignore the last, for taken in this sense, the English and Chinese versions of the law of gravitation would be two or two sets of natural laws. The term is however often used to mean the content of scientific knowledge. When it is said that natural laws have changed from time to time, we have very likely a case in which the term is used to mean the content of scientific thought for in the history of scientific thought scientists do give up certain concepts and adopt certain others, and in so far as the term is used in this sense, and change means the rejection of one set and the adoption of another set of ideas, natural laws do change. We are using the term "natural law" here to mean the object of scientific knowledge. If so, it is simply another name for the interrelated universals and possibilities. Since the interrelatedness is itself a universal or a possibility it cannot change. The term "natural" does not exclude men and the term "law" is here temporarily restricted to the sense of justice. A natural law simply is, and by saying that it simply is, we also mean that it must be obeyed in the sense that other things being equal it has no exceptions to the rule.

When we say that the process of reality flows in accordance with pattern, we mean that objects and events obey natural laws; while natural laws are universal, they are not a priori either in the sense that they cannot but be so, or in the sense that they must be so in any circumstances. They are a posteriori in the sense that they have to be discovered and verified. Each and every one of them simply is. Taken as a totality, there is indeed a mustness about natural laws so that given a certain number of them, others may be inferred, and the more that is given, the more can be inferred. But taken separately each simply is. A natural law may take the form of a statical summary, even when it does so, it has no exceptions. In any given stance however, a natural law may not be realized, for the realization of a given natural law is contingent although the realization of some in the totality of natural laws isn't contingent. We must not take the contingent realization of a natural law as a reason for granting exceptions to the rule. In the case of a person having had a fatal dose of poison without resulting in death, it is the failure of one natural law to realize and

　　"自然律"有时被认为是指客体，有时被认为是内容，甚至在极端的情形之下被认为是科学知识内容的表达。我们将忽视自然律的第三个含义，因为根据这种意义来理解的话，英语的和汉语的万有引力定律就是两个或两套自然律。不管怎么样，这一术语经常被用来指科学知识的内容。当说自然律在不同的时间发生变化的时候，我们很有可能是这样来理解这一术语的，即这一术语被用来指科学思想的内容，因为在科学思想的历史上科学家确实经常舍弃某些概念而采纳另一些概念。如果是在这种意义上来运用这一术语，而且变化是指舍弃某一套概念而采纳另一套概念，那么自然律确实是有变化的。我们运用"自然律"这一术语在此是指科学知识的客体。如果是这样的话，那么它简直就是相互关联的共相和可能的另一名字。由于相互关联本身就是一共相或一可能，所以它是不能变化的。"自然"这一术语并不排除人，"律"这一术语在此暂时局限于指合理性。自然律就是那样，而说它就是那样时，我们也是在说必须要遵守自然律，意即其他条件相同的情况下是没有例外的。

　　当我们说实在的过程根据图案流动时，我们是在说客体和事件遵守自然律。虽然自然律是共相，但是在它们不得不如此的意义上或在任何情况下它们必须如此的意义上，它们并不是先验的。在它们必须被发现或被证实的意义上，它们是经验的。它们中的每一个都是如此。把自然律看作是一个整体，那么我们确实可以说自然律有其必然性。只要其中的一定数量的自然律被给定，那么其余的就可以从中推出来。而且给定的越多，那么可以推出的自然律也就越多。但是分别地来看，每一个就是那样。自然律可能有着静态概括的形式，但即便是如此，它也是没有例外的。然而在任何给定的状态中，自然律可能没有被现实，因为一给定自然律的现实是偶然的，虽然整体中的某些自然律的现实不是偶然的。我们绝不能把自然律的偶然的现实看作是有例外的理由。比如一个人吃了致命的毒药之后并没有死去，这是某一自然律没有现实，而另一个自然律却

the success of another one to do so. Natural laws are universal aspects the realization of which depends upon the presence of equal conditions summarized by the phrase "other things being equal." Since conditions are never quite equal, there is never any telling as to which of the natural laws is to be realized at any particular moment. Here again we have to emphasize the distinction between natural laws taken as a whole and each and every one of them taken separately. We have already mentioned that the realization of contingent possibilities as a class is not contingent, although the realization of any one contingent possibility is contingent. The same is true of natural laws. Only in this connection do we have to put the matter the other way around. Although the realization of natural laws taken together is not contingent, the realization of any one of them is. Where a natural law fails to realize because the conditions are unequal, it does not mean the presence of exceptions, for there are exceptions to a rule only where the rule isn't followed under equal conditions.

There is a good deal of talk about the conquest of nature and there is a sense in which this may be correctly said. If we mean by it that we are able to bring about an actualization of a series of objects and events favorable to ourselves through the operation of certain natural laws where others might have operated, we may correctly say that we have conquered nature to a much greater extent than we ever did before. But if we mean by the conquest of nature the ability to dispense with natural laws or to disobey them we are very likely talking nonsense. The operation of natural laws has never been suspended and it is not more suspended today than it ever was before. The Boulder Dam does not dam nature or natural laws; it merely enables us to encourage the operation of certain natural laws at the expense of certain others. The significant thing for human beings is rather that the operation of natural laws taken as a disjunctive whole is inescapable, while taken separately each can be dodged. It can be dodged however only through the operation of other natural laws. Clearly in this case one cannot say that natural laws have exceptions. Quinine cures malaria not by suspension of natural laws; it is rather the operation of one to offset the operation of another that undesirable effects are avoided. The ability to do so depends upon our theoretical knowledge, our practical ingenuity as well as the capacity to maintain more or less equal conditions. The

现实了的结果。自然律是普遍方面，普遍方面的现实依赖于"假如其他条件相同"的同样条件的存在。由于条件从来不可能是完全相同的，所以就无法知道哪一自然律在哪一特殊的时刻将要现实。在此我们要再一次强调作为整体的自然律和每一个自然律之间的区别。我们已经指出过，作为一类不是现实的可能不是偶然的，虽然它们中的任何一个可能的现实是偶然的。对于自然律来讲也是如此。只有在这种联系中，我们才能以另一种方式来说明这一问题。虽然作为整体的自然律的现实不是偶然的，但是它们中的任何一个的现实却是偶然的。当由于条件不相同的时候一自然律没有现实，这并不意味着例外的出现，因为只有在相同的条件之下没有遵从规律，这时才有所谓的例外。

关于征服自然的话题有充分的讨论，在某种意义上说征服自然是对的。如果我们能通过某些自然律带来有利于我们的客体和事件的实现，而另外一些自然律没能发挥作用，在此意义上我们可以说我们与过去相比更大程度上征服了自然，这样说就是对的。但是如果我们的征服自然意味着摒弃自然律或不遵守自然律，那么我们可能就是在说胡话。自然律的作用是从来就没有失效过，在今天和在过去都是一样的。顽石坝并没有抵制自然或自然律，它只不过是利用了某一些自然律来抑制另一些自然律而已。对于人类来说一件十分重要的事就是，虽然能够逃避个别的自然律，但是作为分离的整体的自然律是不可逃避的。能够逃脱个别的自然律只是因为利用了另外的自然律。从这样的角度来看问题，那么我们就显然不能说自然律是有例外的。奎宁并不是取消了自然律才能够治疗疟疾的，而是靠了某一自然律起作用来抵消其他自然律的作用，从而避免了人们不想要的结果。要能够做到这一点必须依赖于我们的理论知识、我们的实际所已经具有的智慧和确保或多或少相同条件的能力。

hospital is an effort to maintain more or less equal conditions so that certain natural laws can operate towards certain desired efforts and the laboratory is an attempt to maintain more or less equal conditions so that certain natural laws can operate so that certain desired discoveries can be made. If natural laws have exceptions, our world would be a chaos instead of a cosmos.

Concrete reality then unfolds itself in accordance with the pattern of natural laws. This means that reality is thoroughly intelligible. By intelligible we do not mean rational on the one hand, or predicable on the other. Rationality involves adopting adequate means towards an end as well as avoiding anything that does not contribute towards the end. If a person is rational he does certain things and avoids certain others. Reality in its unfoldment does not seem to adopt certain things and avoid certain others even though an end can be attributed to it. Predicability involves such a connection between the past and the future that given the past, the future though unactualized is yet given in some sense also. While we do not say the reality in process is rationed, we do not say that it is irrationed either. It is predictable in some ways and unpredictable in others. The emergence of particulars is unpredictable, while the realization of possibilities may be predicted sometimes with very high degrees of probability. Intelligibility is different; it is understandability if anybody is given the capacity to understand. It involves the explanation of the present in terms of the past as well as of the actual in terms of the universal and the possible. It involves on the part of the person who understands the ability to answer the questions of what, how, why or when concerning the actual. For the present we shall not touch at all understanding in the sense of answering the question how the actual has come to be, for this is a question of history and is therefore outside the subject matter of the present section. If now we confine ourselves to the kind of understanding which involves the ability to answer questions as to how or why or what the actual is cross-sectionally, not historically, we are speaking of understanding in terms of abstract concepts and their interrelatedness. This is another way of saying that when we do understand, we are able to exhibit the natural laws which the actual obeys. Hence when we say that concrete reality unfolds itself

医院建立就是试图确保或多或少的相同条件的尝试，这样做就可以达到使某些自然律起作用从而取得令人满意的结果。建立实验室的目的也是企图确保或多或少的相同的条件使某些自然律能够起作用从而有新的发现。如果自然律有例外，我们的世界就会出现一片混乱，而不再是井然有序的宇宙了。

正是根据自然律的图案，具体的实在才展开自身。这就意味着实在是完全可以理解的。当然我们所说的可以理解，在一方面不是说是理性的，在另一方面不是说是可以预见的。理性意味着运用适当的方法去达到预期的目的，同时也避免不为此目的服务的任何事情。如果一个人是理性的，那么他就会做某些事情，而不做其他的事情。实在在展开自身的过程中似乎并没有做某些事情而避免另一些事情，虽然它也会达到某一目的。预见涉及了过去和未来的关系，即如果给定了过去，那么未来虽然还未现实但在某种意义上也已被给定了。虽然我们没有说在过程中的实在是定量的，但是我们也同样没有说它不是定量的。在某些方面它是可以预见的，但在另一些方面它又是不可预见的。殊相的出现是不可预见的，但可能的现实有时是可以预见的，如果可能的程度很高的话。可理解性却是不同的，如果任何一个人都具有理解的能力那么它就有可理解性。它包含着以过去来解释现在，以共相和可能来解释现实。就有理解能力的人而言，它还包含着回答关于现实的什么、如何、为什么、什么时候等问题的能力。在目前，我们不打算讨论就回答现实是如何成为现实的这个问题的理解，因为这样的问题是历史的问题，所以它在我们目前讨论的主题之外。如果我们现在把自己局限在讨论这样的理解，它包含着从横断面的角度而不是从历史的角度来回答比如实在如何、为什么和实在是什么这样问题的能力，那么我们正在谈论的是在抽象概念和它们的相互联系的意义上的理解。这是在以另一种方式表明，当我们确实理解了，我们就能展示实在所遵守的自然律。因此当我们说具体的实在根据图案展示自身的时候，

in accordance with pattern we are also saying that it is thoroughly intelligible or understandable.

The pattern in which reality unfolds itself is the pattern of the interrelatedness of possibilities and universals, and this in turn is the object of all the "...logies" taken as the content of scientific knowledge. There are a number of questions from the point of view of the different sciences as well as their interrelation. Each science is from the point of view of contents a group of interrelated concepts. Some of these groups give us certain indications of the nature of their interrelatedness. Physics seems to be capable of being organized mathematically and almost deductively though the time to organize it deductively may not yet be ripe. With further advance in physics it might be possible to start with certain fundamental principles from which the whole body of physics can be deduced. If so, this group of concepts can become a deductive system. Are the other branches of concepts like physics? Then again there is the old question of the interrelatedness of the different groups of concepts. Is it possible in future to have an encyclopedia as systematic and deductive as *Principia Mathematica* so that starting with certain sciences others can be deduced? Some years ago there was the question as to whether biology could be deduced from physics. Although the problem has been laid aside or dissolved for a number of years, it does not seem to have been solved, and with further advance in thought, it may be brought forth again. What the answers to these questions are we do not know, but whatever they are, they reflect the interrelatedness of possibilities and universals. The scientific answers to scientific questions reveal the pattern in accordance with which concrete reality unfolds itself. The object of scientific knowledge is not something apart from reality, it is not its "phenomena" or "appearance" and still it is the universal aspects of reality, it is not something from which reality differs.

VI

In this section we shall take up particulars and individual objects or events. Particulars are distinguished from particular or individual objects or events in that the former are an aspect and the latter are concrete wholes; the former can be pointed to, named or referred to, while strictly speaking the latter cannot be expressed since they house

我们也在同时说它是完全可以明白的或可以理解的。

实在在其中展示自身的图案就是可能和共相的相互关联性的图案，这反过来又是所有作为科学知识内容的"XX学"的客体。从不同的科学及其相互关系的观点来看，这里存在不少的问题。每一门科学从内容的角度着眼就是相互关联的一组概念。某些这样的概念向我们揭示了概念之间的相互关联的性质。物理学似乎能够以数学的甚至可以以演绎的方式组织起来，虽然以演绎的方式把它组织起来的时机尚未成熟。随着物理学的进一步发展，物理学有可能从某些基本的原则出发，从中推演出整个物理学知识系统。如果是这样的话，那么这样的一组概念就能够变成一演绎系统。是否其他的概念系统也与物理学相似呢？在这里我们又遇到了关于不同概念相互关联性的老问题。在未来有没有可能出现如《数学原理》那样系统的和演绎的百科全书，可以以某些科学作为出发点，其他的科学可以从中推演出来？几年前就曾出现过生物学能否从物理学推演出来的问题。虽然这一问题多年来被搁置在一旁或者说消解了，但是这似乎并不意味着这一问题已经被解决了，而且随着思想的不断进步，这个问题可能还会被提出来。我们不知道对于这样的问题可能会有什么样的答案。但是不管答案可能会是什么，它们都反映了可能和共相之间的相互关联。对于科学问题所给的科学答案揭示了具体的实在据以展示自身的图案。科学知识的客体并不是脱离实在的某种东西，它不是它的"现象"或"表象"，它仍然是实在的共相方面，它并不是与实在不同的其他东西。

六

在这一部分中，我们将讨论殊相和个体客体或事件。殊相不同于特殊的或个体的客体和事件，因为前者只是一个方面，而后者则是具体性的全体；前者可以被指示出来，可以被命名或被谈论到，而严格地说起来，后者是不可表达的，因为后者包含着不可表达的 x。

or contain the inexpressible x. We shall take up the particulars first. As we have already said a particular is different from a universal only in that it is a particular—it remains an aspect. By itself it is as "bodiless" as a universal. An aspect is particular when it is uniquely a certain position in time and location in space. A set or a nexus of particulars is itself a particular, so also is a series. That is to say, taken as a whole it is also uniquely its position in time and location in space. The composition of a set or a nexus or a series of particulars lies therefore in the scaffolding of space-time, not in the pattern of universals which we discussed in the last section. Since a set or a nexus or a series of particulars is itself a particular, it would be simpler for us to speak merely of particulars. A particular does not endure in time, since it does not persist beyond the period of time for which it is a particular into another period for which it isn't a particular. A particular is finite, that is to say, there is no particular that occupies a point-instant, nor any that occupies the whole of space-time. A particular cannot change since there is no difference in one particular, nor any identity in two particulars. Since it cannot change, it cannot move either. Sometimes we say for instance that this glass has a particular shade of blue, since the glass has been here for a few months and been moved from one place to another, the particular shade of blue might be supposed to have changed and moved. But if we take the whole life of the glass in question to be the period for which the shade of blueness is a particular, this single particular has neither changed nor moved. In this case we are simply taking the whole period as a simple unit of time during which there may be a succession of other particulars but obviously no change of that single particular, since that unit of time does not succeed itself. Similarly its location in space. Each particular we must remember is both a particular and a set or a nexus or a series of particulars. The particular shade of blueness for the whole life of the glass is one particular in one sense, and a set or a nexus or a series of particulars in another sense in which there may be darker shades as distinguished from the lighter shades of blue none of which has changed or moved. No particular is so simple as to cease to be a set or a nexus or a series of particulars, or so complex as to cease to be a single particular. There is no ultimate simplicity or complexity to a particular.

我们将首先讨论殊相。正如我们已经指出的那样，一殊相不同于一共相仅仅是因为它是一殊相，它仍然是一个方面。就它自身而言，它正如共相一样也是"无体的"。当在时间、空间中占据着唯一位置的时候，一个方面就是特定的。一组或一套殊相本身也是一殊相。同样，一系列殊相本身也是一殊相。这就是说，作为整体的殊相在时间和空间中也占有唯一的位置。一组或一套或一系列的殊相的组成因此也在空—时的框架之中，而不在我们在前一章中所讨论的共相图案之中。由于一组或一套或一系列殊相本身也是殊相，那么我们直接说殊相就显得更简单。一殊相没有时间上的延续性，因为它只在自己作为殊相的时间内存在，超过这一时间它就不再是殊相了。一殊相是有限的，这就是说，并没有殊相占据点—时，也没有殊相占据着整个的空—时。一殊相也不能有变化，因为在一殊相中是没有差异的，在两殊相之间也没有同一性。由于殊相不能有变化，所以它也就不能移动。我们可以举例说，这只玻璃杯子呈现出某种特殊的蓝色，因为这一杯子几个月来都在这里，而且从一个地方被挪到另一地方，所以可能认为它的蓝色发生过变化，被移动了。但是如果我们把杯子的整个存在期看作是这一蓝色殊相存在的阶段，那么这一殊相既没有变化，也没有移动。在这一事例中，我们只是把整个的过程看作是一个简单的时间单位，在其中可能有其他的殊相出现，但显然那一殊相并没有变化，因为那一时间单位并不接续自己。它在空间中的位置也有着同样的情形。我们必须记住，每一殊相既是一殊相，也是一组或一套或一系列殊相。对于杯子的整个存在期来说，特殊的蓝色在一种意义上说就是殊相，在另一种意义上是一组或一套或一系列殊相。在后一种意义上，可能有较深的蓝色能够与较浅的蓝色区别开来，但是没有一种颜色发生过任何变化或移动过。没有一殊相简单到不再是一组或一套或一系列殊相，也没有复杂到不再是一个殊相。对于殊相来说，既没有最简单的殊相，也同样没有最复杂的殊相。

Conversely a given position in time at a given location in space is the particular there is at that position and location in the sense that it cannot be anywhere else. For the moment let us separate conceptually the scaffolding from the particulars that occupy it. Particulars are aspects and as such they act and react upon each other in accordance with natural laws. Each is in a complex of internal relations other than the external relations of time and space. Since a particular cannot change or move or persist beyond its time it can hardly be said to have such and such, it can only be said to be such and such. With regard to an individual object, we may say that under such and such influence it has changed, but with regard to any particular we can only say that under such and such influence it ceases to be. The influence mentioned is either the operation of natural laws or the co-temporalness or co-spatiality of other particulars. A particular is not merely a relational property of internal relations but also a relational property of external relations. Change the position of the ink bottle on this desk, and you have a different set of particulars. To borrow a term often used in political science each particular is a "status quo." Change the status in any way, and you have also myriads of death and birth of myriads of particulars. We are trying here to exhibit a certain kind of organicity of particulars in which any change in reality whatsoever brings not merely changes of objects and events, but also births and deaths of particulars. It isn't that a particular has gone through certain changes and to the presence of other particulars, it is rather that some die and others are born, the moment other particulars are introduced. That is to say, with regard to particulars, each is because the others are. This organicity is not limited to the particulars as such, for since each particular is its position and location in space-time, all the positions and locations conceptually separated from the particulars have the same organicity. Thus is the flow or passage of time: we are not merely confronted with different sets of particulars we are also passing through different time-surfaces and occupying different space-time-lines. When it is said that a person is killed in New York City on Nov. 3rd, 1943, the statement sounds extremely simple, but the particular way in which that event took place is so complicated as to baffle any kind of adequate treatment on our part and that is part of the reason that we summarize the whole situation by using the phrase "in New York City on Nov. 3rd, 1943." The reason why we can do so is that

反过来说就是，在空间中给定位置上的一个时间上的给定位置就是一个殊相，这个殊相就在这一位置上，而不能在其他地方。在目前，让我们从概念上把框架和占据框架的殊相区别开来。殊相是方面，因此它们根据自然律而相互作用。每一殊相是时间和空间方面内在关系的综合，而不是外在关系的综合。由于殊相不能变化或移动或超越自己存在的时间，所以不能说殊相具有什么，我们只能说它们是什么。谈到个体的客体，我们能够说在这种那种影响之下，它发生了变化。但是谈到殊相，我们只能说在这种那种影响之下，它不再是原来的殊相了。这里所提到的影响或者是指自然律的作用，或者是指其他殊相的同时发生或占据同样的位置。一殊相不仅仅是内在关系的关系质，而且也是外在关系的关系质。把桌子上的墨水瓶位置变一下，你就会有另一套殊相。借用政治学中经常运用的一个术语，每一殊相都是"现状"。以任何方式改变这样的现状，你就会看到无数殊相无数次的生灭。我们在此努力要说明的是殊相的有机性，即实在的任何变化所导致的不仅仅是客体和事件的变化，而且也是殊相的生灭。这不是说一殊相经过了某些变化变成了其他殊相，而是说当其他的殊相产生时，一些殊相衰亡，另一些殊相产生。这就是说，谈到殊相，每一殊相都依赖于其他殊相。这一有机性并不仅仅局限于殊相，因为由于每一殊相是它在空—时中的位置，从概念上说与殊相分离的所有的空间和时间的位置有着同样的有机性。时间的流或过程也是这样，我们不仅仅遇到不同的殊相，我们也同样经过了不同的时—面，占据着不同的空—时—线。当说到一个人于 1943 年 11 月 3 日在纽约被杀死，这一陈述听起来非常地简单，但是这一事件发生的特殊方式是很复杂的，以至于我们不知如何妥当处理。这就是我们用"1943 年 11 月 3 日在纽约"

the organicity of particulars can be conceptually separated from the organicity of spatial and temporal positions. In practice they cannot be separated. The police may reenact the event but what is reenacted is not the original event.

Let us next take up individual objects and events. They are distinguished from particulars in that they are concrete wholes not aspects, and they house or contain the inexpressible x which we call Stuff. We have already said that in practice we identify an individual object or event with a set of particulars at any particular place and time. This identification is theoretically unsound. None of Hume's arguments is conclusive in establishing identity. But practically we do not have much difficulty. If we ignore the theoretical difficulties for the moment and follow the practice, we can easily see that through the identification of particulars with the scaffolding of space-time, the individual objects and events are also catalogued in it. These are the actualities that form the content of concrete reality in process; they are the things that sift through the pattern, the sun light that flashes through the window curtains. Concrete reality therefore not merely proceeds in accordance with pattern but also fills the scaffolding of space-time with individual objects and events. The latter not only realize possibilities, but also take place at certain times and in certain spaces. They can be understood in terms of the universals they realized and ascertained in terms of their position in time and their location in space. While science discovers or tries to discover the pattern or the natural laws the objects and events obey, history ascertains or tries to ascertain the facts about the objects and events, namely their qualities and relations in terms of their temporal and spatial relations with other objects and events. We are here using the term "scientific knowledge" to mean horizontal knowledge of universal patterns, and the term "historical knowledge" to mean vertical knowledge of particular or general organicness. We have said something about the term "general" previously. Compare the proposition "Native Americans were in America before 1492" with the proposition "Everything heavier than air falls down in air when unsupported." The former is only general, whereas the latter is universal. History deals not only with the particular, but also with the general.

这一短句来总结整个情况的部分理由。我们能够这样做的理由就是殊相的有机性能够在概念上与空间和时间位置的有机性分离开来。当然在实际上它们是不能这样分离的。警察可能重现这一事件，但是重现的事件显然不是原来的事件。

下面我们将来讨论个体的客体和事件。它们是不同于殊相的，因为它们是有具体性的整体，而不是方面。在它们中间包含有不可表达的 x，我们把 x 称为质料。我们已经说过，在实际上，我们认为个体的客体或事件就是在任何特殊的空间和时间中的一套殊相。这样的确认在理论上是站不住脚的。休谟在建立同一方面的任何论证都不具有结论性的意义。但是这样的看法在实际上却没有什么太多的困难。如果我们暂时忘掉理论方面的困难而跟着实际走，那么我们就能很容易地看到通过殊相与空—时框架的确认，个体的客体和事件也就位列其中了。正是这些现实性组成了过程中的具体的实在内容，它们是由图案筛选的事物，是透过窗帘的阳光。因此具体性的实在并不仅仅是根据图案而延续自身，而且也是以个体的客体和事件来充实空—时框架的。后者不仅仅使可能现实，而且也在一定的时间和一定的空间中产生。它们可以根据它们所实现的共相而得到理解，也可以根据自身在时间和空间中的位置得到确定。在科学发现或努力去发现客体和事件遵循的图案或自然律的同时，历史在确定或努力确定关于客体和事件的事实，即以它们与其他客体和事件的时间和空间关系而言的特质和关系。在此我们是运用"科学知识"这一术语来指示共相图案的水平知识，而"历史知识"这一术语则用来指示特殊或普通的有机性的垂直知识。我们在前面曾经讨论过关于"普通"这一术语。在此我们比较一下下面两个命题。一个是"在 1492 年之前北美土著居民居住在美洲"，另一个是"所有比空气重的物体在没有支撑的时候就会下落"。前者是所谓的普通的命题，而后者则是普遍命题。历史不仅仅是处理特殊的情况，它也处理普通的情况。

The use of terms here is sufficiently novel to merit a few words of clarification. While all branches of knowledge are involved or concerned with true propositions not all of them are interested in their discovery. Some of them are disciplines for conduct, others for service, while still others for the expression of creative impulses. Of the branches of knowledge interested in the discovery of truths, science aims at the universal, history aims at the particular and general. Obviously this distinction has little to do with books or persons. An encyclopedia is all of the branches of knowledge squeezed into a book and a Leibniz is a participant in a number of them. There is a history of science, it is history not science; there may be a science to history, if so, it is science not history. A scientist may be at the same time a historian, but in the capacity of a historian, he is interested in particular or general truths. A historian may be at the same time a scientist, but in his capacity as a scientist, he is interested in universal truths. What are known as social sciences now seem to be sciences in name, not sciences in fact; at least they do not seem to have become sciences yet. It seems that they have discovered no universal truth and as yet have developed no technique for discovering universal truth. Almost all of them are mixed branches of knowledge and a large part of their component is history; only what is discovered seems to be mostly general truths. We are using the term "history" to mean those branches of knowledge which ascertain or try to ascertain the particular and general truths. Their object is the interrelatedness of qualities and relations in terms of the scaffolding of space-time.

What have we obtained so far? Our principle of congruence gave us a concrete world which cannot be denied, no matter how skeptical one is in doing so or in trying to do so. The principles of contingency and economy supply us with a reality in process, a changing temporal and spatial world diversified into individual objects and events which realize universals through the births and deaths of particulars and which are catalogued

by the scaffolding of space-time. In broad outline we have essentially the
world we experience. We do not bifurcate reality into the phenomenal
and noumenal or the apparent and real. While we are here not dealing
with epistemology, we may tarry a bit just to say that although we admit

　　这些术语的用法是全新的，因此需要做一番澄清的说明。虽然
所有的知识系统包含着或涉及真命题，但并不是所有的知识系统都
对它们的发现感兴趣。有些知识是行为准则，有些知识是应用准
则，而且还有些知识是表达创造冲动的准则。在对发现真理感兴趣
的知识分支中，科学的目标在于共相，而历史的目标则是特殊的情
况和普遍的情况。显然，这样的区别与书本和个人没有什么关系。
所谓的百科全书是把知识的所有的分支塞进一本书里去，莱布尼茨
这样的人在很多书里都有收录。有科学的历史，这是历史，而不是
科学。可能存在着一门关于历史的科学，如果是这样的话，那么它
就是科学，而不是历史。一位科学家可以同时是一位历史学家，但
是作为一位历史学家，他所关心的是特殊的或普通的真理。一位历
史学家可能同时也是一位科学家，但是作为一位科学家，他所关心
的是普遍的真理。现在被看作是社会科学的似乎是名义上的科学，
而在实际上并不是科学，至少它们似乎还没有变成科学。似乎它们
还没有发现普遍的真理，至今也未发展出去发现普遍真理的技术手
段。它们几乎全部是各种知识分支的结合，其中的很大部分是历史，
已被发现的似乎大部分也仅仅是普通的真理。我们在此所运用的
"历史"这一术语是指确定或努力去确定特殊的和普通的真理的那些
知识分支。它们的客体是空—时框架中的特质和关系的相互联系。
　　我们至此的讨论能够得出什么样的结论呢？我们的和谐原则向
我们提供了一个具体世界，这样的世界是不能否认的，不管你如何
持怀疑态度去否认或试图否认它。偶然性原则和经济原则则向我们
提供了一个在过程中的实在，一个不断变化的时间和空间的世界。
这样的世界分化为个体的客体和事件，这些位于空—时框架内的个
体的客体和事件通过殊相的生灭而实现共相。从广泛的意义上说，
本质上我们所有的这个世界就是我们所经验到的世界。我们没有把
实在分成现象的和本体的两个部分或表面的和实在的两个部分。虽
然我们在这里没有讨论认识论的问题，但是我们可以耽搁一点时
间，就是为了说虽然我们承认在殊相方面对于能感的不同类型来说

a certain relativity of the sensed to the different classes of the sentients in terms of particulars, we do not admit any relativity of the known or the knowable to the classes of sentients as knowers in terms of the universals. That which is red is relative to men, dogs, horses, monkeys, ...as different classes of sentients from the point of view of the particular that is sensed, but redness as a universal, the object of knowledge instead of sensation is not relative to the different classes of sentients as knowers. We are here speaking in terms of universals even when the subject matter of our discussion happens to be particulars. In terms of universals the world supplied by the three principles is essentially the world of our experience. There are different realities but there are neither higher or lower, nor deeper or shallower realities. There are realities for which different values might be prescribed and while as values there are different gradations, as realities none is more valuably real than any other.

The emergence or the evolution of human beings is neither accidental nor final. It is the recognition of these that gives us our essential dignity. Just as individual human beings are stations in human life, so also is humanity a station in the unfoldment of Tao. We subscribe to some of the views expressed in Russell's *A Free Man's Worship*. The span of human life may be very long for us, but the day will inevitably come when human life itself will be just a short period in the past, a short chapter in the unfoldment of Tao. Whether after that the world turns to be inert matter or supermen succeed us seems to be quite immaterial. Although we are not final, we are not accidental either. The universe wouldn't be complete if the kind of entities like human beings are not in it at some time or other. During the span of human life those who are human have to try to behave as human beings, they have to struggle along to perform the function or the role expected of them, to fulfill as much as they can or to approach as near as they can to the most comprehensive and the most essential realization of humanity. None of the Golden Ages would be more valuable if they persisted, and if any persisted till eternity, it probably wouldn't be valuable at all. The destination is not more valuable than the transit, nor is the end more important than the means; it is only when the job is done in the transit that the destination becomes more valuable. Human life as a whole is like individual life: it is not the pompous funeral that gives an individual life its dignity; it is rather the way one lives one's life that makes him dignified.

所感是有相对性的，但是我们却不承认在共相方面对于能感的不同类型来说能知或所知有任何的相对性。比如从所感的殊相的角度看，对人、狗、马、猴子……这些能感来说红色是相对的。但是红性作为共相，它是知识而不是感觉的客体，所以相对于能知来说，它不是相对的。我们正在谈论的是共相，即便我们在此讨论的主题恰巧是殊相。从共相的角度来看，由这三个原则决定的这一世界本质上就是我们所能经验到的世界。有着不同的实在，但是并没有更高或更低的实在，也没有更深刻或更浅薄的实在。有规定了不同价值的实在：作为价值，就有不同的层次；作为实在，就不能说某一实在比其他的实在实在得更有价值。

人类的诞生或进化既不是意外的，也不是最终的。正是这样的认识才赋予我们人类以必不可少的尊严。正如个人是人类生命的驿站，人性也是道得以展开的一个驿站。我们赞同罗素在其《自由人的礼赞》一文中的某些看法。对于我们而言，人类的生命可能是非常漫长的，但是终有那么一天人类生命本身只不过是过去时日中的一个非常短暂的阶段，只不过是道展开过程中的一个短小的章节。在我们之后这一世界是否变成死寂的物质或有超人出现似乎并不是一件重要的事情。虽然我们并不是最终的存在，但是我们也不是意外出现的生物。如果在某些时间中没有像人类这样的实体出现，那么这一宇宙就将是不完全的。在人类生命的过程中，人必须活得像个人，他们必须努力奋斗以完成他们被期待实现的那些作用或角色，尽其可能去完成或接近人性的最全面和最本质的现实。任何黄金时代持续下去都不会更有价值，如果哪个黄金时代持之以恒，那么它可能会毫无价值。目标并不比过程更有价值，目的也并不比手段更重要。只有在过程中完成工作，目标才会变得更有价值。整个人类的生命正像个体人的生命一样，盛大铺张的葬礼并不能给个人生命以尊严，真正给他以尊严的是他的生活方式。

TIME AND ACTUALITY

I

The last chapter has furnished us with a world of objects changing in accordance with pattern and catalogued in the scaffolding of space-time. In terms of the pattern universals are realized and disrealized, and in terms of the scaffolding of space-time particulars appear and disappear. For each particular that appears there is a universal covering it, but since there may be a multiplicity of particulars to one universal, there is a richness to the particulars, which is denied to universals. Hence although reality unfolds itself in accordance with patterns, it has a wealth of particulars in the scaffolding of space-time that is not found in the pattern itself. Thus far we have spoken of reality in its static mood, even when we speak of the changing world or of reality in process we have restricted ourselves to changed states or stations of reality, not change or process itself. In neglecting the dynamic mood of reality, we have also neglected the acting and the acted, or in a word, the actual. We are using the term "actual" here to include the notion of the present. The actual is not merely reality, but also the present reality. Compared to its theoretical version the actual is by far the richer. Let us call the appearance and disappearance of the particulars the drift. Perhaps we can approach the problem of the actual through the drift of reality more easily than through its pattern. It is through the drift of reality that objects and events act upon each other, and although when they so act upon each other in accordance with the pattern it is not the pattern that is actual. The drift is in accordance with the pattern; it obeys natural laws, but while what is obeyed or realized is a natural law or a group of natural laws, that which is there and does the obeying isn't a natural law at all, it is what we usually call fact or facts. The world is like a game of chess, and yet with all the rules of the game and the presence of pawns, the knights, the bishops and kings, a game need not actually be played, though if it were played, it obeys the rules. The question is what is there that is actual.

Ordinarily we attribute this activity to objects and events. We experience the burning of the red hot coal or the scalding of the boiling water, and we conclude that something there is being acted upon while the coal and the water are active. Objects change and move, events take

时间和现实

一

上一章向我们描绘了这样一个客体世界，世界根据图案而变化，并位于空—时框架之中。从图案说，共相现实或成虚；从空—时框架说，殊相出现和消失。对于每一出现的殊相，都有一共相与之相应。但是由于有可能相对于一共相有众多的殊相出现，因此殊相就呈现出多样性，而共相却没有这样的多样性。这样，虽然实在根据图案而展现自身，它在空—时框架内具有殊相的丰富性，但是图案本身却不具有这样的丰富性。至此，我们是从静的角度来谈论实在，即便我们在谈论变化的世界或过程中的实在的时候，我们局限在谈论变化的状态或实在的阶段，而不是谈论变化或过程本身。由于不谈论实在的动态，我们也就同样不谈论行动和受动，或者一句话，不谈论现实。我们在此运用的"现实"这一术语中包含着当前这一观念。现实不仅是实在，而且是当前的实在。相较于它的理论形式，现实显然是更加丰富的。让我们把殊相的出现或消失叫做势。可能我们通过实在的势要比通过它的图案更容易接近现实的问题。正是通过实在的势，客体或事件才相互影响；而且虽然当它们根据图案相互影响时，图案本身却不是现实的。势与图案是一致的，它遵循着自然律。但是被遵循或被现实的是自然律或一组自然律，而存在着的并遵循着自然律的却完全不是自然律，而是我们通常叫做事实的东西。世界如同国际象棋游戏，有游戏规则，有兵、马、象、王，但是游戏也并不必一定要在实际上进行，尽管如果要进行的话，就得遵守规则。问题在于，在那里的所谓现实的是什么。

通常我们把这个能动性归之于客体和事件。我们被红色煤炭烧伤或开水烫伤，我们就会总结，当煤炭和水能动的时候某些东西受

place, and so long as it is convenient for us to identify objects and events with their nexus of particulars or sets of universals which clothe them, we might as well do so. In practical life there is hardly any inconvenience. Theoretically there is a good deal. While objects do change and move, the nexus of particulars neither changes nor moves. The same is true of universals. It is easy to see that other universals aside, the universal change itself doesn't change, nor does motion itself move. If objects were identified with certain nexus of particulars or certain sets of universals, they cannot change or move. If they can neither change nor move, how could they act and be acted upon? The only thing that enables an object to change or move is the Stuff that is housed in it. Basically therefore it is also Stuff that is active. It may have to have the help of the nexus of particulars, or the sets of universals, just as a wearer has to make use of his clothes in order to change his appearance, but it is the Stuff or the wearer that does the changing or is active. Its activity is expressed through the entrance into and departure from possibilities.

There are two ways of entrance or departure, voluntary or involantary, unconditioned or conditioned, free or compelled. None of these terms is adequate, but the idea may be smuggled across through any pair of them. When Stuff is about to enter into or leave, or on the point of entering into or leaving a possibility we call it an occasion or *Chi*. We are using the term in such a way as to rule out on the one hand what we sometimes call a "change of mind" and on the other whatever determination or purpose that may enter into the activity. We are trying to make the term as casual and factual as we can. An occasion is no more than anything being what it has come to be, it simply becomes or is. It is not casual, nor is it purposive. It may result in the realization of a possibility that is previously unrealized, or the disrealization of a possibility that is previously realized, in which case it is an occasion concerning universals as well as particulars. The appearance and disappearance of dinosaurs in natural history belong to this category. Occasion may also result merely in the appearance or disappearance of particulars in which case it is an occasion concerning particulars alone. Thus the disappearance of the green of yesterday and the appearance of the red of today in the history of an apple belong to the second category. Since all occasions concern the appearance or disappearance of particulars, it is with the second category that we are more concerned here.

到了影响。客体是变化的和移动的，事件是会发生的。只要便于我们确认客体和事件与裹覆它们的殊相或共相，我们就能确认。在实际生活中几乎没有什么不方便，但在理论上却有不少的困难。客体确实是在变化和移动的，殊相却既不变化也不移动。对于共相来说也是这样的。很容易看到，且不说其他的共相，变化这一共相本身并不变化。移动这一共相也不移动。如果客体与某些殊相或某些共相完全同一，那么它们也就不能变化或移动。如果它们既不能变化也不能移动，那么它们又怎么能够施加影响或接受影响？唯一能使一个客体变化或移动的是寓存于其中的质料。因此基本上说来，能动的也是质料。质料可能需要殊相或共相的帮助，这正如穿衣者利用服装来改变他的形象。但是，是质料或穿衣者在作出改变或是能动的。它的能动性表现在它的出入于可能之间。

出入有两种方式，自愿的或被动的，无条件的或有条件的，自由的或被迫的。这些术语中没有一个是充分的，但是这些术语中的任一组多少还是表达了我们的看法。当质料即出即入或正要出入于可能，我们把这种情形称为几。我们是在这样的方式上运用这一术语的，即一方面是要排除我们有时叫做"改变主意"这样的东西，另一方面是要排除或许能进入能动性的决定或目的。我们尽可能使这一术语成为临时的和事实的术语。所谓几就是任何东西成为的那个样子，它只是变成或就是那样。它不是偶然的，也不是有目的的。它会使先前未曾现头的可能现实，或使先前现实的可能成虚。这样的话，它就是关于共相或殊相的几。在自然史上，恐龙的出现和消失就属于这个范畴。几也可能会导致殊相的出现或消失。这样的话，它就只是关于殊相的几。因此，一个苹果昨天的绿色消失了，而在今天出现了红色，这样的情形就属于第二个范畴。由于所有的几都与殊相的出现或消失有关，所以我们在此更为关心的是几的第二种情形。

An occasion is not an object or an event, it is not a universal, neither is it a particular. An occasion is not an object, since it is an activity, and while objects are active, they are not activities. Although it is an activity, it is not an event. In the last analysis, events are entrance into or departure of Stuff from possibilities. Events may be comparatively simple or comparatively complex, in which case, you have either simple combinations of entrances or departures or else comparatively complex combinations of entrances or departures. An occasion is not an entrance into or departure of Stuff from possibilities; it is that state in which either is about to or on the point of taking place. If one watches the Leaning Tower without any knowledge of the fact that it has stood for centuries, one may have a sense of something impending, something about to happen or on the point of happening that is distinct from the sense of the happening of that something when it does happen. Only in the case of our present notion of occasion, it is always accompanied by entrance into and departure of Stuff from possibilities, since we have ruled out any "change of mind." That an occasion is not itself a universal need not be dwelt upon at all. It is not a particular either. A particular is an aspect, it is like a universal in being an aspect, its expression is adjectival or adverbial, and it adheres to objects and events. While an occasion is not an aspect, it cannot be said to adhere to objects and events. Perhaps what is even more important is that a particular is what is catalogued in the scaffolding of space and time; it is of the flotsam and jetsam of the flow of time, not the flow itself; whereas as we shall see in a few paragraphs hence occasions are a part of the flow itself.

The change or motion of an object is always accompanied by its occasion in so far as it is occasioned. No change or motion takes place before the appropriate occasion, nor after it. The former is obvious, since before Stuff can enter into or depart from a possibility, it must have had that state of being on the point of entering into or departing from a possibility. It is more difficult to see why change or motion doesn't take place after the appropriate occasion. Our terms "about to" and "on the point of" are inadequate; they suggest a temporal sequence of purpose precedent to action or of action subsequent to purpose. What we need are terms that do not suggest this temporal sequence and we do not know of any such terms. It is here that we need the term "appropriate" to introduce the idea that given any change or motion that

几本身既不是一客体，也不是一事件。它不是一共相，也不是殊相。几不是一客体，因为它是能动性。客体是能动的，但它们不是能动性。虽然几是能动性，但是它不是一事件。总而言之，事件是质料进出于可能之间。事件可能是比较简单的或比较复杂的。如果是这样的话，那么你或者有比较简单的进或出的组合，或者有比较复杂的进或出的组合。几不是质料进入或走出可能，它是将要进入还未进入的一种状态，或者是正要发生的一种状态。如果一个人看着斜塔而不知道它几个世纪以来一直是这样倾斜的事实，那么他就可能有某些事情将要发生的感觉，某些事情即将发生与那件事情确实发生的感觉是不一样的。只有在我们当前的几这一观念之下，几才总是伴随着质料进出于可能，因为我们已经排除了"改变主意"。几本身不是共相这一事实完全不需要进一步讨论，它也不是殊相。殊相是一个方面，正如共相是一个方面，它的表达方式是形容词性的或副词性的，它依附于客体和事件。而几不是某个方面，不能说它依附于客体和事件。或许更为重要的是，殊相是位于空间和时间框架之内的，它是时间之流中的漂浮者，不是流本身。然而我们将在后面看到，几是流本身的一部分。

就一客体来说，它的变化或移动总是与它的几相伴随的。在适当的几之前和之后都不可能有变化或移动。说在适当的几之前没有变化或移动，是因为在质料能够进或出于可能之前，必然有正要进或正要出可能的那个状态。比较难理解的是，为什么说在适当的几之后变化或移动也不会发生。我们在此所运用的"即将"和"正要"这两个术语是不适当的，它们暗示着移动之前的目的所具有的时间顺序或目的之后的移动的时间顺序。我们所需要的术语不应该是暗示时间顺序的，然而我们没听说过这样的术语。在此我们需要术语"适当的"是为了介绍这样的思想，即给定任何不预先规定的

is not preordained, there is an appropriate occasion. A change or motion cannot take place after its own appropriate occasion simply because if it did, it might be detached from its own appropriate occasion, and it might then be without its own occasion or occasioned by something that isn't its own appropriate occasion. What is urged is that there is a one-one correspondence between occasions on the one hand and changes or motions on the other so that for each motion or change that is occasioned, there is an appropriate occasioning and no change or motion that is occasioned is either before or after its appropriate occasion. Just as the world is eternally changing, Stuff is eternally occasioning. There is no temporal sequence between changes and motions on the one hand and their appropriate occasion on the other.

Neither is the occasion the purpose of its appropriate change or motion. No purpose is implied in the notion of occasion. Occasions are random efforts of Stuff. Neither are they caused. They certainly are not caused in the sense that they are inferable from previous occasions in accordance with causal laws. If we take the world at t_1 and the world at t_2, no matter how short the interval may be, we can easily see that the first does not cause the second. There is no caused law in terms of which these worlds could be subsumed and their relation inferred. Besides both are wholes hence neither happens in a background for which the problem of similarity arises, simply because there is no background whatsoever. Hence the occasion appropriate to the world at t_1 does not cause the occasion appropriate to the world at t_2. An event A in the world at t_1 and an event B in the world at t_2 may be causally related, if so, the occasion favors the realization of a certain causal law and not certain others. We merely say that the occasion favors the realization of a certain causal law; we do not say that the occasion appropriate to A causes the occasion appropriate to B. As occasions go, B need never be occasioned. That it does happen under hypothesis merely indicates that it favors the realization of a certain causal law. The causal relation that is appropriate to events is not appropriate to occasions. In terms of causal relations, an occasion is uncaused. If it be said that it is caused by Stuff, we are simply asserting that in so far as anything else is concerned, it is uncaused. And to say that Stuff causes its own occasion is to say nothing at all.

变化或移动，就会有适当的几。变化或移动不能在适当的几之后发生的理由就是：如果它在之后发生，那么它就有可能脱离它自己的适当的几，就有可能没有自己的适当的几或由不是自己的适当的几的东西所引起。这里所要表达的思想是：在几与变化或移动之间存在着一一对应的关系，因此对每一被引起的移动或变化来说都有一个适当的几，没有一被引起的变化或移动是后干或者是先于它自己的适当的几的。正如这一世界是永远在变化的，质料也是永远在引起变化的。在变化和移动与它们适当的几之间是没有时间顺序的。

几也不是它自己的适当变化或移动的目的。在几这一观念之中并不隐含目的这一含义。几就是质料进出可能的随机的努力，它们不是其他事物所引发的。说它们当然不是其他事物引发的，是因为它们不是根据因果律而由先前的几推出的。如果我们以在 t_1 的世界和在 t_2 的世界为例的话，那么不管它们之间的间隔是多么地短，我们都能轻而易举地看出前一个世界并没有引发出后一个世界。没有这样的引发规律可以将这两个世界归属其下，并推导出它们的关系。而且这两个世界都是整体，每一个世界的产生并没有相似性问题的背景，只是因为根本就没有背景可言。因此，适合于 t_1 世界的几并不会引发 t_2 世界相应的几。在 t_1 世界中的事件 A 和在 t_2 世界中的事件 B 可能有因果方面的联系，如果是这样的话，那么几就有利于某一因果律的现实，而不是其他的因果律的现实。我们只是说几有利于某一因果律的现实，我们并没有说适合于 A 的几引起了与 B 相应的几。就几而言，B 并不需要被引发。假设它确实发生了，这也只不过表明它有利于某一因果律的现实。适合于事件的因果联系并不适合于几。从因果联系方面说，几不是被引发的。如果说它是由质料引起的，我们也只不过是在断言，就其他事情而言，它不是被引发的。而且说质料引发自己的几，根本什么也没有说。

Since an occasion is neither caused nor is it purposive, it cannot be known beforehand. So far as occasions are concerned, the world is free. It is free not merely in the sense that our knowledge is not comprehensive enough or detailed enough to predict beforehand what is going to happen, but free in the sense that the world is fundamentally undetermined beforehand so far as occasions are concerned. This has nothing to do with Heisenberg, nor is it a denial of the option of natural laws or causal relations in the world of objects and events. Objects and events must obey natural laws and given the appropriate similarity of conditions obtaining at any time and place, the realization of some law might even be predicted with such an overwhelming degree of probability as to make it approach to certainty. But as to which of the laws is to be realized there is no predetermination so far as occasions are concerned. The certainty of prediction may be approached but it cannot be reached. We must not confuse occasions with the operation of natural laws. The operation of natural laws is indeed obligatory, but the operation of any one natural law at a certain time and place is not itself under the operation of natural laws. If I am hungry, I am bound to eat, but I am not bound to eat at 11:58. If you say that the operation of other laws result in my eating at 11:58, you are not taking any one of them separately and are assuming at the same time that the actual conditions are such as to favor the operation of some of them so as to result in my eating at 11:58. The latter is begging the question from the point of view of occasions since from that point of view the similar conditions given in the argument needn't be given at all, and are only given because they are occasioned.

We have thus far treated *Chi* or occasion from the point of view of Stuff or its activity. Neither Stuff nor its activity is directly experienced by us, and the notion treated in terms of either is liable to be unfamiliar. Fortunately we needn't restrict ourselves to this way of speaking. We have already spoken of an occasion as being appropriate to a changing individual or a moving object. If we take the point of view of the individual object, we find the occasion appropriate to it to be essentially what we sometimes call luck. The notion of luck implies subjectivity and since we take point of view of the individual object to which the occasion is appropriate, we have the subjectivity of the individual object.

由于几既不是被引发的，也是没有目的的，所以我们不能预先知道它。从几的角度来说，世界是自由的。说它是自由的，并不仅仅是说我们的知识不够充分或者不够详细具体，所以不能够预先知道将要发生什么；而且从几的角度看，世界根本上就不是被预先规定好了的。这与海森堡的原理毫无关系，它也并没有否认客体和事件的世界中的自然律或因果联系。客体和事件必须遵守自然律。给定在任何时间和地方能够获得的条件的恰当相似性，那么某些规律的现实甚至可以达到极高的预料概率，以至于接近确定性。但是究竟什么规律可以现实，从几的方面着想，是不能预见的。我们可以不断地逼近预见的确定性，但是不能到达它。我们绝不能把几和自然律的作用混同起来。自然律的作用确实具有强制性，但是某一自然律在某一时间和地方发生作用本身并不在自然律的作用之下。如果我饿了，那么我肯定是要吃东西的，但是我不一定非要在 11 点58 分吃东西。如果你说有其他的规律作用导致我在 11 点 58 分吃东西，那么你就没有把它们区分开来，而是同时假定了现实的条件有利于它们中的某些起作用，因此导致了我在 11 点 58 分吃东西。后者从几的观点进行了假定，由于从那一观点看问题，在这一争论中的相似的条件根本无须给出，只是因为它们被引发了，所以才被给出了。

至此，我们从质料或它的能动性的角度讨论了几的问题。质料及其能动性都不能被我们直接经验到，运用这两个术语来讨论的观念也不是我们所熟悉的。幸好，我们没有必要把自己严格地限制在这样的说话方式中。我们已经说到了与变化的个体或移动的客体相应的几。如果从单个的客体看问题，那么我们就会发现与之相应的几本质上就是我们有时叫做"运"的这个东西。运的观念隐含着主体性的思想，而且由于我们是从与几相应的个别客体的角度谈问题，所以我们就具有了个别客体的主体性。在前面的部分中，

In the preceding paragraphs we have no such subjectivity and we can speak of occasions only in terms of Stuff and its activity. By bringing in this subjectivity we can easily see that occasion is transformed into luck. The notion of luck is essentially that of the occasion, and it contains that element of "needn't be," but simply "is." To some individual object, it also contains the element of good or bad, favorable or unfavorable, but for the present, we needn't dwell on that.

II

Unlike *Chi* or occasion, *Shu* or preordination is when Stuff shall enter into or depart from possibilities. As we have already said, the entrance into and the departure from possibilities may be voluntary or involuntary, unconditioned or conditioned, free or compelled, and we have already pointed out that these are inadequate terms. They are especially so in relation to *Shu* or preordination. We use the term "shall" to mean free and yet decided. The word "will" might be used, but in order to avoid the whole doctrine of free will, we prefer something that is not quite so rich in its implications. What is intended to convey is that on the one hand Stuff is free to enter into and to depart from a possibility and yet on the other it has decided to enter into and depart from one rather than any other possibility. It is free in the sense that it is not determined by anything else, and decided in the sense that it is not casual; that is to say, it is not compelled, but compelling. The flavor of decision herein attributed to preordination furnishes us with the sense that whether a certain course is wise or not, it is yet to be pursued rather than merely entertained or considered. Since an enormous amount of decisions are made as practical measures without conviction or faith or previous knowledge of their consequences, the flavor of decision need not contain the complicated notions which the terms "will to believe" or "will to live" often imply. We may also start from the other way around by considering preordination from the point of view of the changing or moving objects. To them preordination is something that cannot be helped, it just will happen, and the psychological state to receive it is either bland acceptance as if it is properly due when it is favorable or indifferent, or resignation when it is unfavorable or even disastrous. While an occasion is something that simply is actually, preordination is something that actually cannot keep being.

我们还未涉及这样的主体性,我们只是以质料及其能动性来谈论几的。由于引进了主体性,我们就能比较容易地看到,几在此转换成了运。运这一观念本质上就是几的观念,它包含着"不必是"的因素,直接"就是"。对于某些个别的客体来说,它也具有好或坏、有利的或不利的这样的因素,但是在目前我们不必考察这样的问题。

二

与几不一样,数是当质料出入于可能的那个状态。正如我们已经说过的那样,进出于可能或许是自愿的或被动的、无条件的或有条件的、自由的或被迫的。我们也已经指出,这些并不是合适的术语。联系到数来看,这些术语更是如此。我们用"会"这一术语来指自由的,然而是已经决定了的。可以用"要"这一个词,但是为了避免整个的自由意志的学说,我们还是倾向于那些没有很丰富含义的词。在此想要表述的思想是,一方面质料是自由地进出于可能的,然而另一方面它已经决定了要进出于某一可能而不是其他的可能。在不是由其他事情决定的意义上,它是自由的;在不是随意的意义上,它是已经决定了的。这就是说,它不是被迫的,而是主动的。数所具有的决定的意味向我们提供了这样的意义,即不管某一过程是否明智,都必须继续下去,而不能仅仅是斟酌。由于大量的决定作为实际的措施被作出时,对它们可能带来的后果并没有信心或信仰或足够的了解,所以决定的意味不必包含有如"相信的意愿"或"活下去的意愿"这样的术语经常所隐含的复杂观念。我们也可以从另一个方面开始,从变化或移动的客体的角度来考察数。对它们来说,数是某种不得不如此的东西,它就是要发生。对待它的心理状态或者是平和的接受,当它是有利的或无关紧要的时候把它看作是完全应该发生的;或者是屈从,当它是不利的或甚至有害的时候。几就是具有现实性的东西,然而数却是实际中不能持续存在的东西。

The above attempt at a clarification of the notion of preordination may enable us to distinguish it from other things and these distinctions again may clarify the notion. Like an occasion, preordination is not an object or event or a universal or particular. We need not go into these again since the distinction between these and occasion holds equally between them and preordination. What it might be confused with more than anything else perhaps is the effect of the operation of a natural law. If A—B is a natural law and "a" happens at t_1 and let's say "b" happens at t_2, the preordination appropriate to "b"t_2 may be said to be merely the effect of the operation of the law A—B. The event "b"t_2 is the effect of the natural law. It is the effect of the operation of A—B with the help of the appropriate background S in which A—B operates. But if we left ourselves out of the activities, that is to say, if we do not let our ideas be bound by them, we see no reason why S should be realized so that A—B operates instead of let us say A—C another law which might operate under a set of conditions different from S. Hence although the event "b"t_2 is the effect of the operation of a certain natural law under the given circumstances, the preordination appropriate to "b"t_2 is not, since it is a part of the preordinations or occasions responsible for those circumstances as well. The effect of a natural law requires something given, whereas preordination requires nothing given and is responsible for the given. Every move on the chessboard obeys rules, but that any one move should be actually made is not a question of rules, it is either casually made or made with decision. With regard to every event there is an element that is casual or else an element that savors of decision. We call the former *Chi* or occasion, and the latter *Shu* or preordination. It is these elements that chose the possibilities to be actualized at a certain time and place. If natural laws themselves chose the actual, civilization would have been impossible, and it would have been impossible, if natural laws were not operative. Civilization requires a certain maneuverability of the given so that natural laws can operate towards the achievement of the end desired.

We have already said that the actualities are realities, but they are not co-extensive with realities, since some realities can be said to be non-actual. Confucius is in some sense real though he is no longer actual. Some astronomical realities are actual while others are not. The actual

上面讨论的目的是要澄清数这一观念，这会使我们将它与其他的事物区别开来，而这些区别又会反过来进一步澄清这一观念。像几一样，数也不是一客体或事件，也不是一共相或殊相。我们不必在此再讨论这些，因为这些事物与几之间的区别也同样存在于它们与数之间。可能比别的东西更容易引起混淆的是自然律作用的结果。如果 A—B 是一自然律，"a" 在 t_1 发生，让我们假定 "b" 在 t_2 发生，与 "b" t_2 相应的数可以被说成仅仅是自然律 A—B 作用的结果。事件 "b" t_2 是自然律的结果，这是 A—B 作用的结果，当然应该加上 A—B 发生作用的适当的背景 S 的帮助。但是如果我们使自身处于能动性之外，就是说，如果我们的意念不受能动性的束缚，那么我们就看不出为什么 S 应该现实以便 A—B 发生作用，而不是另外的规律比如 A—C 可能在与 S 不一样的条件之下发生作用。因此虽然事件 "b" t_2 是某一自然律在既定的情况下作用的结果，但是与 "b" t_2 相应的数却不是，因为它本身就是促成那些情况的数或几的一部分。自然律所导致的结果要求某种给定的东西，而数却不要求任何既定的东西，相反它能促成所与。国际象棋中每走一步都要遵守规则，但是现实地走出任何一步并不是规则的问题，它或者是随意地作出的，或者是某种决定之下作出的。对于每一个事件来说，都有或者随意或者带有决定意味的因素。我们把前者叫做几，把后者叫做数。正是这些因素对可能作出了选择，使它们在某一特定的时间和地点现实。如果自然律自身选择了现实，那么就不可能有文明。如果自然律不起作用，那么文明也是不可能的。文明要求所与的某种可操作性，这样，自然律才有可能向着所要取得的目标的方向起作用。

我们已经说过，现实就是实在，但是它们与实在并不是并存的，因为某些实在可以说是非现实的。孔子在某种意义上是实在的，虽然他不再是现实的了。某些天文上的实在是现实的，而另外

is always the existent, it has the element of now, and if we are talking of local actualities, and it has the additional element of the here as well. The actual is that which is acting. Taking any slice of time as the present, there is a whole world that is actual, a world of objects and events that act and react upon each other. Since activity is not itself an object or an event it can only work through the actualities as its medium or through the objects and events as its instrument. Objects and events cannot however function as instruments through their universals or particulars, since the former cannot be said to be here and now, while the latter being so uniquely here and now can neither move or change. Basically activity is that of Stuff and Stuff is active in two ways, either through occasions or through preordinations. When it is said in the last paragraph that it is these activities that chose the actualities we also mean that it is they that chose what universals are to be realized and what particulars are to appear at the present. Like all realities actualities obey natural laws, but which of the laws is to be obeyed is not itself the operation of a natural law. Hence while actualities obey natural laws, their being actual is not the effect of the operation of a natural law. This may at least be one sense in which we sometimes say that while we can describe nature we cannot explain it.

Perhaps we can make use of the difference between implication and inference to make the above point clearer. Implication is expressed by a series of if-then statements in which whether the implicant or the implicate is separately true or not is irrelevant. But if any inference is to be drawn some implicant has to be asserted to be true. The truth of the implicant is not supplied by the implications, but is drawn elsewhere. Natural laws are knitted into a pattern very much like the interrelatedness of propositions connected by if-then relations. Any genuine universal proposition is expressed in the form of an if-then sentence. The presence of the actual is like the truth of the second premise to a traditional hypothetical argument; if it is not given in the manner of the truth of the second premise being asserted, no conclusion can be drawn, hence no inference made. Just as a whole set of hypothetical major premises do not yield a conclusion, so the whole set of natural laws do not allow us to infer what actuality is at any particular time or place. The actual obeys the

一些则不是。现实的总是存在的，它有现在这一因素。而且如果我们谈论地域现实，那么它还有在这里这样的因素。现实的就是正在起作用的东西。把某一段时间作为现在，那么就有一整个的世界是现实的，在其中客体和事件相互作用着。由于能动性本身并不是客体或事件，所以它只能通过现实作为中介或通过客体和事件作为工具而起作用。然而客体和事件不能够通过它们的共相或殊相作为工具而起作用，因为共相不能够说在此时此地，而殊相在此时此地具有唯一性，所以是不能够移动或变化的。基本上说来，能动性是质料的能动性。质料在两个方面可以说是能动的，或者是通过几，或者是通过数。上一段落曾说到这些能动性选择了现实，我们的意思也是说，正是它们选择了什么样的共相将要现实，什么样的殊相在现在出现。像所有的实在一样，现实遵守自然律。但是究竟遵守哪一个自然律，这本身不是自然律的作用。因此，虽然现实遵守自然律，但是它们之成为现实并不是自然律作用的结果。这至少说明了一个意思，即我们有时说虽然我们能够描述自然，但是却不能够解释它。

或许我们能够利用蕴涵和推论这两者之间的区别把上述论点解释得更清楚。蕴涵通过"如果——则"这样的陈述得到表达，在这样的陈述中，蕴涵者和被蕴涵者分别是真的还是假的并没有多大的关系。但是如果要作出任何一推论，那么有些蕴涵者必须被断言为是真的。然而蕴涵者的真并不是由蕴涵提供的，而是从其他地方取得的。自然律被编织成一图案，非常类似于由"如果——则"关系联结起来的命题之间的相互关联。任何真正的普遍命题都是由"如果——则"的句子形式表达的。现实的呈现类似于传统假言命题中的小前提的真值。如果它不是以被断言的小前提的真值形式给出，那么就不可能得出结论，因此也就不可能得出推论。正如假言推论中的大前提不能得出结论一样，一组自然律也同样不允许我们推出在特殊的时间或地点有什么样的现实。在下述的意义上，现实

natural laws in the sense that with the truth of the second premise given, the conclusion is inevitably arrived at; it is not determined by natural laws in the sense that the truth of the second premise is not contained in the natural laws themselves, and the actual can only be inferred from the natural laws with the actual given. This is the fundamental stubbornness we find in facts. So far as occasions and preordinations are concerned, we are faced with the purely given. We cannot do anything with it other than to accept it, and therein lies the stubbornness of the given. When it is said that we may explain facts, but we cannot explain them away, part of what is meant may very well be that feeling of stubbornness involved in actualizations that obey natural laws and are yet not dictated by any of them, that are no more intelligible than any other possible alternatives and that no matter how intelligible the other alternatives may be they are yet not actual here and now.

Unlike occasions preordinations can be known beforehand. They are known partly through the operation of natural laws, and partly through the actualization of the background favorable for the operation of certain natural law against certain others. They may not as a matter of fact be predicted, but they are predictable. The reading of actuality may mislead us, and the reasoning may be faulty, but otherwise preordinations may be predicted with some degree of accuracy. The usual inference from cause to effect is both a reading of the actual in terms of causal relations and a prediction of preordinations. Rules may be adopted for doing so and the prevailing theory of relativity helps us to correlate time and space in such a way that given the time interval certain space distances become irrelevant and vice versa. Calculation fails more and more in proportion to the increase of time or space intervals between events. Hence prediction is more or less limited to localities under certain limited time intervals. The point to be emphasized here however is that prediction is not merely based on what we call usually the operation of natural laws, it is also a prediction of preordinations through the reading of the actual. There is a drift as well as a pattern in the actual, and the drift of the actual indicates preordinations if correctly gauged. We are here essentially advocating the common sense view that in order to be able to know the future to any extent we have to know the past and the present. Only in our language we say that the actual indicates preordinations. In order to predict preordinations we have to know natural laws as well,

遵循着自然律，即给定了小前提的真值，那么必然会得出结论。在小前提的真值并不包含在自然律之中的意义上，现实不是由自然律决定的。只有在现实被给定的情况之下，现实才能从自然律推出来。这就是我们在事实中所发现的硬性。就几和数而言，我们面对着纯粹的所与。我们没有别的选择，只能接受所与，因此在这里就存在着所与的硬性。当说我们可以解释事实但却不能够为事实辩解的时候，这么说的部分意思可能就是这种现实中包含的硬性的感觉。这些现实遵守自然律，却不受其控制；跟其他可能的选择一样都不可理解，并且不管其他的选择多么容易理解，在此时此地它们却不是现实的。

与几不同，数是能够预先知道的。数能够知道，部分是由于自然律的作用，部分是由于有利于某一自然律而反对其他自然律起作用的背景的现实。在事实上它们可能没有被预言，但它们是可以被预言的。对现实的理解可能会误导我们，对现实的推论也可能会有错误，但是对数的预见却可以有一些准确性。平常所谓的从原因到结果的推论既是以因果关系来理解现实，也是对数的预言。可以采用某些规则来这样做，现在盛行的相对论可以帮助我们将时间和空间以下述的方式联系起来，即给定时间的间隔，某些空间距离就变得不相关，反之亦然。随着事件之间的时间或空间距离的增长，预测会越来越不准。因此，预言多多少少是在某一限定的时间间隔之内，并且是局限于地点的。然而在此所强调的重点是，预言不仅仅是依据我们通常所说的自然律的作用，而且也是通过理解现实来预言数的。在现实中有势也有图案，而且如果估计正确的话，现实的势就能表明数。我们在此实质上是在提倡常识性的看法，即为了能够在某种程度上知道未来，我们必须知道过去和现在。只是以我们的语言来讲，我们说现实表明了数。为了能够预言数，我们也必须

but knowing them is not sufficient. Here again we may return to a point already mentioned: reality proceeds in accordance with pattern, but it is not propelled by pattern; it is post-facts intelligible, but not anti-facts rational. Besides preordinations there are occasions as well. The sum total of circumstances relevant to a given locality together with the operation of certain laws towards which these circumstances are favorable indicates preordinations relevant to that locality.

To the individual object or event, the preordination appropriate to it is its fate. We have already pointed out that the occasion appropriate to an individual is its luck. Just as an occasion is different from preordination, so luck is different from fate. One difference is felt by the kind of individual, who are endowed with feeling and intelligence. Though related and relevant to the individual alike, luck is external while fate is internal to the individual. An individual without his luck remains that individual whereas an individual without his fate may often be not quite that individual. Luck is what happens to an individual whereas fate is what is bound to happen to an individual; it is a part of his character that actuates his fate. Fighting against one's luck is sometimes ridiculous sometimes comical, since one is often outside the conflict as a spectator, but fighting against one's fate is always a tragedy since one is always fighting against one's self. Luck is what needn't be but somehow is, whereas fate is always bound to be. Just as luck may be good or bad, so also is fate, but we shall not dwell on these aspects. We have been talking of the kind of individuals endowed with feeling and intelligence so as to bring out the difference of feeling attached to luck and fate, but the more general way of speaking is not to limit ourselves to these individuals. We have seen the change or motion that is occasioned does not come before or after its appropriate occasion; we may say that no change or motion that is preordained can escape its preordination. This is another way of saying that no individual whether endowed with intelligence and feeling or not can escape his fate whether it is good or bad.

III

We have already said that the metaphysical principle has provided us with time. This is perfectly true. Time is however quite complex, and although we shall leave a number of senses untouched, we still have to

知道自然律，但是知道它们还不够。在这里，我们可以再次回到前面已经提到过的观点，即实在根据图案而开展，但它不是由图案导致的；它是后事实的可理解的，而不是前事实的合理的。在数之外还有几。与既定地点相应的情形的总和以及情形有利于其的规律的作用都表明了与地点有关的数。

对于个别的客体或事件来说，与之相应的数是命。我们已指出，与个体相应的几是运。正如几不同于数，运也不同于命。有一类个体是既有感觉也有理智的，他们能够感觉到运和命之间的区别。虽然运和命都与个体相关，但是运是外在于个体的，而命却内在于个体。一个体没有运仍然是那个个体，然而作为个体如果没有命，那么这一个体可能就不是那个个体了。运是恰巧发生于个体的东西，而命对于个体来说却是必然要发生的，是他特性的一部分，实现了他的命。一个体与自己的运斗有时是荒唐的，有时是滑稽的，因为个体作为旁观者经常置身于这样的战斗之外。但与自己的命斗总是以悲剧而告终，因为与自己的命斗就是与自我斗。运是不必如此但又不知为何就是如此，而命却总是必然如此的。正如运可能是好的也可能是坏的一样，命也是如此，但我们现在不讨论这些方面的问题。我们至此一直讨论的是禀赋着感觉和理智的个体，这样的个体能够显出与运命相联的感觉的区别。但一个更广泛的范围并不把我们局限于这样的个体。我们已经看到由他物引起的变化或移动既不在几之前也不在几之后，我们也许能说没有一个由数决定的变化或移动能够逃脱它的数。这是以另一种方式说，没有一个体，不管它是否具有理智和感觉，总是不能逃脱他的或好或坏的命。

三

我们已指出，形而上学原则为我们提供了时间。这是千真万确的。然而时间是非常复杂的。虽然我们不准备涉及时间的某些

admit a number of senses in order to do whatever minimal justice there may be to the subject. We have already distinguished the content of time from its scaffolding. Although analogies are misleading we might indulge in them to some extent in order to smuggle certain ideas across. Time may be likened to the railroad together with the running train. The road bed together with milestones is like the scaffolding and the train together with whatever there is in it is somewhat like the content. The scaffolding of time is static if one views it from the outside; its Januaries or Februaries are like the milestones of the road bed. It becomes dynamic only when viewed from the content of time just as the milestones on the road bed run away from us when we are on the train that runs over the road bed. But the content has also two elements, the flow and what is carried in the flow just as the running train consists of running on the one hand and on the other the train and everything that is carried in it. Analogies should not be pushed too far or else dissimilarities will spoil the picture, and ideas other than those that are meant to be conveyed may be brought alone to confuse the issue. Don't think of the train that goes back and forth or the bare track with no running train on it. Time is a one-way traffic.

The content of time then consists of the pure flow and the flotsam and jetsam in it. The former is the series of occasions and preordinations and the latter is the sum total of factualities. The content is always in the present and the flow is irreversable. Such terms as "about to," "on the point of," "shall" used in our discussion of occasions and preordinations are inadequate in some significant senses, but they have the virtue of indicating genuine becoming instead of that which becomes or that which has come to be. The actualities are the realizations or disrealizations of universals, the appearance or disappearance of particulars in the history of objects or events. The time-content is a flow of occasions and preordinations loaded with actualities; it is some old reality in process viewed from the actual and the present; it is congruent, contingent, economical, as well as in accordance with pattern and eternally drifting into a wealth of co-temporal and co-spatial nexus of particulars. This is the content of time as distinguished from its scaffolding. Since there are occasions and preordinations to the flow, there are also luck and

含义，但是为了能最低限度展示这一主题，我们仍然必须承认时间的某些含义。我们已经把时间的内容和时间的框架加以了区别。虽然类比往往容易误导人，但是我们可以略微以此来说明有些问题。时间可以比作有火车在上面奔驰的铁轨。树有里程碑的路基类似于框架，而火车及其内所装载的一切多少有点儿像内容。如果一个人从外面看过去，时间框架是静止的，它的那些 1 月份或 2 月份像树在路基旁的里程碑。只有当从时间内容的角度去看的时候，它才会显得运动起来，正如当我们从在路基上飞驰的火车上去看树在路基旁的里程碑时，才会感到里程碑是向后跑去了。但是时间内容也有两个因素，时间流以及在时间流之中的东西，就像奔驰的火车也是由两方面组成的，一方面是火车的奔驰，另一方面是火车以及它所装载的东西。类比不能太过，否则不同之处就会破坏这种描述，并非想要传达的意念就会出现从而搅乱我们的问题。不要考虑来回奔驰的火车或没有任何火车奔驰的空轨这些情况。时间是单向的轨道。

时间内容是纯粹的时间之流和在其中的杂七杂八的东西构成的。前者是一系列的几和数，而后者是事实的总和。内容总是当前的，而流是不可逆转的。我们在讨论几和数的时候所运用的"即将""正要""将会"这些术语在某些重要意义上是不合适的，但是它们却具有这样的好处，即显示真正的变化过程，而不是变成了什么。现实是在客体或事件历史上的共相的实在或成虚、殊相的出现或消失。时间内容是现实满载于其中的几和数的流，从现实和现在的观点来看，它是在过程中的过去的实在。它是和谐的、偶然的和经济的，而且也遵循着图案，永远在走向众多同时同地的殊相。这就是与时间框架相区别的时间内容。由于时间之流中有着几和数，因此在其中也有着运和命。与理智和感觉不一样，

fate. Quite apart from intelligence and feeling, there is relativity and subjectivity among objects and events in their relations to each other. A landslide brings a change of course to a stream, let us say. In actuality, it is more relevant to some mountain or hill as well as to some stream. So also are occasions and preordinations. They are more relevant to some than to others and in that relevancy we have to distinguish congeniality or uncongeniality. The occasion or preordination appropriate to the landslide is uncongenial to the mountain or hill from the point of view of that mountain's or that hill's continued and comparatively unchanged existence and it may be congenial to a number of other things in the sense that it favored their continued existence such as flowers and trees that were formerly too shaded and are now directly under the sun. While actualities are congruent, the interrelations of the different items in them are not all congenial or uncongenial.

We shall cease to speak in terms of occasions and preordinations and for convenience's sake we shall only speak of time under the proviso that it means the content and the flow as distinguished from the scaffolding. In terms of congenialities or uncongenialities, time retains certain items of what is carried and throws overboard certain others. That is to say, some survive and others perish. In between there are all sorts of degrees of changes varying from those that are extremely slight to those that are quite radical and all, including survival and perishing, are indicated through the appearance or disappearance of particulars. The perishing or survival is often predicated of individual objects, for example: "As a result of the landslide, a certain mountain or hill disappeared." That mountain is regarded as an individual object and so regarded it means more than a particular, but while it is more than a particular, its disappearance is none the less also the disappearance of a particular. The change of an individual object is usually expressed in terms of the appearance and disappearance of particulars, for example: "The apple which was green yesterday is now entirely red." Here we regard the apple as the individual object, green or red as the particular that disappears or appears. In terms of perishing and survival, however, we may just as well say that the apple survived while the green object perished. At any rate as time flows, particulars appear and disappear and individuals survive or perish. Survival and perishing

在客体和事件的相互关系之中有的是相对性和主体性。比如说，山崩当然会给河流带来变化。现实上，更相关的是某座高山或小丘或某条河流。对于几和数来说也是这样的。它们也是与某些东西而不是另一些东西有着更紧密的关系。在这样的相关性中，我们必须区分同质性和非同质性。从高山或小丘持续的和相对不变的存在来说，与山崩相应的几或数和高山或小丘并没有同质性，但是它却可能与一些其他的事物有着同质性，因为它有利于这些事物如花和树的存在。那些花和树以前可能过于遮蔽，而现在却直接暴露在阳光之下。虽然现实是和谐的，但在现实中的不同东西之间的相互关系并不都是同质的或非同质的。

我们从现在开始不再以几和数这样的术语来谈论问题，为了方便我们将只谈论时间，并且是在这样条件之下，即时间意味着与框架相区别的内容和流。根据同质性和非同质性，时间保留某些在其中的东西，却抛掉另外一些东西。那就是说，某些东西保留了下来，另外有些东西则消失了。在保留和消失之间也存在着不同程度的变化，从那些最细微的变化直至最为激烈的变化。所有的变化，包括留存和消失，通过殊相的出现或消失体现出来。对个体客体的消失或留存经常可作出预料，比如说"作为山崩的结果，某一高山或某一小丘消失了"。那座山被看作是个体的客体。这样来看的话，那么它就不仅仅是一殊相。但是虽然它不仅仅是一殊相，然而它的消失却仍然是殊相的消失。一个体客体的变化通常是通过殊相的出现或消失来表达的。比如说："昨天还是绿的那个苹果现在完全变红了。"在此我们把这个苹果看作是个体客体，把绿或红看作或者出现或者消失的殊相。然而，从消失或留存的方面考虑，我们可以这样说，苹果留存下来，但绿色客体消失了。不管怎么样，随着时间的流逝，殊相会出现或消失，个体会留存或灭亡。留存或灭亡或许

may appear in two ways, in one of them it is merely the individual that survives or perishes, while in the other the species to which the individuals belong also survives or perishes. In the latter case we have the appearance and disappearance of species of the kind that happens in natural history. Distinguish an object or an event from its environment we can easily see that time brings forth relative to each object or event an environment with some elements that are congenial and others that are not. This is merely another way of saying that actualities act and react on each other in a way favorable to some and unfavourable to others. Some survive and others perish, and some are the cargos of time while others are its flotsam and jetsam.

This notion of time is not contrary to certain significant usages in ordinary life. When it is said that the time has come to talk of many things, it does not mean that it is now twelve o'clock or March 15th, 1944. It means that certain potentialities of the kind described are about to be actual in an environment in which the given actualities point to their immediate actualization. Whether the "time" has come to talk of cabbages and kings, or to leave your host and go home, or to start a revolution or merely to smoke a pipe, what is meant is that the flow of time will carry with it the actualization of the potentialities described by these phrases. Then again we sometimes speak of a good time or a bad time. It is not the scaffolding that is meant and although it is not the pure flow that is meant either, it is yet the flow together with what is carried in it. When we say that "in 'times' like those when we are fighting for our very lives, we should not expect to eat as well as we did ordinarily," or "if we read the signs of the 'time' correctly, we ...," we are talking of the flow of time together with some of the actualities in it. Something in time is said to be good or bad, or else it is such that certain behavior which might be described as moral or intelligent is called for, or yet it is such that relative to certain measures should be adopted. There is in time a sort of internecine relationship between actualities in which there is subjectivity relative to certain things and objectivity relative to certain other things, so that there is also a conglomeration or convergence of congenialities and uncongenialities. When uncongenialities cut balance than congenialities for an individual, for that individual the time is about over. When a man declares that his time is over, it does not mean any stoppage of the flow of

会以两种方式出现。在一种方式上，仅仅是一个体留存或灭亡；而在另一个方式上，个体所属的物种也会留存或灭亡。在后一个方式中，自然史上物种的出现或消失就属此列。将一客体或事件与它的环境区别开来，那么我们就能容易地看到，相对于每一客体或事件，时间引发了带有同质元素或非同质元素的环境。这只不过是以另一种方式说，现实间的相互作用，有利于一些现实，不利于另一些现实。有些留存，另一些灭亡了；某些是时间所载的货物，而另一些则是它丢弃的东西。

　　这里所说的时间与日常生活中有关时间的某些重要用法并不冲突。当说到了谈论许多事情的时间，这并不意味着现在是 12 点或是 1944 年 3 月 15 日。它只是意味着某些被描述的潜在性在一环境中将要变成现实，在这样的环境中给定的现实表明它们即将变成现实。无论是到了漫谈各种话题的时间，或者到了要作别主人回家去，或发动一场革命或只是抽一支烟的时间，意思无非是说时间之流将会裹挟着这些短句描述的潜在性的现实。然而我们有时又谈到好的时机或坏的时机。这里所说的不是时间框架，也不是纯粹的时间之流，而是时间之流及在其中的一切。当我们说"当我们为自己的生命去战斗，在这样的'时间'里，我们不能指望跟平时那样吃得那么好"或"如果我们能看懂'时间'的迹象，那么我们……"等等的时候，我们正在谈论的是时间流及其中的某些现实。在时间中的某些东西被说成是好的或坏的，或者情况是要求作出某些被认为是有道德的或是聪明的行为，或情况是相关的某些措施应该被采纳。在时间中有一种相互冲突的关系存在于现实之间，其中相对某些事物有主体性，相对其他事物有客观性，因此就有同质性和非同质性现象的汇集。当在一个个体中非同质性超过了同质性，那么对于这一个体来说它的时间也就快要过去了。当一个人说他的时间结束了，这不是说时间之流的停顿，而是

time; it means that he is about to be jettisoned out of the actualities into the limbo of the past.

Time then is essentially an evolutionary process. It is the basic element in what we call in these papers reality in process. It is that flow in which all things change, some survive, others perish, and all the changes take place in terms of particulars that appear or disappear or else of possibilities realized or universals disrealized. We are here merely describing time as evolution, not propounding any specific theory of evolution, or tracing its history. As to what survive, or what they survive from, or whether in the process there is progress or not, or if there were, what is the criterion, etc. are not questions with which we are here concerned. Nor do we start with certain remote ages, for no matter how remote they may be, they cannot be as remote as the beginning of time since for us time has no beginning. Whatever age natural history chose for its starting point of its subject matter, there was time before that age and therefore also evolution. It does not stop with the emergence of men, nor with the arrival of the 20th century. What we are talking now is not a segment of time nor is our actuality confined to the surface of the earth. Since we are essentially talking of reality in process, we are also talking of the unfoldment of Tao. To indicate that time is an evolutionary process is also to say that there is evolution going on in Tao's unfoldment. We may as well say that all the contingent possibilities will be realized in the evolution and this is simply another way of saying that time is endless.

Time as evolution is an infinite process in which all sorts of things imaginable and conceivable will happen. Whatever is imaginable or conceivable is a possibility and unless it is an eternally unrealizable possibility, it will be realized, and unless it is a necessary or an eternally realized possibility, it will be realized in time. This statement is very likely staggering to some, and it certainly sounds incredible. Let us try to make it clear by ruling out that which it does not mean and finding out that which it does mean. One thing it does not mean is that all sorts of imaginable or conceivable will happen in what we sometimes call "this world". Whatever this world may mean, it is a slice of time from t_n to t_m. Whether we speak of geological ages or astronomical ages, or merely in

说他快要被现实弃置于过去的归宿当中了。

这样，时间本质上是一不断进化的过程。它是我们在这些论文中称为过程中的实在的一个基本因素。正是在时间之流中，一切事物都在变化之中，某些事物留存下来，另一些事物则消亡了，而且所有变化的发生都是根据于生灭的殊相或者实在的可能或者成虚的共相。我们在此仅仅是将时间描述为进化过程，并没有提出什么特殊的进化理论，或追溯进化的历史。至于什么留存下来，或从什么东西中留存下来，或在过程中是否有进步，或如果有进步，那么标准是什么，诸如此类的问题不是我们在此所要考虑的。我们也不是从遥远的年代开始讨论的，因为不管年代是多么地久远，它们也不可能与时间的开端一样久远，因为对我们来说时间是没有开端的。不管自然史选择什么样的年代作为它的主题的起点，在这一年代之前总还是有时间的，因此也就有进化。这样的进化并不因为人类的出现或 20 世纪的到来而终止。我们现在正在谈论的不是时间的片段，我们的现实也不局限于地球表面。因为我们在本质上谈论的是过程中的实在，我们也是在谈论道的展开。表明时间是一进化的过程也同样是说在道的展开中也有进化的过程。我们还可以这么说，所有不老是现实的可能将在进化过程之中现实，而这也不过是时间没有终结的另一种说法。

作为进化过程的时间是一无限的过程，在这一过程之中所有可以想象的和可以思议的事情都会发生。可以想象的或可以思议的都是可能。除非它是永远无法现实的可能，否则它就会现实；除非它是必然或老是现实的可能，否则它总是会在时间中现实的。对于某些人来说这样的说法可能令人震惊，听起来简直不可相信。让我们进一步来排除它所不包含的意思而找出它所包含的意思，从而把它的意义弄清楚。它不包含的一个意思是，各种可以想象的或可以思议的事情将会在我们通常叫做的"这个世界"上发生。不管"这个世界"意味着什么，它总是从 t_n 到 t_m 之间的时间阶段。不管我们所说的是地质年代还是天文时间，或仅仅是历史的年代或甚至是世

terms of historical ages or even generations, we are merely assigning values to n and m. If their difference is large, we have a long slice of time and if it is small, we have a short one. In any case what we are really talking about when we talk about this world is merely the sum total of actualities of a slice or a period of time and in that world or during that slice of time, some things happen and others don't. But even in such a world lots of imaginable and conceivable things have happened which we have not imagined or conceived and although lots of things may happen in any such world, we cannot say something imagined or conceived, let us say x, will happen, because t_m may come before x happens, no matter how distant t_m may be from the time x is imagined or conceived. There is no obligation on this part of t_m to postpone its arrival until x happens. When we say ordinarily that certain things will happen or not, we have surreptitiously or unconsciously set limits to time in which it is expected to happen or not to happen. When universal peace is said to be possible or impossible, a certain time limit is brought along with the question or statement. It is doubtful whether most people would be interested in world peace if it comes in ten thousand years. One should not be surprised if the assumed limit of time for most people interested in universal peace is the peace immediately after the present war.

If no time limit is set, the problem is quite different. Anything possible (other than the eternally unrealizable possibilities) will be realized in infinite time, because so long as it is not realized, time simply flows merrily on without limit. It is only when the possibility is realized that a limit to time is set, namely, the time of the realization of the possibility in question. It was, I think, Eddington who suggested that given infinite time a monkey will be able to type out mechanically without knowing what he is doing, let's say Keats' "Ode on a Grecian Urn," provided he does not repeat himself. This may not be accomplished in billions and billions of years, but it will be accomplished in infinite time, because if it weren't accomplished in any finite period of time, typing goes on endlessly; the only limit set is the typing of the ode. The same thing is true of the realization of any possibility that is not itself eternally unrealizable. The statement that such a possibility will be realized in infinite time does

代，我们也只不过是赋值于 n 和 m。如果它们之间的距离是巨大的，那么我们就具有了一个很长的时间阶段；如果它们之间的距离是很小的，那么我们所具有的就是很短的时间阶段。总之，当我们谈论这个世界的时候，我们真正谈论的只不过是在一段时间之中的现实的总和；在那一世界中或者在那一段时间中，某些事情发生了，而其他事情没有发生。但是即便在这样的世界中，仍然有许多可以想象或可以思议的事情发生，然而我们既没有想象到也没有思议到它们。虽然有许多的事情可以在这样的世界上发生，但是我们不能够说某些想象到或者是思议到的事情，比如 x，就会发生。因为 t_m 可能在 x 发生之前到来，无论 x 被想象到或被思议到的时间距 t_m 有多么遥远。从 t_m 的方面说，在 x 发生之前，它是没有责任去延缓它的到来的。当我们在日常生活中说，某些事情是否会发生，我们总是在有意或无意之间对它们预计发生或不发生的时间有所限制。当我们说世界和平是可能的或不可能的，对于这样的问题或陈述是有时间方面的限制的。如果和平将在一万年以后才会姗姗而至，那么绝大多数人是否会对世界和平感兴趣就是一个问题了。如果于绝大多数对世界和平感兴趣的人而言，所说的和平是目前这场战争之后马上就会到来的和平，那么我们就不会感到意外了。

如果没有时间方面的限制，那么问题就会完全是另一种样子了。任何可能的事情（除老是不现实的可能之外）都会在无限的时间中得到现实，因为只要它没有现实，时间就会欢快地向前流淌而毫无任何限制。只有当可能现实的时候，时间方面的限制才确定了，即相关的可能现实的时间。我想是爱丁顿曾经这样说过，如果给一个猴子无限的时间，只要它不重复打字的话，那么它就有可能机械地打出比如说济慈的《希腊古瓮颂》，却不知道自己在干什么。这可能在几十亿年的时间内都不能完成，但是在无限的时间内肯定能完成。因为如果没在有限的时间之内完成，打字的过程可以无限制地进行下去，唯一的限制就是打《希腊古瓮颂》。这样的情形对于老不现实的可能来说也是完全适用的。这样的可

not mean much practically or positively, since it includes the possibility that the said possibility in question may not be realized in any finite time. It may not be realized, that is to say in $t_n—t_m$ no matter how large the difference between m and n is, provided it is finite. To people speaking in the context of ordinary life, this means that some possibilities simply won't be realized. The statement that all imaginable and conceivable things will be realized in infinite time carries with it a number of assumptions, one of which is that reality like history does not repeat itself, or that if it does give the impression of doing so, it does so with a slight similarity of pattern and not identity in drift. Most likely there are other assumptions, but we shall not try to enumerate them here. Time is an infinite flow, that is, it flows ad infinitum partly because the universe is taken to be infinitely rich in variety and more things happen in it than we can ever imagine or conceive.

IV

With the above in mind we can see that in the unfoldment of Tao or in reality and process, an infinity of things have happened and an infinity of things will yet happen unless it is something that is impossible, or if possible, eternally unrealizable. Speaking from the point of view of some slice of time as the present, anything will be realized in infinite time. We cannot say when certain things will happen, but that they will happen sometime or other does not seem to be open to doubt. The attitude here taken needs a bit of further clarification from another angle. We do not attribute the existence of things or the emergence of actualities to the propulsion of any transcendental reason, or the will of a transcendental God, or the fulfillment of a transcendental purpose. Since Tao is co-extensive with the universe, there cannot be anything transcendental to Tao or to its unfoldment. If there is, it is something that is a part of Tao, or something that functions in the unfoldment of Tao and if it is transcendental it is so only to some of the things in reality or process. Since all sorts of things happen in the unfoldment of Tao, all sorts of values will emerge in it. In this section we shall deal with the emergence of purpose and mind. It can be easily seen that Tao is neither purposive or non-purposive, neither knowing or conceiving nor not knowing or not conceiving. But since purpose may emerge in the unfoldment of Tao in

能会在无限的时间之内现实，这一陈述在实际上或实证上没什么意义，因为它还包括这样的可能，即所说的那个可能在任何有限的时间内不能现实。它可能不会现实，就是说不管 n 和 m 之间的区别有多么大，只要这段时间是有限的，它就不可能在 t_n 到 t_m 这一段时间之内现实。对于在日常生活情况之中讲话的人们来说，这就意味着某些可能是绝对不会现实的。所有可以想象的和可以思议的事物将在无限的时间内现实，这一陈述附带着一系列假设。其中的一个假设就是，实在像历史一样是不会重新来过的；或如果确实给人感觉重新来过了，它也只是在图案方面的些微的相似性而不是势的方面的同一性。最有可能的是，还有另外的假设，但是我们不准备在此列举它们。时间是一无限的流，这就是说，它无限地流淌下去，部分是因为宇宙本身就具有丰富的多样性，在其中发生的事情的数量远远超出我们所能想象或思议的范围。

四

记住上面所说的一切，我们就能看到在道的展开过程中，或在实在和过程中，无限的事物已经产生，无限的事物将要产生，只要它们不是不可能，或是老不现实的可能。从现在这样的时间阶段的角度来看，任何事物都会在无限的时间之内现实。我们不能够说某一事情将在何时发生，但它们将要在某时或另外的什么时候产生似乎毋庸置疑。此处所采取的态度需要我们从另外的角度做进一步的澄清。我们没有把事物的存在或现实的形成归之于任何先验理由的推动或先验的上帝的意志或先验的目的的完成。因为道是与宇宙并存的，所以不可能有任何先验于道及其展开过程的存在。如果有这样的东西存在的话，那么它们就是道的一部分，或者是在道的展开中起作用的事物。如果它是先验的，它也只有对实在或过程中的某些事物来说是先验的。由于各种事物都是在道的展开中产生的，因此所有的价值也在此过程中出现。在这一部分中，我们将要讨论的是目的和心的出现。能够很容易地看到，道既不是目的性的也不是非目的性的，既不是知道的或想象的，也不是不知道的或不想象的。但是由于在它出现的范围内，目的

so far as it emerges, the unfoldment in which it emerges becomes partly purposive. The same is true of the emergence of the mind. Tao unfolds itself through the vehicle of the actualities. Nothing can be predicated of Tao-one, while all that can be predicated of the actualities separately is but a functioning of Tao-infinite. If Tao cannot be said to be purposeful itself, it must be admitted at the same time that it cannot but have purposefulness in the unfoldment.

"Purpose" is most generally used to mean desire or need together with the adoption of means towards its satisfaction. In some of the ways in which the term is used it involves consciousness, but since we shall discuss the emergence of mind separately, we might as well rule out consciousness as one of the ingredients. We shall limit the term "purpose" to mean certain ends to be achieved by certain means whether the latter is consciously adopted or not. In this sense, the ends are purposes and the means are the purposive or purposeful action or activities. Thus the bending of the stalk of a sunflower towards the sun is purposeful, because it can be said to be indulged in to achieve an end, namely, the facing of the flower towards the sun. The emergence of purpose brings with it the emergence of the individual capable of purpose as well as of purposive act. These belong to the realm of objects and events. They are different from other objects only through having purpose so far as our discussion is concerned. Purposes involving needs may be considered to be comparatively primitive while those involving policies complex. It is possible to have a gradation of purposes from the comparatively simple to the comparatively complex, but even so it does not mean that evolution proceeds in accordance with that gradation. While a theory of progress may be maintained in relation to specific aspects within certain areas and for a period of time in the scaffolding of space and time, it can hardly be maintained universally. A criterion of value may be adopted upon which values may be assigned to purposes and it is possible to have a gradation of values from the almost valuable to the eminently valuable. Here again we may note that while a progressive growth in valuation may take place in limited spheres, a universal theory of an all-pervading growth can hardly be maintained. The adequacy of means to end may be compared and a scale of adequacy

可能在道的展开过程之中出现，那么它出现在其中的展开过程就部分地有了目的。这也同样适用于心的出现。道是以现实为工具而展开自身的。关于道一不能作出任何论断，然而对现实分别作出的所有论断都只不过是道无限在发生作用。如果不能够说道是有目的的，那么在同时就必须承认道在展开过程中不得不具有目的。

"目的"在日常生活中最普通的用法是指意欲或需要，并要用一定的手段来达到意欲的满足。在某种方式上，"目的"包含有意识，但是由于我们将要专门讨论心的出现，我们最好还是不把意识看作这一术语的一个成分。我们将把"目的"这一术语局限为运用某种手段来实现最终要达到的目标，而不管这样的手段是有意识还是无意识采纳的。在这种意义上，最终要达到的目标就是目的，而手段就是有目的的或有目的性的行动或行为。这样，向日葵的茎向着太阳弯腰就是具有某种目的性的，因为可以说它有达到某种目的的愿望，即面向太阳。目的的出现导致了具有目的和有目的的行动的个体的出现。这些都属于客体和事件的领域。就我们目前讨论的范围而言，它们与其他客体的区别就是因为它们具有目的。包含需要的目的相对而言可能是比较简单的，而包含政策的目的却是复杂的。目的可以分成不同的层次，从比较简单的到比较复杂的。但是即便如此，这也不是说进化就是根据这样的层次来进行的。虽然在某些领域内某些具体的方面，在空—时框架内的某一段时间内，进步的理论是可以成立的；但是从普遍的方面着眼，这样的理论几乎是不能成立的。可以采纳某种价值标准，从而将其归属于目的，而且价值本身也可以被分成不同的层次，从略具价值的直至相当有价值的。在这里我们也可能注意到，虽然在限定的领域内，赋值有渐进性增长，但是全面性增长的普遍理论是不可能成立的。对于目的来说的手段的充分性可能用来比较，而且充分性的级别可能得到强调。

might be urged, but again while adequacy might be gained from the point of view of certain aspects at the expense perhaps of certain other aspects, a universal increase in adequacy along all lines can hardly be read into the evolutionary process of time.

That purpose will emerge in time, we have a doubt after what has been said about time has been made clear. Purposiveness is a possibility, the corresponding concept of which is not contradictory, nor is it such that it is eternally unrealizable. Hence it is a contingent possibility. The realization is contingent from the point of view of any particular time or place; it is not contingent in the sense that it may never be realized. In one way of speaking there is no contingent possibility that will be realized, that is why we say that the sum total of contingent possibilities will be realized as time flows into infinity. The emergence of purpose is dependable, but as to when it is to emerge is quite a different question, and one in which we are not interested, it being a question of history. That there is purpose now is merely a question of fact. Nor are we interested in how long purposiveness stays. There is no reason why it should not stay for a long time, neither is there any why it should stop rather abruptly. There have been ages of inert matters in the past, and there is no reason why it shouldn't be any in future. It must be understood that we are talking of factuatizations and actualities, of the stations of process separately, not of the unfoldment of Tao as a whole. The latter can hardly be said to be purposive or non-purposive, it may be said to be neither or both. When the actualities cease to include purposive individuals, it does not mean that the whole unfoldment of Tao ceases to be purposive just as when glacial ages of inert matter returns, the whole unfoldment of Tao does not thereby become inert. The emergence of purpose affects the interrelations of the actualities; it disturbs the congenialities or uncongenialities of the entities in the actual; it does not modify the unfoldment of Tao itself.

With the emergence of purpose something most significant

happened. There is a minimal bifurcation of reality, a faint separation of the self from the others, or a slight demarcation of the inside from the outside. The whole world of reality actualized at any particular time and place is no longer quite lumpy with the emergence of purpose, and

但是虽然从某些方面来看（这些方面可能要以其他方面为代价而取得）可以得到充分性，然而在时间进化的历程之中不可能得到在所有方面充分性的普遍增长。

关于时间的所说弄清楚之后，我们有一个疑问，即目的将要在时间中出现。目的性是一可能，与它相应的概念不是矛盾的，也不是老不现实的可能。因此，它是不是老是现实的可能。从任何特殊的时间或地点的角度来看，它的现实是偶然的；但是在它可能永远不现实的意义上说，它不是偶然的。以一种方式说，没有会现实的不老是现实的可能，这就是为什么我们说，随着时间无限流逝，不老是现实的可能的总和会现实。目的的出现是可靠的，但是至于它究竟在什么时候出现则完全是一个另外的问题了，而且这不是我们感兴趣的一个问题，它是一个历史的问题。现在有目的存在只不过是一个事实的问题。目的性究竟能够存在多长的时间也不是我们感兴趣的问题。似乎没有理由为什么目的性不应该持续存在很长的一段时间，而且也没有理由为什么有些目的性应该突然停止存在。在过去确实存在过无生命物质的年代，没有理由可以否认在将来为什么不应该再次出现这样的年代。我们必须理解的是，我们正在谈论的是事实和现实，是分别地谈论过程中的阶段，而不是整个儿地谈论道的展开。道的展开不能说是有目的的或者说是没有目的的，只能说它不是这两者，或者说这两者都是。当现实不再包括有目的性的个体的时候，这并不是说整个道的展开不再具有目的性；就像无生命的冰河时代再次出现时，整个的道的展开并不会因此变成无生命的。目的的出现影响了现实之间的相互关系，它扰乱了现实界中实体的同质性或非同质性，但是它并没有更改道的展开本身。

由于目的的出现，某些最为重要的东西也就随之发生了。出现了实在的最低限度的两分化，即自身与他物开始有了最初的区分，或内在的与外在的之间有了细微的划分。在既定的时间地点现实了的整个实在的世界，由于目的的出现也不再是一个整块了，现实中

some of the items in the actualities set themselves apart, not indeed in the sense of taking themselves out of time and space, but in the sense of introducing subjectivity. Since we are not associating purpose with mind, or consciousness, the bifurcation is not conscious and therefore not pronounced, at least not so pronounced as when purposes are aided by mind. But bifurcation is there just the same. The adoption of means towards ends whether conscious or not means that ends would not be accomplished if means were not adopted; hence it means a modification of that part of reality that is other but not self, or that is outside but not inside, or that is object but not the subject. The capacity to adopt means to ends is often accompanied by the capacity to avoid what is harmful. The objectified reality is modified in any case in the direction of what the subjectified reality wants or needs; we should not discuss the success or failure in these modifications of the objectified reality. We want to point out rather that no matter how much or how little modifications there may be, it is only the objectified reality that is modified; reality in the sense of the non-bifurcated totality remains unmodified; it is what it is in the sense that whatever innovations there are they are what occasions and preordinations have actualized them to be.

The term is used in a large number of senses and elaborate theories may be proposed for any of them. We shall use the term here to mean the capacity to abstract, to symbolize and to apply the abstract or symbolic to various data (that of sense included). If one has such capacity, one has a mind. It is something that may or may not function, but if or when it does, its function is entirely intellectual, and it is so quite irrespective of degrees of intellectuality. In this sense a number of animals seem to be endowed with minds since their capacity to symbolize and abstract is undoubted as they do apply the abstract and symbolic to their data. The emergence of mind like the emergence of purpose can be counted on. Again it is not a question of when it does appear. If the world is capable of waiting, it might have waited for ages and ages for the appearance of mind, and it might have waited in vain in all those ages. That we have it now is essentially a point of historical interest quite devoid of philosophical significance. It may also disappear altogether or disappear

的某些东西将自己与他物区别开来。它们并不是使自身离开时间和空间，而是有了主体性。由于我们不把目的和心或意识联系在一起，所以这里所谓的两分化并不是有意识地作出的，因此也不是那样明显，至少不像目的和心结合的时候那样明显。但是两分化仍然是两分化。不管是有意识或是无意识，采用手段来达到目的就意味着，如果不采用手段，那么目的是不可能实现的。因此，这就意味着对实在的某一部分的改造，这一部分是其他而不是自身，是外在的而不是内在的，是客体而不是主体。采用手段来达到目的的能力往往是与避免有害的结果的能力联系在一起的。客体化的实在是沿着主体化的实在的愿望或需要的方向得到改造的，我们不讨论对客体化实在的改造是成功的还是失败的。我们想要指出的是，不管这样的改造是大还是小，得到改造的只是客体化的实在。整体的未经两分化意义上的实在是没有改造过的，它仍是原来的样子。在这样的意义上，不管有什么样的革新，是几和数使它们得以成为现实的。

这个术语可以在很多的意义上使用，而且对于这些意义也都可以提出不同的理论。我们在此所运用的这一术语局限于进行抽象、运用符号的能力，和将抽象或象征的东西运用于各种不同的材料（包括感觉材料在内）的能力。如果一个人有了这样的能力，那么他就具有了心。心可以发生作用，也可以不发生作用。但是当它发生作用的时候，它的功能就完全是理智的，而且是完全与理性的程度不相关的。如果从这样的意义上来看的话，那么许多动物好像也是具有心的，因为无疑它们有运用符号和进行抽象的能力，因为它们确实把抽象和象征的东西运用到了它们的材料上。心的出现与目的的出现一样也是可靠的。当然在此它也不是什么时候出现的问题。如果这世界能够等待的话，那么它就可以花费漫长的时期等待心的出现，它也有可能在这样漫长的时期里徒劳无获。我们现在有心本质上是一历史事实，而完全没有哲学方面的任何意义。同样也有可能它会完全地消失，或者消

only to appear again under quite different conditions, that is to say, in a context of actualities different from these that are actual here and now. There is no worry that the world will always be without minds, neither is there any that it will always be burdened with minds. Although needs and desires need not be associated with minds, minds are associated with needs or desires. Thinking involves the urge to do so, and knowing involves the desire or need for knowing. Even knowing for knowing's sake is merely a case where knowing is itself an end. While mind is active, its activity is not itself directed towards the modification of the objectified reality. What is aimed at is rather what we call understanding of the objectified world. A thorough knowledge of that world leaves it as it was or is or is going to be, that is, it leaves it unmodified. The emergence of mind also bifurcates reality but while the emergence of purpose bifurcates it into the agent and patient, the emergence of mind bifurcates it into the known object and the knowing subject.

The emergence of purpose and that of mind are both significant, each in its own way. But when they are combined, that is, when individuals emerge endowed with purpose as well as with mind, the interrelations of actualities in terms of their congenialities or uncongenialities are enormously changed. Purpose without mind is sometimes effective sometimes ineffective and must of necessity be limited to purposive activities of limited scope. Mind without purpose (other than purely cognitive) merely distinguishes the knowing from the known, and by itself it results in no modification of the known in any way. But when these are combined, the adequacy and the scope of the means adopted towards the ends are both increased by the help of mind; purpose becomes comprehensive, complex and effective. With mind and knowledge it is possible to have a series of ends and means such that the end may be the means to other ends and the means may be the end to other means. The longer the series of means, the more far-removed and complex the end, and the more likely also it is to mistake the intermediate means to be themselves the ends. The link of the means to each other may be based on knowledge, or on what is believed to be knowledge or on what is imagined to be knowledge without its being so; hence the adequacy of means towards ends may not be uniformly increased, but the scope is

失之后又会在完全不同的条件之下再一次出现。这就是说,在与此时此地的现实环境不同的其他现实环境之下出现。我们没有必要担忧这世界始终不会有心,也不必担心永远为心所累。虽然需要和愿望不必与心联系在一起,但是心却是与需要或愿望紧密相连的。思维包含着去做的冲动,知道也包含着知道的需要或愿望。即使为了知道而知道也不过是这样一种情况,即知道本身就是目的。虽然心是主动的,它的主动性本身并不直接指向客体化的实在的改造,真正目的是我们所说的获得对客体世界的理解。对这一世界的完全的了解使世界依然是过去、现在或将来的样貌。这就是说,这样的了解并没有改造这个世界。心的出现也同样把实在两分化了,目的的出现将实在分成施动者和受动者,心的出现则将实在分成被知的客体和能知的主体。

目的的出现和心的出现这两者在各自的方式上都是相当重要的。但是当这两者结合在一起的时候,这就是当禀赋着目的和心的个体出现的时候,现实的相互关系,从它们的同质性或非同质性的角度看,就发生了极其重大的变化。没有心的目的有时是有效的,有时是无效的,而且必定局限于一定范围内的有目的性的行动。没有目的(除了纯粹认识上的目的)的心只能区分能知和被知,仅仅靠其自身并不能使被知得到任何的改造。但是当它们结合在一起的时候,由于得到了心的帮助,为了达到目的而采纳的手段的充分性和范围都有所提升。目的变成了综合的、复杂的和有效的了。由于有了心和知识,这就有可能有一系列的目的和手段。因此,目的可能是其他目的的手段,而手段也有可能是其他手段的目的。手段的系列越长,目的也就变得越远越复杂,而且也更有可能把中间的手段本身误当成目的。手段之间的相互联系可能是以知识为其基础的,或者是以被认为或者是以被想象为是知识的东西为基础的,而事实并非如此。因此为了目的而采纳的手段的充分性不可能是清一色地提升,

bound to be enlarged when purpose is combined with mind. Values may come in to complicate the issue. Upon some criterion of valuation, the end may be eminently valuable while the means might be condemned. Moral problems or issues there may ever be, if mind were not joined with purpose. If there ever was any original sin, it was the alliance of mind with purpose, but then it was through their alliance that both virtue and vice are realized. Enormous numbers of other things emerge with the combined emergence of mind and purpose; culture is born, artifacts are created, and politics, ethics and various sciences make realities more complicated than ever before. But we shall not dwell on any of these, important as they are from the point of view of the growth of civilization. From the point of view of time as an infinite evolutionary process, there is no reason why civilization should endure. Quite a different kind of world, or a different kind of civilization may be actualized through future occasions and preordinations.

What we want to emphasize is rather that reality is more dichotomized with the combined emergence of purpose and mind than by either of them alone. Let us call the bifurcated realities the object and the subject realities. It is easy to have the agent and patient relation of these two realities exaggerated. Mind and knowledge enable the subject reality to be much more of an agent than purpose alone does, hence the object reality becomes also much more of a patient. On the part of agent, it is easy to feel or to be emotionally turned to the feeling that almost anything could be done to the patient in the direction of transforming as to suit the desires or needs of the agent. In doing so, the agent or the subject reality is lifted out of the world of existents or actualities or realities, and it becomes their ruler and a despotic one at that. A good deal can be said for the ascendancy of mind and purpose. An enormous amount of modification of object reality may have been accomplished, an enormous number of artifacts may have been created, values relative to the purpose of the subject reality may be assigned to their modification, creative progress might be maintained and satisfactions might be felt in various lines of endeavor. But the demarcation between object and subject realities becomes more pronounced, their separation becomes further and further apart and a sort of bloated self-importance of the

但是当目的与心结合在一起的时候，范围必然会增大。价值的参与可能把问题变得更加复杂。出于某些价值的标准，目的可以是相当有价值的，而手段可能成为遭谴责的东西。如果心不与目的结合在一起，那么道德问题就会产生。如果确实有原罪的话，那就是心与目的结合。但正是通过它们的结合才使善和恶能够现实。极大数量的其他事物也伴随着心和目的的结合而出现了。文化诞生了，器物产生了，政治学、伦理学和各种科学使实在变得比以前更为复杂了。从文明发展的角度来看这些都是相当重要的，但是我们却无意在此讨论这些。从作为无限进化过程的时间来看，没有理由认为文明是会永远地持续下去的。可能通过未来的几和数，一个相当不同的世界或相当不同的文明会诞生。

我们在此想强调的是，较之目的和心的出现单独导致实在的两分化，二者的结合使实在在两分化得更严重了。让我们把两分化的实在分别叫做客体实在和主体实在。很容易把这两个实在的施动者和受动者的关系夸大。心和知识这两者较之于单独的目的使主体实在更是一位施动者，因此客体实在也更是一位受动者。从施动者的角度看，很容易感觉到或在感情上容易有这样的感觉，即几乎可以以改造的方式对受动者做任何事情，来适应施动者的愿望或需要。在这样做的时候，施动者或主体实在就会被抽离这个存在的世界或现实界或实在，而提升为它们的统治者，而且是独裁者。关于心和目的这一方面的主导地位可以有很多要说的。为数极多的客体实在方面的改造可能已经完成，为数极多的器物可能已经创造出来，与主体实在的目的相关的价值可能已给予了改造，创造性的进步可能已经取得，人类努力的多个方面都令人满意。但是客体实在和主体实在之间的划界也变得越来越明显，它们之间的区别变得越来越大，其结果很可能是施动者的自我

agent may easily become the result. It is also easy to feel that in modifying the object reality, the subject reality is also modifying the whole reality in process or the unfoldment of Tao. The latter is not the case. Mind and purpose are possibilities; they themselves are actualized through occasions and preordinations and whatever modification or creation there may be as a result of the emergence of mind and purpose they are also actualized by occasions and preordinations and the whole subject reality is not any exception. The unfoldment of Tao is just as responsible for the modification of the object reality as the subject reality, since it is responsible for the latter as well.

V

It is about time to say something about human beings in this connection. Up to the present they are the most effective combinations of purpose and mind, if we speak from the point of view of that slice of time that is packed with what we now call natural history. There may have been more effective combinations before and there may yet be afterwards, but if we take the present with the not too distant past and future in mind, men are certainly the actualities of destiny. The emergence of humanity is neither accidental nor final. If it is only at all accidental, it is only so in taking place in this particular slice of time, that is to say, in being occasioned or preordained as it has been or is. Humanity is bound to emerge in time, because it is a possibility that is contingent. On our classification of possibilities, it does not belong to any other category. Obviously it is not necessary, nor is it eternally realized or eternally unrealizable. Since it is a contingent possibility, its realization will come in time. Its emergence need not be heralded with exaggerated glory, nor should its tenure of existence be falsely credited with finality. Compared to other contemporary actualities, or compared to other periods of actualizations in the known span of natural history, human beings and the period in which they function may indeed be glorious. But no matter how glorious human beings may be in comparison with other contemporary species, they are also dependent upon the cooperation of other species, and no matter how glorious the period in which they function may be, it is one station in the unfoldment of Tao and requires other periods to bring it to a focus. There is a sort of mutual dependence

重要性得到恶性的膨胀。我们也很容易地感觉到，在改造客体实在的同时，主体实在也在改造整个过程中的实在或道的展开。后者并非如此。心和目的都是可能，它们本身是通过几和数而成为现实的。作为心和目的出现的结果，不管有什么样的改造或创造，它们的现实也同样通过几和数。整个的主体实在也并不例外。道的展开导致了对客体实在的改造，正如主体实在那样，因为它也同样对后者施加影响。

<h1 style="text-align:center">五</h1>

就此而言，现在是讨论人类的问题的时候了。到目前为止，如果某段时间内充斥了大量我们称之为自然史的东西，从这样的角度来看，那么人类就是目的和心的最有成效的结合体。可能在这之前或之后会有更有成效的结合体，但是如果我们考虑现在时也考虑进不远的过去和未来的话，那么人类的出现就是命定的现实。人类的出现既不是偶然的，也不是最终的。如果人类的出现是偶然的，那么也只是在这个特殊的时间出现的意义上说是偶然的。这就是说，也是像从前或现在一样，在为几和数所决定了的意义上是偶然的。人类在时间中必然要出现，因为它是不老是现实的可能。根据我们对可能的分类，它不属于其他类别。显然，它并不是必然的，也不是老是现实的或老是不现实的。由于它是不老是现实的可能，所以在时间之内它是会现实的。它的出现并不值得给予过分荣耀的赞美，也同样不应该错误地将终结感给予它存在的期限。与同时期其他的现实相比，或与已知自然史上的其他现实阶段相比，人类及他们在其中起作用的时期可能是很辉煌的。但是与其他的同时存在着的物种相比，不管人类是多么辉煌，他们也同样要依靠其他物种的合作；也不管他们在其中起作用的历史时期是多么辉煌，它也只不过是道展开过程中的一个阶段而已，靠着其他时期来衬托成为焦点。在各种不同种类的存在之间是相互依赖和相互渗透的，只是由于思想和

or mutual infiltration of being that is easily neglected through our necessity for economy in thought and action. For practical purposes it is necessary to single out our species from the cumulative effects of other contemporary species as it is to single out any one person from the complex effects of his environment. If we bear in mind, however, this mutual infiltration of being (mentioned already in Chapter II), we are not likely to be excessively modest or excessively boastful.

Human beings are of course immensely important to themselves. To a human being, his desires, his needs, his hopes, his whims and whatnot are all important; they only differ so in degrees that some of them are unimportant compared with others. So also is the satisfaction of these. His mind alone is capable of making him filled with pride. What is more important in this connection is that with the help of the propelling force of his purpose, his mind gives him his power. No species ruled the world with greater power or more efficiency than the human species. Whether the rule has been benevolent or not, there is as yet no prospect of a revolution in sight, and even if the rule were resulted, no species is as yet powerful enough to effect an overturn of human power. With medicine and doctors as the police, germs and diseases are mere thieves and thugs who disturb the peace occasionally but are not likely to be powerful enough to effect a revolution against the human species. Like all rulers human species face more difficulties from within. There is internal strife, there is greediness, desires seem to run rampant, luxuries continue to become needs; society may become so integrated and so differentiated that individual may cease to be and different social or economic strata may become almost like different species. These difficulties may be overcome and a long period of benevolent and despotic rule may take place. From the point of view of the human species, nothing is more desirable. Since the underlings we are not in the habit of looking ahead in terms of millions or billions of years, the complacency of human beings due to their achievements is perhaps securable. Power is liable to intoxicate its possessor into complacency.

There is however a question of value which may fill human beings with diffidence. With regard to value there is of course a choice of criteria. A number of criteria may be adopted, so as to fill human beings

行动方面的经济原则的必要性而使我们忽视了这一点。就实际的目的而言，有必要从其他同时存在的物种的积累效应中挑选出我们这一类，这正如同把某一个人从他所处的环境的复杂影响中挑选出来一样。然而，如果我们记住了这样的存在之间的相互渗透（在第二章中已经提到过这一点），那么我们就不可能过分谦虚，也不可能过分自大。

对于人类自身而言，人类当然是极其重要的。对于一个人来说，他的愿望、他的需要、他的希望、他的某些突发的异想诸如此类都是很重要的。它们只是在程度上有所区别，以至于有的与其他的比较起来显得更重要些。对于诸如此类的满足也具有同样的情形。他的心灵本身就足以使他充满着自豪。在这里显得更为重要的是，在他的目的的驱动力量之下，他的心给予他力量。其他的物种没有人类那样更大的力量或更高的效力来统治这个世界。不管这样的统治是仁慈的还是不仁慈的，到目前为止，我们还看不到在这方面有革命的可能性。即使实现了统治，也没有哪一个物种的力量能够强大到足以推翻人类。有药物和医生作为警察，病菌和疾病也只不过是小偷和暴徒，它们充其量也只能偶尔打破平静，而不可能强大到足以发动一次推翻人类的革命。像所有的统治者一样，人类面临的困难更多来自内部。有内在的倾轧，有贪婪，欲望似乎毫无节制地在蔓延，奢侈品不断地变成必需品。社会可能融合、分化，以至于个人不再是自己，不同的社会阶层或经济阶层可能变成几乎是不同的物种。这些困难有可能被战胜，然后是一段相当长时期的仁慈的独裁统治。从人类的观点看来，没有更令人称心满意的结果了。作为底层百姓，由于我们没有往前看几百万年或几百亿年的习惯，人类通过成就获得的满足或许是牢靠的。权力很容易让掌权者自鸣得意。

然而不管怎么样，还有一个价值问题，它可能会使人感到胆怯。考虑到价值，就当然有一个标准的选择问题。可以选择不同的

with pride. On the adoption of a certain criterion, Indian philosophy is to be preferred to the Greek, but if another criterion is adopted, the Greek intellect is the more valuable. Between Chinese social control and Roman law, we also have a question of the choice of the criteria of values. While granting that a number of criteria might be adopted so as to fill human beings with pride, others might also be selected as to fill them with diffidence and trepidation. On the basis of nicety of instinct, we probably suffer from a comparison with other species. We may prefer to have penguins rather than monkeys as our near relatives. It may have been Rousseau who said that an intelligent being is a depraved animal. On the basis of the cooperation of physical faculties we suffer in comparison with tigers, leopards and even our ancestors the primitive men. In certain ways we can hardly be said to be more moral than certain animals. We are not likely even to attain to the functional beauty of an eagle or the visual beauty of a pheasant. Like individuals, human species are burdened with its strength, for like individual strength, its strength is also its weakness. Mind is probably the strongest asset of the human species and yet it is through having that remarkable mind that human beings are sometimes made more calculatingly immoral, more disgustingly depraved, more painfully and falsely miserable, more unnecessarily and cruelly at war with themselves than any other species. On the basis of values there is no conclusive reason why human species should survive. Fortunately or unfortunately survival does depend not upon prescriptive values.

Human beings may claim that they are not merely important to themselves. With reality dichotomized into the subject and object, there is not merely a question of the subject reality, but also that of the object reality. Compare the difference of the object reality before and after the emergence of man. It is such a difference as to bad men that they have conquered nature. In a large number of ways, this might be truly said. The face of the earth is certainly changed by men, and one might say that were it not for the emergence of men, it would not have changed in that way it did. A considerable part of the object reality might be described as the creations or artifacts created by men. They are the traces of what we call civilization and depend for their preservation and maintenance upon the emergence and continuation of the human species. Nor is the

标准来使人类充满自豪感。选择某一个标准，可能印度哲学要优于希腊哲学。但是如果再采取另外的一个标准，那么希腊的思想可能更有价值。在中国的社会控制和罗马的法律这两者之间，我们也同样面临着一个价值标准的选择的问题。承认一些标准可能使人类感到自豪，其他的标准则有可能使人类胆怯和恐慌。就直觉的精确性来说，我们跟其他生物比较一下可能会感觉受伤。我们可能更愿意选择企鹅而不是猴子做我们的近亲。可能是卢梭这样说过，一个理智的生命存在体是一个邪恶的动物。在身体能力的协调方面，我们与老虎、豹子甚至我们的祖先原始人相比都会败下阵来。在某些方面，几乎不能说我们比某些动物品德更高尚。我们甚至不可能达到鹰所具有的功能上的美，或雉的视觉上的美。正如个体一般，人类因为优势而苦恼。如同个人的优势，它的优势同时也是它的弱点。心灵可能是人类最强的优势，然而也正是因为有了卓越的心灵，与其他物种相比，人类有时才变得更不道德而工于心计、更邪恶而令人反感、更卑鄙而令人羞愧，更容易发动没必要的战争，战斗中对同类更加残忍。从价值的角度而言，并没有任何有说服力的原因可以解释为什么人类应该幸存。幸或不幸，存活可不依赖于规定的价值。

　　人类可能会宣称，他们并不仅仅是对于自己来说才是重要的。由于实在被分成为主体和客体这样两个部分，因此不仅存在着主体实在的问题，而且同样存在着客体实在的问题。比较一下人类出现之前的客体实在和人类出现之后的客体实在之间的区别。对于邪恶的人类来说，这个差别如此之大以致可以说是他们征服了自然。在许多方面，这可能是正确的。由于有了人类，这个地球的面貌发生了变化。可以说，如果不是人类的出现，地球就不可能以它已然变化的方式而发生变化。客体实在的相当大的部分可以说是人类的创作品和器物。它们就是我们称之为文明的踪迹，这些文明踪迹的留存和保持依赖于人类的出现和持续存在。人类的成就并不仅仅局限

human achievement limited to creations; it is even extended into spheres in which it might be said to have changed the course of evolution. Left to itself, the ginkgo might never have survived to their day, and the fate of dogs, horses and cats is certainly questionable if left to themselves. In the language of these pages, certain possibilities which might not have been realized without men are now realized with the emergence of men, certain others which might have been disrealized are now continually realized, while still others which might have been rampant are now disrealized simply because they are harmful to men. Whether more are destroyed than preserved or vice versa, it is of course difficult to say, but changes in object reality seem to have been expedited considerably through the emergence of human beings who are therefore of significance not merely to themselves.

There is however a significant sense in which we can say that nature has never been conquered. Certainly no natural law has ever been suspended merely for human benefit and at humans' will. What is accomplished is the acquirement of capacity to make use of the operation of certain natural laws to prevent the operation of certain others so that the state of affairs desired by human beings may be realized. The pattern in accordance with which reality proceeds is not changed by men. Even without men some natural laws operate in such a way that the operation of other natural laws is prevented. The only difference is that the resultant state of affairs in the one case is desired by men whereas in the other it may have never been desired by any species. While certain changes which have taken place in object reality are due to the emergence of men, these same changes considered from the point of view of the unbifurcated reality cannot be similarly changed due to the emergence of men. Object reality is something set about from subject reality only when reality is bifurcated, but when it is not bifurcated, there is no such thing as object or subject reality. Whatever changes that take place are merely changes that do take place, not such that from a subjective point of view their having taken place could be attributed to the activity of the subject reality. For the unbifurcated reality, any change is change of its own accord. Once we think of the unbifurcated reality, we think also of its organic unity and that unity consists partly of an infiltration of being such that human

于创作品，它已扩展到了一些领域之内，以至于可以说它已经改变了进化的进程。如果仅仅依靠自身，银杏绝不可能存活到繁盛的时候，狗、马和猫如果任其自生自灭，它们的命运也相当成问题。运用这几页的话来说，有些可能如果没有人类或许就不会现实，但是现在由于人类的出现，它们现实了。其他的有些可能或许已成虚，而现在却继续被现实着。还有其他的一些可能或许会变得漫无节制而现在却成虚了，仅仅是因为它们对人类有害处。当然很难说被摧毁和被保存的哪一个更多，但是客体实在的变化似乎在相当大的程度上因为人类的出现而得到加速。由此可见人类的重要性并不仅仅是对人类本身而言。

然而，在某种重要的意义上，我们可以说，自然从未被征服过。当然没有一个自然律仅仅因为人类的利益和人类的意志被中断。人类做到的是获得某种能力来使某些自然律起作用，而抑制其他的自然律起作用，从而人类所想要达到的状态才能够现实。实在运作所依据的图案并没有被人改变。即使没有人，一些自然律也在起作用，而防止了其他的自然律起作用。唯一的区别在于，在一种情形下所得到的结果是人类所想要的，而在另一种情形下所得到的结果可能不是任何物种想要得到的。虽然客体实在方面所产生的某些变化是由于人类的出现，但是如果从没有被两分化的实在的角度来看，这些变化可能不会因为人类的出现而发生同样的变化。只有当实在被两分化之后，客体实在才与主体实在区分开来。实在没有两分化的时候，并没有客体实在或者是主体实在这样的东西。所出现的不管什么样的变化都只不过是实际上所发生的变化，而不是从主体的角度来看，认为它们的发生可以归属于主体实在的能动性。对于没有被两分化的实在来说，任何变化都是主动的变化。一旦我们想到未经两分化的实在，我们也会想到它的有机统一性。这统一性部分地包含了一种渗透，因而人类既沉浸也渗透于与他们并存的

beings are as much soaked and shot through and through with their contemporaneous objects and events as they are shot through and soaked with things human. There is a mutual interdependence of all actualities and without a subjectivity of viewpoints no one is more responsible for the process of reality than any other. The actual is what is brought along in the pure flow of time and if human beings function in it, they like everything else in it are occasioned and preordained in the unfoldment of Tao.

We have said repeatedly that human beings will disappear. They may do so either in the way of abrupt termination or in the way of gradually changing into other species. We are accustomed to saying that nothing is final with however an emotional reservation that we ourselves are the exceptions. There is no reason why we should be the exceptions in the sense of a sort of crowning glory in the pure flow of time. We may imagine ourselves to be valuable cargo, and we may actually be that, but the time will come when we will be stored up in the oblivion of the past. As individuals we come and go, and whether we come from and go to dust or not, no difference is made to the coming and going. The same should be of the species. It is only as Stuffed Form or Formed Stuff that we are immutable; as human beings we are as much in the whirlpool of changes as anything else in the reality of process or in the process of reality. We may of course survive so very very long that even for millions of years we are assured of our tenure of existence or actualization, but the all-comprehensive universe which has tolerated us for so long will not tolerate us ad infinitum. What will succeed us can hardly be predicted. While we may say something on the basis of preordinations we cannot say anything on the basis of occasions. That we are bound to go is however not open to doubt.

The usual objection is that with such a view human beings are bound to become phlegmatic, lethargic and fatalistic and that in the apathy that ensues while whatever that is "bad" may be avoided, whatever that is "good" won't be accomplished either. Civilization wouldn't have advanced to the present stage, it may be said, if such ideas as there were entertained by men, and if we are to entertain them now, civilization will remain stagnant and futile. There may be danger from those who not merely crave for eternity but also make it the condition of their continual

客体和事件，同时既沉浸也渗透于人类的事物。所有的现实之间都是相互依赖的。如果不从主体性的角度看问题，那么没有人比其他人对实在的过程要负更大的责任。现实就是在纯粹的时间之流中带来的东西，如果人类也在其中起作用，那么他们像其他任何东西一样，也是在道的展开过程中由几和数所决定的。

我们已经不断地指出，人类将来会消失。他们可能会突然消失，或者逐渐地演变成其他物种。我们习惯于说，没有什么东西是终极性的，但是在感情上我们却有所保留，认为我们自己应该是一个例外。然而却没有理由表明我们应该是例外，我们在纯粹的时间之流中并不享有某种至高无上的辉煌。我们可能想象自己是贵重物品，而且我们在事实上可能也是，但是我们成为过去的收藏品被束之高阁的时间终究是会到来的。作为个体，我们有生有死，我们是否来自或归回尘土，这并不影响我们的生死。对于人类这个物种而言也是一样的。只是作为有质料的式或有式的质料，我们才是永恒不变的。作为人类，我们正如在过程中的实在或实在的过程中的任何其他东西一样都处在变化的漩涡之中。我们当然可能生存很长一段时间，甚至可以保证生存几百万年，但是容忍我们生存这么长时间的整个无所不包的宇宙却不可能容忍我们无限地生存下去。至于究竟什么将会取代我们，现在是不可能预料到的。虽然我们可以根据数预言某些东西，但是却不可能根据几预言什么。我们人类必定会消失是毋庸置疑的。

通常所遇到的反对意见是，根据上述的看法，人类必定要变成毫无感情的、懒洋洋的命定论者。在随之而来的无动于衷里，可能避免所谓的坏东西之时，所谓的好的东西也不会再现实。可以说，如果心存这样的观念，文明将不可能发展到我们今天这样的地步；而且如果我们现在就考虑这些观念，那么文明将会保持静止和无效。危险可能会来自这样的一些人，他们不仅仅追求永恒，而且也将永

existence. Most people would not be affected in any undesirable way. Life after all consists of activities and no one commits suicide merely because life is to be followed by death. Consciousness of death has never prevented anyone from enjoying the present, or creating forms of beauty, or working towards a more desirable future or seeking for truth or thinking about the ultimate. If sometimes we drink because tomorrow we die, we sometimes also work for the same reason. It may even be argued the other way around and say that we are destined to eternity we won't do a thing today since there is always a tomorrow. Neither can be urged and accepted since life is actual and active, and the essence of any form of living is to function in the role that is given or assigned. A living man is the functioning or actuating towards the essence of man just as a living. Aristotle is a functioning or actuating towards Aristotelianness.

恒作为他们持续存在的条件。绝大多数的人将不会受到任何不理想的方式的影响。生活毕竟是由能动性组成的，没有人会仅仅因为死亡是不可能避免的而去自杀。知道会死，但这却从来没有妨碍过人们享受今天的生活，或去创造美的各种形式，或努力工作去争取更为理想的未来，追求真理或思考终极性的存在。如果在某些时候因为我们明天就会死所以我们现在要饮酒，那么我们有时也为了同样的理由去工作。也可以反过来说，比如说我们注定是永恒的，所以在今天我们用不着做任何事情，因为总会有明天。两种看法都不应提倡也不能接受，因为生活是现实的和能动的，生活方式的本质是按照被给予的或被分配的角色去发挥作用。一个活着的人就是朝着人作为生活的本质去发挥作用或成为现实。亚里士多德就是向着亚里士多德性而发挥作用或成为现实的。

NATURE AND MAN

I

There is a doctrine in Chinese philosophy which may be summarized as that of the unification of nature and man. It is a doctrine that is perhaps more emphasized in some philosophies than in others, but it is not merely a technical idea, being entertained as well by the average educated man. It is a complicated pattern of ideas and we do not intend to deal with it in the manner of systematic exposition, nor do we claim that what we say here represents exactly the doctrine actually held by any thinker or any school of thinkers in the past. What is intended in those pages is rather to present some similar idea in terms more or less of our present day language through reasoning that is somewhat indicated by the previous chapters. It is not our purpose here to introduce a historical doctrine in its historical perspective, to trace its origin or to delineate its development, neither do we intend to present the cause of its development in terms of the physical environment of its propounders.

It is perfectly likely that some such doctrine as we are dealing with here is peculiarly wedded to an agricultural society or civilization in which technical knowledge hasn't advanced enough to afford people with the idea of their power over nature, in which their consciousness of their dependence upon their environment has sufficiently developed so as to give them instead the idea of the power of nature over man. Perhaps a more nomadic life in which hunting predominates brings out much more the idea of the importance of individual initiative, since the success of hunting depends much more upon the capacity to perceive what is coming, to gauge the chances accurately, to seize the moment of decision and to act accordingly with adequacy and courage. With the idea of the importance of individual initiative firmly established, the idea of the power of man over nature is much more likely to follow than it is in a civilization in which people follow seasonal changes, watch the weather passively and are entirely helpless in the face of floods and draughts. The kind of civilization which China has had for thousands of years may have been responsible for the doctrine of the unification of nature and man. Semple and Huntington may be able to account for the emergence of this

自然和人

一

中国哲学中有这样的一种理论，我们可以把它概括为"自然与人合一"。这一思想在某些哲学中得到了更多的强调。但是这一意念不只是一种技术性的意念，它几乎为每一个普通的接受过教育的人所信仰。它是一个很复杂的意念图案，我们不打算在此运用系统阐述的方法来处理这一思想，我们也不能说我们所说的一切是完全准确地表达了历史上的思想家或某些思想流派所持有的这一思想。在此，我们的目的是多多少少用我们现在的语言，并通过在前几章已经显示出的推论方法来介绍类似的意念。我们的目的不是从历史的角度来介绍一历史上的思想，来追踪它的源头或来描述它的发展，我们也不打算根据提出这一思想的思想家的自然环境来介绍它的发展的原因。

我们在此讨论的这一思想很可能是与农业社会或农业文明尤其相关的。在这个农业社会或文明中，技术的知识还未得到充分的发展，还不足以使人们认识到他们的力量可以征服自然。即，他们对环境的依赖意识得到了充分的发展，知道自然的力量胜过人。在游牧生活中狩猎是主导的方面，这样的生活更能激发出个人主动性的重要性的观念，因为狩猎的成功更多地要依靠一些能力，如观察所来为何物、准确地判断可能性、及时作出决断和恰当勇猛地行动的能力。由于个人主动性的重要性的观念已牢固树立，所以更容易产生人的力量胜于自然的观念。而在另一种文明中，人们遵从季节性的变化，被动地观望着天气，完全无望地面对着洪水和干旱。从这样的文明中比较难得出人定胜于自然的观念。几千年来中国社会所具有的文明可能导致了"自然与人合一"的思想。森普尔和亨廷顿可能运用他们分析和处理其他理论的同样方法来解释"自然与人合一"

doctrine in ways similar to what they have done concerning a number of other ideas. This may very well be true, but if it is, it is a historical truth, not a philosophical doctrine.

How ideas come to be is quite different from what they are. For all we know, Euclid might have been a psycho-analytic case; he might have had an obsession with figures traceable to a psychosis for which his childhood experiences were responsible; but even so, his obsession is not a part of his geometry; and while it is relevant to the historian, it's irrelevant to the geometer. It has become somewhat fashionable to speak of the falling apple in connection with Newton; the story is interesting, and may even be instructive; but it is not a part of physics. Given the history of law an idea has come to be, we have yet to face the problem as to what it is. Quite a large number of ways of dealing with it remain. There is for instance a question of its truth or falsehood, its consistency or inconsistency, or its tenability when no decision can be arrived at concerning its truth or falsehood, or else its fruitfulness or wisdom when judged in terms of what consequences there may be when the idea is seriously entertained. The doctrine of the unification of nature and man may owe its historical origin from the kind of civilization China has always had for ages; it is none the less a pattern of ideas which should be examined in some of the ways mentioned. It is besides an idea to which a large number of people are emotionally attached, and whether or not it is otherwise acceptable, it is as such a part of the fund of beliefs and main springs of life of a section of mankind.

We should distinguish knowledge from belief. Human actions up to the present are not always guided by knowledge. On the one hand, we may say that our knowledge is as yet limited; we are ignorant of so many things that even if we do want to be guided by knowledge we have not sufficient knowledge to guide us. On the other hand, even if we have sufficient knowledge to guide us we are not always so guided. In some cases, there is a willful persistence in what we do, in others, a tendency to follow the line of best resistance; and in extreme cases, there may even be an indulgence in action or behavior in defiance of what knowledge foresees to be the consequence. Perhaps our actions should be guided by knowledge, even though they often are not. From the point

思想的出现。这可能是非常正确的。但是如果是这样的话，那么这也就是一个历史的事实，而不是一种哲学的理论。

意念是怎样演变而成的和它们是什么样的意念是不同的。就我们所知，欧几里得本可以作为一个心理分析方法的实例。他对数字的着迷可以追溯到孩提时代的经历导致的精神失常。但是尽管如此，他的着迷并不是他的几何学的一个部分。虽然它与历史家是相关的，然而它与几何学家却是不相关的。现在有一种相当流行的说法，说的是下落的苹果与牛顿的关系。这一故事是十分有趣的，而且也很有启发性。但它却不是物理学的一部分。给定了规律史，一个意念形成了，我们却面临着这样一个问题，即这样的意念是什么。可以有相当多的方式来处理这个问题。比如，有它是真或是假的问题，它是一致或是不一致的问题，或当它的真或假还不可能作出断定的时候它是否能站得住脚的问题，或当这一意念被认真考虑的时候从这一意念能引出什么样的结果方面看，它是富有成果的还是充满智慧的的问题。自然与人合一的思想历史上起源于中国几千年来所拥有的文明，它仍然是一意念图案，应该运用已经提到的方式来考察这一图案。此外，它还是相当数量的人们情感依恋的一个意念，不管它的其他方面是否可以被接受，它却是一部分人类众多信念的一部分，是他们生命的主要源泉。

我们应该区分知识和信念。迄今为止的人类行动并不总是为知识所引导的。在一方面，我们可以说，我们的知识到目前为止是有限的；我们对很多事情一无所知，所以尽管我们想要以知识来指导我们，但我们却没有足够充分的知识来指导。可是在另一方面，即使我们有了足够充分的知识来指导，我们也不总是在知识的指导之下的。在某些事例中，在我们所做的事情中有着固执己见的倾向；在另外一些事例中，有遵从最小阻力的倾向；而在极端的事例中，有人沉湎于行动和行为，无视知识预言的结果。可能我们的行动应该由知识来引导，

of view of the efficiency in obtaining the kind of result desired, there is no question at all; knowledge should guide our action and behavior. On some other criterion, the question is not so simple. As a matter of fact we are guided by habits, by custom, by law and in the mental basis of our actions we are as much guided by beliefs as by knowledge. Knowledge is of course accompanied by beliefs, but belief is not always accompanied by knowledge or even based on it; and what is more significant, the efficaciousness of belief does not suffer even though it is not accompanied by or based on knowledge. Every one of us has a fund of such beliefs, and excluding an idea from the sphere of knowledge does not mean excluding it from the sphere of beliefs. Even if the doctrine of the unification of nature and man should be rejected as knowledge, it may yet be accepted as belief, and even though the question of truth and falsehood is to be ruled out, the question of fruitfulness and wisdom remains.

I am not a student of Chinese philosophy or history, and so far as ideas are concerned, I'm interested only in their cross-sectional pattern not in their historical development. I'm emotionally somewhat attuned to the feeling or flavor of Chinese philosophy and frankly partial to the ideas soon to be presented. In the previous chapters we have said that in the unfoldment of Tao, human beings are bound to appear; their emergence is neither accidental nor final, and while their tenure of existence is limited, their essence requires a function that is both earnest and real. So long as they function in actuality, they have to function in what we call the democracy of co-existents. For as we individually have to get along with our neighbors, human beings have to get along with their co-existents. Intellectually there is a question as to what attitude to take on the part of human beings and emotionally there is a question of harmony between what we have been describing as the subject and object realities. Here we must introduce the term "t'ien." We have conveniently but inadequately called the doctrine the unification of nature and man. "Nature" is not a synonym of "t'ien." If we speak analytically, it is a bad policy to use the term "nature," for it is obviously capable of many and diverse meanings. But it has the closest flavor to the term "*t'ien*" which is itself ambiguous. The latter may be combined with different terms to

尽管它们经常并不是这样的。从想取得理想结果的效率的角度来看，是不存在什么问题的，知识应该指导我们的行动和行为。从其他的标准来看，问题就并不这样简单了。事实上，我们是由习惯、习俗、法律来引导的。在我们行动的精神基础方面，我们由信念引导和由知识引导是一样多的。知识当然伴随着信念，但是信念却并不总是伴随着知识或甚至并不是以它为基础的。更为重要的是，尽管信念并不伴随着知识或以知识为其基础，信念的效验并不因此而有仕何的影响。我们中的每一个人都有很多这样的信念，从知识的领域内把一意念驱逐出去并不意味着把它从信念的领域内也驱逐出去。因此尽管我们可以拒斥作为知识的自然与人合一的思想，但是它却可以被当作信念来接受。而且尽管真和假的问题可以排除，但是成果和智慧的问题却依然存在。

我不是中国哲学或历史的研究者。就意念而言，我所感兴趣的也不是它们的历史发展，而是意念的截面的图案。在感情上我熟悉中国哲学的感觉或韵味，而且坦率地说对将要在此介绍的中国哲学思想我是偏爱的。在前几章中，我们已经说到，在道的展开过程中，人类是必定会出现的。他们的出现既不是偶然的，也不是终极性的。虽然他们存在的历史时期是有限度的，但是他们的本质要求他们发挥认真和实在的作用。只要他们在现实中起作用，那么他们就必须在我们称之为共存者的民主中发挥作用。因为正如对于我们个人而言，我们必须与我们的邻居友好相处；对于人类来说，他们也必须与他们的共存者友好相处。在理智上有这样的一个问题，即人类应该采取一种什么样的态度。在感情上的问题则异，在我们一直描述的主体实在和客体实在之间的和谐问题。在这里，我们必须引进"天"这一概念。至此我们一直是为了方便但不很恰当地把这一思想叫做"自然与人合一"。但是"自然"不是"天"的同义词。如果我们从分析的角度来看问题的话，那么运用"自然"这一词就是一个不好的策略，因为显然这一个词可以有很多不同的意义。但是它具有与"天"最相近的意味，"天"本身的意思也含糊多样。

mean entirely different things, and what appears in the doctrine of the unification of *t'ien* and man, it expresses more than the term "nature" expresses in English. Perhaps the phrase "nature and nature's God" is more nearly equivalent to *t'ien* than any other term or phrase, if we bear in mind that the God mentioned is not the Christian God. We shall use the term "mere nature" to mean dichotomized nature which falls into the realm of the subject or object and reserve the term "nature" to mean both nature and nature's God.

The difference between nature and mere nature is that with the former men are subsumed under it, while with the latter either men are excluded from it or it is set apart from men. No matter how the deity part of nature is conceived, whether Christian or not, it permeates both men and mere object nature; it enables men to be conscious that they have a nature of their own and that mere human nature is part of nature just as mere object nature is. The significance to be emphasized in the case of nature is located not in the concrete and discrete things, but rather in the interrelated pattern in which men can hardly set themselves apart. Conceive nature to be not merely nature but also nature's God, natural law is no longer merely the invariant relation which holds between bits of matter or describes the change and motion of discrete objects or things, but also law of conduct so far as purposive and conscious human beings are concerned. The law of nature includes not merely *jus naturale* but also *lex naturalis*, provided we do not attribute the imperative element to the will of a God who assumes the human form. Inanimate objects merely obey invariant relations, they are neither blessed nor cursed with purpose or knowledge to land them in inextricable difficulties, their virtues being merely their qualities are not their vices, nor is their strength their weakness. The strength of a tree that shoots into the sky is not the weakness of its being torn by the wind; in either case, it merely obeys invariant relations; but bless that tree or curse it with knowledge and purpose, a number of if-then propositions may be entertained informing the tree that if it doesn't aim too high, it won't be torn up; that if it doesn't want to be torn up, it had better not shoot too high; that if it cannot resist the temptation of shooting above the shoulder of other trees, it must be prepared to be torn up by the winds, etc. In the latter case the tree would begin to have spiritual struggle, and like Hamlet, it would be tormented

"天"可与不同的词结合在一起而指示完全不同的事物。在"天人合一"这一理论中的"天"这一概念所表达的思想要比英语中的"自然"一词丰富得多。可能"自然和自然神"这一短语要比其他的术语更接近于"天"，如果我们记住这里所说的神并不是基督教的上帝的话。我们将要运用"纯粹的自然"这一术语来指称两分化为主体的领域和客体的领域的自然，而保留"自然"一词，专门用来指示自然和自然神。

自然和纯粹的自然之间的差异在于，对于前者来说，人类是包含在内的；而对于后者来说，或者人类被排除在它之外，或者它与人类相离。不管自然的神性部分被如何看待，是否被认为是基督教的，它渗透于人和纯粹的客体自然之中。它使人们意识到他们具有自己的本质，意识到纯粹的人性正如同纯粹的客体自然一样是自然的一部分。我们所要强调的自然的重要性不在具体的和互不相关的事物中，而是在一种相互关联的图案中，在这种图案中人们与其他事物几乎不可分。如果认为自然不仅仅是自然，而且也是自然神，那么自然律就不再仅仅是存在于物质之间不变的关系或者描述互不相关的客体或事物的变化和运动的不变的关系；从具有目的性和自觉意识的人类来考虑，自然律也是行为律。自然律不仅仅包括自然的规律而且也包括自然法，只要我们不把强制的因素加于与人同形的神的意志之上。无生命的物质仅仅遵循着不变的关系，它们不享有目的或知识，也不因目的或知识的烦恼而置身于不可摆脱的困境之中。它们的品质仅仅是它们的特质，这不是它们的恶。同样，它们的优势也不是它们的弱点。高耸入云的树的优势并不是它被风吹折的弱点所在；任一情况下，它仅仅遵循着不变的关系。但是赋予它知识和目的或使它饱受知识和目的之苦，那么就会产生很多关于树的"如果——则"的命题。如果它没想长太高，则不会被风吹折；如果它不想被风吹折，则最好别长那么高；如果它抵挡不住要比别的树长得高的诱惑，则必须准备着被风吹折，如此等等。在后一例子中，那棵树就会开始进行精神斗争，并且

by the question "to shoot high or not to shoot high;" and what is even more to our point, a single invariant relation invokes precepts and rules on the one hand and invokes wisdom of choice on the other. Natural law so interpreted if not richer than the traditional *jus naturale* is the modern invariant relations.

II

But why unify nature with men? Are they not already unified? If they can be unified, why aren't they? If they cannot be unified, why advocate their unification? What is meant by unification anyhow? We must present the problem of disunification. We have already pointed out that with the emergence of purpose and knowledge, reality is dichotomized into subject and object realities. Since human beings are endowed with both purpose and knowledge, they not only demand modifications of object reality, but also know to an increasing extent how these are to be brought about. Object reality often resists these modifications and it succeeds or fails in accordance with the power the subject reality wields, and his power is proportionate to his knowledge. What we call mere object nature is what we have been calling object reality, and what we have been calling subject reality, we now limit to mere human nature. There wouldn't be resistance on the part of mere object nature if there weren't purposive men, for the reality wouldn't have been dichotomized. Once reality is dichotomized, struggle and resistance are inevitable. So far as mere object nature is concerned, the issue seems to be more or less decided; the victory so far belongs to man. From some other point of view to be later presented, the result is not quite so conclusive; it may even turn out that the victor is also the vanquished.

There is of course a good deal to be said on behalf of the plight of man. They acquire purpose and knowledge after they are conceived or born; none of them becomes a human being with his own consent, and yet being assigned the human role, he has to function as a human being. He has to exist, to eat, to propagate, and to be clothed. There are basic desires and needs, and their satisfaction is not always easy, for obstacles there are and often are such that they cannot be overcome. He has to struggle for his existence, to gain power over his adversaries. He has to gain knowledge and its power in order to exist and he has to exist in order

就像哈姆雷特一样，它也会被要长太高还是不要长太高这样的问题所折磨。对于我们来说更重要的一点是，一种不变的关系在一方面产生了规律和规则，在另一方面则产生了选择的智慧。这样来解释的自然律，即使不比传统的自然规律更丰富，至少体现了现代的不变的关系。

二

但是为什么自然与人要合一呢？难道它们还未合一？如果它们能够合一，为什么它们还没有合一呢？如果它们不能够合一，为什么要提倡它们的合一？所谓的合一到底是什么意思呢？我们必须提出不合一这一问题。我们已指出，随着目的和知识的出现，实在被两分为主体的实在和客体的实在。由于人类既具有目的也具有知识，所以他们不仅要求改造客体实在，而且也越来越知道如何进行改造。客体实在经常拒绝这些改造，它的拒绝是成功的还是失败的就要看主体实在所能够利用的力量，而主体的力量又与其知识相称。至今一直被叫做客体实在的，我们现在称之为纯粹的客体自然。而至今一直被叫做主体实在的，我们现在将其仅仅局限于纯粹的人性。如果不存在具有目的性的人类，那么纯粹的客体自然就不会有抵制，因为实在就不会被两分化。一旦实在被两分化，那么斗争和拒斥就成为不可避免的了。就纯粹的客体自然讲，问题似乎多少已有定论，那就是胜利至今是属于人类的。从我们后面将要讨论的观点来看，结果并不具有这样的确定性，甚至可能胜利者同样也是失败者。

当然关于人类困境这样的话题可以说上很多。怀胎或诞生之后，人类就获得了目的和知识。他们中没有一个经自己同意而成为一个人，但是既然被赋予了人的角色，他就必须像一个人那样发挥作用。他必须存活，必须吃饭，必须繁殖，必须穿衣。他们有很多基本的欲望和需要，这些欲望和需要的满足并不总是很容易的一件事，因为总有不少的障碍，而且经常是很难克服这样的障碍的。为了存活，他必须斗争，必须获得力量来征服他的敌手。他必须获取知识，

to fulfill the function required of him. Whether conscious of it or not, his own mere nature, the mere nature of being human, drives him towards the acquisition of power. He cannot very well renounce his desire to push forward without also curtailing the mere nature of his own being. However different he may be from the other animals or objects, he is not different from them so far as the fact that his existence is shaped by his essence is concerned; he has to be human just as a log has to be loggish or a horse to be horsy. But whereas a stone does not require any effort to be strong or to achieve stoniness, it is also the essence of human beings to make efforts, since he is endowed with purpose and knowledge. He is bound to modify mere object nature to suit his needs or desires and to adopt means towards achieving end. Here again he can hardly help this any more than a horse can escape being horsy or a piece of stone from stoniness. In his efforts, he is all too human. Being human means in the language of preceding chapters merely fulfilling the essence of humanity or realizing the possibility of Humanness. So far as the struggle for existence is concerned, being human is also being merely natural.

But the combination of purpose and knowledge affords human beings power and while power needn't be dangerous, it often is. It breeds the desire for greater power and instead of being merely a means to an end, it has the tendency to become itself an end. The struggle for existence may turn into a struggle for power. As means, power is limited; it ceases to function when the end is achieved. If stamps are used for letters, we need only as many stamps as the letters require; if money is needed to maintain a certain standard of living, we need only the amount required for the maintenance of the standard. But if stamps and money are collected for their own sake, there is no limit to their collection. The same is true of power. With the accumulation of power, there is also an expansion of desires along lines that may never have been dreamed of before, and far beyond the requirement for existence. With mere human nature driving, there is no guarantee how the power is to be used. It may be used against obstacles in mere object nature or it may be used against fellow human beings, or it may even be used against oneself. One is liable to agree with Rousseau that man is everywhere in chains whether or not there ever

用知识的力量来争取存活，他必须存活下去来完成赋予他的使命。不管他意识到还是没有意识到，作为人的纯粹本性迫使他去获得力量。他不可能成功地抛却他前进的欲望而丝毫不影响他自己纯粹的本性。不管他可能与其他动物或客体之间有多大的区别，只要考虑到他的存活是由他的本质决定的这样的事实，那么他与动物或客体之间就没有区别。正如木料必须有木料性或马必须有马性一样，人也必须有人性。一块石头不需要做任何努力来变得强壮或获得石头性，而人却不一样，人的本质要求他去努力，因为他被赋予了目的和知识。他必定要努力改造纯粹的客体自然来满足他的需要或欲望，要采取手段来达到目的。在这方面他身不由己，正如马不能避开是马的事实、石头不能避开石头性一样。在他的努力下，他太是个人了。用我们前几章所运用的语言来说，是人就意味着要完成人的本质或就是要实现人性这一可能。就为了存活而进行的斗争而言，为人也仅是为自然而已。

但是，目的和知识的结合给人提供了力量。虽然力量并不必然是危险的，但它却经常是危险的。它引发了想得到更大权力的欲望。而且它不满足于仅仅作为某种目的的一种手段，而有着使自己成为目的的倾向。为了生存的斗争可能会演变成为了权力而进行的斗争。作为手段，权力是有局限的，当某种目的达到之后，它也就不再发挥作用了。如果邮票是为了邮寄信件，那么有多少信件我们就需要多少邮票；如果钱是为了维持一定的生活水准，那么我们所需要的也仅仅是能够达到这一生活水平的钱的数量。但是如果我们收集邮票和金钱仅仅是为了它们本身，那么对于邮票和金钱的收集就是没有限制的了。对于权力来说也有着同样的情形。随着权力的不断积累，也就出现了欲望的不断膨胀，这种膨胀以前从来不敢想象，已完全超过了生存所需要的程度。在纯粹人性的驱动之下，我们不能保证如何使用权力。它可能被用来清除纯粹客体自然中的种种障碍，或者可能被用来针对自己的同胞，甚至可能被用来针对他自己。人们可能会倾向于同意卢梭的看法，人无处不在枷锁之中，不管原来是否存在着他享受其中自

371

was once a state of nature in which he was free. Knowledge by itself is harmonious, but purposes often conflict with one another not merely between states or races or different men but also in single individual himself. An individual with conflicting purposes is the enclosed battle ground for spiritual struggle, and although stone walls do not make a prison, nor mere object nature any obstacle to his yearnings, he is yet his own prisoner. The more power one acquires, the more one may be enslaved.

We have already pointed out that with the aid of knowledge purpose may become extremely complicated. There may be a chain of means to ends such that some ends are means to other end and some means end to other means. If one tarries in this chain, one is liable to take means for end. And value may come in to complicate the issue. The question of the justification of means by end may be raised and if one tarries with certain means so long that the ends are lost sight of, the means which was formerly justified by the ends is no longer so when the end is no longer in view. If the ends are not supposed to justify the means, then no matter how far removed the ends may be, whether or not they are lost sight of, they do not affect the means, since the latter will have to be justified on their own ground. But then the power to achieve ends is greatly diminished. Secondly, the longer the chain of means to ends, the more conflict of ends there is likely to be. Conflict with mere object nature is a straightforward issue—one could march into it with a stout heat, conflict with other human beings is liable to be accompanied by misgivings, and conflict with one's self may result in tragedies, since it is here that one's strength is also one's weakness, one's victory also one's defeat, and where a person is himself a house divided, nothing can possibly console. In the third place, with the aid of knowledge, purposes multify, desires increase. Some desires are transformed into needs while whims are changed into desires. The transformation may be highly satisfying, though it need not be so. But whether it is so or not, something is lost in the process. What was once only a whim or a wish or a hope with the softness, the lightness and the poetic quality that accompany it, is transformed into desires and needs with all the grossness and coarseness that accompany the will to achieve. If we

由的那种自然状态。就知识本身而言，知识是和谐的，但是目的却是经常相互冲突的。这样的冲突不仅仅存在于国家之间或种族之间或不同的人之间，也同样存在于单独的个人本身。有着相互冲突的目的的个人是一封闭的精神斗争的战场。石砌的围墙并不是真正的监牢，纯粹客体自然对他的欲望也不构成障碍，然而他却是他自己的囚犯。个人所取得的权力越多，那么他就可能被奴役得越多。

我们早已指出过，在知识的帮助之下，目的可能变得极其复杂。可能存在着目的和手段之间的链条，某些目的成了其他目的的手段，而某些手段却成了其他手段的目的。如果一个人在这样的目的与手段的链条之间徘徊，那么他就有可能把手段看作是目的，而且价值的加入会使这一问题变得更为复杂。由目的来证实手段的合理性问题可能会出现。如果一个人长期停留在手段上而忽视了目的，由于目的被遗忘，那么以前由目的证实的合理的手段也不再合理了。如果目的不来证实手段的合理性，那么不管目的挪到多远，也不管它们是否在视野中消失，它们都是不会影响手段的，因为后者将不得不在自己的基础之上得到证实。但是如果情形是这样的话，那么实现目的的力量也将大大地降低。第二，手段与目的之间的链条越长，目的之间的冲突也就可能越多。与纯粹客体自然的冲突是一个直截了当的问题，一个人可以勇敢地走进这样的冲突中去。与人之间的冲突常常伴随着疑虑担忧。与自己的冲突可能会导致悲剧性的结果，因为正是在这里体现了一个人的优势同时也是他的弱点，他的胜利同时也是他的失败。当一个人自己内心已经崩溃，那么就没有什么东西可以给他以安慰。第三，有了知识的帮助，目的便层出不穷，欲望也不断地增长。某些欲望转变成为需要，而突发奇想则变成了欲望。这样的转变可能是很令人满意的，但是并不必如此。然而不管它是否会如此，某些事情在这一过程中失掉了。曾经带有柔和的、轻松愉快的、富有诗意的特质的冲动或愿望或希望，现在则转变成了伴随着粗野鄙陋性质、坚决要实现的欲望和需要。如果我们有在月亮上举行野餐的能力，那么我们身

ever gain the capacity to have picnics on the moon, it will be welcome by some element in us and resulted by others, for the whimsical wish of enjoying solitude on the moon is transformed into a gross desire, resulting in a struggle for tickets and jostling at the gangplank with perhaps a notion as clear and distinct as Cartesian ideas that no solitude is to be had even on the moon.

But perhaps the most important result of increased desires is that we are more enslaved by them. With the increased facility to satisfy, desires tend to increase in a geometrical ratio. In simple and naive desires we may not feel enslaved, for the end is in view and the means direct. If we merely walk down a few steps to a brook for a drink, we won't feel that our drink or the few steps we have to walk encroaches upon our freedom. But if we have to do it scores of times in order to carry water for different families so as to support our own, we are liable to feel that walking up and down these steps interferes with our conversation or quiet afternoon at the tea house. Where the end is not a sensed or felt need of the present, even a simple desire may give rise to a feeling of enslavement. Imagine the enormous number of desires that accompany modern civilization, and the long chain of means to ends they involve! One cannot help feeling that a man is like a silkworm that spins a cocoon to enslave itself. While on the one hand we have to admit that the scope of human activities is greatly increased, things that formerly were incapable of accomplishment are now easily done; on the other, desires and needs also multify so that one is driven and enslaved by them more than ever before. It may be poetic sublimation to proclaim that an "ironmaster" drives us; obviously it cannot, unless human beings drive themselves. One may revolt against being driven by others, but when one drives one's self, there is no possibility of redress. The chance of self-enslavement is greatly increased by the increased power over object nature and fellow human beings. Whether there is any struggle against the domination of desires or not depends upon the individual, but even when there is any struggle, one cannot help feeling that one is not chained. The question is: do we conquer mere object nature to make ourselves slaves? Does the greater freedom to do things compensate for the greater enslavement of and by ourselves?

上的某些因素会因此感到很高兴，而另外的有些因素则会促使它实现，因为欢享月亮上的孤独的荒诞想法转变成了粗俗浅陋的欲望，会导致为了争夺门票而发生的斗争，会出现在步桥上拥挤不堪的现象，还可能会出现像笛卡儿的观念一样清楚分明的观念：即使在月亮上也不会再有孤独了。

但是，可能不断增长的欲望所带来的最重要的结果是我们更多地被欲望所奴役。由于满足欲望能力的不断增长，欲望也呈现了以几何级数增长的趋势。如果欲望是简单的、素朴的，那么我们可能不会有被奴役的感觉，因为目的就在眼前，而手段也是直接的。如果我们只是走了几步路到溪边喝水，那么我们就不会感觉到喝的水或我们必须要走的那几步路侵犯了我们的自由。但是如果我们要反复做这样的事情，必须把水送到不同的家庭中去是为了我们自己的生存，那样我们就会感觉到这种来回走动会影响我们的谈话或在茶馆消度宁静的下午。如果目的不是当下感觉到的需要，那么一个简单的欲望就会引起被奴役的感觉。想象一下与现代文明相伴随的大量的欲望，以及这些欲望所包含的目的到手段的漫长的链条。人们就禁不住会感到，人就像蚕那样在作茧自缚。虽然在一方面我们必须承认人类活动的范围大大地扩展了，以前不可能完成的事情现在很容易就能做到。但在另一方面，欲望和需要也在不断增长以至于人们比以前更多地被这些欲望和需要所驱使，被它们所奴役。如果我们说"钢铁厂厂长"在驱使我们，这可能非常富有诗意；显然这是不可能的，除非人自己驱使自己。如果有人驱使自己，人们可能会反抗；但是当一个人自己驱使自己的时候，那就没有纠止的可能了。由于征服客体自然和他人的力量的不断增长，人的自我奴役的可能性也在极大地增加。是否有任何反对欲望主宰的斗争在于个人，但是即使有这样的斗争，人们也不禁觉得他们并没有被束缚。问题是：我们对纯粹客体自然的征服是为了使我们自己成为奴隶吗？我们有更多的自由来做事情，这是否抵消了我们自身更多的奴役及自我奴役呢？

There is then a problem that is essentially human. Some things might be done through social economic and political measures. To start with, however, a choice is involved. The great society may be organized for power or for happiness. By happiness we mean the synthetic harmony of the different ingredients in the makeup of a man. It is not to be confused with pleasure which may be unhappily enjoyed or with the mere satisfaction of desires which may be such as to disturb harmony. If the great society is to be organized merely for power, whether military or industrial, the above problem can hardly be solved. If the great society is to be organized for happiness, individuals will have to cooperate in making positive efforts towards their own salvation. The great society can merely provide for the conditions, under which individuals may rescue themselves, but in the last analysis they will have to do their own rescuing. Formerly it was religion that performed the task of individual salvation, but religion seems to have lost a good deal of its former effectiveness, and since what is relevant to our problem is only that part of religion that deals with the human, we may set formal religion aside in our present discussion. Even the relevant part has to be taught to the individual, to be experienced, meditated and divined by him. The problem is not merely human but also individual.

III

We shall use a term in the following paragraphs to mean something more than the dictionary allows. The word "vista" according to *Webster* means "firstly a view or prospect commonly through or along an avenue as between rows of trees, or secondly a mental view or prospect extending over a series of events." We shall keep the view or prospect part of the meaning and discard the tree or the event part. We are not interested in what is seen or heard but in the significances gathered from experience. It may be that the kind of significances gathered depends upon individual characteristics as well as their relation to their environment; and they may in turn be due to mere subject nature or nurture; but whether this is so or not, we need not try to ascertain, since we are here only interested in the kind of significances gathered. What is known to any individual as the meaning of life is on our account the total amount of significance, gathered and organized into a pattern; it is

这样就出现了一个本质上是人才具有的问题。有些事情可以通过社会经济和政治措施得以完成。然而首先，这里就有一个选择的问题。一个大的社会可能为了力量或为了幸福而组织起来。所谓幸福，我们是指构成人的各种要素间的综合性的和谐。我们不应该把幸福与所谓的消遣混淆起来，因为消遣可能并不能给人们带来幸福，或者把它与欲望的满足混淆起来，因为这样的欲望的满足可能会扰乱和谐。如果一个大的社会仅仅是为了力量而组织起来的，不管是军事的力量还是工业的力量，那么上述的问题是几乎不可能得到解决的。如果一个大的社会是为了幸福而组织起来的，那么个体就必须联合起来，共同作出积极的努力，设法自助自救。社会只能够为我们提供一定的条件，在这样的条件下个人可能做到自救。但是归根到底，他们必须自救。以前是宗教担负起了拯救个体的使命，但目前宗教似乎已经丧失了它以前所具有的许多效用。由于与我们的问题相关的仅仅是解决人类问题的那部分宗教，因此我们在当前的讨论中把正式的宗教暂且放在一旁。即使是有关的那一部分也必须传授给个体，由个体去体验，去沉思，去推测。这里的问题不仅仅是人类的，而且也是个体的。

三

在下面的部分中，我们将使用一个术语来指示某些事物，其含义要远远多于词典所能包含的。根据《韦氏英语词典》，vista 一词的意思是"首先是指通常从或沿着两排树之间的道路看到的景色或视野，其次指关于一系列事物的前景或展望"。我们将保留这一词意义中的前景或展望的部分，而舍弃树或事物的部分。我们的兴趣并不在于所看见的或所听到的，而在于从经验中所收集到的意义。可能这样收集到的意义依赖于个人的特点及其与环境之间的关系，它们可能转而归因于纯粹的主体自然或教养。但是，事实是否这样，我们无须努力去确定，因为我们在此的兴趣仅仅是所收集到的意义。任何一个人所知道的生活的意义，就我们而言，是指收集到或组织进图案中的整体的意义，

not merely the conceptual meaning of the term "life," nor the emotional content of living, nor the flavor with which one's life is lived; it is all things combined with something in addition, something that motivates or guides or directs the basic promptings of one's heart. In fact the usual word to describe it is "philosophy" in the sense in which one often says that everyone has his own philosophy; but in order to preserve the term for the formal and conceptual approach to fundamental problems as it is now used in colleges and universities, we call the pattern of significances one's vista.

We have already said that either mere subject nature or nurture or both may be responsible for the kind of vista one entertains. It may be that a certain minimal instinctive endowment is neglected in order that certain vista may be attainable. It is *t'ien* however that nurture has to assert its effects even though the required instinctive endowment is given. The statement that everybody can be a sage means to assert also the importance of nurture. Even if some vistas are born, others are achieved. The achievement of some vistas must be accompanied by conscious and strenuous efforts and these may fail, if they are misdirected. It is with views and prospects that we are concerned, not acts or instincts or impulses. If our efforts are directed towards the stoppage of certain propensities that are about to be actualized, the suppression of certain instincts which struggle for expression, or the frustration of certain impulses which have already manifested themselves, our efforts are liable to be misdirected, and instead of gaining vistas, we may become psycho-analytic cases. But if our efforts are directed towards working out a view and maintaining it, we may succeed in allowing certain instincts to function without others manifesting themselves, in encouraging certain feelings to be entertained so that others won't emerge, or certain acts to take place so that others may be nipped in the bud. In the simplest language possible, we may live as every other person in the world of facts and yet so lifted out of it that our world of significance is quite different from many of our contemporaries. One's problem in gaining vista is not to change the object or the man; it is rather to fulfill as much as possible the man in the animal or object. It is only the vulgar who erect idols of worship or expect the coming of superman to solve essentially human

而不是仅仅指"生活"这一术语的概念意义，也不是指生活的情感的内容，也不是指每一个人生活所具有的某种韵味。它是指所有的事物及所附带的某些事物，这些事物或激励或引导或指引着一个人精神的基本动机。事实上，常用来描述它的词是下面意义上的"哲学"一词，即人们经常所说的每一个人都有他自己的哲学。但是为了保留"哲学"这一术语在学院或大学用来处理基本问题的那种正式的和概念上的方法，我们还是把这种意义图案叫做人生的观点。

我们已经说过，或者是纯粹的主体自然，或者是教养，或者是这两者，对一个人所持有的人生观有影响。为了达到某一人生观，可能要忽略某些最为基本的本能的禀赋。即使所要求的本能的禀赋被给予了，也是"天"来使教养发挥作用。"人皆可以为尧舜"这一句话表明了教养的重要作用。即使某些人生观天生就有，其他的人生观却需要达成。某些人生观必定要通过有意识的和艰苦的努力才能够达成。如果这样的努力被误导了，那么这样的人生观可能就会失败。我们现在关心的是前景和展望，而不是行动或本能或刺激。如果我们努力的目的是阻止将要成为现实的某些癖好，是压抑某些极力要得到表达的本能，或挫败已经得到表达的某些刺激，那么我们的努力极有可能被误导，我们不仅不能得到某一人生观，反而还有可能成为心理分析的对象。但是如果我们的努力是指向得到某一人生观并坚持这一人生观，那么我们就可能成功使某些本能起作用而使另一些本能不表现出来，成功地使某些感情得以发泄而其他的感情不许露头，或者使某些行动发生而使另外一些行动消灭于萌芽之中。以一种可能是最简单的语言来说，我们可能像在事实世界中的任何一个人一样地生活，然而超脱之后，我们的意义世界是非常不同于我们同时代的很多其他人的。人们得到人生观的问题不是去改变客体或人，而是设法尽可能多地去完成存在于动物或客体中的人性。只有粗俗的人才试图树立崇拜的偶像或期待着超人来帮助

and even somewhat earthy problems.

There are probably large varieties of different vistas. If one thinks of the different "philosophies" of different men, how various and multitudinous they are, one has a rough idea of how many combinations and permutations there are to vistas. We are however only interested in three main and somewhat platonic types: the naive, the heroic and the sagely. These terms describe vistas, not a person's occupation, or character, or capacity, or mere ideas. Obviously a great scientist or musician may have a heroic vista although his interest in science is single tracked or his interest in music purely emotional expression. When it is said that great men are basically simple, it is probably not meant to convey that they are simple in the various ways in which they are great, more likely it is meant that in spite of their greatness or even responsible for it, there is a simplicity of vista. A hero in war may be a man of naive vista; his heroism may consist of bagging as many enemies as he can while his vista is naive. It is probable and even likely that a man with a naive vista is a naive man in many ways, and a man with a heroic vista a hero in the eyes of his contemporaries. None the less a distinction should be made. Whether Plato's artisans, warriors and statesmen who are supposed to embody the respective vistas of industry, honor and wisdom are meant to describe vistas or not, our terms here are not meant to describe social strata or individual virtues. If vistas are the products or the corresponding virtues of professions or stations in life, one can hardly lift oneself out of the world of facts in which one happens or chooses to function.

A naive vista is one in which the dichotomy or bifurcation of reality as well as that of self and others is reduced to a minimum. It is such that a person who achieves it is free from egocentric predicament. While it is perfectly true a child cannot be said to have a vista since he has gathered no significances, it is none the less profitable to compare the child-like quality in his behavior with the attitude of a sophisticated man. A child enjoys a certain harmony with his environment. He is not likely to revolt against his environment or to want to conquer it. If he is frustrated, he probably cries wholeheartedly, and if immediately he is moved to laughter, he does not hesitate to do so. He is not affected by any desire

解决本质上是人类自身的甚至多少是世俗的问题。

可能存在着相当多的不同的人生观。如果人们想到不同的人有着不同的哲学，它们是如此不同和多种多样，那么人们就会对有那么多的人生观的排列组合有了大致的想法。然而我们感兴趣的是三种多少具有柏拉图性质的人生观，即素朴人生观、英雄人生观和圣人人生观。这些术语描绘的是人生观，而不是个人的职业或特点或能力或意念。显然，伟大的科学家或音乐家可能具有英雄的人生观，虽然他对科学的兴趣是单向度的或他对音乐的兴趣纯粹是感情的表达。通常所说的伟大的人物本质上是简单的，这可能不是说这些伟大人物在他们伟大的方面是简单的，而更可能是说尽管他们伟大，他们的人生观具有素朴性，或是他们素朴的人生观成就了其伟大。战争中的英雄可能是具有素朴人生观的人，虽然他的英雄主义可能表现在他尽其所能杀死了很多的敌人，然而他的人生观还是素朴的。很有可能的是具有素朴人生观的人在许多方面都是素朴的，一个具有英雄人生观的人在他同时代的人看来是个英雄。但是在这之间必须作出区别。不管被认为分别体现了勤奋、忠诚和智慧的人生观的柏拉图的工匠、武士和政治家是否有意描述不同的人生观，我们在此所运用的术语却不是用来描述社会阶层或个人的品德的。如果人生观是职业或生活阶段的产物或相应的品德的话，那么人们就很难从他们碰巧或经过选择而在其中起作用的事实世界中超脱出来。

素朴人生观是这样一种人生观，在其中实在的两分化和自我与他人的两分化被降至最低的程度。具有这种人生观的人，会从自我中心的困境中解脱出来。由于一个孩子还没有收集到人生意义，所以不能说他具有一定的人生观，这是非常正确的。然而把他在行动中表现出来的孩子气的特质拿来和一个有经验的人做比较却是有意义的。一个孩子享有他与环境间的某些和谐。他不可能起来反抗他的环境或想要征服环境。如果他受到了挫折，他可能会痛快地大哭；如果他受到触动想要笑，他就会毫不犹豫地去笑。他不会因为行为

for consistency of behavior, neither is he possessed by spiritual struggle. The child-like qualities of his behavior may be achieved by a man with a vista. A man with a naive vista is one who has achieved this child-like simplicity; it is not the simplicity of a simpleton or a dullard. It consists of being humble, of entertaining desires without being enslaved by them, of having a certain consciousness of self without egocentricity, so that one is neither unduly elated by success or unduly humiliated by failure. He is not likely given to comparisons with other men. Whether he is dull, devoid of talent, or lacking in social grace, or else sparklingly witty, extraordinarily talented, or intensely intellectual, he accepts himself; he accepts himself as being merely given and fulfills his function in life with equanimity in either case. So far as he himself is concerned, he is merely conscious of a charge to keep what he is, and so far as his environment and fellow human beings are concerned, he demands so little of them that he is not likely to be obstructed by them. He is not estranged by them. The vista enables him to achieve what is often called "peace of mind."

A heroic vista is one in which dichotomy of reality is almost at a maximum. Again it is the vista that is heroic, not necessarily the person. The heroic vista has a large number of varieties and is also permeated with more psychological complications than any other vista. There may be anthropocentric heroism. One may be fired with the idea of the conquest of mere object nature by man and emotionally propelled towards its achievement. Here the dichotomy is between mere object nature and man and the obsession is with the conquest of the former. So far as the mere object nature is concerned, the victory thus far belongs to man; but so far as mere human nature is concerned, the issue is as yet uncertain. It is quite likely that the victor may turn out to be himself equally the defeated. There seems to be on the one hand an intrinsic unwillingness to deal with men, to solve their problems, and on the other to whip them into a concerted action towards the conquest of mere object nature is just as a nation harrowed by internal dissention often seeks unification through external aggression. But just as external aggression does not solve the problem of the internal dissention of a nation, so the conquest of mere object nature does not solve the intrinsic

一致性的欲望而受影响，也不会纠缠于精神方面的斗争。他的行动所具有的孩子气的特质可能被一个具有某种人生观的成人习得。一个具有素朴人生观的人是这样的一个人，他具有孩子气的素朴性，这种素朴性并不是蠢人或笨伯的素朴性。它表现为谦卑，虽然有欲望却不为欲望所控制，有明显的自我意识却没有自我中心。正因为如此，他不会因为胜利而得意忘形，也不会因为失败而羞愧万分。他不会拿自己与别人相比。不管他是愚蠢、缺乏智慧，或者举止并不优雅，还是妙趣横生、才华横溢，或者才智过人，他能够接受自己。他接受他自己既定的状态，在生活中发挥着自己的作用，对于上述的两种截然相反的情形他都安之若素。就他本人来说，他完全地意识到要保持自我的责任。就他的环境和同胞的方面来说，他对于他们要求如此之少，以至于他也不可能为他们所阻挠。他也不为他们所疏远。这样的人生观引导他达到经常被称之为心静的境界。

英雄的人生观中实在的两分化几乎达到了最大的程度。而且这里所说的是人生观是英雄的，并不必然指这个人是英雄。英雄人生观有着各种不同的类型，而且与其他人生观相比充满了更多的心理学方面的难题。人类中心的英雄观就是英雄人生观中的一种。具有这种人生观的人可能在内心中燃烧着由人来征服纯粹客体自然的热情，而且为强烈的情感所驱动来达到征服自然的目的。在这里，纯粹的客体自然和人一分为二，人所着迷的是要征服纯粹的客体自然。如果从纯粹的客体自然的角度来看，此刻胜利是属于人的；但是从纯粹人的本性来看，问题却并没有这样确定。事情很可能是这样的，胜利者可能同样会成为失败者。似乎在一方面从内心讲人们不愿意来处理人的问题，来解决他们所面临的问题；但是在另一方面，激励人们同心协力来达到征服纯粹客体自然的目的，正如同内乱纷扰的国家经常是通过发动对外侵略来达到统一的目的。但是，正如对外侵略并未解决国内纷扰问题一样，对客体自然的征服也同

problems of man. Problems may be ignored for a time, they may even be temporarily dissolved, but emerge they will, and when they do, they are likely to do so with a vengeance. Human desires may become rampant for which the conquest of mere object nature is not a solution, but instead an aggravation. To use a phrase so often employed in military strategy, the initiative may be lost; human beings may be driven not merely by the mere object nature they have conquered, but also by their own mere nature which they have ignored.

There may be egocentric heroism. Here the line of demarcation is drawn between the human environment and the ego. External achievement is again the predominant element; only it is not aimed at the conquest of mere object nature; instead it is directed towards the human environment. Satisfaction is derived from making or imagining the individual ego, the victor over circumstances that are chiefly human. Such doctrines as "Wherever there is a will, there is a way," or "One is the sum total of what one has achieved," or "With concentration and effort one always succeeds" are expressive of their brand of heroic vista. One may be the most un-heroic sort of person and yet believes that it is only through the conquest of one's human environment that one finds one's individual realization. The heroic vista is not limited to an individual society, but it is there that the single-tracked heroism is most predominant. The multitudinous and yet definitely channeled opportunities enable a person to identify his personal worth with his success or failure in a single line of ambition or achievement. The qualities required for success are quickness of perception, facility for projects, capacity for seizing opportunities and ruthlessness in carrying out one's projects; and although the resultant effects of success may sometimes be sound and fury devoid of deep human significance, yet since nothing succeeds like success, one is likely to make heroes out of ruthless, capable and successful men. And in an important sense they are heroes. Most of the great statesmen, soldiers, or industrialists or even some of the religious leaders were men with heroic vistas. Civilization might have been a static affair, if there weren't a galaxy of such men. They are necessary to civilization, more especially perhaps to its environment, but they are not sufficient; they are victors in wars, not preservers of peace, and so far as their vista is concerned,

样不能解决人内在的种种问题。可以暂时忽略这些问题，甚至它们可能在目前得到了解决，但是问题会不断地出现。如果它们出现了，那么它们就会变得极其严重。人类的欲望可能会变得毫无节制，征服纯粹客体自然对于这样的欲望来说并不是真正的解决办法，相反却会使情况恶化。借用军事战略学中经常说的一句话就是可能丧失主动权。人类不仅仅为纯粹客体自然所驱动，而且也同样为被他们所忽视的自己的本性所驱使。

可能会有自我中心的英雄主义。在这里界线是划在了人类的环境和自我之间。外在的成绩依然是主要的因素，所不同的是它的目标不是要征服纯粹客体自然，而是要指向人类的环境。满足感来源于营造或者想象自我，那个征服了环境（主要是征服他人）的自我。下面的这些说法如"有志者事竟成"，或"人就是他所成就的一切的总和"，或"只要专注和努力，你就会无往而不胜"表达的就是他们这种英雄人生观。一个人可能最不像是一个英雄，但是他却坚信只有通过征服人类的环境人才能获得自我实现。英雄人生观并不局限于个体的社会，但正是在个体的社会中狭隘的英雄主义最为普遍。大量的然而有明确导向的机会使人沿着抱负或成就这一维度将自身价值等同于成败。成功所需要的特质是感觉的敏锐、计划的能力、抓住机遇的能力和执行计划的冷酷无情。虽然由此导致的成功的效果可能是不包含深刻人生意义的喧哗与骚动，然而由于一事成百事顺，所以人们可能会认为无情的、有能力的和成功的人就是英雄。在某种重要的意义上说，他们是英雄。许多伟大的政治家、士兵或实业家或者甚至某些宗教领袖就是具有英雄人生观的人。如果人类的文明没有众多这样的英雄人物，那么它就可能只不过是一种静止的状态。对于人类的文明来说，这些英雄人物是必不可少的，对于人类的环境来说更是如此，但是仅仅有他们是不够的。他们是战争的胜利者，而不是和平的维护者。从他们的人生观的角度来看，

the significance gathered are partial to one aspect of the essence of being human.

IV

The sagely vista is somewhat like the naive except that its *apparent naïveté* is arrived at through advanced meditation and contemplation. The behavior of a man with a sagely vista may appear naive as a man with a naive vista, but the discipline behind it is based upon meditation that transcends the human function with the result that one is not merely free from egocentricity but also of anthropocentricity. It is not necessary here to dwell at length the idea that among human beings in the concrete each is because the others are. It is only in the abstract that individuals are independent of each other. The question as to what Aristotle might have been if he were in ancient China for instance is a speculation concerning Aristotelianness; the actual and concrete Aristotle was, because his local contemporaries were. We are not talking of the dependence of each other for certain purposes such as security, protection, food and employment, etc., we are rather speaking of the very core of each individual character. We are all of us in varying degrees Laurels and Hardies, or Mutts and Jeffs, or Bradleys and MacArthurs, or even Simon twins. The more intimate the relation between individuals, the more each is integrated with the other, and the more one projects oneself into the other, the more one is because the others are. There is in the concrete a mutual permeation or infiltration of individual characters and once this is realized, there is a democracy of giants and pygmies since each wouldn't be if the others weren't so that both the strong and the weak suffer the same fate or inherit the same world. Individual differences there are and must be, and while for certain purposes, they are usefully accentuated through labels and abstractions, they shouldn't be emphasized to the extent as to obscure the mutual interpenetration of individuals in actual and concrete life.

Since the very being of each is soaked through and through with the very being of his intimate contemporaries, where is the line that divides people into selves? To be sure, physiologically each one of us is a unit, but then to single out the physiological aspect is surely an abstraction. Certainly some of us have mental qualities that are not shared by many

所获得的意义只是人类本性的一个方面。

四

圣人的人生观在某些方面类似于素朴人生观，所不同的在于它表现出来的素朴性得自于高级的沉思和冥想。具有圣人观的人的行为看起来像具有素朴人生观的人一样素朴，但是在这种素朴性背后的自律是以超越人类职责的沉思为其基础的，这就使得个人不仅仅能够摆脱自我中心主义，而且也能够摆脱人类中心主义。在这里没有必要详细地讨论这样的思想，即每一个具体的人因为他人而成为自己。只有在抽象的意义上，个人才可以说是相互独立的。关于"如果亚里士多德生活在古代中国将会是什么样的"这个问题是一个关于亚里士多德性的沉思；实际而且具体的亚里士多德是因为他当地的同时代的人而成了亚里士多德本人。我们现在谈论的不是每一个人为了某些目的如安全、保护、食物和职业等等而相互依存，我们现在正在谈论的是每一个个体特点的核心。我们所有的人在不同的程度上都像劳雷尔和哈迪，或者是马特和杰夫，或者是布拉德利和麦克阿瑟，或者甚至是西蒙兄弟这样的好搭档。个人之间的关系越是紧密，那么每一个人也就与他人更紧密地结合在一起。一个人越是把自己投射到他人之中，他也就越因别人而成了他自己。实际上，个体的特点之间是相互渗透或相互弥漫的。一旦这种情况实现，那么巨人和侏儒之间就有了民主状态，因为如果没有对方，那么他自己也就不可能存在了。因此强者和弱者有着同样的命运或获得了同样的世界。个人之间确实存在着差异，也肯定会有差异。虽然为了某种目的，通过标签和抽象的方法可以强调差异，并且也很有用，但是不应该过分地强调个人之间的差异，因为这可能会在现实的和具体的生活中妨碍个人之间的相互渗透。

由于每一个人的存在都深深地浸透着或渗透着与他息息相关的同胞的存在，那么把人类划分成个体的界线在什么地方呢？诚然，从生理上讲，我们中的每一个人就是一个单位，但是挑选出这样的生理的方面无疑就是一种抽象。确实，我们中的某些人具有某种精神特质，

others, and whether we call them extraordinary or remarkable or peculiar, they are at any rate distinct; but surely this is description if not valuation, and to describe is after all to abstract. Can we distinguish a man's qualities from those of his forefathers and of his contemporaries or determine what portion of them is due to history, to the cultural environment and to the zeitgeist? If we cannot so distinguish or determine, one's mind is a jumble, a complex, or a welter of multitudinous ingredients and no longer an individual. If we can so distinguish and determine, there is either a residue which is hardly the whole individual, or else there is nothing left so that the concrete individual has evaporated. It may be said that each individual has a soul distinct from the soul of any other individual. Whether this is true or not, we need not ascertain, for unless we think of souls as being windowless or else in vacuum, we can hardly end the problem of their interpenetration. The crux of the whole matter is that what is known as the individual is itself an abstraction; in the concrete it is a mobile area of accentuation where an enormous number of events take place in action and reaction. A mind that is aware of this universal penetration is bound to entertain a vista that transcends individual differences and while admitting them intellectually, a mind so lifted out of itself in such awareness refuses to have any emotional vested interest in any single self.

This mutual interpenetration is not limited to human beings. Each particular object reflects the whole particular world to which it belongs in the sense that each is because the others are. Such particular object is related to every other particular object in different ways and while some of these relations are internal and others external, the qualities and relational properties of any single object depend upon the qualities and relational properties of every other particular object. So far as the particularity is concerned no object can change or move; the particular stays put. What is repeatable elsewhere and at different times in any particular object is either the set of universals realized by the object or else its own illusive identity. We are so accustomed to abstraction that it is difficult for us to reason or even to talk about the particular. Take the desk on which I now write. We are accustomed to thinking that it could be moved; we may indeed say that as a matter of fact it was moved only

是其他的人所不具有的，不管我们是否称它们是非凡的或卓越的或特殊的，无论如何，它们总是独特的。但这确实是在描述而不是评价，描述毕竟就是一种抽象。我们能够把一个人的特质与他前辈的特质、与他同时代人的特质区别开来吗？或者我们能够断定这些特质中的哪些部分是属于历史的，哪些是属于文化环境和时代精神的吗？如果我们不能够作出这样的区别或者断定，那么一个人的心灵就是杂乱的一堆，就是一个复合体，或者是不同的诸多因素的综合，而不再是个体的了。如果我们能够作出这样的区别和断定，那么就会有几乎不是作为整体的个体的剩余物，或者是什么东西也没有遗留下来，那么作为具体的个人就消失了。我们可能会这样说，每一个人都有自己的与他人不同的心灵。这一说法不管是正确的还是不正确的，我们在此无须确认，因为除非我们认为心灵是没有窗户的或者是在真空之中的，否则我们就几乎不可能终止它们相互渗透的问题。全部问题的关键在于，被认为是个人的事物本身就是抽象的；实际上它就是一个强调的活动区域，在其中有数量众多的事件在作用和反作用中发生。一个人的心灵如果能够意识到普遍的渗透，他就必定能够怀有超越个人差异的人生观。虽然在理智上承认个人之间的差异，但是有这种意识并超越了自身的心灵就会拒绝任何情感上的个人既得利益。

这种相互渗透的情形并不仅仅局限于人类。在每一客体因为其他客体的存在才能存在的意义上说，每一个特殊的客体都反映它所隶属的整个的特殊世界。这样的特殊客体在不同的方式上与每一其他的客体相互联系着。这些关系中有的是内在关系，有的则是外在关系。任何一单独的客体的特质和关系质都要依赖于每一其他的特殊客休的特质和关系质。就特殊性的角度来看，没有一客体是可以变化或移动的；殊相留在原地。在其他的地方和在不同的时间在任何一特殊客体中可以重复的东西，是那套由客体实现了的共相或者它本身虚幻的同一性。我们习惯于谈论抽象的东西，因此对我们来讲，推论或者甚至谈论殊相就感到非常地困难。以我现在正在写字的书桌为例。我们通常以为它是能够来回移动的；我们可能说，事实上它在昨天就被移动了。

yesterday. It could be moved as an enduring object, but so far as its particularity is concerned, we insist that the term "this desk" covers a series of particulars first at a certain original position, then in transit and finally in a new locality, and none of the particulars has either changed or moved. To say that an object has changed either its qualities or its location is merely to affirm either that it has gone through a set of different and dissimilar particulars or that its internal and external relations with other particular objects are no longer the same as before. In either case, the pattern of the whole world in its particularity is also different.

There are other ways in which a particular object reflects the particular world, but we shall not dwell on them. What we must not forget is that a man is also an animal and an object. It is perfectly true that one is different from some objects in being an animal, and from some animals in being a man, and from the man in being oneself, but if one realizes that what is known as oneself is permeated with other men as well as other animals and objects, one can hardly be much excited about being a particular self. The realization enables him to feel at one with the world and everything in it. He acquires universal sympathy. He does not despise other objects for he is himself one of them, and in a democracy of existents, he gives as much as he takes. He does not frown upon other animals for like him they are merely functioning in accordance with their respective essences; and he doesn't condemn certain animalistic proclivities in himself since being a man does not release him from the function of realizing the essence of an animal. While a number of senses might be urged in which the man in him may be regarded as being better or worse than other objects or animals in the concrete flow of life, or in the actual passage of time, he is merely different from the others just as they are different from each other among themselves, the humanity in a person gives him the most serious of problems for it is the capacity of a human being that his relations with others of his species are most complicated; there he is liable to enjoy the keenest pleasure or else suffer the most poignant pain. If he is incapable of either, it must be due to a certain lumpiness in himself, and the uttermost he could achieve is the naive vista. If he is capable of both, he must be a keen

　　它可以作为一个持续存在的客体来移动，但是如果从它的特殊性的角度来看，我们坚持认为"这张桌子"这一术语包含着一系列的殊相，首先最初在某一地方，在途中经过的地方，也在最终达到的新的地点。没有一个殊相发生变化或移动。说一个客体改变了它的特质或者是改变了它的地点，仅仅是在断言它经过了一套不同的殊相或者它内在的和与其他特殊客体的外在的关系已经与以前的不一样了。在这两种情况下，整个世界图案的特殊性也是不同的。

　　特殊的客体还有另一种反映特殊世界的方式，但是我们不打算在此谈论它。我们不应该忘记的是，一个人同时也是一个动物和一个客体。作为动物，人是不同于某些客体的；作为人，他又不同于某些动物；作为自己，他又不同于他人：这是千真万确的。但如果他认识到，被认为是自我的东西是与其他的人、其他的动物和其他的客体相互渗透的时候，他就不会因为自己的特殊自我而异常兴奋。这一认识会引导他看到他自己与世界及世界中的每一事物都是一体的，他会因此而获得普遍同情。他不会歧视其他的客体，因为他自己就是它们中的一员。而且在这种存在者的民主状态之中，他给予多少，也就获取多少。他不会对其他的动物表示不满，因为像他一样，这些动物也只不过是根据各自不同的本质来发挥自己的作用。他也同样不会谴责某些在他身上表现出来的动物性的倾向，因为作为一个人并不能使他自己从实现其动物本性的作用中得到解脱。虽然需要鼓励一些感官，在这些感官里他身上的人性可能会比具体的生活之流中其他的客体或动物优越或糟糕；或者在现实的时间阶段中，他只不过是不同于其他的人，正如其他的人相互之间也有区别一样；但是一个人所具有的人性给他带来的问题最为严重，因为正是由于人类的能力使得他与他的种族中的其他人的关系变得非常复杂；因此他有可能享受极度的欢乐或者遭受最为强烈的痛苦。如果他不能够有以上这样两种感受，那么可以肯定，他本人是一个极其麻木不仁的人。对于他而言，他最多所能得到的是素朴的人生观。如果他能够有上述的两种感受，那么他就是一个

as well as a passionate man; either blind passion spells his doom, or sublimated and wisely directed passion guides him towards salvation. If one struggles against one's own passions, one is a cornered animal, an imprisoned man, immersed in a maze of conflicting emotions from which one can hardly extricate oneself. One must have significant knowledge and relevant wisdom in order to cope with the problem; and the man with the sagely vista does not solve the problem in the usual sense, for him the problem is dissolved so that it is no longer there to plague him.

Perhaps the most unselfish at all emotions is sympathy. In its pure sincerity, it is obviously selfless. With the realization that one is permeated with the qualities and relations of one's co-existents, one is capable of universal sympathy in all its sincerity and purity. In ceasing to be anthropocentric one may also cease to be egocentric. Once free of egocentricity, one is no longer plagued by the problem of self-enslavement. It is the vested interest in a person that makes him the slave of his own desires, and it is his desires that disturb the peaceful relation between him and other men. It is also his desires that render him struggling within himself. Desires however are burdened in themselves only when they breed other desires that strive for satisfaction with equal persistency. Once they are given the chance of island hopping, there is no way of preventing them from hopping on ad infinitum. Nor is the problem one of curbing one's desires. The only way to do is to know one's destiny, to be at peace with one's station in life in a much more comprehensive than the merely social or political sense. Obviously some desires will have to be satisfied, but if in satisfying or trying to satisfy them, one is at peace with one's destiny, one is reconciled with one's limitations; whatever destiny or station that is given, it is for him a charge to keep, a function to fulfill in the democracy of mutually dependent co-existents. He admits neither self-satisfaction, nor self-deprecation. He does not struggle against what is within his function, nor does he crave for what is beyond it. Since he is a man, he has to realize the essence of his being, and whatever is given him in addition as a separate self he accepts with as much good grace as he accepts his humanity. What is needed is not saintliness which involves being Godly and therefore other

敏锐而富有激情的人。如果是这样的话，那么不是盲目的激情给他带来厄运，就是得到升华并有理性指导的激情会引导他达到自我拯救。如果一个人反对自己的激情，他就成了困兽囚徒，陷于感情冲突的迷津之中而不能自拔。为了处理这些问题，一个人必须具有相当的知识和相关的智慧。一个具有圣人观的人，并不是以一种常见的方式来解决这样的问题，因为对于他来讲，这样的问题消解了，所以这些问题不会困扰他。

可能最无私的感情就是同情。在它的最真诚的意义上说，它显然是无私的。由于一个人与他的其他共存者的特质和关系相互渗透的实现，他就能够有最真诚和最纯粹的普遍同情。如果一个人不再以人类为中心，那么他也就不再以自我为中心了。一旦脱离了自我中心的困境，那么他也就不再会为自我奴役这样的问题所困扰。正是个人身上的既得利益使他成为自己的欲望的奴隶，也正是他的欲望扰乱了他与其他人之间的那种和平的关系，也正是他的欲望使他与他自己进行着斗争。只有当欲望滋生出其他努力以同样的固执求得自己的满足的欲望的时候，欲望才会为欲望所累。一旦它们有机会进行跳岛之旅，那么我们就根本没有办法可以阻止它们无限制地跳下去。这也不是一个遏制欲望的问题。唯一可行的方式就是认识自己的命运，以更加全面的意识而不只是社会和政治上的意识来平和地对待自己的处境。显然某些欲望会得到满足，但是如果在满足或试图满足它们的过程中，人们能够平和地对待自己的命运，那么他就能够与自己的局限达成和解。不管是处于什么样的命运或阶段，对他而言那就是要履行的责任，在与相互依赖的共存者的民主状态中所要完成的作用。他既不承认自我的满足，也不承认自我的批评。他不会起来反对自己职责范围内的任何东西，也不会渴求职责范围之外的东西。由于他是一个人，他就必须实现他的存在的本质。作为独立的自我所给予他的一切，他都会有风度地接受，一如他接受自己的人性。他所需要的不是如上帝般的圣洁，因此不成其

than man, but sagacity which involves the transcendence of the mere nature in man so as to approach that nature in man which is also *t'ien*. The latter is within the possible reach of any man. Once it is reached, one may be in vista different from most men and yet in every other aspect the same as any Tom, Dick or Harry. In him object nature and subject nature are unified and in the unification there is harmony.

It must be emphasized that we are talking of vistas, not classes of men. We do not urge upon the creation of a class of sages any more than the institution of a class of heroes. In our present day society, there is so much differentiation and integration of function that people can hardly be stratified into any simple hierarchy of classes. There is no reason why a pedlar or a shoemaker or a lawyer or a doctor shouldn't be a man with the sagely vista. A man with such a vista is equally at home with shoe-making as with statecraft, for in either of them he is fulfilling the function that is given, that contributes to the pattern of the particular world in which he lives, and in making such a contribution he allows no distinction between the humble and the pretentious. Nor is there any particular profession that is never suited to the achievement of the sagely vista—everybody is capable of it. Of course not everybody will succeed. The important problem is not so much as to make everybody a sage or to lead or to encourage them to entertain it as an ideal. With this ideal in mind, one is not likely to mistake power, knowledge, wealth, etc., for human wisdom; useful as these are for certain specific purposes, it is yet the latter that enables a person to live a life that leads to social harmony and individual peace of mind. Take knowledge for instance. It has become objective, reliable and eminently useful for the maintenance and improvement of the conditions of life; but it has not been equally successful in supplying human beings with such wisdom as to direct the kind of life to be lived. The advance in knowledge has thus far resulted in the heroic and tragic enslavement to one's desires, whether good or bad or indifferent, and knowledge itself has become so neutral that saints and devils could make use of it alike. And power and wealth do not face any better. The fundamental problem of today may be one of social legislation or economic rearrangement so as to better the conditions of life, but that of tomorrow is bound to be one of individual salvation so as to improve

为人，而是超越人的纯粹本性的聪慧，使他能够接近称为"天"的本质。后者是任何人都可能达到的。一旦达到了，那么此人可能就具有了不同于绝大多数人的人生观，然而在其他的一切方面他却像任何一个张三李四一样。在他身上，客体自然和主体自然是统一的，这样的统一就是和谐。

必须强调的是，我们在此所讨论的是人生观，而不是人的阶层。我们并不是极力在提倡要创造圣人这样阶层的人，也不提倡英雄阶层的人。在我们今天这样的社会中，人们的职责有着太多的分化和综合，因此几乎不可能把人们分为简单的阶层。没有理由说明为什么一个小贩或一个鞋匠或一个律师或一个医生不可以是具有圣人观的人。一个具有圣人观的人既可以是制鞋好手又可以是管理国家的能手，因为在任何一种情形中他都是在实现所给予他的职责，即努力为他生活于其中的这个特殊的世界的图案做贡献。在这样做的时候，他对那些卑贱者或狂妄者一视同仁。也并没有什么特殊的职业不适合去达到圣人观，每一个人都可以达到。当然，并不是每一个人都能成功地达到这样的境界。在这里，重要的问题并不是要使每一个人成为圣人或引导或鼓励他把圣人观当作一种理想去追求。有了这样的理想在心中，人们就不会将权力、知识、财富等误认为是人的智慧。尽管它们对于某些特殊的目的来说是非常有用的，然而只有人的智慧才能使人们过一种通往社会和谐和个人心灵平和的生活。以知识为例。对于维持和改善生活条件来讲，知识是客观的、可靠的和极其有用的。但是它在给人们提供能够指导他们生活的智慧方面却并不是同样成功的。至今知识方面的进步使人英勇地、不幸地沦为欲望的奴隶，不管这些欲望是好是坏还是一般。知识本身已经成为了中性的，天使和魔鬼都同样可以利用它。权力和财富方面的情形也并不见得更好。我们今天所面临的最为基本的问题，可能是制定社会法律或经济重新调整的问题，以达到改善人们的生活条件的目的。但是明天的基本问题就肯定是个人自救的问题，以便

the quality of living. What is needed is not a class of sages, but a section of people in different functions achieving the sagely vista. Socially as well as individually the trouble is not with our stars but with ourselves, and to prevent the social organism from being dominated by the heroic vista which is going to sweep the world, it is necessary to permeate it with the sagely vista.

V

The West seems to have been dominated by the heroic vista. While it is occasionally asserted that the meek shall inherit the world, the predominant attitude is one of self-assertiveness, of striving towards the satisfaction of desires and of identifying it with the pursuit of happiness. The resultant social organization is one of power and achievement. Achievements alone stagger our imagination, their number is tremendous, their scope exceedingly wide and their significance far reaching. They are in fact such that in the West one lives almost in a created environment of artifacts. New York City is a crowning glory of human achievement; subjective nature seems to have dominated to such an extent that object nature is almost missing. And the power of knowledge, of industry and of social organization is even more terrifying. While its constructive side is expressed in achievements, its destructive side is expressed in the tottering effect or civilization by the present global war. Civilizations in the past may have been wiped out by glaciers, by floods, by earthquakes or landslides, or by desiccation and decay, but they are not likely to be wiped out through any such agency in the near future; if their destruction ever takes place, it is likely to be effected through human beings themselves. Progressives everywhere are looking forward towards an individual organization for security; some are even planning and working for a world state. This is indeed as it should be. There is however no assurance that the world state will soon emerge, and even when it does, there is no assurance that there won't be any civil war or that the future civil war will be less destructive than the present international wars. There seems to be an attempt to externalize human problems, to solve them with a sort of intellectual legerdemain; the attempt is probably based upon our reluctance to look at problems from the angle of the human material. Terrifying as the power over us is, it is

改进生活的质量。现在需要的并不是一个圣人阶层，而是一部分获得圣人观的在履行不同职责的人。社会方面和个人方面的麻烦不在于我们的灵魂人物，而在于我们自己。为了防止社会机体被即将要蔓延整个世界的英雄观所控制，很有必要以圣人观来席卷社会。

五

西方世界似乎一直是英雄观占着统治地位。虽然在西方偶然也有人断言温顺的人将会接手这个世界，但是占统治地位的态度仍然是过分自信的态度，是努力使欲望得到满足的态度，是将满足欲望等同于追求幸福的态度。结果，社会的结构就是一个权力和成就的社会结构。仅这些成就就足以颠覆我们的想象：它们数量惊人，范围极其广泛，影响十分深远。事实上，这些已经取得的成就形成了这样的一个局面，即在西方人们几乎是生活在一个被创造出来的人工产物的环境之中。纽约可以说就是人类所取得的辉煌成就的一个顶峰。主体自然的主宰几乎达到了这样的程度，即客体自然几乎正在消失。而且，知识的力量、工业的力量和社会组织的力量更是令人不寒而栗。它的建设性方面通过其成就表现了出来，然而它的破坏性方面也通过目前全球性的战争下摇摇欲坠的后果或文明表现了出来。过去的文明可能由于冰河、洪水、地震或滑坡，或者是由于干旱和腐朽而遭到摧毁。但是在最近的将来，文明不可能由于这些影响而遭到摧毁。如果它被毁灭的话，那么很有可能这样的破坏者就是人类自身。随处可见的进步人士是希望建立一个旨在安全的个体的组织，有些人甚至在计划和努力建立一个世界性的国家。这确实是应该做的事情。然而，我们却不能肯定，这样的世界性的国家不久就会出现。而且即使出现，我们也不能保证，再也不会有内战或者将来的内战的危害性要比现在的全球性的战争的危害更小。似乎有把人类所面临的问题外化的企图，并准备运用理智魔术来解决这些问题。这样的企图可能是由于我们不愿意从人类物质的角度来看待这些问题。能够征服我们的力量尽管令人毛骨悚然，然而运用

yet wielded by human beings, and how it is to be used depends ultimately upon the kind of persons we are going to be. We cannot externalize our problems for we are ourselves a part of them.

That the West has been dominated by the heroic vista does not seem to be open to doubt. The ideological evidence seems to be overwhelming. The doctrines that man is the measure of all things, that the essence of a thing is our perception of it, that understanding makes nature are all offshoots of a basic anthropocentricity which one accepts almost as a matter of course. Even the Bible is not free from it. Without anthropocentricity and even egocentricity who would believe that God created man according to his own image, or want Him to do so? If we really had a lively sense of humility we certainly would not want to humiliate Him with our own image, the image of underlings that we are and underlings that we will continue to be. It seems safe to conclude that not only in Hellenic light but also in Hebraic sweetness there is a strain of human assertiveness, of pride in being what we are, of deep-seated belief in ourselves as the salt of the earth. The role of human beings is so glorified that one seems to be eternally smiling with an almost militant satisfaction over one's biological heritage. Social varieties there certainly are and cases of extraneous dissatisfaction with oneself are occasionally found. But even in self-mortification and self-torture there is no real sense of anthropocentric humility; what is motivating behind it is likely to be a militant desire to be other than oneself. The normal person is one who is anthropocentric if not egocentric and his normal attitude is to regard object nature either as an enemy to be conquered or as plastic material to be shaped according to his desires. In doing so, he may succumb to the mere nature in man. He may proceed to "construct" objective nature in philosophy and try to "conquer" it with all the sources at his command. He may become a conquering hero in one sense, but if he succumbs to the mere nature in man, he is also the vanquished in another and probably more significant sense.

That the heroic vista has advantages is not open to doubt. That it has worked wonders in the way of achievements has been mentioned earlier. There certainly should be more of it in the Far East, but in order that the advantages of such a vista should be unaltered, it has to be tempered

这些力量的却是人类自身。如何来运用这些力量，最终说来是取决于我们将会成为什么样的人。我们不能够把自己的问题外化，因为我们本身也是其中的一部分。

西方世界一直以来都是由英雄观占统治地位的，这似乎毋庸置疑。我们可以在这方面找到无数的思想方面的证据。比如说人是万物的尺度，物质的本质是我们对它的感知，理解决定着本质——所有这些说法都是基本上以人类为中心的产物。人们几乎理所当然地接受了这些思想。即使是《圣经》也是以这样的思想为基础的。如果没有人类中心论，甚至没有自我中心论，谁还会相信上帝是根据自己的形象创造了人，或者希望上帝去这样做呢？如果我们确实具有敏锐的谦卑的意识，那么我们就不会以自己的形象来羞辱上帝，因为这样的形象是我们这些下手的，是我们这些将永远是下手的人的形象。这样，我们就可以比较稳妥地得出这样的结论，即不仅仅在希腊的明朗中，而且也在希伯来的美妙中都有人的过分自信的成分，有因为自身定位而自傲的成分，有深入骨髓的自认为是社会中坚的成分。因此，人类的角色被大加赞扬，似乎永远微笑着，带着激进的生物性遗传的自鸣得意。社会当然呈现出多样性，有时也能发现对自我的外在的不满，但是即使在自我羞愧感和自我折磨中也没有真正意义上的以人类为中心的谦卑，在其背后的真正动机可能是要成为非我的激进欲望。正常的人，如果不是以自我为中心，就是以人类为中心的。他的一般的态度是要把客体自然看成或者是要被征服的敌人，或者是根据自己的欲望加以改造的具有可塑性的材料。在这样做的时候，他可能屈从于人的纯粹本性。他进而可能会来"建构"哲学上的客体自然，而且会努力调动自己所有的资源来"征服"它。在某一种意义上，他可能会成为胜利的英雄。但是如果他屈从于人的纯粹本性的话，那么在另一种意义上，也可能是更为重要的意义上，他也是被征服者。

英雄观具有它自己的长处，这是没有疑义的。在前面已经提到在英雄观的指导下人类所创造的种种辉煌成就。远东社会应该有更多这样的英雄观，但是为了使得这种英雄观带来的长处不打折扣，我们

with the basic humanness of the sagely vista. The so-called conquest of nature would be saluted if it did not result in the greater enslavement of human beings by themselves. In a sense objective nature has never been conquered, no "natural law" has ever been suspended or nullified for human benefit and merely at human's will; what has been done is to bring about a state of affairs such that certain natural laws operate against certain others so that the result desired by human beings are realized. Human beings play one part of object nature against some other part in order to satisfy their desires. Since desires breed other desires, the more nature is "conquered" the more rampant our desires also become. Achievements succeed achievements and power generates power. We may of course say that there is a good and bad or a constructive and destructive side to the "conquest" of object nature, but while some useful purpose is undoubtedly served in looking at the problem in this eclectic sort of way, a more important truth is likely to be ignored. The root of the problem is the same—achievement and power are but different expressions of the same impulse, and if one hankers after the constructive, one also brings with it latent destructions. The heroic vista regards the will to achieve as given and final, and unless this will is itself tempered by the sagely vista at the source, there is no assurance that it won't destroy humanity through that chain of desires and satisfactions.

The East certainly has not solved the problem of human misery and the West may not have solved the problem of human happiness. Once the Indian or the Pacific is crossed in different directions, human misery is probably agonizing to the Western traveler. Life there still depends upon climate, upon recurring floods and draughts as it did ages ago. Live and let live seems to go hand in hand with die and let die. Life is not valueless, for even with the humble, a good deal of fuss is individually made over birth, but it may indeed be said to be cheap for even death on a large scale does not give rise to much social and political concern. Between birth without one's consent and death not always against one's will, life is a stolid and squalid affair following the line of least resistance to what fate dictates. And yet incredible as it may seem, in the midst of all this misery happiness is not necessarily absent. There is little regret or resentment; seldom is there anguish or agony, since there is little desire to be other

不得不用圣人观中基础的人性部分来冲淡缓解它。如果没有更严重的人类的自我奴役的现象，那么我们应该向对自然的所谓的征服致敬。在某种意义上，客体自然从来就没有被征服，没有一个"自然律"因为人类的利益、仅仅在人类意志的支配下而被暂时取消或者宣布无效。实际做到的只不过是，为了使某种自然律起作用而使其他的自然律暂时不起作用，因此人类预期的结果得以实现。人类在客体自然中发挥作用来反对其他作用，其目的是为了满足自己的欲望。由于欲望会滋生其他的欲望，因此自然被征服得越多，那么我们的欲望也就变得更加毫无节制。成就接着成就，力量产生力量。我们当然可以说，对客体自然的"征服"有好的也有坏的方面，或者说有建设性的也有破坏性的方面。但是折中来看这一问题，显然达到了某些有用的目的，然而似乎一个更为重要的真理被忘记了。这一问题的根源也是同样的，即成就和力量是同样动机的不同表达。而且如果一个人追求建设性成就，与此同时也会带来潜在的破坏。英雄观把取得成就的意愿看作是既定的和最终的。除非这样的意愿在其源头上为圣人观所调和，否则我们就不能确定它不会通过欲望和满足的链条来摧毁人性。

当然，东方社会没有解决人类的苦难的问题，而西方社会可能也没有解决人类的幸福问题。一旦西方旅游者从四面八方越过太平洋或印度洋，他们在东方看到的人类的苦难可能会令他们极其痛苦。在那里，人们的生活还像多少世纪以前那样依赖于天气，取决于一再出现的洪涝灾害。一荣俱荣，一毁俱毁。生活并不是毫无意义的，因为即便对卑微的人来说，生命的诞生也会给个人带来无穷的惊喜。但是确实也可以这样说，生命是不值钱的，因为即使大规模的死亡也并没有引起社会和政治方面的同情。人的诞生并没有经过本人的同意，他的死亡也并不总是违背他本人的意志，在这样的生死之间，生命是一种麻木悲惨的状况，对于命运的主宰遵循着最小抵抗力原则。然而似乎令人不可置信的是，在如此苦难的生活之中也并不一定缺少幸福。在这里，很少有后悔或者愤愤不平；很少有苦恼或者痛苦，因为几乎没

than oneself; hardly ever is there tragedy, for tragedy involves such a war of passions as to render the possessor of them, always the vanquished, no matter which side wins, and contrary to popular belief, such a war is on the whole alien to the oriental. The heroic vista is not absent in the East, but in the anthropocentric form it is so seldom entertained as to be of no practical significance. Objective nature still overwhelms mere man. It is this fact in the East that impresses upon the Western mind with greater force than anything else. Undoubtedly more anthropocentric heroism should be encouraged, greater efforts should be made towards the "conquest of nature," undoubtedly also a higher standard of living should be the aim of every man, but it must be understood that these things would be a blessing only if in having them accomplished certain naivete or sagaciousness is not lost together with its natural naturalness or contented contentedness.

The Western civilization will sweep over the whole world, perhaps for its own excellence, but also for its power. Once given a start, it rolls on of its own momentum. It has obvious virtues: it raises the standard of living to a previously undreamed-of level, it insures a condition of life that is almost free from natural calamities, and while miseries due to human management have not been eradicated, they will undoubtedly diminish as improvements are made in social and political reorganization. For the achievements, the oriental has nothing but admiration; he may feel wonderment and awe for the speed and efficiency with which the world becomes transformed; but so far as the destination is concerned, he might yet have his misgivings. Is there any guarantee that the whole civilization wouldn't be something like getting all dressed up with no place to go, or making elaborate preparations for a journey that doesn't take place? If happiness is to be identified with the mere satisfaction of desires, it is doubtful whether anyone in the brand new world will be happier than the early Greeks or Chinese or the Elizabethan Englishmen. Happiness is both harmony within and the ability to get along without; the latter is an asset only when it contributes to the former. But if the heroic vista is allowed to dominate our thought and behavior, with all its pungency, all its vigor and rigor, it may drive people into a beehive of activity so that each is stressed, strained and torn between numerous and ever

有非我的欲望；也很少有什么悲剧，因为悲剧蕴涵着这样的感情冲突，无论哪一方面获胜都会使这些感情的拥有者常常成为失败者。而且与通常的信念不同，从整体上讲，东方对这样的冲突是完全陌生的。英雄观在东方并不是没有，但是很少有以人类为中心的形式出现的英雄观，所以在东方这样的英雄观并没有实际的重要性。客体自然仍然使纯粹的人不知所措。在东方正是这样的事头给西方人的心灵留下了比任何其他事情更为深刻的影响。无疑，以人类为中心的英雄观应该得到更多的鼓励，"征服自然"需要付出更多的努力，更高的生活标准无疑应该成为每一个人的目标。但是我们必须理解的是，当这些事情实现的时候，某些素朴性或明智性没有与它的自然的自然性或令人满意的满足性一起失掉，仅仅这种时候这些事情才是福气。

西方的文明将会席卷整个世界，或许是因为它的优秀，也是因为它的影响力。一旦开始席卷，它就会以其磅礴的气势滚滚向前。显然它具有自己的优势，它使人们的生活水平提到了以前想象不到的程度，它保证人们的生活条件几乎能免除自然灾害。虽然人类管理所带来的苦难并没有从根本上得到消除，但是这样的苦难无疑会因为社会和政治方面改革的成绩而不断地减少。对于这些成就，东方人除了表示敬佩之外没有什么可说的。对于世界变化的速度和效率，东方人感到极大的好奇和敬畏。但是考虑到所要达到的目的，他却不得不感到担忧。整个文明是否能够保证不会像盛装打扮之后却无处可去或者为实际上不会发生的旅程做精心的准备？如果把幸福等同于纯粹欲望的满足，那么生活在新世界的人是否要比古代的希腊人或中国人或伊丽莎白时代的英国人更幸福，就非常值得怀疑了。幸福既是内部的和谐，也是与外在融洽相处的能力，只有当后者能够对前者有所贡献的时候它才能成为有利条件。但是如果允许英雄观及其所含有的尖刻、活力和严密来主宰我们的思想和行动，那么它就有可能驱使人们进入行动的漩涡之中。每一个人都处在重压之下，紧张无措，在无数的不

increasing desires with the net result that the absence of misery does not mean the presence of happiness. What is needed in the West is greater sagaciousness, admitting only that kind of assertiveness that is neither anthropocentric nor egocentric, an assertiveness that is consonant with human dignity and yet does not give rise to false human pride. The belief in democracy, the conception of human worth, the striving towards an equalization of the conditions of life should be accompanied by the realization that man cannot set himself apart from mere object nature and lord over it, for in doing so he is merely giving aid and comfort to the mere nature in him which he must transcend in order to save himself.

断增长的欲望之间难以取舍。最终结果就是没有苦难并不意味着幸福的出现。西方人所需要的是更多的明智性，仅仅只承认既不是人类中心也不是自我中心的自信，那种与人类尊严相一致但却不会产生虚假的人类自傲的自信。对民主的信念、人类价值的观念、朝着生活条件平等的奋斗应该伴随着如下目标的实现，即人不能使自己脱离纯粹的客体自然并主宰它，因为当他这样做的时候，他仅仅是将帮助和满足给予了纯粹本性。为了拯救自己，他必须超越纯粹本性。

NOTES 注释

Chinese Philosophy 中国哲学

1 This paper was written in Kunming in 1943 and was mimeographed for limited circulation. —The author

本文 1943 年写于昆明，曾油印少量分送。——作者注

2 本文首次公开发表于 *Social Sciences in China* 第 1 卷第 1 期，1980 年；后收入《金岳霖文集》第 2 卷，第 531—549 页。钱耕森译，王太庆校。

译者附识：本文是我的老师金岳霖先生于 1943 年用英文撰写的。1980 年文章发表时，仅为便于自学起见，我曾约元枚同志尝试合译了一份初稿，并呈送金先生指正。不料，稿件于呈送过程中不慎遗失。1984 年尊敬的金先生不幸病逝。我的老师周礼全先生、我的老同学诸葛殷同同志与《哲学研究》编辑部共同约我重译此文。并且，我的老师王太庆先生欣然同意亲予校对。遂勉力重译，谨向金先生深表缅怀之情；谨向王、周两位先生和元枚、诸葛两位同志以及编辑部的同志深表谢忱。

Philosophy and Life 哲学与生活

3 本文是作者 1943—1944 年访问美国期间撰写的。英文手稿收入《金岳霖文集》第 2 卷，第 550—567 页。陈静译。

Prolegomena 逻辑的作用

4 本文原是作者为自己一本"未完成的书"写的绪论，载于《哲学评论》第 1 卷第 1、2 期，1927 年 4 月、6 月；后收入《金岳霖文集》第 1 卷，第 233—282 页。王路译。

Tao, Nature and Man 道、自然与人

5 本文是作者 1943—1944 年访问美国期间撰写的，生前未发表。英文稿收入《金岳霖文集》第 2 卷，第 568—749 页。胡军译。

6 即《论道》，商务印书馆 1940 年 9 月版。

7 原稿中缺第一章的标题及第一节的标号，为了统一体例，现添加标题和第一节的标号"I"。

8 原稿中"II"下面有一个标题"The Realm of Expressibles"，为了统一体例，现删去。

9 作者在《论道》一书和以后的论述中都将"质料"表述为"能"。